Integrating Counselling and Psychotherapy

Directionality, Synergy, and Social Change

Integrating Counselling and Psychotherapy

Directionality, Synergy, and Social Change

Mick Cooper

Los Angeles | London | New Delhi
Singapore | Washington DC | Melbourne

Los Angeles | London | New Delhi
Singapore | Washington DC | Melbourne

SAGE Publications Ltd
1 Oliver's Yard
55 City Road
London EC1Y 1SP

SAGE Publications Inc.
2455 Teller Road
Thousand Oaks, California 91320

SAGE Publications India Pvt Ltd
B 1/I 1 Mohan Cooperative Industrial Area
Mathura Road
New Delhi 110 044

SAGE Publications Asia-Pacific Pte Ltd
3 Church Street
#10-04 Samsung Hub
Singapore 049483

Editor: Susannah Trefgarne
Assistant Editor: Talulah Hall
Production Editor: Anwesha Roy
Copyeditor: Sarah Bury
Proofreader: Sunrise Setting
Indexer: Martin Hargreaves
Marketing Manager: Camille Richmond
Cover Design: Sheila Tong
Typeset by: C&M Digitals (P) Ltd, Chennai, India
Printed in the UK

© Mick Cooper 2019

First published 2019

Apart from any fair dealing for the purposes of research or private study, or criticism or review, as permitted under the Copyright, Designs and Patents Act, 1988, this publication may be reproduced, stored or transmitted in any form, or by any means, only with the prior permission in writing of the publishers, or in the case of reprographic reproduction, in accordance with the terms of licences issued by the Copyright Licensing Agency. Enquiries concerning reproduction outside those terms should be sent to the publishers.

Library of Congress Control Number: 2018949163

British Library Cataloguing in Publication data

A catalogue record for this book is available from the British Library

ISBN 978-1-5264-4002-0
ISBN 978-1-5264-4003-7 (pbk)

At SAGE we take sustainability seriously. Most of our products are printed in the UK using responsibly sourced papers and boards. When we print overseas we ensure sustainable papers are used as measured by the PREPS grading system. We undertake an annual audit to monitor our sustainability.

For Shula, with all my love

CONTENTS

Acknowledgements ix
Web resources x
About the author xii

1 Introduction: Towards a common framework for counselling and psychotherapy 1

Part I A Common Framework for Counselling, Psychotherapy, and Social Change: Describing the elephant 13

2 Directionality: Philosophical foundations 15
3 A phase model of directionality: From fantasy to action 29
4 Wellbeing and emotions: A life 'on track' 43
5 Goal dimensions: What we strive for counts 61
6 A structural model of directionality: What we really, really want 75
7 Effectiveness: Better ways of getting to where we want to be 93
8 Synergies are good 105
9 From intrapersonal to interpersonal levels of organisation: Playing to win–win 119

Part II Resources for an integrative practice: Putting the elephant back together 135

10 Psychodynamic approaches within a directional framework: Change through awareness 141
11 Humanistic approaches within a directional framework: Helping directions unfurl 151
12 Existential approaches within a directional framework: Choosing to choose 171
13 Cognitive-behavioural approaches within a directional framework: Effective strategies for life 181

CONTENTS

Part III: Directional practices: Riding the elephant   195

14   Goal-oriented practices   197

15   Working with directions in counselling and psychotherapy   213

16   Developing interpersonal synergies   231

17   Conclusion: Towards better   247

References   253
Index   289

ACKNOWLEDGEMENTS

I am very grateful to Diane Bray and the Department of Psychology at the University of Roehampton, who have been so supportive of my work, including a sabbatical term in which much of this text was written.

Many thanks to the following colleagues who took the time to read through and comment on earlier drafts of this book: Petra Kagleder, Emma Kay, Lizzie Lumsden, John McLeod, Melanie Mitchell, Rolf Sundet, Biljana van Rijn, and Tamara Vaughan.

I am extremely grateful to Hanne Oddli, who was a source of dialogue and encouragement throughout the writing of this book. Thanks, also to Gina di Malta who led on, and contributed to, a range of research projects that informed this text; to Christopher Lloyd and Charlie Duncan for their work on the goals measures review; and to Liz McDonnell for her support, suggestions, and insights.

Thanks, as always, to Susannah Trefgarne, Talulah Hall, Anwesha Roy, Sarah Bury, and the team at Sage, who have been an enduring source of support for my writing. Thanks to my mum, Kitty Cooper, who has been an enduring source of love, support, encouragement, and Scrabble. To Helen Cruthers; and to our children – Zac, Shula, Ruby, and Maya – who give me direction and meaning in life.

Figure 15.1 is Reprinted with permission from *Plan analysis* by Franz Caspar, ISBN 0-88937-117-2 ©1995 Hogrefe & Huber Publishers (now Hogrefe Publishing) www.hogrefe.com

WEB RESOURCES

Visit **https://study.sagepub.com/counselling** to find a range of online resources:

1.1 The Golden and Platinum Rules

1.2 Cooper, M. (2006). Socialist humanism: A progressive politics for the twenty-first century. In G. Proctor, M. Cooper, P. Sanders & B. Malcolm (Eds.), *Politicising the person-centred approach: An agenda for social change* (pp. 80–94). Ross-on-Wye: PCCS Books.

1.3 Cooper, M. (2000). Person-centred developmental theory: Reflections and revisions. *Person-Centred Practice, 8*(2), 87–94.

1.4 Cooper, M. (2012). *A hierarchy of wants: Towards an integrative framework for counselling, psychotherapy and social change*. University of Strathclyde, Glasgow.

1.5 Glossary

2.1 Directional orientation of interpersonal perceptions

2.2 Are our directions becoming increasingly socialised?

3.1 Table of directional phases

3.2 Directional constructs

3.3 Moderators of the helpfulness of feedback

4.1 The directional role of emotions

4.2 Directionality and flow

5.1 Goal taxonomies

5.2 Promotion and prevention focus

6.1 Are our highest-order directions 'given'?

7.1 Ego depletion

8.1 Classic conflicts

11.1 Life scripts

15.1 The plan formulation method

15.2 Why therapies fail: A directional perspective
16.1 Are interpersonal dysergies inevitable?
17.1 Socialist humanism
17.2 Is there a natural tendency towards synergies?

ABOUT THE AUTHOR

Mick Cooper is Professor of Counselling Psychology at the University of Roehampton, where he is Director of the Centre for Research in Social and Psychological Transformation (CREST). Mick is a chartered psychologist, a UKCP registered psychotherapist, and a Fellow of the BACP. Mick is author and editor of a range of texts on integrative, person-centred, and existential approaches to therapy, including *Working at relational depth in counselling and psychotherapy* (2nd ed., 2018, Sage, with Dave Mearns), *Pluralistic counselling and psychotherapy* (2011, Sage, with John McLeod), and *Existential therapies* (2nd ed., 2017, Sage). Mick has led a series of research studies exploring the processes and outcomes of humanistic counselling with young people, as well as clients' preferences and goals for therapy. Mick is the father of four children and lives in Brighton on the south coast of England.

1

INTRODUCTION

Towards a common framework for counselling and psychotherapy

This chapter discusses:

- The rationale for writing this book.
- The development of integrative, eclectic, and pluralistic perspectives in counselling and psychotherapy and their relationship to the present book.
- The desire to develop a common framework for understanding distress and change, inclusive of both psychological and sociopolitical factors.
- Ethics as a starting point for developing a common framework for counselling and psychotherapy.
- The structure of this book.

It's Wednesday afternoon, quarter past three. The therapy session was supposed to start at three o'clock, but Mei has still not turned up. I'm beginning to worry that she'll miss the session entirely. Then I remember that I thought that last week, and the week before, and then actually she did turn up – just, it seems, later and later each week. I hear footsteps past the door to our university-based therapy centre... they go on; no Mei. I sit in my chair, trying to do what I know I should do: use the time to reflect on Mei and what might be going on for her. But I'm distracted, agitated – a bit annoyed, although I can never feel too annoyed with Mei. Then a knock, Mei's at the door, smiling apologetically. She rushes in, apologises again, backpack down, handbag down, Sainsbury's bag to the side, sits, asks if she can go to the bathroom, rushes out, rushes back, sits, smiles. It's nice to see her.

Mei and I have been working together for just over two months. A housing officer in her late-thirties, Mei came to therapy saying that she wanted to work out what to do in her marriage and to find some satisfaction in her life. 'It's a question,' she said, smiling wryly, 'of whether I should "dump the lump".' The 'lump' that she was referring to was her husband, Rob, whom Mei had known from college and married in her mid-twenties. 'He's a good man,' she said, 'a really good man; and a loving dad to Olivia [their 12-year old daughter]. But... Oh my G... he– *we've* just got so... boring.' With a half-grimace/half-smile, Mei told me that she and Rob had not had sex for over two years, and that they had both acknowledged the relationship as 'pretty much over'. In addition, for the last three years, Mei had had a 'thing' for a younger colleague at work, Saul. 'We did– kind of– something happened one drink's night,' she said, 'but it was really nothing. I just wish he'd– he's so ambivalent, so anxious; you see his lovely face for a few seconds and then he just scurries back under his blanket.'

In our assessment session, Mei also said that she hoped therapy would help her cut back on her 'spendaholism'. 'Rob and I are terrible with money,' she said. 'When we first met, we were both really into punk music, and we've always spent far too much buying old vinyl records that we never bother listening too.' And then there was her mother. 'God knows, she should have been put down years ago,' said Mei. 'But I just don't want her to die and feel that, really, I could have been a better person to her. She did– I suppose– she did do her best. It wasn't easy for her getting disowned by her middle-class, home counties family for marrying someone Taiwanese.'

So how can I, as a therapist, be of greatest value to Mei? How can I help her make sense of her difficulties and move towards the things that she wants in life? With over 500 different varieties of counselling and psychotherapy now available (Lillienfeld & Arkowitz, 2012), our field offers a plethora of different understandings and methods that may be of use. From a person-centred perspective, for instance, I might support Mei to connect with her 'true' feelings towards Rob; behaviourally, I might help Mei develop her assertiveness skills; or, from a psychodynamic perspective, I might encourage Mei to notice how her behaviours towards me – such as arriving later and later for each session – mirror past and present patterns of relating.

This diversity of understandings and methods makes the counselling and psychotherapy field a treasure trove of possibilities. But it also means our field can tend towards the fragmentary, disjointed, and disconnected: a 'Babel' of different models, languages, and beliefs (Miller, Duncan, & Hubble, 1997). This can make it difficult for therapists to draw on understandings and methods from other orientations – even if they may seem particularly appropriate for particular clients at particular times. For instance, it might seem helpful to encourage Mei to explore 'transference' issues around her lateness, but how do you do that if you are only trained in CBT or humanistic therapies? The diversity of approaches in our field can also increase the likelihood of an unproductive *schoolism* (Clarkson, 2000), in which advocates of different orientations 'defend passionately the "truth" of their own school and attack with vigour the "error" of rival schools' (Hollanders, 2003, pp. 277–278). Clients, too, may find this diversity and heterogeneity of therapies and therapeutic languages confusing or overwhelming. They may be left wondering, for instance, 'Which therapy is best for helping me with my problem?' and 'How do these different approaches fit together?'

THE DEVELOPMENT OF INTEGRATIVE AND ECLECTIC APPROACHES

From the 1930s onwards, therapists have attempted to overcome these challenges through the development of *integrative* and *eclectic* approaches to counselling and psychotherapy (Goldfried, Pachanakis, & Bell, 2005). Here, 'pure form' therapies have been combined in four main ways (Norcross, 2005; Stricker & Gold, 2003). First is *theoretical integration*, in which aspects of two or more approaches are synthesised together to form a new therapy. A classic example of this is 'cognitive analytic therapy' (Ryle, 1990). Second is *assimilative integration*, in which therapists introduce new understandings and methods into their pre-existing orientation. In contrast to theoretical integration, this is often on an individual basis (for instance, a person-centred therapist drawing in psychodynamic and Gestalt understandings and methods) and is likely to proceed over the course of a professional career. Third are *common factors* approaches, which attempt to identify active ingredients across a range of therapies. This approach is based on the assumption that, 'Therapies work not because of their unique explanatory schemes of specialized language; on the contrary ... their success is based on what they have in common' (Miller et al., 1997, pp. 22–23). For instance, Miller et al., drawing on the psychotherapy research evidence, argue that all forms of therapy have four common curative elements: (1) client factors and the clients' environment; (2) the therapy relationship; (3) the therapy technique; and (4) expectancy and hope. Finally, there is *technical eclecticism*, such as Lazarus's (1981) multimodal therapy, in which the therapist draws on a wide range of therapeutic methods, without any single theoretical model underlying their practice.

By combining two or more pure form therapies in these ways, integrative and eclectic approaches help to create more common languages in the counselling and psychotherapy field, and reduce the likelihood of schoolism. However, they still have their limitations. Theoretical and assimilative forms of integration combine just a small handful of different orientations, leaving the vast majority outside their scope. In addition, theoretically integrative forms of therapy, as specific combinations of different pure form therapies, can become schools of therapy in themselves. At the other extreme, while eclectic therapies offer a more inclusive framework, their lack of unifying, underlying theory may mean that they tend towards *syncretism*: the haphazard, uncritical, and unsystematic combination of theories and practices (Hollanders, 2003). This means that, as with common factors models, practitioners may struggle to know which methods to adopt when. As Mei's therapist, for instance, I may know that change is dependent on her engagement with therapy, the quality of our relationship, the particular methods I use, and her levels of hope – but what do I actually do with her?

THE DEVELOPMENT OF PLURALISTIC PERSPECTIVES

In an attempt to overcome some of these issues, John McLeod and I – along with other colleagues, such as Windy Dryden – have articulated a *pluralistic* approach to counselling and psychotherapy integration (Cooper & Dryden, 2016; Cooper & McLeod, 2007, 2011; McLeod, 2018b). This is based on two fundamental premises: (a) 'Lots of different things can be helpful to clients'; and (b) 'If we want to know what is most likely to help clients, we should talk to them about it' (Cooper & McLeod, 2011, p. 6). In our work, we have distinguished between a *pluralistic perspective* and a *pluralistic practice*. The former refers to a general sensibility: an inclusive attitude towards the whole scope of therapeutic understandings and methods, including pure form, integrative, and eclectic ones. By contrast, the latter 'refers to a specific form of therapeutic *practice* which draws on methods from a range of orientation, and which is characterised by dialogue and negotiation over the goals, tasks and methods of therapy' (Cooper & McLeod, 2011, p. 8).

The inclusivity of the pluralistic approach comes from its grounding in a pluralistic philosophical outlook (e.g., Berlin, 2003; James, 1996), which holds that 'any substantial question admits of a variety of plausible but mutually conflicting responses' (Rescher, 1993, p. 79). This means that a pluralistic approach to therapy can embrace a multiplicity of seemingly contradictory truths. For instance, from a pluralistic standpoint, one might understand Mei's problems with her mother in psychodynamic terms (that her mother was neglectful when she was a child) and also in behavioural terms (that her problems with her mother fester because she is not, at the present time, sufficiently assertive with her). Hence, psychodynamic and/or behavioural approaches may both be considered suitable for working with this client, depending on the client's own personal preferences. As with eclectic and common factors approaches, however, the downside of a pluralistic framework is that it may not provide strong guidance on how different understandings or methods should be drawn together, or what should be used when – particularly in the absence of client preferences. And, indeed, research shows that trainees in a pluralistic approach can struggle with knowing how the different orientations can be fitted together (Thompson & Cooper, 2012).

TOWARDS A UNIFYING THEORETICAL FRAMEWORK

From a common factors perspective, a fitting parable for the therapeutic field may be that of the blind men and an elephant. In this tale, originally from India, one blind man feels the elephant's trunk and says that the entity in front of them is a snake. Another feels its ear and says it is a fan. A third feels the elephant's side and says it is a wall, etc. Eventually, in some versions of this story, the blind men come to blows, never realising that they are all, actually, describing facets of the same thing. Similarly, it could be claimed, each of the different therapy orientations 'see' people's problems, and their solutions, in different ways and miss out on the common principles and processes behind them all.

Without wanting to mix metaphors, this is, perhaps, the 'elephant in the room' and the basis for the present text: that behind all our different theories and concepts, there is, actually, a great deal of commonality in how we understand clients and how we try to help them. So the aim of this book is to try to describe something of what that elephant might be like: to articulate a common framework – and vocabulary – for counselling and psychotherapy that can:

- support the integration of understandings and methods from across orientations;
- help to improve communication and collaboration between the schools;
- bring greater clarity and cohesion to the field.

As with common factors and pluralistic approaches, this is not about creating a 'new' and 'improved' brand of therapy (Miller et al., 1997). Rather, the aim is to try to show how the present orientations might be brought together to better effect.

Although the framework developed in this book, and its ethical foundations, are highly consistent with Miller et al.'s (1997) common factors approach, it adopts a somewhat different starting point (see Chapter 2, Directionality). In contrast to other common factors models, it also tries to identify – and describe – the specific, 'pantheoretical' (i.e., across orientation) pathways by which change can happen in therapy. In this respect, it might be termed a 'common functions' framework, rather than a 'common factors' one (Caspar, 1995).

Probably, the therapeutic approach that comes closest to the present framework is Grawe's (2004) psychological therapy. Grawe, based at the University of Bern in Switzerland, was a brilliant psychotherapy theorist and researcher, who developed a comprehensive model for understanding psychological distress and change. Unfortunately, along with his untimely death (in 2005, at the age of 62), little of Grawe's work has been translated into English, and what there is – his *magnum opus*, *Psychological therapy* (Grawe, 2004) – is a dense, somewhat cacophonic mix of perspectives and voices. Fortunately, many of his ideas and interests have been developed by members of his school, including Caspar, Grosse Holtforth, and Michalak, who are now among the leading lights of the psychotherapy research world. In addition, the present framework shares many features with a range of contemporary psychotherapeutic and psychological approaches: Snyder's 'hope therapy' (Lopez, Floyd, Ulven, & Snyder, 2000), 'motivational counseling' (Cox & Klinger, 2011c, 2011d), and 'Motivational Systems Theory' (Ford, 1992).

In relation to the pluralistic approach, the framework and practices developed in this book can be considered both a step forwards and a step back. In terms of moving forward, the present text strives to go beyond the pluralistic approach by providing specific ideas on which understandings and methods should be used with which clients, and when. The present book also strives to refine, and extend, a key premise underlying the pluralistic approach: that human beings are oriented towards 'goals', and that these should be a principal focal point for the therapeutic work (Cooper & McLeod, 2011, chapter 3). This focus on 'goals' has been a key criticism of the pluralistic approach and, to be honest, neither John McLeod nor I were entirely happy with the term when we adopted it. In our pluralistic approach, we focused on 'goals' because we wanted to emphasise the active, future-oriented nature of human being, and to put the client's own agenda at the centre of the therapeutic work. However, we also knew that this term had a somewhat mechanistic feel to it and could be seen as over-emphasising outcomes over processes, as well as conscious deliberations over unconscious desires. In the present book, therefore, the concept of *directionality* is used to describe this forward-moving, active quality of human being – in the hope that this provides a more encompassing, less mechanistic, conceptual foundation (see Chapter 2).

The framework developed in this book, however, is also a step back from a pluralistic approach, in the sense that it presents one particular understanding of how psychological difficulties emerge and how they can be addressed in counselling and psychotherapy. That is, the model aims to be all-inclusive – to account for all change across all orientations – and this striving for totalisation might be seen as contradicting the basic pluralistic principle of differentiation: that different people change in different ways at different points in time. Such a totalised account, however, can sit within a pluralistic framework, provided that it is not proposed as some ultimate, 'meta-narrative' truth. In this respect, the relationship between totalising frameworks, such as the present one, and a pluralistic approach might best be characterised as *dialectical* (that is, opposing forces which, together, lead to a more advanced synthesis). Here, totalising frameworks help to specify and concretise our understandings and practices, while a pluralistic perspective reminds us that there is always more to know.

ETHICS AS 'FIRST PSYCHOTHERAPY'

In most cases, counselling and psychotherapeutic approaches – whether pure form, integrative, or eclectic – start with psychological theories, observations, and evidence. Cognitive therapy, for instance, is founded on an understanding of the biases and errors that can afflict human thinking (Beck, Rush, Shaw, & Emery, 1979), while Gestalt therapy is derived from an appreciation of the holistic nature of perceptual processes (Perls, Hefferline, & Goodman, 1951). Other frameworks, such as the person-centred approach (Rogers, 1942, 1957), are primarily founded on clinical and empirical observations. Existential therapy, probably uniquely, is derived from a set of philosophical assumptions (Cooper, 2017a).

The pluralistic approach that John McLeod and I developed was somewhat different, in that it was explicitly grounded in ethics and a politically progressive standpoint. In particular, what we wanted to develop was a therapeutic framework that, at its core, 'emphasised an egalitarian client–therapist relationship: client as "agentic", intelligent being; and therapist as "fellow traveller"' (Cooper & McLeod, 2011, p. viii). The present framework is similar, in that its starting point is not 'What are my clients like?', or even 'What will work best with my clients?', *per se*. Rather, it starts with the question 'How can I engage with my clients in a deeply valuing and respectful way?' (Cooper, 2007, 2009)?

Such an approach is rooted in the philosophy of the French post-existential thinker Levinas (1969, 1982), who argued for the 'primacy of the ethical' (1969, p. 79). By this, he meant that the question of how we relate to an other is not a 'superstructure' – lying on top of other, more fundamental philosophical questions – but an 'irreducible structure upon which all other structures rest' (1969, p. 79). So, from this perspective, the issue of how we relate to others takes precedence over other issues, like logic, meaning, or the nature of reality. No doubt, Levinas's own experiences of 'witnessing the unspeakable horrors of the Holocaust' profoundly affected his views on this matter (Atterton, Calarco, & Friedman, 2004, p. 20).

Transposed to the therapeutic field, this means the starting point for our theories and practices is the question 'How can I engage, ethically, with my client?' Other questions, like 'How can I understand my client's psychological distress?' or 'What therapy techniques should I use?' may well inform this, but these questions should be in the service of, rather than prior to, the question of how to relate well. So, for instance, when we think about how to respond to Mei's lateness, we might want to draw upon theories of transference, or research evidence regarding low self-esteem, but first and foremost we need to ask 'How should I be treating Mei?' That is, 'How can I engage with Mei in a way that is deeply respectful and valuing to her?'

Of course, in reality, nearly all therapeutic approaches – and nearly all therapists – would view things in a similar manner: that the way we treat our clients is, ultimately, more important than any particular theory or technique. As suggested above, however, such ethical 'first principles' are rarely made explicit. Perhaps this is because, like the air around us, they are so all pervasive that we simply take them for granted. Yet if we are aiming to develop a shared framework for counselling and psychotherapy, they may be an important starting point for seeing what is common to all.

This commitment to valuing and respecting clients – as we would want to be valued and respected ourselves (see Web Resource 1.1, The Golden and Platinum rules) – means that the starting point for the present framework is that clients should be engaged with as active, subjective, *directional* agencies (Berlin, 1958; Buber, 1958; Levinas, 2003). This is Buber's (1958) *I–Thou* stance; and it contrasts with his conception of the *I–It* attitude, in which the other is treated as a natural object that can be scrutinised and analysed (see Chapter 2, this volume; Cooper, 2015a). Here, then, we are not asking, first and foremost, 'What is Mei's problem?' or 'Who is Mei?' but 'Where is Mei trying to get to?' We are brought alongside Mei – as an intelligent and *intelligible* human being – as she strives towards doing things in her world. Understanding clients in terms of their directions is also ethical in the sense that it puts the client's own desires for therapy, and therapeutic change, at the heart of the counselling and psychotherapeutic work. We will explore this much more fully in the subsequent chapter.

INTEGRATING THE SOCIOPOLITICAL REALM

As an approach grounded in ethics, the present framework – like some other 'directional' ones (e.g., Little, 2007) – also strives to integrate an understanding of sociopolitical factors, processes, and structures into psychological ones. Ethics is never about just one individual: it is about how we, as a society, relate to each other, and the principles and behaviours that can be most beneficial for all. And it is clear from the research that a range of sociopolitical factors – like income, work, family life, community, political freedom, and wider social values – can have a powerful impact on an individual's wellbeing (Layard, 2006). Mei's life history is just one example of this. As the only non-white child in her primary school, Mei was teased and bullied from the age of six to her mid-teens, and it left lasting scars. 'It wasn't the worst when the kids had a go at me,' said Mei, mid-way through our fourth session, 'it was when the teacher joined in.' Mei described a time when her primary school teacher, frustrated with Mei for mispronouncing an English word, had made Mei stand up in front of the rest of her class. 'Mei,' the teacher said, 'do you know why people don't like you?' Mei described how she stood there, confused, not knowing how to answer: burning up with humiliation. The class stared. Eventually, the teacher told her to sit down again. She slunk back. 'I think I learnt', said Mei, 'that even the people who are supposed to be there for you just aren't. You're totally– you're just on your own. I'll never ask for anything.'

A *politically-informed* approach to therapy (McLeod, 2013) stretches back to the likes of Adler and Reich (see Totton, 2000), and continues to evolve today (see, for instance, the journal *Psychotherapy and Politics International* and Box II.1 Politically-informed approaches, in the introduction to Part II of this volume). A particularly significant contemporary development here is the *Power Threat Meaning Framework*, published by the British Psychological Society's Division of Clinical Psychology, which sets out a non-diagnostic understanding of emotional distress in terms of the threats that 'the negative operation of power may pose to the individual' (Johnstone & Boyle, 2018, p.9.). However, these approaches stands in contrast to the 'magical voluntarianism' implicit in most contemporary therapy models (including, it has been argued, the pluralistic framework; Vermes, 2017), which holds that individuals can overcome their own psychological distress without wider social and political change (Smail, 2005). Hence, the present approach explicitly aims to understand how the intrapersonal and interpersonal worlds interact; and to develop understandings and methods that are suitable for change at interpersonal levels of organisation, as well as intrapersonal ones.

THEORETICAL DEVELOPMENT

The framework that I present in this book has been in gestation since the early 2000s, and is present – in some form – in pretty much everything I have ever written. It is what really matters to me: how we can create a more caring, respectful, equal society, both through therapy and through wider social change (see Cooper, 2006).

An initial attempt to sketch out some of these ideas and experiences was published in 'Socialist humanism: A progressive politics for the twenty-first century' (Cooper, 2006, see Web Resource 1.2). This, itself, emerged from an earlier analysis of, person-centred developmental theory (Cooper, 2000, see Web Resource 1.3), and led to a subsequent critique of the humanistic split between 'intrinsic' and 'extrinsic' goals and motivations (Cooper, 2013). Around this time, I also authored an extended monograph in which many of the ideas were fleshed out for the first time: *A hierarchy of wants: Towards an integrative framework for counselling, psychotherapy and social change* (Cooper, 2012, see Web Resource 1.4). An accessible summary of these initial ideas was published in the British Association of Counselling and Psychotherapy's (BACP) *Therapy Today* magazine, as 'Social change from the counselling room' (Cooper, 2015c). More recently, these ideas have been applied to consider the nature of a 'fully functioning society' (Cooper, 2016), as well as their value in helping to address issues of world suffering (Cooper, 2017b).

As indicated above, the central concept in this book, directionality, is derived from earlier work on goals, as developed with John McLeod in the pluralistic approach (Cooper & McLeod, 2007, 2011). More recently, I reviewed the evidence on the psychology of goals, as applicable to clinical practice (Cooper, 2018), as part of an edited text with Duncan Law on *Working with goals in counselling and psychotherapy* (Cooper & Law, 2018b). This chapter has been incorporated into the present book (primarily in Chapters 4 and 5), though with numerous revisions and developments.

Over the years, I have also published work on the parallels between intrapersonal and interpersonal processes (Cooper, 2003, 2004; Cooper, Chak, Cornish, & Gillespie, 2012; Cooper & Hermans, 2007; Cooper & Ikemi, 2012; Cooper & Spinelli, 2012), which forms an important premise for the current book.

ABOUT THIS BOOK

Following this introduction, this book is divided into three parts. Part I presents the theoretical foundations of the framework: a description of 'the elephant'. Part II shows how each of the principal therapeutic approaches articulate with, and can help to develop, this framework: putting the elephant back together again. Part III then describes some specific, integrative therapeutic practices that come out of this framework: riding the elephant, itself.

To give some more detail, Part I begins with a chapter on the core philosophical premise underlying this framework, that human being is *directional* (Chapter 2). The phases of this directionality are explored in Chapter 3, and then the relationship between directionality and affect are discussed in Chapter 4, with psychological wellbeing being conceptualised as the *actualisation* of our directions. Chapter 5 develops this further, by looking at different types of direction (for instance, conscious versus unconscious), and how these may mediate the relationship between directionality and wellbeing. Chapter 6 then introduces a *structural* model of directionality, in which *lower-order* directions are conceptualised as means towards more significant *higher-order* directions, such as relatedness and self-worth. Using this model, Chapter 7 looks at how problems may emerge if people's lower-order actions are ineffective at achieving higher-order desires and goals, and Chapter 8 looks at how problems can also emerge if directions are in conflict. Finally, in this part of the book, Chapter 9 looks at how this whole framework can be transposed to an interpersonal level, helping us to understand dynamics in couples, groups, and society as a whole.

As indicated above, Part II of the book takes the four main therapeutic approaches – psychodynamic (Chapter 10), humanistic (Chapter 11), existential (Chapter 12), and cognitive-behavioural (Chapter 13) – and shows how they articulate with the present framework, as well as the unique contribution that they can make to it. Each chapter in this part of the book is divided into four main sections: the approach's model of the human being and how this sits with the present framework; their assumptions about the highest-order human directions; their formulation of the core conflicting directions; and their practices, as viewed through a directional lens. These chapters focus primarily on individual therapies, rather than therapy for couples, families, or groups. However, Chapter 9 explores how the basic framework developed in this book could be extended to these multi-person modalities.

Part III of the book begins by looking at goal-oriented therapeutic practices: an approach to counselling and psychotherapy that is particularly consistent with (though not essential to) the present framework (Chapter 14). Chapter 15 then considers a range of other therapeutic practices closely associated with the present framework: helping clients to identify higher-order directions, directional formulation, and a summary of different practices that can be used at different phases of the directional process. In Chapter 16, this is again transposed to the interpersonal plane, looking at particular practices that can help to develop synergies between people and larger social groupings. Finally, Chapter 17 brings the book to an end by considering how therapists can act towards wider social change, the limitations of the present framework, and the kind of research that is needed to take it forward.

Along with the Web Resources, a Glossary is available online which defines key terms.

The book draws from a wide range of sources, including theory and research from psychology, psychotherapy, and the wider social sciences. Chapters 9 and 16 draw particularly from *game theory* to explore interpersonal cooperation and communication; and I am particularly interested in how such 'extra-therapeutic' theories can be used to inform therapeutic insights and methods. However, to ensure that the book remains relevant, at all times, to real-world therapeutic practices, I relate the ideas back to two particular case studies: Mei and Logan (introduced in Chapter 7). To preserve anonymity, and because these cases need to be relevant to a wide range of understandings and methods, they are primarily fictional. However, they are informed by experiences with clients over more than 20 years of clinical practice.

Throughout the book, various self-development questions and exercises are proposed. As these invite readers to explore issues at a personal level, readers should only undertake those with which they feel comfortable, and ensure that there is adequate personal support available should they need to 'debrief' after the exercises.

SUMMARY

This book is about developing a common framework for understanding how problems emerge, and how they can be addressed. Its aim is to build bridges between different therapeutic orientations – and with the wider sociopolitical field – and to show how there may be much more compatibility, and 'integrate-ability', than is often assumed. Through doing so, my hope is that practitioners will find a more coherent way of combining understandings and practices across the different therapies – and with wider social justice actions and concerns. This, I hope, will help us find better ways of learning from each other, and developing new and improved therapeutic understandings and methods that can build on the knowledges and competences of all. This is a common-factors approach that is open to all the different forms of integration; one that both develops, and sits within, a pluralistic perspective. Most fundamentally, though, the book strives to develop a way of thinking about, and practising, counselling and psychotherapy that starts from an ethic of respect and responsibility. This is the question: How can I engage with my clients – and with the wider world – in a deeply valuing and respectful way?

QUESTIONS FOR REFLECTION

- As a therapist, what is *your* sense of how Mei may be most helped with her difficulties? What does this say about the particular therapy orientation (pure form, integrative, eclectic, or pluralistic) that you are most aligned with?
- To what extent do you think it is possible, or helpful, to create a single, unified framework for understanding – and addressing – problems in people and in society?
- To what extent do you agree that ethics should be the basis for developing therapeutic understandings and practices? How important do you think it is compared against theory, evidence, or the therapist's own personal experiences?
- What do you want from reading this book?

FURTHER READING

Berlin, I. (1958). Two concepts of liberty. In H. Hardy (Ed.), *Liberty* (pp. 166-217). Oxford: Oxford University Press. Outlines the nature of *value pluralism* as part of a wider discussion on the nature of human freedom.

Cooper, M., & McLeod, J. (2011). *Pluralistic counselling and psychotherapy*. London: Sage. Practical and succinct summary of the pluralistic framework.

Grawe, K. (2004). *Psychological therapy*. Gottingen, Germany: Hogrefe & Huber. A 639-page tome detailing Grawe's comprehensive psychotherapy. Brilliant and impenetrable in equal measure.

Johnstone, L., & Boyle, M. et al. (2018). *The Power Threat Meaning Framework*. Leicester: British Psychological Society. Comprehensive review of the relationship between emotional distress and social inequalities, setting out a framework for psychological practice that puts social justice issues at its core.

Norcross, J. C. (2005). A primer on psychotherapy integration. In J. C. Norcross & M. R. Goldfried (Eds.), *Handbook of psychotherapy integration* (pp. 3-23). New York: Oxford University Press. Valuable and accessible review of the different forms of integration and eclecticism.

PART I
A COMMON FRAMEWORK FOR COUNSELLING, PSYCHOTHERAPY, AND SOCIAL CHANGE
Describing the elephant

2

DIRECTIONALITY

Philosophical foundations

This chapter discusses:

- The core philosophical premise underlying this book: that human experiencing is *directional*.
- The meaning of directionality:
    - on-the-way-to-somewhere
    - future-oriented
    - agentic
    - intelligible
    - unconscious as well as conscious, embodied as well as cognitive
    - in-the-world.

Do you like roller coasters? Possibly not. But you have probably been on one, and you probably know that feeling of something starting to shunt forward: an acceleration, an energy, a force.

The starting point for the framework developed in this book is that human being is such a force. That is, that we are in motion, a process of forward movement: a reaching out from where we are to where we want to be. Imagine Mei, then, as a 'journeying forward', but not one single journey. Rather, multiple journeys in multiple directions, like the delta of a river, criss-crossing and winding: towards Saul, towards being a 'good' mother for Olivia, towards trying to live more fully.

What should this quality of human being be called? Terms like 'drive' or 'force' capture much of the energetic elements of this phenomena, but have a somewhat mechanistic quality, and do not quite convey the 'self-propelled' nature of this journeying (Wellman & Phillips, 2001). 'Will', 'volition', or 'agency', on the other hand, focus too exclusively on consciously-determined strivings (see below). 'Intentionality', in many respects, is an ideal term, and is widely used in the philosophical literature to describe the human quality of intending forward (e.g., Dennett, 1987). Unfortunately, however, it has a second – albeit related – meaning from phenomenological philosophy (Malle, Moses, & Baldwin, 2001): that all mental states are directed towards some object (Brentano, 2015, see below). 'Intent' also implies a commitment to a particular action, and is not inclusive of those desires or wishes that may exist prior to a definite decision (Perugini & Bagozzi, 2004, see below). *Motivation*, a widely used term in psychology (e.g., Ford, 1992), is also near ideal, in that it describes 'the internal states of the organism that lead to the instigation, persistence, energy, and direction of behaviour towards a goal' (Klinger & Cox, 2011, p. 4). However, as this definition suggests, the term tends to emphasise internal processes rather than the 'in-the-world' nature of our journeying forward (see below). Traditionally, the term 'motivation' has also been associated with a more mechanistic and deterministic understanding of human being, with early motivational theories viewing humans 'as machine-like entities driven by internal or external forces beyond their control' (Ford, 1992, p. 6).

For the purposes of the present text, the term that will be used to describe this forward-moving quality of human being is *directionality*, with the term *direction* used to describe specific forward orientations. The word 'direction' is used by the existential-relational philosopher Buber (1964) to describe the 'primal tension of a human soul' to 'choose and realise' certain possibilities and not others. Angyal (1941), a major influence on Rogers, also uses the term 'direction' to describe '*intrinsic pattern of a certain movements*' (p. 54, emphasis in original), and writes about a 'directional' trend in the human organism. Rogers (1980) himself uses the term 'directional' to describe a human tendency equivalent to his 'actualising' drive: towards constructive fulfilment of inherent possibilities. There are also many parallels here with Wadsworth and Ford's (1983) concept of *self-direction*, referring to 'the many aspects of human functioning that collectively indicate that human beings actively influence their own destinies' (p. 514). In addition, the term 'direction' is quite commonly used in everyday language to refer to people's orientation and purpose: for instance, 'Is my life going in the right direction?' or 'I don't have any sense of direction in life'. In many respects, this is similar to the lay concept of being 'on track'.

This directionality has been described as the hallmark of living systems (Woodfield, 1976). Rogers (1963), for instance, states that it is only the presence or absence of a directional process 'which enables us to tell whether a given organism is alive or dead' (p. 3). My computer, for example, can process information far faster than me. And it can do incredible statistics and images and link me up with people all over the world. But, in doing all these things, it is not pursuing a particular direction; it is not trying to make something happen; it does not care about getting my calculations right; it has no purposes or aim. By contrast, I do. When I write these words, for instance, it is because I want to communicate something to you, and because *I hope* to contribute towards a more respectful and responsible world. My computer can help me with these things, but it cannot desire them. It has no purpose, orientation, direction.

Note, as in existential philosophy, directionality is not being described here as something that people can have more or less of (i.e., in 'ontic' terms, see Glossary). Certainly, people can be more or less motivated, or have greater or fewer goals. However, in this book, the term directionality is being used to describe a universal feature of human existence (i.e., in 'ontological' terms, see Glossary). In other words, we are all, always, directional – just as we are all, always, breathing, or embodied, or sensing the world around us. So, from this perspective, a depressed young person is as directional as a highly functioning adult. This is not, in any way, to suggest that they experience the world in the same way, or have similar levels of hope, freedom, or control. But that, as human beings, each is responding proactively to their worlds – and, as will be argued below, in the best ways that they know how.

This fundamental directionality of human beings – indeed, of all species – can be seen as being rooted in evolutionary processes. '[T]he disposition to live purposively is built into the most fundamental architecture of zoological organisms', writes Klinger (2013, p. 26), it is 'an inexorable result of the way the human brain is organized' (p. 23). Why would that be the case? Klinger, like other authors in the meaning-centred field (Aron & Aron, 2013; Steger, 2013), argues that a purposive, directional way of being provides species with an essential evolutionary advantage: that is, a greater ability to survive – and thereby procreate – in their environment. Imagine, for instance, a bee species that was directionless: there would be no seeking nectar, no choosing of a nesting site, no building of a hive – annihilation would be swift. From this perspective, then, directionality is hardwired into us, as human beings, at a neurobiological level, and not something that we can switch off. Klinger and Cox (2011) write: 'Everything about humans must have evolved in the service of successful goal striving – including human anatomy, physiology, cognition, and emotion' (p. 5). (See Dawkins, 2009)

So what does it mean to say that human beings are directional? The following sections explore some of its interrelated qualities.

ON-THE-WAY-TO-SOMEWHERE

To describe human beings as directional is to say that we are more than static, object-like 'things' (Heidegger, 1962). Rather, as with existential philosophy, it is to conceptualise human existence as a dynamic, emerging 'flow' (Cooper, 2017a). And it is a flow that is always 'intending beyond itself' (Husserl, 1960): self-transcendent, a moving beyond what it has been to what it will be. In other words, from this perspective, human being is not only on the way to somewhere, but 'on the way to somewhere else' (Macquarrie, 1972, p. 48). This is what Sartre (1958) calls *being for-itself*: the dynamic, groundless, upsurging of consciousness that 'nihilates', and transcends, our fixed *being in-itself*.

While we might say, then, that Mei is experiencing a profound stuckness in her life, she is not simply a stagnated 'thing'. Rather, in so many ways, she is an intending beyond what she already is. She is a 'wanting-to-sort-out-her-relationship-with-Rob', a 'trying-to-find-different-ways-of-relating-to-her-mother', a 'hoping-to-deepen-her-intimacy-with-Saul'. From this perspective, even the most avoidant or catatonic clients can be understood as striving to get somewhere, even if it a striving to get back to where they have already been.

TELEOLOGICAL: BEING AS FUTURE-ORIENTED

An understanding of human being as on-the-way-to-somewhere is closely related to a *teleological* perspective. The term 'teleology' has been used in many senses, but all refer to 'descriptions or explanations of phenomena in terms of final causes, that is, ends, goals, purposes' (Reese, 1994, p. 75). Teleological perspectives are widespread in the biological and social sciences. They date back to Aristotle (Woodfield, 1976), who identified four causes of being, the last of which was *final causes*: 'that for the sake of which a thing is done' (Reese, 1994, p. 86). Accounts of behaviour, then, are teleological to the extent that they attempt to explain things in terms of the intended outcome. For instance, we might hypothesise that Mei turned up to the session late because, at some level, she wanted to avoid feeling ashamed of wanting help.

This teleological understanding of human being can be contrasted with a causal account, in which human experiencing and activity is explained in terms of past determinants. For instance, a therapist might hypothesise that Mei turned up late to her session *because* she had been shamed by adult figures in her past. Here, the behaviour, *x*, is explained in terms of a preceding cause, *y*. By contrast, a teleological explanation accounts for behaviour *x* in terms of its intended antecedent: *z*. Of course, a teleological perspective does not rule out the importance – or influence – of past factors.

For instance, we might say that Mei wants to avoid talking about herself because, as a child, she experienced shame when she was the focus of attention. Here, however, we are not asserting a direct causal chain from past to present, as if the past was a billiard ball that knocks into the 'ball' of the present and causes it to move forward. Rather, we are viewing the client as a directional, purposive being, who draws on her past as a source of information and guidance on how best to actualise her desired future.

In this way, a teleological perspective is fundamentally *futural* (Heidegger, 1962): oriented towards, and shaped by, what is to come. And, as with directionality *per se*, it has been argued that '[t]he pursuance of future ends and the choice of means for their attainment are the mark and criterion of the presence of mentality in a phenomenon' (Austin & Vancouver, 1996, p. 338). As human beings, from this perspective, we 'hurl ourselves' towards our futures (Sartre, 1958): imagining ourselves at some point ahead, and then acting towards that. So we project forward goals, hopes, and fear; and our behaviour is an attempt to approach – or avoid – what we have posited there. This means that our present is not simply the here-and-now, but also the 'not yet' (Heidegger, 1962).

The teleological nature of human being is evidenced by two particular human characteristics: *persistence* and *plasticity* (Woodfield, 1976). Persistence refers to the fact that we tend to continue in our actions until a particular endpoint is reached, and then the action ceases. So, for instance, I write and rewrite this sentence until I feel (just about) happy enough with it, and then I move on to the next sentence. And, indeed, if people's goals become blocked, they may pursue that goal even harder or become obsessed with them (Baumeister, 1991). Such activity is hard to explain purely in terms of past determinants: What past experiences could cause me to stop at that particular point; and why would I be striving even more when I cannot get what I want? Rather, my activity would seem oriented towards, and shaped by, a particular end. Plasticity refers to the fact that, if I do not reach the goal through one method, then I may adopt another method to do the same thing (also known as *equifinality*, see Chapter 6). Indeed, human activity can be seen as series of constant readjustments to achieve a particular effect. So, for instance, if I cannot find the right words to express what I want to say, I may try another set of words. And, in fact, I might even abandon this paragraph, or this chapter, or this book, if I do not feel it is communicating what I want to communicate. What this shows, again, is that my activity is oriented towards, and shaped by, a particular desired endpoint (communicating a certain understanding to my readers). Such plasticity would be very hard to explain in terms of starting conditions alone.

AGENTIC

Closely connected to this teleological perspective is an understanding of human being as *agentic*. 'To be an agent is to intentionally make things happen by one's actions'

(Bandura, 2001, p. 2); that is, to be an 'active initiator' of one's actions in the world (Rogers, 1963). From this perspective, then, human beings are proactive and generative, striving to make things happen rather than being merely reactive to their circumstances. Layard (2006) writes, 'We are not blank slates on which our situation operates to make us happy or sad. We are active agents who both shape our situation and control our response to that situation' (p. 73). Of course, this is not to suggest that everything that happens to us is our 'responsibility' or 'fault'. Mei, for instance, cannot be held responsible for the racist bullying that she endured. But it is saying that, even under such circumstances, we have the capacity to respond in a range of ways. For instance, Mei could have responded with violence, or she could have allowed herself to show her hurt, or – as she did – she could have tried to protect herself by becoming more wary of others. This is similar to the view of human beings and human emotional distress put forward by the BPS's *Power Threat Meaning Framework*, which views human beings as 'active agents in our lives at the same time facing many very real limits and barriers to the changes we can bring about (Johnstone & Boyle, 2018, p.17).

Agency is also closely related to the capacity to *self-organise* – another distinguishing feature of animate entities (Ryan, 2012). Self-organisation means that we are not just a bundle of fragmented and incoherent responses. Rather, something 'within' us – something agentic – marshals our resources to respond in coordinated, coherent, and meaningful ways. When we speak of human directionality, then, we are not just saying that human beings move along particular paths, like arrows that have been fired from a bow. Rather, human beings create their own direction: an 'internal teleology' (Corning, 2003, p. 172). This, again, distinguishes animate beings from inanimate beings. The latter must always be moved by something else, but animate organisms move themselves.

Within the therapeutic field, recent years have seen a number of attempts to apply this agentic understanding of human being to clients. Most notable here is Bohart and Tallman's *How clients make therapy work: The process of active self-healing* (1999), which critiques theories of psychotherapy for not construing clients in active, generative terms. They write: 'It is as if, in therapists' eyes, clients have been lobotomized when they enter therapy. ... Clients are not granted the ability to think in the same active, generative way therapists do' (pp. 208–209). By contrast, Bohart and Tallman emphasise the client's ability to plan and initiate action, and to choose their own goals. Along similar lines, Duncan, Miller, and Sparks (2004), in their book *The heroic client*, describe a 'client directed' approach to therapy in which the client, and not the therapist, is seen as the 'hero' of the therapeutic drama. This perspective is well supported by the empirical evidence, which shows that the majority of change in therapy is, indeed, due to client factors (such as levels of motivation and engagement), rather than anything specific to the therapist (Cooper, 2008).

To say that human being is directional, then, is to say that we are not passive sponges that soak up our worlds, or machine-like automata, controlled by laws or by the environment (Koestler, 1967; Rogers, 1963). Rather, it is to suggest that, as human beings, we are active organisms, always 'up to something', always striving and seeking (Rogers, 1963). Hence, for instance, if we want to understand Mei's lateness, we need to strive to understand what she is trying to do: where she is wanting to get towards. Not, necessarily, in terms of her deliberately wanting to be late, but in terms of her lateness emerging from the various ways in which she organises herself towards her world: for instance, her strivings to avoid feeling shame.

INTELLIGIBLE

Intelligibility means that human behaviour is 'always a meaningful and comprehensible response towards the world: there "for a reason", and not something that is simply irrational, ad hoc or meaningless' (Cooper, 2015a, p. 58). In other words, human beings should be understood as 'rational agents', who act to further their goals in the light of their beliefs (Dennett, 1987). This does not mean that people should be understood as always acting in a logical way, or consistently doing the things that are most helpful for them. Indeed, in Chapters 7 and 8, we will see how, from a directional standpoint, people can end up behaving in ways that are highly illogical, contradictory, and self-destructive. However, the principle of intelligibility holds that people tend to behave 'in a fashion they construe to be the best adaptive alternative given their current perception of themselves and the situation' (Greenberg, Rice, & Elliott, 1993, p. 80). That is, people try to do their best, even if doing their best is not always the best thing that they could be doing. Again, this is consistent with the *Power Threat Meaning Framework* (Johnstone & Boyle, 2018), which strives to communicate to service users the overall message that:

You are experiencing a normal reaction to abnormal circumstances. Anyone else who had been through the same events might well have ended up reacting in the same way. However, these survival strategies may no longer be needed or useful. With the right kind of support, you may be able to leave them behind. (p. 18, emphasis in original)

This understanding of human activity as intelligible stretches right back to the very beginnings of psychotherapy – indeed, it can be considered its very *raison d'être*. For Freud (1962), dreams, symptoms, and neuroses all had a sense, and it was the task of the psychotherapist to unravel this 'true' meaning. In the case of 'Little Hans', for instance, Freud (1909) suggests that the boy's phobia of horses – seemingly a random, meaningless fear – was actually an expression of his desire to ward off his father, who he feared would castrate him. Freud (1962) wrote, 'even the delusional ideas of the insane would certainly be found to have a sense if only we understood how to translate them' (p. 296). This is, perhaps, most powerfully demonstrated in the work of the existential psychiatrist R. D. Laing, who showed how psychotic symptoms made sense within the context of a disturbed and invalidating family context (e.g., Laing, 1965; Laing & Esterson, 1964).

This assumption of intelligibility can also be seen in *rational choice theory*, one of the foremost models of social and economic behaviour. This approach assumes that:

> [P]eople have desires (goals, wishes, etc.) and beliefs (convictions, vague ideas, etc.) and based on these they chose the alternative that best satisfies their desire (achieves their goal), given what they believe about various actions' possible consequences and their likelihood. (Eriksson, 2011, p. 28)

UNCONSCIOUS AND CONSCIOUS, EMBODIED AND COGNITIVE

Directions may be entirely conscious: for instance, 'I want to order the carbonara rather than the Bolognese'. As will be evidenced in Chapter 5, however, directions may be wholly unconscious. Mei, for instance, may have little awareness of her deep yearning for relatedness with others, just as she may be unaware that her lateness to sessions is rooted in a desire to avoid shame. In this respect, then, a directional understanding of human beings is not the same as 'voluntarism', which assumes that the human, conscious will is the primary determinant of actions (May, 1969a).

Closely related to this, as the existential philosopher Merleau-Ponty (1962) has argued, directionality does not simply exist at a disembodied, cognitive level, but as a somatic, embodied 'rising up' towards the world. Mei's yearnings for intimacy with Saul, for instance, are rooted deep within her body: a psycho-somatic-sexual whole. Here, the body is not simply a passive receptacle to the world, but a directional agency itself, responding and acting towards its world in meaningful ways.

In the therapeutic field, this embodied directionality has been most clearly articulated and applied in *focusing-oriented psychotherapy* (Gendlin, 2003). This is an approach that evolved from the person-centred field and strives to help clients 'take forward' their bodily 'felt senses' (see Chapter 11). Gendlin (1996) writes, '*Every experience and event contains implicit further movement*' (p. 15, emphasis in original), and the task of the focusing-oriented therapist is to help that forward movement unfurl. For instance, a client who notices a tightness in their stomach might be asked, 'What is this tightness saying?' or 'What happens when you just allow that tightness to be? Where does it go to?' In this respect, focusing-oriented psychotherapy invites clients to cut beneath their conscious goals and tasks, and to reconnect with a deeper, more embodied directionality.

As with Buber (1964), we might also consider directionality at the spiritual level: the 'inner song' of the soul (p. 56). For Buber, this is the essential 'we': the being-with and -towards others that unites us at the transcendental plane. For Buber, 'God' is not outside human relating, but is manifest through it (Buber, 1958). In other words, in our directionality towards others, and in our receiving of that other's directionality, we touch our spiritual essence. He writes, 'Spirit is not in the *I*, but between *I* and *Thou*. It is not like the blood that circulates in you, but like the air in which you breathe' (pp. 57–58).

IN-THE-WORLD

In rational choice theory, as with the majority of the psychological literature, there is a tendency to understand our desires and goals as something that exists within us (though see Cavallo & Fitzsimons, 2012; Deci & Ryan, 2012; Heckhausen, Wrosch, & Schulz, 2010). Therapeutic approaches, too, have tended to conceptualise the relationship between goals, desires, and psychological distress at the individual level alone (see Part II, this volume). However, a person's directionality can be considered fundamentally embedded in their *world*. Here, 'world' refers to a person's context: his or her environment (Moran, 2000). This is consistent with a *biopsychosocial* understanding of the person (Engel, 1977), in which '[o]rganism and environment are the two indispensable poles of a single process – life' (Angyal, 1941, p. 32). Such an understanding is central to the present text because if people's directions are fundamentally in-the-world, then the actualisation of these directions may require changes in the world, as well as 'in' the person.

This *in-the-world*-ness of directionality is manifested in several ways.

Directionality as towards something

Directionality, as described above, is something that comes *from* the person – not something that happens *to* them. And yet, the worlds that people inhabit are not mere appendages to their directions. For every goal, by necessity, requires a 'goal object' (Elliot & Niesta, 2009, p. 59), every desire needs something desired, and these 'directional objects' are an essential component of the direction itself. We can see this in the fact that directional objects are non-substitutable. 'I want a cup of tea', for instance, is a different direction from 'I want a cup of coffee'. It has a different 'texture', a different feel. In this respect, then, there is no objectless 'I desire…' or 'I intend…': there is no 'internal' directionality without an external correlate.

This understanding of directionality, as towards something, is consistent with a *phenomenological* understanding of consciousness (Husserl, 1960). For Brentano, a key predecessor of phenomenology, all mental acts are *intentional*, in the sense of being related to some object (Moran, 2000). So consciousness, from this perspective, is always consciousness *of* something (Spinelli, 2005): it is characterised by an 'aboutness' (Moran, 2000), an opening on to 'alterity' (Crossley, 1996).

Helpfully, here, phenomenologists distinguish between the *noesis* and *noema* of an intentional act (Langdridge, 2012; Smith & Woodruff Smith, 1995; Spinelli, 2005).

The former is the act of perceiving: for instance, my *seeing of* the kitten. The latter, by contrast, is the perceived as perceived: that is, *the kitten* as I see it. In the same way, then, we might distinguish between two poles of directionality – the *movement* towards something (e.g., wanting, desiring, striving for) and the *phenomenon* towards which we move (e.g., the tea, the coffee) – always remembering that these two facets are fundamentally inseparable. For Ford (1992), in discussing goals, this is the difference between *goal process* and *goal content*, respectively.

Given the embodied nature of directionality, it may also be appropriate to draw parallels with Heidegger's existential-phenomenological understanding of being-in-the-world as *care* (Guignon, 1993; Heidegger, 1962; Polt, 1999). Care describes our enmeshment in the world in the sense that 'external' things matter to us: we are not indifferent to them (May, 1969a). I experience a sense of calm, for instance, as I watch the green fields from my train window; or experience despair as I watch the nightly news. Such 'moods' reveal how the world affects me: my 'innermost' feelings are intertwined with – and attuned to – what is 'outside'. In the same way, we can say that my directionality emerges in response to a world I care about: where it matters to me what I do – or do not do. Take away a world that matters and I would have no directionality left: no goals, no desires, no strivings.

The social construction of directions

Directionality is also in-the-world in the sense that the directions we adopt are often – and, perhaps, always – infused with the meanings, values, and directions of those around us (Eriksson, 2011; Freund, 2007). This might be from family, friends, or our wider communities and society. From her mother, for instance, Mei 'internalised' the belief that she should be deferential to others – a direction reinforced by society's wider gender norms. And, from her girlfriends, Mei learnt that she should prioritise having fun and getting out in the world. The hypothesis that our directions are influenced by social factors is well supported by the research. For instance, there is evidence that goal pursuit may be automatically triggered by the goals that we infer in the behaviour of others: *goal contagion* (Aarts & Custers, 2012). In a fascinating example of this, Gillespie (2007) showed how tourists in Ladakh, north India, desired particular types of experience (such as travelling over the Himalayas on motorbike) that were derived from iconic images and meanings in the public sphere (such as the film *Easy Rider*). More insidiously, in the case of eating disorders, young girls may be internalising such values as thinness from their parents, peer groups, or from the media (Irving & Cannon, 2000).

Such 'extrinsic' directions may overlay more 'intrinsic' wants and goals (see Chapter 5). However, from a Heideggerian (1962) perspective, these socially-infused directions may be at the very core of our being. Heidegger argues that, from birth, we are 'fallen' into a world of ready-made meanings and purposes (Dreyfus, 1997), and tend to adopt these, ourselves, without ever asking why. It is as if we wake up in the middle of a running race and chase off in the same direction as everyone else without ever knowing – or asking – where we are all going. In our contemporary digital age, it could be argued that this process is becoming ever more prevalent (see Web Resource 2.2).

Building on Heidegger (1962), a 'postmodern' perspective holds that the social construction of our directionality is unavoidable. Philosophers like Derrida (1974) and Wittgenstein (1967) have argued that we can never wrest ourselves free from language, a socially constructed media. Hence, we can never find some personal, 'non-social' directions. For as soon as we try to think about, or express, our directions, we are recaptured in the play of language. I desire 'intimacy', for instance, or I desire 'success', but these words do not stand in for some pre-verbal, 'actual' wants. Rather, from this perspective, as I 'name' these desires, so they are constructed.

In contrast to this, however, humanistic and existential perspectives tend to hold that socially constructed layers of meanings and purposes can be peeled away, such that people can find more authentic, 'intrinsic' directions. Fromm (1942), Laing (1967), and Rogers (1959), for instance, all write that human beings are often hugely alienated from their genuine directions, left 'a shrivelled, desiccated fragment of what a person can be' (Laing, 1967, p. 22). From these perspectives, however, there is also the possibility – through therapy, or through political activity – of overcoming this alienation, and of re-accessing more natural, authentic wants.

'Socialist humanists' like Fromm (1942) and, to a great extent, Laing (1967), base much of this thinking on Marx's (1988) early writings (see Web Resource 17.1). Marx argued that capitalism and its means of production reduced people to 'crippled monstrosities' of what they could be. Here, where workers are yoked and subjugated to their machines, they become little more than machines themselves: devoid of even their most basic desires. And, argues Marx, in a society where labour is divided down into discrete, specialised activities, each of us become alienated from our natural desires for diversity and creativity at work. Furthermore, for Marx, capitalism fundamentally estranges us from our natural wants because it idolises one 'good' above all else: 'money'. For Marx, this is a 'refinement of needs', but also a 'bestial barbarization, a complete, unrefined, abstract simplicity of need' (p. 117). That is, our natural tendency to progress towards multiple goals – our heterogeneity, both within people and between people – gets bottled down to one, all-pervasive objective (Walzer, 1983; Chapter 16, this volume). And for Laing (1967) and Marx – as for Heidegger (1962) – it is not just that society alienates us from our authentic directions, but that it 'covers up' this alienation: alienating us from the reality of just how alienated we are.

Interpersonal directionality

Our directionality is also fundamentally in-the-world in the sense that it is always intertwined with the directions of others. Mei's directions towards Rob, for instance, are shaped by Rob's own directions (e.g., for spending money on records), which are themselves shaped by Mei's directions. In this sense, then, we can never entirely disentangle one person's directions from others.

This intertwining and interdependence also means that, while we have started with an analysis of directionality at the individual level, it would be just as legitimate to analyse it at the dyadic level, or at the family, group, community, or societal levels (as we will go on to do in Chapter 9). That is, we might focus on Mei's directions or Rob's directions, but we could also focus on the directions of 'Mei–Rob' as a couple, or of their family 'system' with Olivia.

Directionality as towards someone

Directionality is also in-the-world in the sense that many of our most important strivings are *about* others. For instance, Pöhlmann (2001), in one survey of 620 adults, found that 'intimacy – having a personal relationship which is based on mutual affection and trust – was the most important goal for nearly all of the participants' (p. 74). This is clearly illustrated in the case of Mei, who, like so many clients coming to therapy (Grosse Holtforth & Grawe, 2002), wanted to improve her relationships: with Rob, with her mother, and with Saul.

Contextual factors

Finally, our directions are in-the-world in the sense that the extent to which we can *actualise* them – that is, facilitate their achievement (see Chapter 3) – is very much dependent on our 'external' context. Ford (1992) writes that our environment must be 'responsive': that is, 'have the material and informational resources needed to facilitate goal attainment' (p. 131). For instance, the racism that Mei experienced as a young girl made it very difficult for her to actualise her desire for safety, or for self-worth. This is a critical point for the present text, because it means that improvements in wellbeing may require change at the social level, as well as at the psychological one. As the *Power Threat Meaning Framework* states, for instance, 'reducing economic and social inequality is probably the single most effective step we can take to improve the mental health of the population' (Johnstone & Boyle, 2018, p. 265).

CONCLUSION

Directionality can be defined as the agentic, forward-moving, intelligible quality of human beings and human systems. The term, itself, is relatively uncommon in the literature. But the basic assumption that human beings strive towards things – and that this directionality underpins much of human thought, feeling, and behaviour – is widely accepted (Ford, 1992; Kiresuk, 1994). In the psychological field, this can be seen in such well-recognised models as the *theory of planned behaviour* (Ajzen, 1991), in which intentions are conceptualised as direct precursor to actions. It is also evident in the vast array of motivational and goal-directed theories, which are 'being more intensively studied today than ever before' (Ryan, 2012, p. 3). As we have also seen, there are parallel developments in such areas as philosophy and economics (e.g., Dennett, 1987).

Empirically, there is also a growing body of evidence to support a directional perspective. Research shows, for instance, that a person's behaviours are directly influenced by their intentions, and that these intentions are directly determined by a person's desires (Bagozzi & Kimmel, 1995; Perugini & Bagozzi, 2001). It also shows that human beings spend much of their time thinking about how to reach their desired goals, and the particular means by which they might do so (Klinger & Cox, 2011; Snyder, 2000).

Research also shows that directional phenomena – such as wants, desires, and intentions – are among the earliest, and most basic, ways in which children make sense of themselves and others: for instance, 'want spoon' or 'want a pet snake' (Wellman & Phillips, 2001; see Web Resource 2.1). Indeed, there is evidence to show that children as young as six months can infer intentions in an adult's behaviour (Meltzoff, 1995): imitating, for instance, what an adult seems to be trying to do, rather than the actuality of their behaviour. As adults, too, 'there is a tremendous body of evidence' supporting the idea that people tend to seek out the meaning intentions of others (Gibbs Jr, 2001, p. 108), habitually and effortlessly 'reading' beneath the surface of others' – as well as our own – behaviours to discern the desires and intentions underneath. When Mei, for instance, sees Rob on his couch, she is not just perceiving a man, and a couch, and a TV. Rather, she is inferring a directional system: husband-wants-to-slob-doesn't-want-to-connect-emotionally.

To summarise, then, the framework developed in this book starts from the assumption that human being is essentially directional. This means that, as people, we are always on the way to somewhere, agentic, and acting in meaningful ways. This directionality, however, is not simply a conscious phenomenon residing inside of us. Rather, it is an embodied being-towards-the-world, acting at all times and in ways we might not be aware of.

QUESTIONS FOR REFLECTION

- Is the concept of 'directionality' meaningful for you? Is it something that you can, or cannot, 'connect' with? How would you describe directionality in your own terms?
- At a personal level, what are the main directions in your life?

FURTHER READING

Bohart, A. C., & Tallman, K. (1999). *How clients make therapy work: The process of active self-healing*. Washington, DC: American Psychological Association. One of the great psychotherapy texts, with theory and evidence on the agency of clients.

Buber, M. (1964). *Daniel: Dialogues on realisation* (M. Friedman, Trans.). New York: Holt, Reinhart and Winston. One of Buber's earlier, and lesser known, works, but beautifully written, and meditating 'on direction' (pp. 49-78).

Duncan, B. L., Miller, S. D., & Sparks, J. A. (2004). *The heroic client: A revolutionary way to improve effectiveness through client-directed, outcome-informed therapy*. San Francisco, CA: Jossey-Bass. Radical and rhetorical treatise on the agency of the client.

Ford, M. E. (1992). *Motivating humans: Goals, emotions, and personal agency beliefs*. Newbury Park, CA: Sage. An in-depth, integrative framework for understanding human motivation, including a review of over 30 different theories of motivation.

Heidegger, M. (1962). *Being and time* (J. Macquarrie & E. Robinson, Trans.). Oxford: Blackwell. Immensely tough reading, but profoundly deep philosophical reflections on the nature of being, care, and directionality.

3

A PHASE MODEL OF DIRECTIONALITY

From fantasy to action

This chapter discusses:

- Directionality as a series of overlapping *phases*.
- The phases of a *directional arc*:
    - Emergence
    - Awareness
    - Evaluation
    - Intention
    - Planning
    - Action
    - Feedback
    - Termination.

For the purposes of Chapter 2, directionality was conceptualised as a single, homogeneous force. A closer analysis, however, suggests that it can be seen as consisting of a number of distinct, albeit related, *phases*. This is supported by empirical research (Gollwitzer, 1990). Mei's directionality towards Saul, for instance, might be manifest as a desire to be close to him, as a choice to spend time with him, or as actual physical actions to be with him. And while Mei's desires might lead to choices and actions, it is quite possible that they would not. Indeed, while Mei feels a constant desire for Saul, she rarely does anything about this.

How, then, should we conceptualise these different elements of directionality? Over the last few decades, a range of different models of motivation, experiencing, and behavioural change have been proposed that can help to develop a more in-depth and nuanced understanding of directionality (e.g., Austin & Vancouver, 1996; Clarkson, 1989; Gollwitzer, 1990; Little, 1983; May, 1969b; Prochaska & DiClemente, 1986). These models conceptualise this phenomenon – or aspects of it – in terms of a sequence of phases: in linear progression, but with the recognition that different phases may overlap or, in some cases, be bypassed entirely. Here, there is also a recognition that the completion of one 'cycle' inevitably leads to the emergence of subsequent 'cycles' (hence, for the purposes of this book, we will refer to a *directional arc*).

Probably the best known of these models is Prochaska and Di Clemente's (1986) *stages of change*, developed specifically in relation to health behaviours such as drug addiction. This conceptualises directionality in terms of five main stages: pre-contemplation, contemplation, preparation, action, and maintenance. The 'Rubicon Model' is another very well-developed – and well-evidenced – model of 'action phases', developed in the social psychological field by Heckhausen and Gollwitzer (1987; Gollwitzer, 1990). This puts particular emphasis on the transition from 'predecisional' to 'postdecisional' phases ('crossing the Rubicon'), as the individual moves from desire and deliberation to planning and action. Clarkson's (1989) *cycle of Gestalt formation and destruction* is another phase model, derived from Gestalt therapy (Perls et al., 1951), which focuses on the micro-processes of here-and-now experiencing.

Although such models have emerged from very different traditions, there is a great deal of commonality in how they conceptualise the directional process (see Web Resource 3.1, which presents a table of six different models). Bringing these models together, we can propose eight phases of a directional arc. These are presented, graphically, in Figure 3.1. For readability sake, the arc is presented as a straight line, but a curved or spiralling line would be a more appropriate way of representing the cyclical nature of this process.

EMERGENCE

The initial phase of the directional arc can be seen as the *emergence*, or emanation, of impulses towards – or away from – something. These are our *desires*, *wants*, *wishes*, and

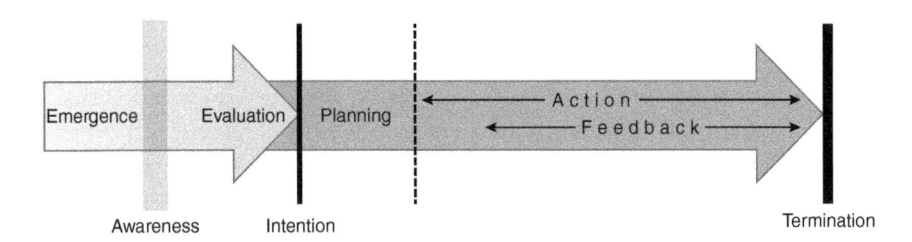

A PHASE MODEL OF DIRECTIONALITY: FROM FANTASY TO ACTION

Figure 3.1 The directional arc

hopes (see Web Resource 3.2, Directional constructs) – or, if away from somewhere, our fears and anxieties. In most instances, this process may be involuntary and unconscious. Mei does not choose, for instance, to experience sexual desire towards Saul. Rather, phenomenologically, it is something that she feels – and then notices in her consciousness.

Such impulses may emerge from deep 'within' us. In Freudian (1965) terms, these are the wishes and wants that bubble up from the 'id', that 'cauldron of seething excitations' (pp. 105–106), as it strives to meet its instinctual needs. We might also locate these emerging desires in our 'phantasy' world of 'imagining, daydreaming, [and] fancying' (Rycroft, 1995, p. 131). Alternatively, in focusing terms, we can see this emergence of directionality as the organising, mobilising, agentic *body*, striving to actualise its organismic potential in implicit, pre-conscious ways (Gendlin, 2003; see Chapter 2, this volume).

From the research, it is still not clear how 'internally' generated desires emerge (Austin & Vancouver, 1996), or why particular desires emanate at particular times. However, from Freudian psychoanalysis to Powers's control theory (1973, 1992; see Box 6.1), it has been hypothesised that they emerge in response to unmet needs, expectations, or standards. So, for instance, we might hypothesise that Mei, like all human beings, has an inherent need for relatedness, and that her desire for Saul emerges in response to deficits in this area of her life. In addition, however, there is the more humanistic view that desires are not just compensatory but emerge as manifestations of a positive, growth-oriented tendency (e.g., Deci & Ryan, 2000).

Research also shows that desires can be 'activated', or 'primed', through external sources (Austin & Vancouver, 1996). Mei's yearning for Saul, for instance, is not something that is constantly 'on'. Rather, it is triggered by stimuli associated with him: for instance, the aroma of his aftershave, or going back to the pub where 'something happened'. Here, research suggests that desires residing in our long-term memories are transferred into our short-term memories: that is, they are made 'accessible' (Moskowitz & Gesundheit, 2009). This activation may take place through a variety of external sources – for instance, words, images, objects, and people – some of which may be universal, others culturally-derived, and others specific to the individual (Kruglanski & Kopetz, 2009).

AWARENESS

Awareness is the conscious recognition of particular directions. This is, perhaps, the most 'bypassable' of the directional phases in that directional impulses can be evaluated, intended, and acted upon without any conscious awareness at all. However, it is essential to identify here because the conscious recognition of hidden desires is the lynchpin of many different therapies. More specifically, through developing a reflective awareness of their desires, it is hypothesised that clients are enabled to 'stand back' from them (i.e., hold a 'meta-perspective', 'mentalize'; Fonagy, Gergely, Jurist, & Target, 2004; Hermans & Kempen, 1993), and make more considered, balanced, informed, and 'free' decisions about how to move forward in their lives (the evaluation phase, see below). Ferrucci (1982) likens this to the difference 'between being impotently transported by a roller coaster and, instead, driving a car and being able to choose which way to go and for what purpose to make the journey' (p. 51). Another way of putting this is to say that, through awareness, we mobilise our conscious mind to support us in achieving the things that we want. From a therapeutic standpoint, developing an awareness of directions may also be important in helping clients find effective and synergetic ways of actualising them (see Chapters 7 and 8); gain a sense of purpose and meaning (see Chapter 12); accept, and feel more compassionate towards, them (Gilbert & Irons, 2014); feel that they are more manageable (Barber, Muran, McCarthy, & Keefe, 2013); and communicate them to others (including their therapists) in clear and effective ways. By contrast, the denial of desires, for many therapies, may be seen as a form of pathology in itself (e.g., May, 1969a).

It may also be important to note, however, that a 'hyper-awareness' of our directions may not be a good thing: creating anxiety about achieving our goals, which could then inhibit performance (Ford, 1992). In addition, there may be a danger that, through consciously defining our directions in the awareness phase – and subsequently in the evaluation and intention phases (see below) – we do not allow them to evolve in a more 'organic' way. In other words, if we consciously symbolise, and operationalise, our directions prematurely, we may create a false and superficial understanding of what they are – disconnected from their more nuanced, subtle, and fluid nature.

EVALUATION

A third phase of the directional arc can be termed *evaluation*, or what Gollwitzer (1990) calls 'deliberation'. This is the weighing up of our initial directions – along with other internal and external factors – to determine how we will choose to act. This process is likely to be conscious, particularly where people are aware of their directions, but research suggests it can also operate at an unconscious level (see Chapter 5, this volume). In certain circumstances, such as immediate physical threat, there may also be very little evaluation at all.

A PHASE MODEL OF DIRECTIONALITY: FROM FANTASY TO ACTION

How do people go about deciding on what they want to do? Probably the best established accounts are *expectancy–value* theories. These are common within psychology and other disciplines, such as behavioural economics (Correia, Murphy, & Butler, 2011), and supported by psychological and neuroscientific evidence (e.g., Ajzen, 1991; Klinger & Cox, 2011; Malle & Knobe, 2001). Grawe (2004) describes them as significant for psychotherapy, though they have probably been under-utilised to date.

As the name suggests, expectancy–value theories suggest that our choices are determined by two particular factors. First is the relative *value* of a particular direction: that is, the extent to which it fulfils our most fundamental, 'highest-order' wants (Tolman, 1932, in Custers, 2009; Gollwitzer & Oettingen, 2012; Moskowitz & Grant, 2009a; and see Chapter 6, this volume). For instance, Cox and Klinger (2011b) argue that people will only stop drinking if the perceived gains of this action (e.g., health, family cohesion) are weighed more positively than the perceived losses (e.g., drowning out painful feelings). To some extent, as rational choice theory suggests, this weighing up will be based on a logical 'cost-benefit' analysis (Layard, 2006). However, research also shows that this *decision utility* – 'the weight that is assigned to the desirability of an outcome' (Kahneman, 1999, p. 17) – can be biased by a number of factors (see Chapter 7, this volume). For instance, 'delay discounting' means that an alcohol abuser may over-value the immediate mood-altering effects of alcohol, while under-valuing the longer term benefits of sobriety (Cox & Klinger, 2011b).

In expectancy–value theories, the second key evaluation factor is *feasibility*: the expectation, or belief, that a particular goal can be reached (Tolman, 1932, in Custers, 2009; Moskowitz & Grant, 2009a). This is closely connected to an individual's perception of 'behavioural control' (Ajzen, 1991). So, for instance, Mei may feel that she would be better off in her life if she left Rob, but if she does not feel able to make this separation, this outcome is much less likely. Psychologically, *self-efficacy* (or personal agency beliefs; Ford, 1992) plays a critical role here. This is a person's belief in their ability to succeed in specific situations or with specific tasks (Bandura, 2001), and its impact is constantly encountered within therapy. If, for instance, a client does not really believe that they can improve things in their lives, they may be very reluctant to try to take the first steps in this direction.

This self-efficacy may be particularly important because it can be the basis of virtuous, or vicious, cycles. Jacey, for instance, was a client who experienced depression and found it incredibly difficult to get out of bed in the mornings: 'It's too painful', 'What's the point?', 'I can't do it'. What Jacey found, however, was that if she could get herself up and doing just small things – like making a cup of tea – her sense of efficacy would improve. This, then, made it more possible for her to go on to do other things, like take her dog for a walk, which then further improved her sense of self-efficacy. By contrast, if she stayed in bed all morning, this deepened her feelings of uselessness, making it even more difficult for her to act.

What we also see with Jacey is the role of past experiencing in determining a person's expectations of success. If we have failed, repeatedly, at a task, we are less likely to believe that success is possible for the future; and are therefore less likely to aim towards those goals. Such an understanding is central to many therapeutic theories, such as Bowlby's (1969) concept of *internal working models*, which are mental representations of self, other, and relationships. If, for instance, we have not been able to achieve the closeness with our carers that we wanted, then we may come to believe that such goals are not achievable. Consequently, we may withdraw efforts at trying to achieve them through, for instance, an 'avoidant attachment' style. This may protect us from disappointment, but it is also likely to reinforce a belief that such goals are not achievable. Hence, we are left without the deep relatedness that, at some level, we may continue to crave.

However, while perceived behavioural control is, ultimately, a perception, it is also fundamentally shaped by the resources and opportunities that are actually available to a person (Ajzen, 1991). If a young black woman, for instance, has low expectations of progressing in her career, this may reflect a very real sexism and racism that exists in her chosen field. Hence, as Ford (1992) points out, a third critical factor in determining how people evaluate their directions is the 'responsiveness' of their particular context. This means that our social and political worlds are not external to, but implicated in, every choice that we make.

INTENTION

'Right,' says Mei, at the start of Session 20, 'I am- I have- I am going to talk to Saul about what's going on. I need to get this sorted.'

Here, out of the evaluation of directions may come a *goal intention*: 'I intend to perform Behaviour X/to reach Outcome Y' (Park-Stamms & Gollwitzer, 2009, p. 362). Desires, as the research shows, predict intentions (Bagozzi & Kimmel, 1995); and intentions are then one of the strongest predictors of how we actually act (Ajzen, 1991). This is the 'crossing of the Rubicon' – like Caesar passing the point of no return – for, at this point, the goal pursuit begins, and therefore must be either successfully accomplished or failed (Gollwitzer, 1990). In existential terms, this can be considered the point of choosing: where, against the backdrop of desires, perceptions, and beliefs, we commit ourselves to one particular path.

In their *mindset theory of action phases*, a corollary to the Rubicon model, Heckhausen and Gollwitzer (1987; Gollwitzer, 1990, 2012) argue that this 'transition from the motivational state of deliberation to the volitional state of implementation implies a qualitative leap with respect to an individual's cognitive functioning' (1987, p. 103). This is the movement from 'desires', 'wants', and 'hopes' to 'plans' and 'goals' (see Web Resource, 3.2). This claim is relatively well supported by the empirical evidence, which shows that *preintentional* (i.e., before a decision is made) and *postintentional* (i.e., after a decision is made) 'mindsets' operate in relatively different ways. In the preintentional, deliberation phase, for instance, people's evaluation of information tends to be more balanced, accurate, and open-minded, while in the postintentional, implementation phase, people's thoughts become more focused and their behaviours more persistent (Gollwitzer, 2012). Similarly, research shows that there are qualitative differences in how lay-people conceptualise preintentional 'desires', as compared with postintentional 'intentions'. Here, intentions are seen as having specific 'action content', and as being more feasible, controllable, and time-framed than desires (Malle & Knobe, 2001; Perugini & Bagozzi, 2004). Interestingly, however, research suggests that, at a very young age, toddlers may not differentiate between these two concepts, having a more synthesised sense of 'desire–intentions' (Astington, 2001). This suggest that, beneath our knowledge of how desires and intentions differ, we have a more basic sense of directions as a unified phenomenon.

PLANNING

In themselves, however, intentions and choices are not enough to get something done. Mei, for instance, is determined to talk to Saul, but is she actually going to do this? The fact, for instance, that just 9% of New Year's resolution are actually kept over a one-year period (see Sheeran & Webb, 2012) shows that intending to do something and actually doing it can be very different things.

The next phase of the directional arc can be termed *planning*: that is, 'the development of specific alternative behavioral paths by which a goal can be attained (i.e., a strategy)' (Austin & Vancouver, 1996, p. 350). In structural terms (see Chapter 6, this volume), this can be conceptualised as setting *lower-order* subgoals to achieve *higher-order* goals (Austin & Vancouver, 1996, p. 350). 'I think', says Mei, 'next time I'm back in the office I'm– I'll ask if we can have a bit of time to talk together. Better than surprising him with it. I could say, "let's go out for lunch".'

This planning phase, however, may not be laid out in such explicit terms, and may be entirely unconscious. It might also be bypassed entirely, with individuals moving straight from intention to action. For instance, Mei might see Saul in the office corridor, feel an impulse to sort things out with him, and blurt out there and then that she loves him. Such plan-less actions, however, may not be particularly helpful in bringing about the intended outcomes. Indeed, another principal focus of much therapeutic work is on helping clients to plan more effectively (see Chapter 7): that is, working out ways of actually fulfilling their higher-order desires (Glasser, 1965). For instance:

THERAPIST So what do you think, Mei, how might you talk to Saul about that?
MEI I think– I might just– I'm tempted to just grab him there and then but, actually, he gets really 'antsy' if he feels under pressure. I think– better to tell him I want to talk a few days before, then find somewhere quiet and calm….

Psychological research has also begun to identify more effective planning strategies, such as *implementation intentions* and *mental contrasting* (see Box 3.1).

BOX 3.1

Implementation intentions and mental contrasting

One area of planning that has been particularly well-examined in the psychological research is **implementation intentions** (Gollwitzer, 1999; Park-Stamms & Gollwitzer, 2009). This refers to 'if-then' plans that individuals can hold for responding to particular concrete situations in particular ways. For example, a client who wants to develop his self-confidence might think, 'If my colleague at work puts me down, I will ask him not to do that again.' This is similar to the technique of 'goal-rehearsal' in multimodal therapy, in which clients are invited to deliberately and thoroughly visualise each step towards a goal, imagining how they will cope with challenges along the way (Lazarus, 1981). Research indicates that implementation intentions are an effective means of supporting goal attainment, with data across 94 independent studies showing a medium to large effect (Gollwitzer & Sheeran, 2006). By establishing implementation intentions, it is hypothesised that people become more sensitized to when the critical situation is emerging (e.g., recognising that they are being put down by their colleague), and then automating the initiation of the planned behaviour (e.g., naturally responding in a more assertive way). Interestingly, a consequence of this automisation is that implementation intentions seem to be particularly effective when the individual is **ego depleted** (i.e., mentally tired; Gollwitzer & Sheeran, 2006).

Mental contrasting is a self-regulatory problem-solving strategy in which the individual first imagines a desired future (e.g., 'Being able to respond assertively'), and then reflects on their current negative reality that stands in the way of that (e.g., 'Getting anxious and flustered when people put me down') (Gollwitzer, Kappes, & Oettingen, 2012; Oettingen & Stephens, 2009). Within 'the theory of fantasy realisation', mental contrasting is compared against **indulging**, in which the person solely fantasises about the positive future; and **dwelling**, in which the person merely ruminates on the negative reality. Mental contrasting has been shown to lead to greater goal commitment and goal-directed behaviour, and it is thought to do this by activating positive, but realistic, expectations of what can be changed and how (Oettingen & Stephens, 2009). Mental contrasting seems to energise the individual, and then helps them begin to consider strategies for overcoming the obstacles they may face.

ACTION

The next phase of the directional arc, consistent across all the different phase models, involves putting our plans into action. Mei walks over to Saul's desk. 'Hiya,' she says, 'Is it OK if we– maybe chat about things? I'd really like to. Maybe next Tuesday we could nip out for lunch?' For Bugental (1987) and May (1969a), this is the shift from the *subjective phase* of the directional arc to the *objective phase*: where our desires, intentions, and plans take on concrete, external form. Action begins with a crossing of the *action initiation* demarcation line (Heckhausen & Gollwitzer, 1987), and may continue until the goal is achieved (Sheeran & Webb, 2012). Although it is just one of eight directional phases, in reality it may be far longer than all the other phases combined.

As with planning, psychological research is beginning to develop a more detailed understanding of how actions can be carried out effectively (see Box 3.2).

BOX 3.2
Goal shielding and goal balancing

Goal shielding is the process of inhibiting the activation of alternative goals and keeping energy directed towards focal goals (Cavallo & Fitzsimons, 2012). It can be considered a normal, healthy, and automatic means of protecting the coherence of goal-directed actions (Klinger & Cox, 2011). For instance, as I am working on this book, I need to shield myself from my desire for relatedness by texting my partner every few minutes. Research shows that this process is often unconscious, with people automatically responding to threats to their attention by re-orienting themselves to the focal goal (Sheeran & Webb, 2012). This process of goal shielding can also be described as 'persistence' (Lewin, 1947) or 'resisting temptation', and is associated with the capacity to delay gratification, which, in children, 'is highly associated with a host of outcomes in later life, most notably later social and emotional competence' (see Cavallo & Fitzsimons, 2012, p. 274).

At the same time, it would also seem essential to have the skill of **goal balancing**. This is shifting from active goals to alternative goals depending on particular circumstances and priorities (Cavallo & Fitzsimons, 2012). For instance, if I stick rigidly to my goal of finishing this paragraph and ignore the ringing doorbell, I may then end up spending the next week having to retrieve my parcel from the post office. This flexibility has also been described as **tabling**: temporarily disengaging from particular goal pursuits (Ford, 1992). The principal determinant of goal balancing and tabling may be when we feel that sufficient progress, or sufficiently speedy progress, has been achieved towards the active goal – then we may start to 'coast' (Carver & Scheier, 2012). And, indeed, research shows that after a given goal has been achieved, the accessibility of that goal decreases and the accessibility of other goals increases (Cavallo & Fitzsimons, 2012). However, there may also be individual differences in how able people are to disengage from goals (see below).

FEEDBACK

'Feedback is essential for pursuing goals', write Fishbach and Finkelstein (2012), 'It enables individuals to adjust their efforts and decide which goals to pursue and which to let go, at least temporarily' (p. 203). Similarly, Woodfield (1976) has argued that feedback is the *sine qua non* of goal-related systems, without which *plasticity* (the switching of methods, depending on whether or not they are successful; see Chapter 2) would not be possible.

This feedback phase may follow on from an action phase. For instance, after Mei has asked Saul out for lunch, he might email her back to say, 'Thanks– definitely. Let's do it.' More commonly, however, this feedback will occur throughout the action phase: an informal, unconscious, nuanced, ongoing 'tuning' of action and response. As Mei starts to say 'Maybe next Tuesday....', for instance, she can see a nervousness glance across Saul's face. He looks down at his monitor. 'Yeah, um... Definitely', he says, 'But will...' Mei immediately picks up on his ambivalence: 'It's OK. You don't have to, you know,' she says, 'it's not an...'

Saul interrupts her, 'No, definitely, let's d...'

'It's– Let's just leave it,' says Mei, hurt, shame, and anger rising in her chest. She strides off.

As Custers, Eitam, and Bargh (2012) write, then, '[O]ur actions are continually modified based on incoming feedback about their effects' (p. 251).

Although feedback, and subsequent adjustment, is often an automatic process, individuals may also differ in how open they are to feedback, and how much they draw on it to inform action. For instance, in writing an essay, a student might regularly ask peers for feedback on drafts, or they might 'plough on' regardless and hope for the best from their assessors. Here, research suggests that the former strategy – regularly drawing on feedback – tends to be more effective in helping people to reach their goals (Harkin et al., 2016; Locke & Latham, 2002; Locke, Shaw, Saari, & Latham, 1981; Michie, Abraham, Whittington, McAteer, & Gupta, 2009). In a classic study, for instance, Polivy, Herman, Hackett, and Kuleshnyk (1986) found that people were more able to moderate the amount of chocolate that they ate when they could see the wrappers of the chocolates that they had already eaten, as compared to when they threw the wrappers away in a wastebasket. Feedback, argue Locke and Latham (2002), allows the person to adjust the level and direction of their efforts to match what the goal requires. This, then, allows them to intensify efforts if they feel that they are not progressing and conserve resources (as well as acknowledge their successes) if they are achieving their goals. At the same time, however, too much feedback and monitoring may have an inhibitory potential (Liberman & Dar, 2009). For instance, if a student were to ask for feedback on their essay every hour or two, it might become impossible to 'shield' a consistent and coherent set of goals for the assignment (as well as driving their peers crazy!). Web Resource 3.3 gives a more detailed discussion on moderators of the helpfulness of feedback.

TERMINATION

Finally, there is termination, the ending of the directional process. This might be when the goal has been achieved, or achieved to such an extent that another direction becomes more salient. However, it may also be mid-way through a process of goal-directed activity when that goal no longer feels achievable: 'Sod it,' thinks Mei, 'Saul can go and f… himself'. Such *goal disengagement* (e.g., Heckhausen et al., 2010) can be problematic. As Csikszentmihalyi (2002) writes, 'The price one pays for changing goals whenever opposition threatens is that while one may achieve a more pleasant and comfortable life, it is likely that it will end up empty and void of meaning' (p. 223). In other words, goals are never seen through: there is never a building up towards a more coherent and consistent purpose. On the other hand, however, goal disengagement 'can often be an adaptive response to situations in which further investment of time and resources is in undue proportion to the expected outcomes' (Jostmann & Koole, 2009, p. 337). In other words, as the idiom states, it is sometimes unwise to 'throw good money after bad', with evidence that the inability to disengage from untenable goals and 'move on' can lead to such distressing experiences as depression, stress, and reduced life satisfaction (Carver & Scheier, 1990a; Klinger & Cox, 2011). Anorexia and bulimia, for instance, have been described as a persistent, unwavering drive to follow a narrow range of thinness and appearance goals, without the capacity or willingness to disengage from them (Irving & Cannon, 2000).

Interestingly, research suggests that disengaging from goals is less about forgetting or deleting a goal from memory, and more about inhibiting responses to all but the most central cues associated with it (Klinger & Cox, 2011). When a person disengages from a relationship, for instance, they may retain a strong sense of the loved one but inhibit goal-directed responses towards them. In this sense, re-engaging with new and alternative goals may be more important to promoting wellbeing than disengaging from lost or failed goals (Klinger & Cox, 2011). If Mei wants to move on from Saul, then, the issue may be less about trying to forget him, and more about focusing on new directions that can take his place. Or, perhaps, it may be about trying to reconnect with the 'higher-order' directions, of which her desire for Saul is just one manifestation (see Chapter 6).

DISCUSSION

'The central "business" of human life', writes Bugental (1987), 'is the translation of intentions into actuality as we try to have the living experience which we believe we need and want' (p. 232). Similarly, Little (2007) writes, 'Human flourishing is contingent on the sustainable pursuit of individual's core projects' (p. 43).

Directionality, as proposed in Chapter 2, is an inherent quality of human being. We cannot not propel ourselves forward in our lives, even if it is against the tide of time or change. However, Chapter 3 has introduced the idea that the way in which we propel ourselves forward may be more or less *salutogenic*: that is, facilitative of our psychological wellbeing. More specifically, as will be argued throughout this book, we can direct ourselves forward in ways that can help us to actualise our 'highest-order' desires and goals, or propel ourselves forward in ways that are chaotic, contradictory, and self-defeating. In this chapter, we have seen that each of the different phases of the directional arc have a role to play in supporting the former process. In other words, if we bypass, or attenuate, particular phases of the directional arc, we may make ourselves more vulnerable to frustration, failure, and distress.

This raises the interesting question of whether people may have characteristic ways in which they omit – or, perhaps, over-indulge in – particular directional phases, to the detriment of their overall psychological wellbeing and functioning. For instance, if I think about myself, I am pretty good at recognising my desires, initiating acts, and using feedback to optimise the effectiveness of my actions. But what I so frequently skip over is a really thorough evaluation of what to do, and then carefully and systematically planning how I am going to do it. Essentially, I get bored with evaluation and planning, and am anxious to get on with action. The upshot, however, is that I can end up doing the wrong thing, or else trying to do it in ways that are poorly thought through, so I don't get to where I want to be. This is illustrated in Figure 3.2, and might be termed an 'impulsive' directional style (Ford, 1992). Figure 3.3, however, presents an opposite – but, potentially, equally problematic – directional arc. Here, there is awareness, evaluation, and perhaps even planning, but these phases are so torturously extended that the person never actually gets to the point of initiating action. Ford (1992) describes this as 'paralysis through analysis'.

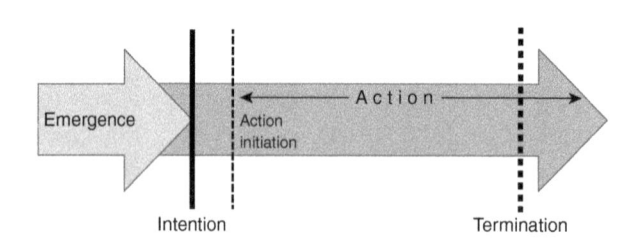

Figure 3.2 A potentially problematic directional arc: Impulsivity

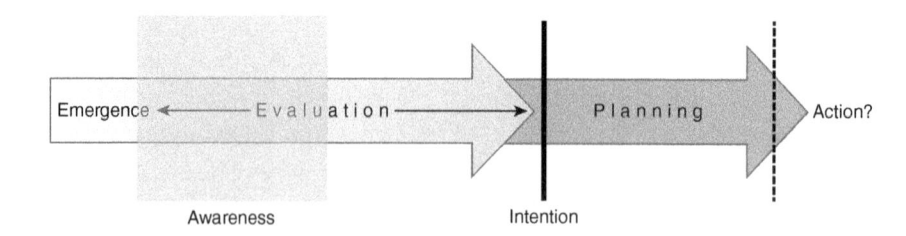

Figure 3.3 A potentially problematic directional arc: 'Paralysis through analysis'

From this standpoint, then, actualising our highest-order directions may be more likely if we can:

- recognise what these desires are (awareness)
- weigh them up effectively against each other (evaluation)

- choose to take forward our most salutogenic desires (intention)
- work out the best way of doing this (planning)
- get going with it (action)
- see how we get on, and revise accordingly (feedback)
- stop at the right time (termination).

In Part II of this book, it will be argued that this is what all our therapies essentially try to do, albeit with a focus on different phases of the directional arc. But why might it be so important to actualise our directions? This is the focus of the next chapter.

QUESTIONS FOR REFLECTION

- How would you profile yourself on the directional arc? What phases do you think you are particularly 'good' at, which ones do you struggle with, and which ones do you tend to bypass? Now consider these questions in relation to a client you are working with.

FURTHER READING

Gollwitzer, P. M. (1990). Action phases and mind-sets. In E. T. Higgins & R. M. Sorrentino (Eds.), *Handbook of motivation and cognition: Foundations of social behavior* (Vol. 2, pp. 53–92). New York: Guilford Press. An in-depth review of motivational phases and the accompanying 'mind-sets'.

Prochaska, J. O., & DiClemente, C. C. (2005). The transtheoretical approach. In J. C. Norcross & M. R. Goldfried (Eds.), *Handbook of psychotherapy integration* (2nd ed., pp. 147-171). New York: Oxford University Press. Concise summary of the 'stages of change' model and its applicability to therapeutic practice.

4

WELLBEING AND EMOTIONS

A life 'on track'

This chapter discusses:

- The role that emotions play in supporting our directions.
- The specific aspects of the directional process that are associated with wellbeing and positive affect:
    - Having *a sense of direction*
    - Viewing our directions as *attainable*
    - *Approaching* our goals (at a reasonable rate)
    - *Achieving* our desires and goals
    - *Appreciating* our achievements.
- The importance of expectations in shaping our wellbeing and affect.
- Vicious and virtuous cycles between directions and affect.

Take a few moments to reflect on how you are feeling right now. For instance, are you stimulated, bored, happy, or anxious? Now consider how that might relate to the different directions in your life, either in the here-and-now present moment or more generally. If you are feeling good, for instance, is that because you feel that you are progressing along a particular direction? Or, if you are feeling anxious, is it because some important goal is under threat?

Over the last century, a number of psychologists and psychotherapists have proposed a *telic* approach to understanding human affect and wellbeing (Diener, 1984). This asserts that our emotions are closely related to how much we feel we are 'actualising' our directions (e.g., Emmons, 1986; Ford, 1992; Frijda, Kuipers, & ter Schure, 1989; Grawe, 2004; Mansell, Carey, & Tai, 2013; Powers, 1992). As Snyder (2000) puts it, '*emotions are a by-product of goal-directed thought* – positive emotions reflecting perceived success in the pursuit of goals, and negative emotions reflecting perceived failures' (p. 11, emphasis in the original). Indeed, from a telic position, it might be argued that, behind every emotion, there is always something that we want (or do not want): that, without some direction, we would not feel. Would we experience shame, for instance, if we did not care about being positively viewed by others, or grief if we did not mind our 'loss'?

From this perspective, then, wellbeing comes from a feeling that we are actualising key desires and goals. This does not mean that we are always progressing towards, and achieving, the things that we fundamentally want in our lives, but it does mean that there is a general propensity towards doing so. For instance, as Little (2011) writes, 'The quality of lives is directly related to the sustainable pursuit of core personal projects' (p. 79). Conversely, from this telic perspective, psychological difficulties are associated with a pervasive inability to 'actualise' key desires and goals. That is, we cannot get to where we want to be, feel hopeless, or experience the world as 'blocking us' at every turn.

This telic approach to affect and wellbeing, as we shall see, is supported by a 'multitude of research findings' (Bagozzi & Pieters, 1998; Freund, 2007; Grosse Holtforth & Michalak, 2012; Wiese, 2007). As just one example, research participants who achieved body weight goals experienced more positive affect and less negative affect than those who did not, with the intensity of affect correlated to the degree of goal achievement (Bagozzi & Pieters, 1998).

This is not to suggest that our directions are the only determinants of how we feel. For instance, it is a well-established fact that our temperament, inherited through our genes, plays a key part in determining our levels of affect and wellbeing (Diener & Lucas, 1999). However, as research by Emmons and Diener (1986) suggests, the role of directional processes is substantial and may be greater than dispositional factors alone.

So why might our emotions be a product of the actualisation, or non-actualisation, of our directions? This can be explained in evolutionary terms (see Chapter 2), with emotions understood as 'the indispensable evaluative component of a motivational system' (Klinger, 2013, p. 35). Goldman (2016) writes, 'emotion is fundamentally adaptive in nature, helping the person process complex situational information rapidly and automatically to produce action appropriate for meeting organismic needs' (p. 319). Emotions do this in several ways (see Web Resource 4.1 for a more detailed discussion). First, they signal to us whether things are on track or not. For instance, Mei's jolt of hurt and shame when she sees the ambivalence on Saul's face 'tells' her that things are not going according to plan. Second, and closely related to this, emotions orient us to what needs attending to (Rogers, 1959). Mei's feelings of hurt and shame, for instance, draws her attention to Saul's face – and not, for instance, to his specific words. Third, emotions motivate us. This may be to do something different (like getting away from Saul), or to keep doing the same thing (for instance, to maintain a pleasurable internal state) (Bagozzi & Pieters, 1998). Fourth, at a very physiological level, emotions mobilise us, they organise us for particular kinds of actions (Greenberg & Paivio, 1997): what Frijda et al. (1989) term 'action readiness'. Mei's increased heart rate, for instance, prepares her, physically, to move away from Saul. Finally, emotions can be a means of communicating to others what we are wanting. As she strides away from Saul's desk, for instance, Mei is very clearly expressing to him how she feels. The specific motivational function for our basic emotions is discussed in Box 4.1.

BOX 4.1

The motivational function of emotions

Ford (1987) argues that there are 14 basic emotional patterns, each of which motivate us to act in specific, evolutionarily adaptive ways. These are grouped into four over-arching functions.

Regulation of behaviours/focus of interest

- Satisfaction-pleasure-joy: 'Continue behaviour towards that goal.'
- Downhearted-discouragement-depression: 'Stop doing that – you won't get anywhere.'
- Curiosity-interest-excitement: 'Find out about this new thing.'
- Disinterest-boredom-apathy: 'Don't bother attending to that - you won't get anything out of it.'

Coping with potentially dangerous situations

- Startle-surprise-astonishment: 'Focus on this new thing - what is it?'
- Annoyance-anger-rage: 'Get rid of that obstacle.'
- Wariness-fear-terror: 'Be careful - it's a threat.'
- Dislike-disgust-loathing: 'Avoid it - it's noxious.'

(Continued)

Establishing interpersonal bonding

- Sexual arousal-pleasure-excitement: 'Let's reproduce.'
- Acceptance-affection-love: 'Build bonds and relationships.'
- Loneliness-sorrow-grief: 'Try to reunite with something that's gone.'

Maintain social cohesion

- Embarrassment-shame/guilt-humiliation: 'Stay within social norms.'
- Scorn-disdain-contempt: 'Reject social transgressors.'
- Resentment-jealousy-hostility: 'Coerce social transgressors.'

As Goldman (2016) writes, above, these emotional process are not deliberate, and they are often not conscious. Rather, they are a rapid, automatic *apprehending*: a 'sensing of things' which precedes 'any form of conscious symbolic thought' (Greenberg & Paivio, 1997, p. 27). When Mei, for instance, strides away from Saul's desk, she is not consciously thinking 'His ambivalence means that he is never going to commit... I am wasting my time... This is really annoying... I should just walk away.' Rather, what she experiences is an immediate and visceral flush of burning hot hurt–anger–shame, which propels her away from Saul. Today, research in the neurobiological field is beginning to uncover some of the mechanisms through which these automatic and unconscious processes can take place (Custers, 2009; Reeve & Lee, 2012).

ASPECTS OF THE DIRECTIONAL PROCESS AND CORRESPONDING EMOTIONS

Emotions, then, can be seen as a basic biological mechanism that helps us move forward along valued lines. Psychological research and theory, however, suggests that these emotions, and feelings of wellbeing, may emerge in relation to five particular aspects of directionality (Cooper, 2018). These are five As: *a sense of direction* in life, viewing one's directions as *attainable*, *approaching* one's goals, *achieving* one's goals, and *appreciating* one's achievement of particular goals. These aspects of the directional process are distinct from the phases of the directional arc (see Chapter 3, this volume, and Figure 4.1), in that they describe an individual's *perception* of their movement and possibilities, rather than the *actual* unfurling of directionality. Nevertheless, they are closely linked, and the aspects of this directional process can be approximately mapped on to the phases of the directional arc as per Figure 4.1.

A sense of direction

Research shows 'abundant links between meaning in life and a very wide range of other indicators of well-being' (Steger, 2013, p. 172). Individuals who endorse items

WELLBEING AND EMOTIONS: A LIFE 'ON TRACK'

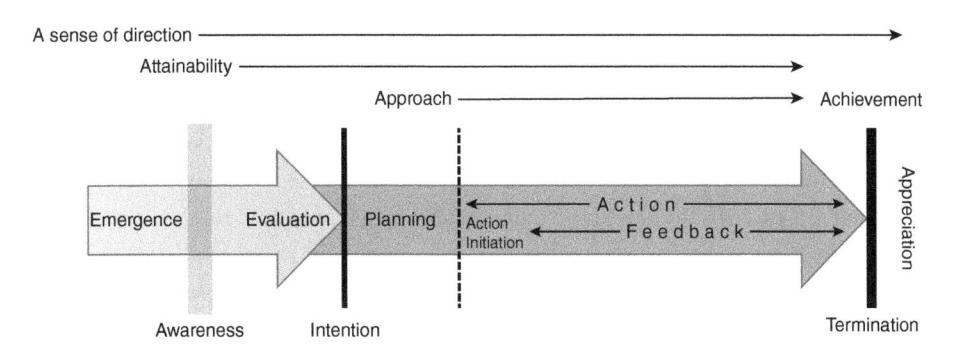

Figure 4.1 Aspects of the directional process associated with wellbeing and affect

such as 'My life has a clear sense of purpose', for instance, on the 'Presence of meaning' subscale of the Meaning in Life Questionnaire have higher levels of happiness, life satisfaction, and positive affect (Park, Park, & Peterson, 2010). By contrast, people with lower levels of meaning and purpose in life have lower levels of negative affect and depression. They also have more substance-related problems, more disruptive behaviour, poorer physical functioning, and more psychopathology (King & Hicks, 2013; Klinger, 2013; Park et al., 2010; Steger, 2013; Vos, 2016a). Indeed, in the nineteenth century, Durkheim proposed that meaninglessness was a risk factor for suicide (Henry, Lovegrove, Steger, Chen, Cigularov, & Tomazic, 2014). In support of these associations, research shows that therapies which focus on helping clients to develop meaning in life can bring about improvements in wellbeing and quality of life, and reduce depression and anxiety (Vos, 2016b; Vos, Craig, & Cooper, 2014).

In terms of the framework developed in this book, meaning and purpose in life can be conceptualised as having *a sense of direction*. This is a feeling of knowing where we want to go in our lives. In terms of the phases of the directional arc (Figure 4.1), this may be facilitated through an evolving awareness of our directions, or through choosing directions in the evaluation phase that align with our highest-order wants. However, it may also be a more embodied, less conscious 'sense' of orientation or focus. That is, a feeling that our emerging wants and desires – or our intentions, goals, and actions – are significant and of value: reaching beyond our individual selves to some higher-order 'good' (see Chapter 6). Conversely, a sense of meaningless can be conceptualised as a feeling that there are no significant directions underlying who, or what, we are. 'What's the point?', says Mei, 'I could be here… I could not be here. Saul's in his own little world. And I'm wasting my life in a crappy relationship with a man who'd rather be watching *Top Gear*.'

When we do not have any sense of direction in life, it can feel like running forward blindly, without any real idea of where we are going. This can be deeply disorientating. As van Deurzen (2012b) writes, 'Many people become desperately confused and depressed when they lose the northern star of the passionate purpose of their life' (p. 176). It can also mean that we get immobilised, unable to see how we can go forward; or disorganised and engaging in 'a helter-skelter quest for gratification which may lead to activity – but not gratification' (Polster & Polster, 1973, p. 228). If we do not feel that we know where we want to go to, we are also likely to feel hopeless about making any positive changes in our lives, and with that apathetic and aimless (Yalom, 1980). In this respect, having a sense of direction is important for actualising subsequent phases of the directional arc. This is because it directs our attention towards particular intentions and goals, energises us, and helps us to persist in what we are doing (Locke & Latham, 2002).

Having a sense of direction may also reduce feelings of suffering and make them feel more bearable (Baumeister, 1991). In the words of Nietzsche, 'He who has a *why* to live can bear with almost any *how*' (in Frankl, 1984, p. 97). Famously, Frankl gives the example of the Nazi death camps, where his attempts to restore his campmates' 'inner strength' was focused on helping them find meaning in their suffering. He writes, 'Woe to him who saw no more sense in his life, no aim, no purpose, and therefore no point in carrying on. He was soon lost' (p. 98). As a more contemporary example, Henry et al. (2014) found that the negative effects of bullying on boys were reduced as their sense of meaning in life increased.

Attainability

Along with having a sense of direction, research shows that it feels good to know that our desires and goals are attainable. A study by Brunstein (1993), for instance, found that participants' subjective wellbeing was associated with prior beliefs that they had the control, opportunity, and support to attain important personal goals. Believing in the attainability of our desires and goals can give us a sense of hope, optimism, excitement, expectation, and possibility. By contrast, if we know where we want to go, but feel it may be unattainable, we may experience such negative feelings as hopelessness, despair, futility, and demoralisation (Emmons, 1986; Frank & Frank, 1993; O'Hara, 2013). Mei, for instance, wants to experience intimacy with Saul, but after the lunch incident she is feeling that it is just not a goal she is ever going to be able to get to.

Attainability is closely related to our sense of expectancy: a key issue in the evaluation phase of the directional arc. In this respect, the extent to which we feel that our directions are attainable is likely to be shaped by our sense of *self-efficacy* (Bandura & Locke, 2003; Brunstein, 1993); the skills, abilities, and competences we do have (Wilson, 1990, in Little, 2007); and, also, our actual, in-the-world opportunities, resources, and support (Brunstein, 1993; Epton, Currie, & Armitage, 2017). However, this question of whether or not we can expect to attain our desires and goals is likely to emerge from the very first moment when we become aware of what we want, and remains until we are very close to completing our goals. As every runner will know, even seconds from the finish line, it can still feel like completing the race is in question.

Here, anxiety might be conceptualised as uncertainty about whether or not we are going to attain important goals: that is, where a negative outcome is not felt to be inevitable (Frijda et al., 1989). A few weeks after striding away from Saul, for instance, Mei says in therapy that she is now really worried about what he makes of her. 'He probably thinks I'm an emotional nutbag,' she says, 'I'm sure he looks down every time he sees me.' Here, her ongoing desire to establish an intimate relationship with Saul is threatened, but she does not know for sure, and it is the not knowing that makes her feel worried. We can see this because, if she knew, for certain, that Saul was not interested in her – that is, the failure to attain her goal was inevitable and uncontrollable – she would not feel anxiety about this situation. Rather, she would feel sadness, frustration, loss, or sorrow (Frijda et al., 1989). In Mei's present situation, then, the goal is still 'on', but it is under threat. Reflect, for a moment, on your own anxieties. Which particular goal is in danger of not being attained?

BOX 4.2

Attainability and expectations in the therapeutic process

Believing that we can attain our goals is associated with wellbeing in regard to the therapeutic process too (Snyder, Michael, & Cheavens, 1999). Research shows that **outcome expectations**, which 'reflect patients' prognostic beliefs about the consequences of engaging in treatment', have a small but significant positive correlation with outcomes (Constantino, Glass, Arnkoff, Ametrano, & Smith, 2011). In other words, clients who have hope and faith in the therapeutic process tend to do better than those who are sceptical about it (Beutler, Blatt, Alimohamed, Levy, & Angtuaco, 2006; Glass, Arnkoff, & Shapiro, 2001). Research also indicates that the more credible clients believe a therapy to be, the more they tend to improve (Ilardi & Craighead, 1994). This may be because it engenders hope within the client, or what has also been termed 'remoralization' (Frank & Frank, 1993). Indeed, Wampold and Imel (2015) argues that therapy 'works' by instilling in clients confidence and belief that change is possible, and they point to the placebo effect as evidence of this. In other words, one of the main ways in which therapy might help people is by increasing the perceived attainability of their goals; something that, as we have seen, is associated with positive benefit. This may be particularly important for clients for whom a substantial part of their problem is that they feel hopeless about ever being able to progress in their lives (Teasdale, 1985).

However, as with reference standards outside therapy (see below), research shows that extremely high and unrealistic positive expectations of the therapeutic process tend to be related to poorer outcomes (Piper, Joyce, McCallum, & Azim, 1998; Sloane, Staples, Whipple, & Cristol, 1977). For instance, clients who 'do not anticipate pain or embarrassment' in therapy tend to respond negatively to therapeutic interventions (Mohr, 1995).

(Continued)

And clients with high levels of perfectionism (as assessed prior to therapy) showed less improvement on a range of indicators than those with lower levels of perfectionism (Blatt, Quinlan, Pilkonis, & Shea, 1995; Blatt, Zuroff, Bondi, Sanislow, & Pilkonis, 1998). Linked to this, research suggests that clients who have a relatively clear understanding of the process and goals of therapy and their role within it tend to get the most out of the therapeutic work, while those who have a more ambiguous understanding of role are less satisfied, less productive, and more defensive (Bednar, Melnick, & Kaul, 1974).

Approach

Once the action phase of the directional arc is initiated, people can begin to progress towards their goals. Here, research shows that the subjective perception of moving towards our goals is strongly associated with feelings of wellbeing and positive affect. For instance, Sheldon and Kasser (1998) asked university students to identify five of their most relevant personal projects, and then to rate how much progress they had made towards them over 12 five-day periods of time. They found that students who rated themselves as making greater progress towards their goals showed increased positive affect, decreased negative affect, and increased overall wellbeing. Consistent with this, in the most comprehensive meta-analysis published to date, Koestner, Lekes, Powers, and Chicoine (2002) found that 'Participants reported significantly more positive affect and less negative affect over time when they had made greater goal progress' (p. 233).

Feeling that we are making progress towards our desires and goals is likely to evoke many of the same feelings as anticipating that our goals are attainable: for instance, hope, optimism, excitement, and expectation. In addition, however, it may also begin to evoke feelings associated with goal attainment *per se*, such as happiness, satisfaction, achievement, and enhanced self-worth. Conversely, failing to progress towards our goals – or moving further away from them – may evoke both the feelings associated with unattainability (e.g., hopelessness, futility, despair, demoralisation), and those associated with failure to achieve our goals (e.g., sadness and shame, see below). When Mei thinks about her relationship with Rob, for instance, she feels a profound sense of loss. 'When we were students,' she says in therapy, 'we used to lie in bed together, listen to music, talk about all the bands we'd love to go and see: electropunk thrash metal in Berlin, post-punk psychedelia in Osaka.... There was so much adventure and love we'd talk about – music journalists – but now it just seems further and further in the distance.' In addition, when our progress towards goals feels 'blocked', we may experience frustration, and anger if that blocking feels unfair (Frijda et al., 1989).

Interestingly, Carver and Scheier (1990a, 2012), drawing on Powers's (1973) control theory (see Box 6.1), suggest that affect may be less related to progress *per se*, and more to the rate of progress compared against some internal standard. That is, people will experience positive affect when they are moving towards their goals at a higher rate than expected, negative affect when the rate is lower than expected, and no affect when they are progressing at an expected rate. This theory makes some intuitive sense. In many ways, for instance, Mei is progressing towards her goal of being clearer about her relationship with Rob. She is starting to talk about it in therapy, she is beginning to broach it with Rob, and she is clearer than before that she does want some kind of separation. But the problem, for her, is that the pace of progress is just agonisingly slow. 'It's– with everything with Rob,' she says, 'it's just at a snail's speed. He has to think over everything like he chews his food. It's like watching a cow eat grass. So... achingly... painfully... torturously... slow...'. However, although, to date, there is some evidence to suggest that positive affect may be associated with velocity of progress (e.g., Hsee & Abelson, 1991), evidence remains 'sparse' (Wiese, 2007).

Achievement

As we move towards the termination phase of the directional arc, so we can begin to experience a sense of achievement for reaching our goals, and this can have an important impact on how we feel. As Carver and Scheier (2012) put it, 'A truism is that affect pertains to whether one's desires are being met' (p. 32). This is an explicit assumption within a range of humanistic (e.g., Glasser, 1965; Maslow, 1971, 1987), existential (May, 1958), and cognitive-behavioural theories (e.g., Mansell et al., 2013), and is well supported by the empirical research (Sheldon & Elliot, 1999; Wiese, 2007). Emmons and Diener (1986), for instance, found a large positive correlation between the achievement of goals and positive affect. In addition, neurological research suggests that the achievement of goals may be associated with the release of the pleasure-producing neurotransmitter dopamine (Koepp, Gunn, Lawrence, & Cunningham, 1998).

When we achieve our objectives, we may experience such positive affects as satisfaction, happiness, pride, accomplishment, fulfilment, and relief. Conversely, if we do not, we may experience such negative feelings as dissatisfaction, failure, sadness, loss, frustration, anger, and regret. Several decades ago, Maslow (1943) suggested that the basis for psychological distress – and 'psychopathology' – may be the thwarting of basic desires and goals. Depression, for instance, has been characterised as the consequence of abandoned plans (Miller, Galanter, & Pribam, 1960), or a chronic failure to achieve goals (Strauman et al., 2006). In some cases, then, clients may be caught between the Scylla of sadness that comes with accepting an irrevocable loss (Grawe, 2004) and the Charybdis of anxiety that comes with trying to hold on to an uncertain goal.

Through achieving our goals, we not only experience the positive affect associated with their completion, but also the positive affect associated with the desire or goal itself. If Mei, for instance, finally has sex with Saul, she both experiences the satisfaction of achieving this goal, and also the pleasure of the sexual intimacy itself. This conceptualisation is similar to Dolan's (2014) theory that 'happiness = purpose + pleasure'.

That is, happiness comes through the process of actualising particular directions (the principal focus of this book), but also through achieving particular states that are pleasurable in themselves. In this way, the theory presented in this book, as with Dolan's, can be seen as encompassing both 'eudaimonic' (authenticity- and growth-oriented) and 'hedonic' (pleasure-oriented) theories of wellbeing (Ryan & Deci, 2001). For Dolan (2014), these two sources of happiness are distinct. But to the extent that people strive for pleasure, and experience positive affect when actualising their purposes, they are clearly very interlinked.

Achieving our directions may also contribute to our wellbeing indirectly through the benefit it may give at higher 'levels of organisation': for instance, to our families or communities (Cantor & Sanderson, 1999). Through achieving goals such as volunteering or bringing about greater social equity, for instance, we help to build more supportive and synergetic social networks, from which we also benefit. This will be discussed in much more depth in Chapter 9.

Although the evidence shows that goal achievement is associated with wellbeing, it is important to bear in mind that this experience may be relatively transient. As Maslow (1987), Dolan (2014), and many others have suggested, the nature of directionality is such that, once one direction is actualised, we will start to move along other directions. This may only be a problem, however, if our focus is exclusively on the achievement aspect of the directional process (for example, 'I must be in an intimate relationship to be happy'). If, on the other hand, our focus is also on the process of approaching our goals and having a sense of direction (for example, 'I'm going to try to get close to people and enjoy it along the way'), then we are less dependent on the transience of goal achievement *per se* (or the abjectness of goal failure).

Appreciation

Once the directional arc is completed, there is also the possibility of appreciating our achievements. This is about savouring what we have done, being mindful of our successes. It is closely linked to an attitude of 'gratitude', which involves recognising that one has obtained a positive outcome, but also recognising that this has been brought about by an external source (Emmons & McCullough, 2003). Although there is less direct evidence of a link between appreciation, wellbeing, and positive affect, research shows that a gratitude outlook can heighten wellbeing (Emmons & McCullough, 2003). Research also shows that taking notice, savouring the world around us, and being mindful are predictive of positive mental states (Aked, Marks, Cordon, & Thompson, 2008; Seligman, 2002).

At a macro level, appreciation has parallels with Erikson's (1950) concept of 'ego integrity', which he contrasts against 'despair'. Here, in the last of his 'eight ages of man', he depicts the ability to accept the life cycle as it has been, rather than fear that it has not been done sufficiently and needs to be redone. For Erikson, this capacity to appreciate what we have achieved may be particularly important for people coming towards the end of their lives. The work of meaning-centred therapists has a similar emphasis. Indeed, to a great extent the process of identifying meanings in life might be understood as developing an appreciation of past goals and achievements. The following is an example from Frankl's (1988) work with a woman who had cancer and had become depressed.

FRANKL What do you think of when you look back on your life? Has life been worth living?
PATIENT Well, Doctor, I must say that I had a good life. Life was nice, indeed. And I must thank for the Lord for what it held for me: I went to theatres, I attended concerts, and so forth...
FRANK You are speaking of some wonderful experiences; but all this will have an end now, won't it?
PATIENT (*thoughtfully*) Yes, everything ends...
FRANKL Well, do you think now that all the wonderful things of your life might be annihilated?
PATIENT (*still more thoughtfully*): All those wonderful things...
FRANKL But tell me: do you think that anyone can undo the happiness that you have experienced? Can anyone blot it out?
PATIENT No, Doctor, nobody can blot it out. (pp. 120–121)

Appreciation may be of value because it is a means of standing back from the transience of our achievements and prolonging such associated feelings as satisfaction and pride. In addition, appreciation may lead us to such feelings as acceptance and calm. If we can acknowledge what we have achieved, then a *metagoal* (see Chapter 5) of wanting to achieve our goals may feel more actualised. Finally, appreciation may be of benefit to us because it can enhance our sense of self-efficacy – that we can achieve our goals – hence boosting our willingness to act towards them.

Discussion

Table 4.1 presents a summary of the emotions that may be associated with particular aspects of the directional process: both the 'positive' emotions when these aspects are present, and the 'negative' emotions when they are absent. This is, of course, only very tentative, and there is a great deal of overlap between different aspects and emotions. Nevertheless, such a table may still be useful because 'the quality and intensity of emotional experience can provide information about the salience of a particular goal' (Kennedy-Moore & Watson, 1999, p. 96). That is, this table – as well as the functional understanding of different emotions presented in Box 4.1 – can give us clues about the particular directions and directional processes that may underlie a client's emotions and feelings. For instance, if a client is feeling frustrated, we might try to trace back to the important goal that is being blocked (Grawe, 2004; Snyder & Taylor,

2000), or if they are feeling ashamed, we might wonder about the social norm that they feel they have transgressed. As Mei, for instance, talks more about her sadness and disappointment in relation to Rob, so it becomes clearer what she wanted – and still wants – in her life. 'It's the– it was the promise of feeling *alive*,' she says, 'getting out there. Being in the world. Music. Festivals. Adventure. Bliss. Just the awe of it all. That's what we meant to each other. That was our promise. Not effin' *Top Gear*.' Hence, as van Deurzen-Smith (1997) states, 'It is by working with the emotional dimension of clients' experience that we can most effectively draw out these hidden and deeply felt levels of their selfhood that betray their original project and that give them a sense of direction' (p. 241). And the less aware that clients are of their particular directions, the more valuable that emotions may be in this role (Ford, 1992). Ford writes, 'learning how to interpret a person's emotional life in terms of the goals and contexts that organize those feelings and give them meaning is a particularly important skill for psychotherapists who must deal with "unconscious" goals' (p. 142). And the more intensely that a client experiences these emotions, the more they may signal that a person is 'on' or 'off' track (Bagozzi & Pieters, 1998; Rogers, 1951).

Table 4.1 Feelings associated with the presence or absence of different aspects of the directional process

	Presence	**Absence**
A sense of direction	Orientation, clarity, purpose, flow, energy, resilience	Disorientation, confusion, depression, hopelessness, apathy, aimlessness
Attainability	Hope, optimism, excitement, expectation, possibility, comfort/relaxation/ease, acceptance	Hopelessness, futility, despair, demoralisation, uncertainty, anxiety
Approach	Hope, optimism, excitement, expectation, happiness, achievement, satisfaction, pride	Hopelessness, futility, despair, demoralisation, dissatisfaction, sadness, loss, frustration, shame, anger
Achievement	Happiness, satisfaction, pride, accomplishment, fulfilment, gratitude, acceptance; experiencing of the desired state (e.g., pleasure)	Dissatisfaction, failure, sadness, loss, frustration, envy, anger, regret, shame, despair
Appreciation	Satisfaction, pride, accomplishment, fulfilment gratitude, calm, acceptance, meaning	Dissatisfaction, failure, sadness, loss, frustration, envy, anger, regret, shame, despair, meaninglessness

Wellbeing, then, can be conceptualised as the experience of actualising our directions. Here, we have a rough sense of where we are going, feel that our goals are attainable, feel we are moving towards them (at a decent enough pace), and have the experience of achieving our goals, with time to appreciate this. This is a flowing, fluid being: new directions emerge, old directions fade, but there is a general sense of moving forward in life towards the things we really want (see Web Resource 4.2, Directionality and flow). Conversely, psychological distress is a sense that we are not actualising our directions: that we do not know where we are going, or that our desires and goals are unattainable, or that we are blocked in making goal progress, or never achieving – or appreciating the achievement of – our goals. And, importantly, this is not just the issue of whether we are actually progressing through the phases of the directional arc (as described in Chapter 3), but how we perceive it (Ford, 1992). As many of us will know from our clients, for instance, an individual may actually have achieved many of the things they wanted in life – for instance, career, status, and family – but still have a feeling that they have failed. And, if so, the associated feelings are likely to be disappointment and despondency rather than satisfaction and pride. This relates closely to the issue of expectations.

EXPECTATIONS/REFERENCE STANDARDS

As suggested above, the feelings that we have in relation to our directions are not just determined by how much we have done, but also by our expectations of how much we should do. This has been termed our *reference standards* (Kahneman, 2011). So if we set high expectations for ourselves, then our desires and goals are less likely to feel attainable, we are less likely to feel that we are approaching or achieving our goals, and we will be less able to appreciate what we have achieved. Very high expectations, then, means that we may be less likely to experience wellbeing and positive affect. In clients (and particularly those experiencing depression), such high reference standards may take the form of a highly critical or demanding 'inner voice', constantly telling the person that they are not good enough and falling short (Caspar, 1995; Elliott, Watson, Goldman, & Greenberg, 2004). At its extreme, such high standards can also take the form of perfectionism, whereby our expectations are way beyond our – or anyone else's – reach. It can also take the form of continually setting harder and harder goals for ourselves such that, as with the 'hedonic treadmill' (Kahneman, 1999; Seligman, 2002), we are never satisfied in our lives because we are constantly feeling that we can never get close to our goals. In support of this, research suggests that having modest expectations is generally better for our happiness (Dolan, 2014), and that people who are unrealistically optimistic about what they can achieve end up having higher levels of disappointment (Armor & Taylor, 1998). As Schopenhauer (1969) puts it, 'all suffering really results from the want of proportion between what we demand and expect and what comes to us' (p. 88).

From an existential standpoint, one of the most problematic reference standards we can set for ourselves may be with respect to happiness itself (van Deurzen, 2002, 2009). Cox (2009) writes, 'Some of the most unhappy people in the world are those who hold firmly to the false belief that complete happiness is achievable' (p. 15).

Along these lines, van Deurzen (2009) states, 'Most of us have secret fantasies about a state of safety and never ending good experiences, in a place where resources do not run out and we get everything we want and need' (p. 77). She describes this 'brave new world of sublime and enduring well being' (van Deurzen, 2009, p. 71) as a utopian 'pipedream', such that, when people come up against the reality of the world, with all its roughness, toughness, challenge, and 'boundary situations' (such as death and suffering; Jaspers, 1932), they feel 'robbed' and 'cheated' of the happiness to which they are 'entitled'. There is some research to support this. For instance, a study found that those with high expectations and plans for the millennium celebrations were less happy on the night than those with lower level expectations and plans (Schooler et al., in Dolan, 2014).

This is closely connected to the argument, presented in Web Resource 2.2, that in contemporary society we are increasingly socialised to the expectation of absolute control of our lives. Farber (2000) describes our epoch as the 'Age of the Disordered Will', in which '[d]ay in, day out, every citizen is instructed by the public media that there is no portion of his life that is not wholly within his control or … wholly subject to his will' (p. 79). Moreover, for Farber, such 'willing what cannot be willed' (p. 77) is the fundamental source of anxiety in our lives. Perhaps this is because, while consciously we may believe in the controllability of our lives, at an unconscious level we may sense their absolute contingency.

Setting very high reference standards may also be problematic because, if people experience despondency at 'failing', they may then tend towards abandoning their directions, rather than finding alternative means towards more modest goals. As the therapeutic work with Mei progresses, for instance, she begins to see that the loss of her dreams – music, passion, excitement – was not just down to Rob's 'slovenliness', but also because she has so easily accepted this. 'I think I just gave up', she says. 'I could have tried to make it happen more.'

'And also,' I suggest to her, 'I wonder if you tried to just replace it by finding it elsewhere. Maybe it's easier to focus on with Saul than make what you wanted to happen with Rob.'

In this respect, the work of the therapist is not just in helping people to move closer towards their reference standards, but also to revise – and where appropriate reduce – their expectations (Grawe, 2004).

VICIOUS AND VIRTUOUS CYCLES

To this point, we have explored the relationship between directionality, affect, and wellbeing in a unidirectional manner: people experience themselves as actualising, or failing to actualise, their desires and goals, and this leads to particular felt-responses. However, people's directions may also be shaped and impacted upon by their emotions: that is, the direction of causality can also be reversed. This is particularly important because it can then lead on to a range of vicious, or virtuous, cycles. The impact of this may be far greater than any single effect alone, and once activated, these cycles may begin to take on a life of their own (see Rogue goals, in Chapter 8).

First, people's directions may be towards particular emotional states. This capacity may be unique to the human species. As Greenberg and Paivio (1997) write, 'the emotion system initially only had to deal with organism–environment interactions. However, with the development of the ability to reflect on ourselves, to represent, imagine, and consciously remember, emotions also become responses to our own processes' (p. 50). Most commonly, as above, people may want to experience 'positive' emotions, like happiness, excitement, or calm, and avoid 'negative' emotions, like sadness, hurt, or anxiety. Indeed, Caspar (1995) writes that 'The effort to create positive emotions and to cope with or avoid negative emotions determines a significant proportion of human behaviour' (p. 184). One of Mei's most salient therapeutic goals, for instance, was to find some satisfaction and pleasure in her life. This, however, sets the person up to experience *secondary emotions* (Greenberg & Paivio, 1997; Greenberg et al., 1993) – reactions to more primary emotional responses – which can then lead to the emergence of vicious or virtuous cycles. Mei, for instance, feels that she is not progressing towards the satisfaction that she wants in her life, and therefore feels dissatisfied. This, then, makes her feel that she is failing even more to progress towards her reference standard of satisfaction, which evokes further feelings of dissatisfaction, etc. Here is another example. Logan, who we will meet in Chapter 7, wants to feel 'chilled', calm, and in control. So when he begins to experience some anxiety (for instance, at a party), his reference standard of 'in controlness' feels under threat, making him more anxious, which then further threatens his reference standard. For Logan, this can then spiral down into a full-blown panic attack.

Closely related to the above, research shows that when people are in a more positive mood, they are more likely to experience life as purposive and meaningful (Klinger, 2013). Conversely, if they are feeling depressed, they are less likely to feel that there is a purpose to their lives (Klinger, 2013). This might be because, at some level, they want to feel positive and happy. Hence, when they are experiencing this, they are more likely to feel that this goal is attainable, that they are approaching it, and that there is direction and meaning to their lives. It might also be, however, a more basic neurobiological process, with brain pathways between positive affect and goal striving overlapping (Klinger, 2013). Hence, when we feel good in the former, we also feel good in the latter. Either way, though, the results can be virtuous cycles (positive affect leads to greater actualisation of directions leads to greater positive affect) or vicious ones (negative affect leads to reduced actualisation of directions leads to greater negative affect).

Third, positive affect tends to stimulate goal-directed behaviour whereas negative affective inhibits it (Gollwitzer et al., 2012; Gollwitzer & Oettingen, 2012). This might be because negative feelings lower the person's sense of self-confidence (as we saw with Jacey in Chapter 3), distract them, or reduce their levels of motivation or energy.

Finally, when people are in a negative mood, they may tend to focus on short-term goals, rather than long-term ones, in an effort to 'repair' their feelings (Sheeran & Webb, 2012). The more frustrated Mei feels with her life, for instance, the more she fantasises about having sex with Saul. This is, of course, an intelligible response, but, as we will see later in this book, short-term strivings often pull against the actualisation of longer-term, more sustainable achievements.

CONCLUSION

Research and theory suggest that our emotions and our sense of wellbeing are intimately associated with a feeling that we are actualising our directions. When we are oriented and moving in the direction we want to be, we feel good; when we are blocked and frustrated, we feel bad. In part, this sense of actualisation is determined by how far we get, but it is also fundamentally shaped by our expectations of how far we should be getting. And because of the potential for virtuous and vicious cycles, small moves towards, or away from, our goals can trigger much larger changes in our psychological states. However, what the research also shows is that the relationship between wellbeing, affect, and the actualisation of our directions is fundamentally mediated by the directions that we are striving for. This is the subject matter of the next chapter.

QUESTIONS FOR REFLECTION

- Identify one of your key directions in life and consider the following questions:
    - To what extent do you experience those desires/goals as attainable?
    - To what extent do you feel that you are approaching that goal?
    - To what extent do you feel that you have achieved that goal?
- What kinds of feelings does your relationship to this goal, as described above, evoke? Do these match the feelings described in Table 4.1?
- Consider the above questions in relation to a client that you are working with.
- To what extent are you able to appreciate your achievements? What are the implications of this in terms of your capacity to experience wellbeing?
- Are there particular vicious, or virtuous, cycles that you experience between directions and affects? If vicious, how might you find a way out of them?

FURTHER READING

Klinger, E., & Cox, W. M. (2011). Motivation and the goal theory of current concerns. In W. M. Cox & E. Klinger (Eds.), *Handbook of motivational counseling: Goal-based approaches to assessment and intervention with addiction and other problems* (2nd ed., pp. 3-48). Chichester: Wiley. Valuable overview of the relationship between goals and wellbeing, and implications for therapy.

5

GOAL DIMENSIONS

What we strive for counts

This chapter discusses a range of goal dimensions that have been found to moderate the relationship between the actualisation of our directions and wellbeing:

- Intrinsic–Extrinsic
- Approach–Avoidance
- Conscious–Unconscious
- Long-term–Short-term
- Important–Unimportant
- Difficult–Easy
- Specific–Vague
- Process–Outcome
- Primary–Secondary

In Chapter 4, we saw how wellbeing and positive affect tend to be associated with the actualisation of our directions. Intuitively, however, it seems likely that this relationship will be mediated by the kind of directions that someone is acting towards. Mei's satisfaction at feeling like she has been a good mother to Olivia, for instance, vastly outweighs her satisfaction at changing the oil in her car. Indeed, her achievement of the latter goal can evoke as much disappointment ('Is this what my life has come to!') as a sense of fulfilment. That different directions have different effects on wellbeing is borne out by the psychological research, which shows that 'Not all [goal] progress is beneficial' (Sheldon & Kasser, 1998, p. 1319).

So what kind of goals are most – and least – likely to facilitate a feeling of wellbeing when they are actualised? In this chapter, we will explore this question by looking at the different dimensions along which people's desires and goals can be categorised, and the theory and research on how this moderates the relationship between their actualisation and wellbeing (for taxonomies of different types of goals, see Web Resource 5.1). For the purposes of this chapter, we will refer specifically to 'goals', rather than the broader 'directions'. In part, this is because the research in this area almost exclusively uses the 'goals' construct. More importantly, though, it is because the focus in this analysis is on the noematic, 'content' end of the directional pole – which is best articulated by this term.

Within the psychological literature, many different dimensions of goals have been proposed, and research suggests that participants' ratings of goals, along such continua, are relatively stable (Emmons, 1986). In his Personal Project Analysis, for instance, Little (1983) identified 27 goal dimensions (such as levels of 'visibility', 'challenge', and 'control'), while Fujita and MacGregor (2012) suggest four over-arching dimensions: abstract versus concrete goals, approach versus avoidance goals, intrinsic versus extrinsic motivation, and mastery versus performance goals. Austin and Vancouver (1996), in probably the most comprehensive review of the empirical and theoretical literature to date, suggest six main goal dimensions: (a) importance–commitment, (b) difficulty–level, (c) specificity–representation, (d) temporal range, (e) level of consciousness, and (f) connectedness–complexity.

Building on these reviews, this chapter discusses nine key dimensions of goals that are of particular relevance to psychological wellbeing and distress – and hence therapeutic practice. We start with those dimensions where there is most evidence of direct effects, working down to more complex, indirect, and less well-evidenced moderators of the actualisation–wellbeing relationship.

INTRINSIC–EXTRINSIC

In recent years, a growing body of evidence suggests that goal actualisation is more salutogenic when goals are *intrinsic* to the person rather than *extrinsic*. Intrinsic, or *self-concordant*, goals (Sheldon & Elliot, 1999; Sheldon & Houser-Marko, 2001) are 'those that are likely to satisfy basic and inherent psychological needs' (Kasser & Ryan, 1996, p. 280), such as the need for relatedness and autonomy (Ryan & Deci, 2000; and see Chapter 6, this volume). By contrast, *extrinsic* goals are those that 'primarily entail obtaining contingent external approval and rewards' (Kasser & Ryan, 1996, p. 280). In other words, extrinsic goals are dependent on the reaction of others: for instance, the desire for wealth, appearance, and fame. Most people are likely to have both. For instance, Mei has a strong, extrinsic goal of being approved of by others, but she also has more intrinsic goals, such as her love of music. 'That's when I feel most alive', she says. This intrinsic–extrinsic dimension links closely to humanistic theories and its distinction between 'organismic needs' and needs that are based on the desire for positive regard, respectively (e.g., Rogers, 1959; see Chapter 11, this volume). Confirmatory factor analysis has demonstrated the validity of this intrinsic–extrinsic dimension across a range of cultures (Grouzet et al., 2005).

Research suggests that the intrinsic–extrinsic dimension is a critical moderator of the relationship between the actualisation of goals and wellbeing, because only the actualisation of intrinsic goals seems to lead to positive outcomes (Sheldon & Kasser, 1998). More specifically, the pursuit of intrinsic goals is associated with higher levels of psychological wellbeing, greater satisfaction, and greater achievement of goals, while the pursuit of extrinsic goals is associated with lower wellbeing, lower vitality, and more anxiety, depression, and physical symptoms (Kasser & Ryan, 1993, 1996, 2001; Koestner et al., 2002; Sheldon & Elliot, 1999; Sheldon & Kasser, 1998). Mei illustrates this. She feels nourished and stimulated listening to punk music in the morning, but earning the approval of others – like her manager – gives only a very temporary 'high', which is quickly replaced by feelings of shame. Paradoxically, an extrinsic orientation also seems to be associated with more difficult and less satisfying relationships. In part, these associations may be because greater goal self-concordance leads to more sustained effort, which then leads to greater goal achievement (Sheldon & Elliot, 1999). There is also evidence that greater goal self-concordance is associated with more goal progress (Koestner et al., 2002).

This intrinsic–extrinsic dimension bears many similarities to a widely studied distinction between *learning* (or *mastery*) *goals* and *performance goals* (Ames, 1992; Dweck & Leggett, 1988; Elliott & Dweck, 1988; Fujita & MacGregor, 2012; Grant & Gelety, 2009; Moskowitz & Grant, 2009b; Murayama, Elliot, & Friedman, 2012). Learning goals, like intrinsic goals, have an end in themselves: for instance, to acquire new knowledge, skills, and competencies. By contrast, performance goals, like extrinsic goals, are focused on achieving outcomes as a means of displaying competence to others: oriented towards external benchmarks and rewards. As with the intrinsic–extrinsic dimension, there is evidence that learning goals tend to be more beneficial to the person than performance goals. For instance, performance goals are more likely to lead to feelings of helplessness after a failure, while learning goals facilitate persistence and mastery-oriented behaviours (Moskowitz & Grant, 2009b).

BOX 5.1

Personal and interpersonal goals

Extrinsic goals are not things that we do to benefit others. They are things that we do to benefit ourselves, based on the anticipated responses of others. However, we can also identify a goal dimension that ranges from entirely self-focused objectives (e.g., wanting an ice cream) to those that are for the benefit of others or the wider community (e.g., striving for social justice). Paradoxically, research suggests that the latter may actually bring about greater wellbeing than the former. For instance, Eigner (2001) reported that people who actively do something to protect the environment have a higher sense of wellbeing, and Sohr (2001) also found that 'hyperactivists' report very high levels of wellbeing. Drawing together the evidence, Sheldon and Schmuck (2001) conclude that 'the source of individual happiness lies in caring for something greater than oneself' (p. 221). Perhaps this is because, through such strivings, individuals can nurture the tendrils of meaning and purpose that seem to be so intrinsic to psychological health (see Chapter 4, this volume).

APPROACH–AVOIDANCE

A goal dimension relatively orthogonal to (i.e., independent of) the intrinsic–extrinsic one, but also with evidence of moderating the goal actualisation–wellbeing relationship, is approach–avoidance (Elliot & Friedman, 2007). 'Approach goals are focused on a positive, desirable outcome or state and regulation entails trying to move toward or maintain the outcome or state' (Elliot & Church, 2002, p. 244). Examples of Mei's approach goals would be 'To get back into music again', 'To have a better relationship with my mother', and 'To be closer with Saul'. By contrast, 'avoidance goals are focused on a negative, undesirable outcome or state and regulation entails trying to move or stay away from the outcome or state' (Elliot & Church, 2002, p. 244). Examples of Mei's avoidance goals would be 'To stop spending', 'To feel less stuck', and now also 'To get away from Saul' (note the direct conflict between this and her approach goal, 'To be closer with Saul'). Approach goals involve a sensitivity to gains, in which the person is trying to reduce the discrepancy between their current state and a desired one. By contrast, avoidance goals involve a sensitivity to losses, in which the person is trying to maximise the discrepancy between their current state and a feared one. In humanistic terms, approach goals can be considered similar to 'higher needs' (such as self-respect and self-actualisation; Maslow, 1943), which strive to enhance the organism (Rogers, 1959). By contrast, avoidance goals can be considered equivalent to 'lower needs' (such as hunger and safety), which are 'deficiency-based' and strive to maintain the organism. This dimension also has strong parallels with Higgins' (1997) distinction between 'promotion' and 'prevention' foci (see Web Resource 5.2).

This distinction between approach and avoidance goals is of particular importance to a therapeutic context because 'Recent research has linked avoidance goal regulation to a host of negative processes and outcomes' (Elliot & Church, 2002, p. 244). For instance, Elliot and Sheldon (1997) found that a focus on avoidance goals, rather than approach goals, was associated with lower subjective wellbeing, adjustment, and experience. More specifically, within the therapeutic context, Elliot and Church (2002) showed that clients who adopted more avoidance goals evidenced smaller increases in wellbeing from the start to the end of therapy, experienced less goal progress, and were less satisfied with the work. Similarly, Wollburg and Braukhaus (2010) found that clients with more avoidance goals showed less reductions in depression symptomatology. More generally, clients coming into therapy seem to have more avoidance goals than a general population, and a greater number of avoidance goals in clients is associated with more psychological problems and lower wellbeing (Elliot & Church, 2002; Tryon, 2018). Consistent with these findings, across the course of therapy, levels of avoidance motivation tend to decrease (Berking, Grosse Holtforth, Jacobi, & Kröner-Herwig, 2005). Indeed, Vieth and colleagues (2003) have developed a psychotherapeutic approach – 'Self–System Therapy' – which specifically aims to help clients find more effective ways of achieving approach goals. Here, therapeutic methods may include asking clients to set one approach goal per day and then evaluate how effectively they were able to progress towards it.

Avoidance goals may be 'ineffective regulatory devices' (Elliot & Church, 2002, p. 245) for a number of reasons. First, while successfully achieving an approach goal may boost our sense of self-worth and efficacy (see Chapter 4, this volume), successful avoidance may evoke more ambivalent feelings. For instance, we may experience relief, but also such feelings as weakness or cowardliness. Second, and closely related, as with all avoidant behaviour, any 'successes' are likely to make the thing that is being avoided seem even more daunting. The more, for instance, Mei avoids contact with Saul, the more he becomes a rejecting, hurtful, untrustworthy figure to her – after all, why else would she be avoiding him. Third, and again closely related, to avoid something we have to call it to mind, and that can then evoke negative affect, while calling to mind something that we want can improve how we feel. Fourth, avoidance goals may be less clear to imagine than approach goals, and therefore less easy to plan towards. Mei knows, for instance, what it would look like to ask Saul out for a drink, but what would it mean to avoid him for ever? How could this actually happen? Finally, in many instances, the desire to avoid or eradicate something is just not realistic. A client, for instance, might want therapy to stop them from ever feeling anxious again, but such an avoidant goal is not achievable (Dryden, 2018). And, to the extent that it sets an unrealistically high reference standard (see Chapter 4), it may end up making them feel worse.

Interestingly, however, research suggests that human beings, in general, may have a natural tendency to orient towards avoidance goals, rather than approach ones

(Kahneman, 2011). This may be because feelings of loss are often stronger and more compelling than feelings of gain. This makes good evolutionary sense: to survive, our priority needs to be to avoid threats and danger, whereas being drawn towards good things is of less immediate concern. The development of wellbeing, then, may require us to turn away from our natural avoidance focus, and to proactively and deliberately orient ourselves towards approach goals.

At the same time, however, there is good evidence that some people have a more approach-oriented 'regulatory style', while others engage in the world in a more avoidance-oriented way (Higgins, 1997). Strauman and colleagues (2006) suggest that these characteristic styles may be related to an individual's socialisation histories. More specifically, if an individual's parents do not emphasise approach goals (e.g., 'Let's do something fun today', 'What shall we discover?'), but instead centre development around avoidance goals (e.g., 'Watch out for that', 'Don't do that'), then the person may fail to develop promotion goals in adolescence and adulthood.

So do you consider yourself to be a more approach-oriented or avoidance-oriented person? You might also want to consider where that regulatory style comes from – does it fit with your upbringing?

CONSCIOUS–UNCONSCIOUS

'In many everyday cases,' write Chun, Kruglanski, Sleeth-Keppler, and Friedman (2011), 'people's choices are guided by volitional goals of which they are acutely aware' (p. 1124). However, one of the most influential developments in the contemporary motivational literature is the recognition that people's choices and behaviours – as argued in Chapter 2 – can be influenced by unconscious goal intentions (e.g., Marien, Custers, Hassin, & Aarts, 2012). In other words, we do not need to be aware of our desires or intentions to act towards specific goals (Moskowitz, 2012). Indeed, it has been argued that unconscious goal-directed activity may be the norm rather than the exception (Austin & Vancouver, 1996; Moskowitz & Grant, 2009a).

Although the notion of unconscious directions is particularly aligned with a psychodynamic perspective (see Chapter 10), it is relatively consistent with the viewpoint of many other approaches. The existential therapist Farber (2000), for instance, writes about two realms of will: the 'unconscious will' and the 'conscious will'. Similarly, in the cognitive field, Kahneman (2011) conceptualises two systems of thinking: *System 1*, which operates automatically and quickly, with little or no effort and no sense of voluntary control; and *System 2*, associated with agency, choice, and concentration, which allocates attention to effortful mental activity. And Epstein (1998), in his integrative cognitive–experiential self-theory, distinguishes between the holistic, affective 'experiential system' and the analytical, logical 'rational system', both of which can drive behaviour.

Numerous research studies, initiated by Bargh and colleagues (e.g., Bargh & Ferguson, 2000), support the argument that goals can be triggered, selected, and pursued without people being consciously aware of these processes (Chun et al., 2011; Moskowitz, 2012). For example, in a classic experiment, Bargh, Gollwitzer, Lee-Chai, Barndollar, & Trötschel (2001) first 'primed' some participants by asking them to undertake a sentence completion task that contained cooperation-related terms, such as 'helpful' and 'fair'. Subsequently, these participants behaved more cooperatively on a resource allocation 'game' than participants who had not had this priming. Critically, however, these participants were not aware of any link between the two activities. In other words, they were acting towards cooperative goals, but had no awareness of what this goal was, or that they had been directed towards it by the priming task. What this study also demonstrates, as discussed in Chapter 2, is that we can be 'primed', unconsciously, into accessing, choosing, or following particular intentions, based on the cues in the environment around us. For instance, research shows that people talk more softly when looking at pictures of a library, or are more likely to choose cleaning goals when exposed to the citrus-like scent of an all-purpose cleaner (Custers et al., 2012; Holland, Hendriks, & Aarts, 2005).

Furthermore, research shows that unconscious goal pursuit can have many of the complex and adaptive features of conscious goal pursuit. For instance, people acting towards unconscious goals can display goal-related behaviour in novel settings, overcome obstacles, and use monitoring, feedback, and 'goal-shielding' processes (see Box 3.2) to achieve their objectives (Aarts & Custers, 2012). When Mei starts to reflect on her anger towards her mum, for instance, she begins to recognise that it is underpinned by a complex goal-oriented strategy: 'I thought it was just about finding her really annoying. But actually, really, I think I want to push her away. Create space from her. It's actually just too painful to think she matters to me… or that I might matter to her.'

As illustrated here, this conscious–unconscious dimension is closely related to a distinction between *self-attributed* (or *explicit*) motives and *implicit* motives (McClelland, Koestner, & Weinberger, 1989). The former is the conscious motives that a person attributes to themselves (e.g., 'disliking mum'), while the latter is those fundamental – and generally unconscious – needs that arise early in a person's development (e.g., 'avoidance of pain'). Crucially, McClelland et al. have argued that implicit motives (as assessed by such projective tests as the Thematic Apperception Test) and self-attributed motives (as assessed by self-report surveys) are independent. In fact, subsequent meta-analyses has shown some degree of association, but it is small (a correlation of .09; Spangler, 1992), equivalent to about 1% overlap.

Research, then, tends to support the hypothesis that the goals we consciously believe we have may be very different from those that are actually driving our behaviour. Furthermore, research suggests that it is the implicit motives, rather than the self-identified ones, that tend to be more predictive of real-world behaviour (Spangler, 1992). This is particularly the case where the behaviour is intrinsically rewarding. Consistent with much psychodynamic thinking, then, research suggests that, in many instances, consciousness lays false conclusions and interpretations on our actual, unconscious motivations (Moskowitz & Grant, 2009a). Fromm (1942) states, 'A great number of apparently insoluble problems disappear at once if we decide to give up the notion that the motives by which people *believe* themselves to be motivated are necessarily the ones which actually drive them to act, feel and think as they do' (p. 118, emphasis in the original). This point is a critical one we shall come back to when we look at the issue of working with goals in therapy (see Chapter 14).

However, evidence also exists that people vary quite considerably in the degree to which their goals are unconscious. Thrash, Maruskin, and Martin (2012) describe this as *motive congruence*: the degree of concordance between implicit and explicit motives. Drawing on the evidence, they suggest that motive congruence is higher in individuals who are more self-determining (i.e., regulating in accordance with their true, intrinsic motives), and whose early environment supported the development of self-determination by meeting their basic needs for autonomy and relatedness. They also suggest that individuals who are higher in motive congruence are more sensitive to their bodily states, less monitoring of others' expectations, and more concerned with self-consistency. Thrash et al. (2012) also cite research that lower levels of motive congruence are associated with lower levels of affective wellbeing over time.

In contrast to the intrinsic–extrinsic and approach–avoidance dimensions, there is no direct evidence that the existence of either conscious or unconscious goals is related to wellbeing *per se*. And, indeed, we would not expect there to be. Almost certainly, it would be impossible to be conscious of all our goals and desires, and probably not desirable, in itself. Nevertheless, as discussed in Chapter 3, developing a conscious awareness of our directions may be essential in helping us find more effective and synergetic ways of actualising them. If what Mei really wants, for instance, is to re-experience passion in her life, then recognising this is likely to open up the possibility of actualising it in a myriad of ways.

Consciousness of our true goals and desires, however, is not always easy, because we may have a *metagoal* (see below) of driving them 'underground'. For Mei, for instance, it may feel incredibly painful to acknowledge that she wants her mum's love and attention. Hence, she may strive (unconsciously) to avoid this awareness. Therapeutically, this can be termed *resistance* (Bugental, 1978; Rycroft, 1995). In addition, recognising our unconscious goals may require mental effort and, as research suggests, we may have a natural direction towards avoiding mental exertion (Kahneman, 2011). It is hard work for clients, for anyone, to dig down to why they are really doing the things that they want in their lives.

LONG-TERM–SHORT-TERM

The distinction between conscious and unconscious goals leads on to a closely related dimension: 'temporal range' (Austin & Vancouver, 1996). This is the degree to which goals are long-term, distal 'life goals' (Pöhlmann, 2001; Schmuck & Sheldon, 2001) as opposed to short-term, proximal objectives. This temporal extension can be defined in terms of how far in the future the goal object is (Miller & Brickman, 2004), as well as the amount of time needed to know whether success or failure has been achieved (Fujita & MacGregor, 2012). Mei's goal of experiencing closeness with Saul, for instance, seems to be a short-term goal in the sense that it is about achieving something in the immediate now. By contrast, her goal of finding greater passion and excitement in her life is a much more long-term aim: something she can only judge the success of in months or years to come.

Within the therapeutic field, we can make a specific distinction between *life goals* (what the person wants to achieve, generally, in life) and more proximal *therapeutic goals* (Mackrill, 2011), *therapy goals* (Elliot & Church, 2002), or *treatment goals*. These are 'intended changes in behaviour and experience to be attained by therapy' (Michalak & Grosse Holtforth, 2006, p. 353). At a more proximal level still, we can also identify 'session goals': what a client specifically wants to achieve in that particular session (May, 1969a).

While short-term goals, like unconscious ones, would seem essential to human functioning (see below), the focus of many therapeutic approaches is on helping clients move away from a 'short-termist' orientation towards a greater focus on mid- and longer-term goals. Dryden (1999), for instance, writes:

> Frequently ... we defeat ourselves by attempting to satisfy our short-term goals while at the same time sabotaging our long-term goals. Thus, for example, we often strive to avoid discomfort when it would be advisable for us to experience discomfort because doing so would help us to achieve our long-term goals. (p. 3)

Indeed, it might be argued that many psychological difficulties boil down to a tendency to prioritise short-term directions over long-term ones. As we will see in Chapters 10 and 13, for instance, the cognitive therapies encourage clients to put effortful and rational ways of thinking and planning – which can lead towards longer-term goals – over immediate cognitive gratification, while, in the psychodynamic and insight-based therapy, there is an emphasis on helping clients put longer-term life improvements over shorter-term avoidance of emotional pain (i.e., resistance). Indeed, the very act of coming to therapy could be seen as a process of putting long-term goals before short-term ones: prioritising ongoing psychological wellbeing over the shorter-term costs of emotional, financial, and time expenditure.

At the same time, however, proximal subgoals (for instance, 'to go for a run') are essential for longer-term, distal objectives (for instance, 'to stay healthy'). And, indeed, psychological research suggests that the setting of more proximal goals generates more success than the setting of distal goals (Locke & Latham, 2002). If Mei, for instance, wants to resolves things with her mother, she is generally better off setting a proximal and *time-bound* goal (the T in SMART goals – see Chapter 14), such as 'Skype her next week and tell her what I find difficult', rather than a more proximal and diffuse goal, such as 'Get to a better place in the relationship with her'. This suggests, then, that proximal goals may form a very important function, but are salutogenic to the extent that they lead towards – rather than away from – more distal, higher-order goals. We will explore this further in Chapter 14.

IMPORTANT–UNIMPORTANT

At a most basic level, goals can vary in their importance to a person. Some of Mei's goals, for instance, are very important to her, like being close to Olivia. Other goals, like arriving on time for therapy, are of less significance. And, as we saw in Chapter 3, the importance of a goal for a person – in terms of the strength of its desirability – is a principal determinant of whether it becomes intended, and then actioned.

Not surprisingly, research shows that satisfaction from goal-oriented activities is higher when those goals are important (Zaleski, 1987). It also shows that the presence of more important goals is associated with greater positive affect and well-being (Emmons, 1986). Little (2007) states that 'individuals experience well-being to the extent that they are engaged in projects that they appraise as estimable, meaningful undertaking' (p. 40). This is similar to our proposition, in Chapter 4, that people need to have a sense of direction in their lives. However, research also demonstrates that goal commitment mediates the relationship between goal attainment and subjective wellbeing (Brunstein, 1993). This suggests that goal importance, or goal commitment, may only be associated with positive affect if we feel that these goals are attainable, and that we are progressing towards – and achieving – them. If, on the other hand, we feel that important goals are unattainable, or that we are not getting closer to them, we may feel worse than if these goals were not important to us.

The importance of goals to a person is closely connected to a range of other dimensions, such as the attractiveness, relevance, and the degree of energy associated with them (Austin & Vancouver, 1996; Sheeran & Webb, 2012). In addition, important goals are likely to be 'higher-order' goals (see Chapter 6) as well as longer-term goals (Zaleski, 1987). Critically, however, as with Caspar (1995), we can distinguish between the importance of a goal, in terms of how urgent, phenomenologically, it feels (i.e., 'intended to be done at once'; Zaleski, 1987, p. 31), and how high-order it is, in terms of how fundamental it is to the person's overall, global directions. This distinction is important because, as in the example earlier, Mei might feel it is of the utmost importance to avoid feeling love towards her mother, and yet, in terms of her most fundamental directions, this may be exactly what she wants. Hence, while goal importance may fluctuate in the short term, its order – as part of a structural configuration (see Chapter 6) – remains relatively constant. The potentially negative consequences of this – in the form of *rogue goals* – will be explored in Chapter 8.

DIFFICULT–EASY

Goals vary in their level of difficulty (Austin & Vancouver, 1996), and this can be defined as the 'level of knowledge and skill that is required to achieve a goal' (Sheeran & Webb, 2012, p. 178). A really difficult goal for Mei, for instance, would be to stop buying records entirely. An easier goal for her would be to reduce her spending to three records per week. Or perhaps not. Perhaps, for instance, Mei would actually find it easier to give up spending entirely than to cut down in stages. The point here, however, as discussed in Chapter 3, is that the feasibility of a particular direction is a major component in how we experience it, as well as whether it is actualised.

In terms of research, there is some evidence that goal difficulty mediates the relationship between goal success and wellbeing, with people experiencing stronger positive emotional responses when actualising more difficult goals (Wiese, 2007). This makes intuitive sense. If, for instance, it was 'hell' for Mei not to spend money on records for a year, she would likely experience much more satisfaction and pride in its achievement than, for instance, giving up spending for a day. Related to this, one of the strongest and most consistent findings in the goal-setting literature is that people tend to show greater progress when they act towards more difficult goals as compared to easier ones (Epton et al., 2017; Locke & Latham, 2002; Locke et al., 1981; Wiese, 2007). So, for instance, Mei is likely to spend less money overall on records if she decides to give up entirely, as compared, for instance, with planning to buy only three records per week.

However, the benefits of difficult goals are likely to be moderated by the degree to which a goal is realistic (one of the SMART characteristics – see Chapter 14). In fact, evidence suggests that goals that are somewhat unrealistically optimistic, to the extent that they lead to higher levels of striving, may enhance goal progress (Sheeran & Webb, 2012). However, extremely unrealistic goals, as overly high reference standards (see Chapter 4), can be expected to lead to lower feelings of goal achievement and more disappointment. Each New Year's Eve, for instance, Mei sets her resolution to spend less money on records. But she does not really plan how she will do it – she just hopes that she will have the 'willpower' to succeed. She manages one day, then another, but after a few weeks the task feels impossible, and with no strategies or supports to draw on, she gives up and starts overspending again.

Hence, the most salutogenic goals may be those that are challenging but also realistic to attain. As Layard (2006) puts it, 'The secret is to have goals that are stretching enough, but not too stretching' (p. 73). This is the essence of *flow* (see Web Resource 4.2), when the challenges meet our abilities (Csikszentmihalyi, 2002).

SPECIFIC–VAGUE

Goals can be specific, precise, and definite or they can be nebulous, open-ended, and vague. The former are more likely to be quantitative; the latter qualitative (Austin &

Vancouver, 1996). An example of the former might be: 'To reduce my record spending down to £20 per week'. An example of the latter might be, 'To spend less'. This dimension is closely related to the degree with which a goal is *concrete*, as opposed to *abstract*. Here, 'Concrete goals detail specific, tangible rewards achieved by particular behaviours in response to particular contexts. Abstract goals, in contrast, reflect more global, general aims that transcend specific situations and apply to multiple contexts' (Fujita & MacGregor, 2012, p. 86). The specificity of a goal is also closely associated to its simplicity, as opposed to its complexity. A complex goal, like enjoying life more, is linked to a wide range of other goals, subgoals, and behaviours (Austin & Vancouver, 1996). It can be achieved through multiple pathways (see equifinality, below). By contrast, a simple goal is relatively distinct and can be achieved through only a small number of means.

Research generally shows that people make more goal progress when they aim for specific, measurable, and simple goals, as opposed to goals that are vague and complex (Austin & Vancouver, 1996; Locke & Latham, 2002; Locke et al., 1981; Sheeran & Webb, 2012). Research also shows that concrete goals are associated with more persistence and satisfaction (Zaleski, 1987). Specificity is the S of SMART goals (see Chapter 14). However, this does not necessarily mean that therapists should strive to set specific goals with clients. Although such goals may be more likely to be attained, they are only salutogenic to the extent that they help the person achieve the higher-order goals that really matter to them. We will explore this in more depth in Chapter 14.

PROCESS–OUTCOME

Another distinction of potential relevance to the therapeutic field is between *process goals* and *outcome goals*. Outcome goals are closed-ended and 'consumable', in the sense that once they are achieved that is it. Examples for Mei might include 'leaving Rob' and 'resolving things with my mother'. Process goals, on the other hand, are open-ended and always subject to discrepancies and correction. Examples for Mei might include 'being more assertive with Rob' and 'making the most of the time I have with my mother'. Outcome goals have an 'ideal focus', compared with the 'vector preference' of process goals (Austin & Vancouver, 1996).

In terms of the relationship between this dimension and wellbeing, evidence is limited. However, both types of goals may have strengths and limits. An outcome goal may be experienced as more specific, and hence more attainable (Locke & Latham, 2002). On the other hand, an outcome focus may mean that positive affect only comes with goal achievement, whereas, if we have a process focus, we can also feel good from our progress towards them. As the saying goes, 'Happiness is a journey and not a destination.' A process focus may also foster a greater sense of self-acceptance, self-efficacy, and calm as we can experience 'micro-achievements' along the way. By contrast, a final, all-important outcome point may heighten anxieties and feelings of being judged.

PRIMARY-SECONDARY

A final dimension of goals – less explored in the psychological field, but closely related to the issue of vicious and virtuous cycles – is the 'metalevel' of the goal. This is the question of whether the goal is just a goal, or whether it is a goal about a goal: a *secondary goal* or *metagoal*. Most goals are of a *primary*, basic type, in that the goal object is a particular state or object. For instance, 'I want to talk to Saul'. Dennett (1987) refers to this as a *first-order* intentional system. However, it is also possible that the goal object is a goal, or a goal-related process, itself, in which case we can refer to it as a *secondary* goal – or a *second-order* intentional system. Mei has a secondary goal, for instance, that she does not want to want Saul. She also has a secondary goal that she wants to find a sense of purpose and direction in life. As we can see here, secondary goals can both be avoidant and approach, respectively. Another example of an avoidant secondary goal would be 'I don't want to have un-finished goals in my life', while another secondary approach goal could be 'I must succeed in achieving my goals'.

Note, as with this latter example, all goals related to achieving competence (see Chapter 6) might be considered metagoals. In addition, to the extent that emotions can be considered the results of goal-related processes (see Chapter 4), it could be argued that goals that have emotions as their goal objects are essentially metagoals. So, for instance, if my goal is that 'I want to be happy' (and if, as argued in Chapter 4, happiness comes from actualising my goals), then, essentially, my goal is to actualise my goals.

Although metagoals are neither good nor bad, like secondary emotions (see Chapter 4), they have the potential to catalyse vicious, as well as virtuous, cycles. Suppose, for instance, that I have a secondary goal that I should not fail on any of my goals. Then, if I do fail (if, for instance, I don't go out for a run), then not only do I feel bad about failing at my primary goal, but I also feel bad at the metagoal level (I have failed at warding off failure). This, then, can spark a vicious spiral: I feel that I have failed for failing, which makes me feel more of a failure, which then increases my feeling of failure, etc. Compare this with the person whose metagoal is to accept themselves whether they fail or succeed. Here, the person may still experience a sense of failure for not going for a run, but this does not trigger a downward emotional spiral. Rather: 'I feel that I have failed' … 'Oh well, that's fine'. End of story.

CONCLUSION

In this chapter, we have looked at a number of goal dimensions and how they mediate the relationship between goal actualisation and wellbeing. In summary, what the research seems to suggest is that it is more helpful to strive towards intrinsic, approach goals and to have some conscious awareness of the goals that are most important to us. Goals that are difficult but realistic, and specific without being trivial, may also be important to aim for, as might a focus on process goals. Noticing when secondary goals may lead us to spiral upwards, or downwards, in our wellbeing may also be of relevance. In Chapter 14, we will look at how this knowledge can be applied to the process of working with goals in therapy.

QUESTIONS FOR REFLECTION

- Identify a goal that is currently salient for you. Jot it down below. Now, for each of the following dimensions, put a mark on the line indicating where you would locate it. For instance, if it is a strongly intrinsic goal, mark that end of the intrinsic–extrinsic continuum. Which of these dimensions seem to most strongly relate to the wellbeing, or psychological difficulties, associated with this goal?

My goal is...

Intrinsic	|	Extrinsic
Approach	|	Avoidance
Conscious	|	Unconscious
Long-term	|	Short-term
Important	|	Unimportant
Difficult	|	Easy
Specific	|	Vague
Process	|	Outcome
Primary	|	Secondary

--- **FURTHER READING** ---

Aarts, H., & Elliot, A. J. (Eds.). (2012). *Goal-directed behavior*. New York: Psychology Press. Offers a range of psychology chapters covering all aspects of goals.

Austin, J. T., & Vancouver, J. B. (1996). Goal constructs in psychology: Structure, process, and content. *Psychological Bulletin, 120*(3), 338–375. Somewhat dated, but a very comprehensive overview of goal dimensions and other aspects of goals.

Moskowitz, G. B., & Grant, H. (Eds.). (2009). *The psychology of goals*. New York: Guilford Press. A second very useful collection of chapters on the psychology of goals.

6

A STRUCTURAL MODEL OF DIRECTIONALITY

What we really, really want

This chapter discusses:

- A 'structural' model of directionality, which allows for a hierarchical conceptualisation of multiple directions and the relationships between them.
- Highest-order directions: what we most fundamentally desire and strive for in life.

Mei wants to be close to Saul; but she also doesn't. She wants to get more into music; but she also wants to spend less money on it. To this point, we have considered individual directions in isolation. However, as we can see here, in reality, multiple directions are likely to be in existence at any one time (Riediger & Freund, 2004). Grawe (2004) writes, 'human experience and behavior are always determined by multiple intentions' (p. 160). So how can we conceptualise these directions together? What are the relationships between these different desires and goals, and how do these relationships affect our overall wellbeing? In this chapter, we will begin to try to answer these questions by outlining a *structural* model of directionality and applying it to an understanding of psychological wellbeing and distress.

HIERARCHICALLY ORGANISED DIRECTIONS

A basic assumption among many theorists and researchers in the philosophical (e.g., Woodfield, 1976), psychological (e.g., Angyal, 1941; Austin & Vancouver, 1996; Carver & Scheier, 2012; Ford, 1992; Koestler, 1967; Little & Gee, 2007; Miller et al., 1960; Powers, 1973), and clinical fields (e.g., Caspar, 1995) is that desires and goals can be conceptualised as existing in a hierarchical structure (also referred to as a 'motivational structure' [Klinger & Cox, 2011] or 'goal hierarchy'). Here, there are a small number of *highest-order* directions, beneath which are *lower-order*, 'sub-directions'. These, then, have further 'sub-sub-directions', cascading down to the lowest-order desires and goals. Koestler (1967) described this multi-levelled, hierarchically-ordered system as an 'inverted tree branching downwards' (p. 39). Individual hierarchies may vary in the number of levels (from 'shallow' to 'deep' hierarchies) and they may also vary in the 'breadth' or 'span' of the levels (Koestler, 1967) from 'narrow' to 'broad'.

Within such structures, lower-order directions can be considered the *means* – or 'strategies', 'methods', or 'pathways' – through which higher-order directions can be actualised (Caspar, 1995; Cooper & McLeod, 2011; Kruglanski & Kopetz, 2009; Miller et al., 1960; Moskowitz, 2012; Snyder, 2000). Conversely, higher-order directions form the *reference value* for lower-order directions: the 'value', the reason why they are undertaken. Caspar (1995) likens this to the weather where, to understand ground-level features (like wind strength, humidity, and temperature), we need to understand what is going on at higher altitudes. Hence, as we go up the hierarchy, we ask 'why?' something is done (Mansell et al., 2013). By contrast, when we go down the vertical hierarchy, we ask 'how?' something is done.

For instance, we could hypothesise that one of Mei's highest-order desires is to experience relatedness in her life (Figure 6.1). To achieve that, she is trying to establish a relationship with Saul; and, to achieve that, she is going to have one last go at sending him an email saying everything she feels towards him. But to do that, she needs to switch on her computer first; and to do that, she needs to flex her finger muscle towards the computer.

A STRUCTURAL MODEL OF DIRECTIONALITY: WHAT WE REALLY, REALLY WANT

Higher-order direction — Relatedness
↕
Establish relationship with Saul
↕
Write Saul an email
↕
Lower-order direction — Switch on computer

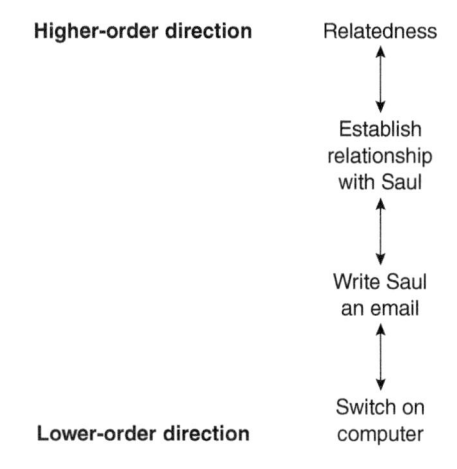

Figure 6.1 A single vertical hierarchy

As Grawe (2004) suggests, to some extent, we can conceptualise this structural model of directionality as a 90 degree clockwise rotation of the phase model (see Chapter 3, this volume). Here, then, the underlying desires (previously at the left end of the phase model) are now at the top of the hierarchy, while the more concrete plans and actions (previously at the right end of the phase model) are lower down (Perugini & Bagozzi, 2004). However, the difference between these two models is that the phase model describes the development of a direction over a particular period of time, whereas the structural model describes the underlying, relatively consistent organisation of the directions. This means that while the phase model focuses only on active directions, the structural model is inclusive of directions that may be latent. For instance, while Mei, that morning at work, is acting on her desire to establish relatedness with Saul, she also has an underlying desire for stability in her life, and this higher-order direction plays an important part in understanding Mei's internal dynamics. However, this desire for stability would not feature in a phase-based understanding of Mei's actions, which focuses solely on the unfurling of her desire for relatedness.

In terms of goal dimensions (Chapter 5), higher-order directions are likely to be intrinsic, long-term, and important (e.g., experiencing relatedness), while lower-order directions are likely to be short-term, specific, and concrete (e.g., switch on computer). Interestingly, Caspar (1995) suggests that both our highest-order and lowest-order directions are likely to be unconscious and automatic, while middle-order directions are more likely to be conscious and deliberate. We can see this in the example above: Mei may not be particularly conscious of her highest-order desire for relatedness, and her lowest-order switching on of the computer may just be an unconscious, reflex-like action. But she may be very aware of, and focused on, her desire for closeness with Saul, or the email that she plans to write to him.

Although this structural model is based around directions, *beliefs* – the second component of an intentional system (Dennett, 1987) – play a critical role in mediating between different levels (Miller et al., 1960). As will be discussed later, this may then play an essential role in the development of psychological problems (Curtis, Silberschatz, Sampson, & Weiss, 1994; Silberschatz, 2017), because beliefs can be more or less accurate. Mei, for instance, believes that if she were really honest with Saul about her desires for him, she would experience rejection and shame. In therapy, however, she explores the possibility that this might be based on past experiences, and that, actually, she really does not know how Saul would react to such an approach. 'Have you thought,' I say to her, 'Have you– What about if actually the best way of getting somewhere with Saul was just to be up front with him? Tell him what's actually going on for you.'

Of course, as suggested at the start of this chapter, more than one vertical hierarchy can exist at any one time (see Figure 6.2). Mei wants relatedness, and she strives for this through a relationship with Saul. But she also wants stability, and her means towards this is through staying with Rob. And, as with getting closer to Saul, there are lower-order things that she does to try to achieve this goal. For instance, when she feels angry towards Rob, she tries to deal with this by suppressing her feelings and walking out of the room.

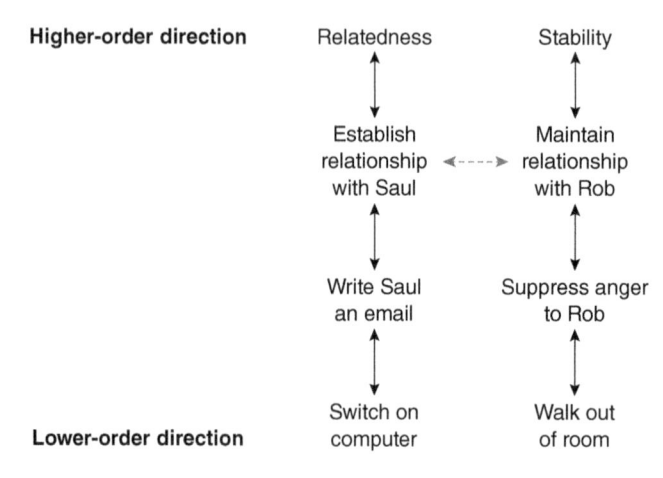

Figure 6.2 Multiple vertical hierarchies

Note: Dashed line indicates conflict between directions

Crucially, once we start to introduce additional vertical hierarchies into this model, we can begin to consider the *horizontal* links between different directions (Kruglanski, Shah, Fishbach, Friedman, Chun, & Sleeth-Keppler, 2002). As we can see in Figure 6.2, for instance, Mei's desire to establish a relationship with Saul directly conflicts with her desire to maintain a relationship with Rob (illustrated by the dashed line). If she gets one, she has to sacrifice the other, and vice versa. This, then, depicts one of the fundamental problems that Mei is facing. In Chapter 8, we will argue that such conflicts are at the heart of many psychological problems.

Two principles that are fundamental to this structural model are those of *equifinality* and *multifinality* (Austin & Vancouver, 1996; Kruglanski & Kopetz, 2009; Moskowitz, 2012).

Equifinality: One goal, multiple means

Equifinality is the principle that the same direction can be actualised through a range of lower-order sub-directions (Austin & Vancouver, 1996). So, for instance, Mei strives for relatedness by being close to Saul, but she also strives to achieve this through spending time with Olivia, and by being close to her girlfriends (Figure 6.3).

```
                    Relatedness
                    ↗    ↑    ↖
              ↙          ↓          ↘
        Spend time   Establish    Be close
        with Olivia  relationship to girlfriends
                     with Saul
```

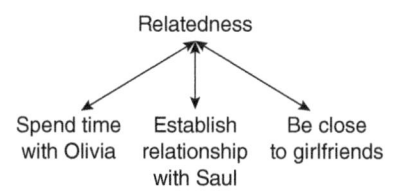

Figure 6.3 Equifinal means to the same higher-order goal

This equifinality is equivalent to plasticity (see Chapter 2), and can be considered one hallmark of a directional system (Woodfield, 1976). However, it also seems reasonable to assume that levels of equifinality can vary from person to person. A person who is high in this capacity might be described as *flexible* (or with 'highly differentiated intentional schema'; Grawe, 2004, p. 288), in that they have a range of different means to actualise their directions (Caspar, 1995). By contrast, someone who has only a few ways of doing things could be described as *inflexible*, 'rigid', or 'myopic'. In terms of psychological wellbeing, such low levels of equifinality may be problematic (Caspar, 1995). We can understand this in terms of people being poor at actualising their directions, because if one means towards a goal is thwarted, they have few further means to draw on (Moskowitz, 2012). An example of this might be disordered eating, where a person's only strategy towards feeling in charge of their lives is by controlling their eating (Irving & Cannon, 2000). In addition, where people have inflexible structures, they may distort reality to fit their pre-existing means and beliefs (Caspar, 1995). So if a person can only feel in charge of their lives by controlling their eating, they may come to believe that this is the only way to do so: relationships, therapy, or other self-development work are not seen as having the potential to help. At the same time, however, equifinal means may only be as salutogenic as the particular alternatives adopted. In Chapter 5, we have already seen how some goals may be more helpful than others, and we will make some important additions to this analysis in Chapters 7 and 8.

Multifinality: One means, multiple goals

For once, Mei has arrived on time for the session. She sits down and shuffles, excitedly, in her chair. She looks down at the carpet, smiling. 'So how's your week been?' I ask.

Mei's smile broadens: a mixture of embarrassment and glee. Over the next ten minutes, Mei tells me all the things that had happened to her that week. She had sent Saul her 'last ditch' email after our last session. And, as discussed in therapy, she had just been very up front. 'Saul', she had written, 'I want us to spend some time together, to talk, to try and see what's possible.' He had replied, telling her that he was in love with her, it was just that… it was 'complicated'. They had gone for a drink (Rob and Olivia were away); she had spent the night at his flat; they had had 'just the most loving, beautiful, tender sex'; they had met the next day; had sex again; talked 'about everything' until the early hours of the morning. 'It's been amazing', says Mei, 'I sort of feel bad towards Rob, but now– for the first time– it's like the clouds in my head have just parted and I know what I want.'

Multifinality (or 'heterarchy'; Austin & Vancouver, 1996) refers to the principle that the same lower-order direction may achieve multiple higher-order directions. Through spending time with Saul, for instance, Mei not only actualises her higher-order desire for relatedness, but also for sexual pleasure and for intellectual stimulation (see Figure 6.4). Multifinal means can be seen as having a high value because, compared with 'unifinal' means (that strive towards just one goal), they are likely to bring about greater overall benefits. Such a system, in which there are high levels of multifinality, can be described as *synergetic* (Cooper, 2012). We will explore the importance of this structural configuration in much more detail in Chapter 8.

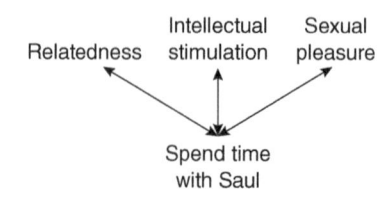

Figure 6.4 Multifinal lower-order means achieve multiple higher-order goals

A STRUCTURAL MODEL OF DIRECTIONALITY: WHAT WE REALLY, REALLY WANT

BOX 6.1

Powers's perceptual control theory

One of the earliest – and perhaps most widely-cited – attempts at developing a structural model of directionality is Powers's (1973) perceptual control theory. This theory has formed the basis for a number of integrative models of clinical practice (e.g., Carey, 2006; Goldstein, 1990; Grawe, 2004; Mansell, 2005), most specifically the method of levels (see Box 13.2). Perceptual control theory has also formed the foundations for some highly-respected theory and research in the psychological field (Carver & Scheier, 1981, 2012).

Perceptual control theory proposes 11 hierarchical levels (Mansell et al., 2013; Powers, 1973). These range from the lowest, physiological level of 'intensity control' (Powers, 1973), such as the basic spinal reflex loop, up to the highest level of 'systems concepts', such as an idealised sense of self or society (Carver & Scheier, 1990b; Powers, 1973).

For Powers (1973), each of these different levels exists as a *TOTE* unit – Test-Operate-Test-Exit – a concept taken from Miller et al. (1960). A TOTE unit begins with the person testing their perception of how things are (consciously or unconsciously) against their reference standard (see Chapter 4, this volume). For instance, Mei wants a certain level of relatedness in her life, and she compares her current perception of how well she is doing here against her desired-for expectation. If a discrepancy is found (and in Mei's case it is), this then leads to behaviour in an attempt to bring her perception back in line with her reference standard (operation). Once changes take place, there is then a further test phase, as the person checks again against their reference standard: for instance, has a relationship with Saul actually brought about the relatedness she was hoping for? If so, the loop is exited. If not, there are further operations to try to reduce the discrepancy between the reference state and actual state.

As with other structural models, perceptual control theory hypothesises that people strive to bring about change, at one level, through means and strategies at a lower level (Powers, 1973). More specifically, Powers proposes that the operation phases of the TOTE cycle involve 'altering the definition of the reference condition for the level below' (p. 51). What this means is that, if we find an incongruity between our perceptions and our reference standards, we set new reference standards at the lower level to try to compensate for that deficiency. Mei, for instance, compares her current closeness to Saul to her reference standard (a proper relationship) and finds she is lacking, so she sets new reference standards at a lower level to try to address this ('Write Saul an email'). And when she compares her current activity to this reference standard, she again finds she is lacking ('I'm just sitting here, staring at a blank computer screen'), so she sets a reference standard at a lower level ('Switch computer on'). This then leads to new reference standards at the lowest, most physiological levels, until behaviour happens and, ideally, changes get made. When the person's perceived reality now matches their reference standards, no further action is required.

(Continued)

Hence, what we have in Powers's (1973) model is a hierarchy of 'negative feedback loops', each aiming to reduce discrepancies in relation to higher reference standards. As Carey (2008) writes, 'Life, then, is like a constant game of "hotter colder". Whenever things start to move away from how we'd like them to be we act in whatever way we need to bring them back' (p. 16). Another analogy frequently used by Powers (1992) is that of driving a car, where we are constantly turning and adjusting the steering wheel to keep ourselves going in the right direction.

Although Powers's (1973, p. 52) control theory has both cybernetic and psychodynamic elements (with its focus on homeostatic regulation), it was strongly rooted in humanistic principles and ethics, and therefore has a broadly phenomenological stance. More specifically, reference standards are defined in terms of how people perceive their 'state of affair' (Powers, 1973, p. 46), rather than the actual state of affair *per se*. So, from this perspective, it does not matter whether Saul does or does not 'genuinely' want a relationship with Mei. What is important is Mei's perception of it, and how close or far away this is from what she is wanting. In Powers's model, then, it is quite possible that people may be striving for goals (for instance, 'to make a difference to other people's lives') – and feeling hopeless and despairing – that they have, in reality, achieved long ago. If we consider perceptions as a form of belief, this again highlights the importance of cognitions – and their accuracy – in determining how effectively we might function in the world.

HIGHEST-ORDER DIRECTIONS

The Spice Girls did not just ask us what we wanted. They asked us what we *really, really* wanted. This structural model of directionality begs the same question: What are our *highest-order directions*? That is, What are the desires and goals that every other direction leads to, but 'behind which we cannot go' (Maslow, 1987, p. 47), and that we would be least willing to give up? (Little, 2011).

Within the literature, these highest-order directions have been described using a wide variety of terms: 'major life goals' (Bleidorn, Kandler, Hülsheger, Riemann, Angleitner, & Spinath, 2010), 'superordinate goals' (Pöhlmann, 2001), 'ultimate goals' (Csikszentmihalyi, 2002; Elliot & Church, 2002), 'fundamental goals/projects/motives' (Klinger & Cox, 2011; Maslow, 1987; Sartre, 1958), 'meta-needs' (Maslow, 1968), 'terminal values' (Austin & Vancouver, 1996; Little & Gee, 2007), 'core projects' (Little, 2007), and 'original projects' (Sartre, 1958).

In many classic philosophies and psychologies, all human beings are hypothesised to have just one highest-order direction, such as meaning (Frankl, 1984) or actualisation (Rogers, 1959). This is illustrated in Figure 6.5, with all directions, and their subordinate directions, leading up to a single, superordinate direction. Other models suggest two basic directions, such as purpose and pleasure (Dolan, 2014), or agency and communion (McAdams, 1985).

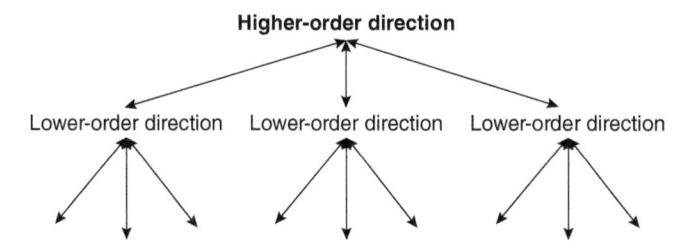

Figure 6.5 A single highest-order direction

Broader still, many contemporary psychological theories propose three or more highest-order directions, such as relatedness, competence, and autonomy (Ryan & Deci, 2000). Here, as depicted in Figure 6.6, a range of lower-order directions serve as the means to actualise these higher-order directions, with some lower-order directions serving to actualise two or more higher-order directions (multifinality). Most broadly, theorists such as William James have argued that there are thousands of highest-order drives (Angyal, 1941) that are irreducible to any smaller number of basic directions.

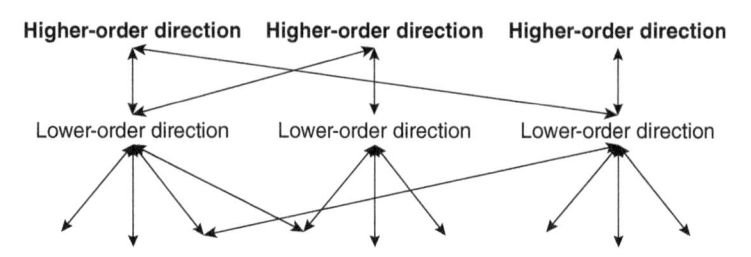

Figure 6.6 Multiple highest-order directions

What are the highest-order directions?

A review of several well-established taxonomies of highest-order needs, wants, or drives (albeit, primarily from a Western cultural context) identifies a number of commonly-posited directions. These are presented in Table 6.1. Most of these taxonomies focus on psychological directions (e.g., Ryan & Deci, 2000). However, some models are also inclusive of the physical and physiological domain (e.g., Maslow, 1987).

Pleasure/pain

From the earliest days of civilisation, the pursuit of pleasure – and the avoidance of pain – have been considered, by many, the most fundamental human direction. The fourth-century BC Greek philosopher Aristippus, for instance, 'taught that the goal of life is to experience the maximum amount of pleasure' (Ryan & Deci, 2001, p. 143). This 'hedonic' tradition has continued through such philosophical movements as utilitarianism, with Bentham (1789) stating that 'Nature has placed mankind

Table 6.1 Taxonomies of highest-order directions

	Maslow (1987)	McClelland & Burnham (2008)	Self-determination theory (Ryan & Deci, 2000)	Epstein (1994)	Flanagan (2010)	Reality therapy (Brickell & Wubbolding, 2000)	Human givens (Griffin & Tyrrell, 2013)
Pleasure/pain				Pleasure principle		Fun and enjoyment	
Growth	Self-actualisation				Change		
Autonomy/control		Power	Autonomy	Coherent conceptual system	Autonomy	Freedom Self-worth/power	Autonomy, privacy
Competence/self-worth	Esteem	Achievement	Competence	Self-esteem	Desirability/positive self-image	Self-worth/power	Status, competence, achievements
Relatedness	Belongingness and love	Affiliation	Relatedness	Relatedness	Connection	Love and belonging	Emotional connection, community, attention
Safety	Safety				Stability		Security
Physiological directions	Physiological					Survival, health and reproduction	
Meaning and purpose							Meaning

under the governance of two sovereign masters, *pain* and *pleasure*' (in Gregory, 1987, p. 308). In the twentieth century, many of the dominant psychologies continued to assume that pleasure and pain were the ultimate drivers of human behaviour: Freud (1963), for instance, with his pleasure principle, and Skinner with his emphasis on the shaping role of rewards and punishments. Today, many contemporary psychological and therapeutic perspectives, from bioenergetics (Lowen, 1975) to CBT (Layard, 2006), still see happiness as the foremost driver of human behaviour.

The hypothesis that human behaviour and experiencing is, ultimately, directed towards pleasure and away from pain can explain a wide variety of phenomena. Why, for instance, is Mei late for her session? Because she wants to avoid the pain of talking about her difficulties. Why does she want to avoid pain? This question does not intuitively seem to make sense, suggesting that the avoidance of pain is a direction 'behind which we cannot go'. Throughout history, however, there have been challenges to this perspective. Aristotle, for instance, considered hedonism 'a vulgar ideal, making humans slavish followers of desires' (Ryan & Deci, 2001, p. 145). More recently, Nozick critiqued the hedonic assumption through his 'experience machine' thought experiment (Nozick, 1977, in Dolan, 2014). Nozick asks us to imagine a machine that could simulate in our brains a state of constant pleasure, so we believe that we have a perfect relationship, a fabulous partner... whatever we desired. The question then is would we want it, or would we prefer to stay with the reality of our actual lives, with their mixture of ups and downs? Nozick suggests, like Keanu Reeves choosing the red pill over the blue pill in *The Matrix*, that most of us would want reality over pleasure, and if so, then how can pleasure be our highest-order direction? In support of this argument, Dolan (2014) found that three-quarters of people would not even choose a pill that could *increase* their happiness. As with the fact that many people are reluctant to take anti-depressants, this again suggests that there is something more important for many people than pleasure.

Growth

From the times of antiquity, this *hedonic* view of highest-order directions has been contrasted against a *eudaimonic* view (Ryff & Singer, 2008). This perspective, widely embraced by the humanistic psychology field, holds that the highest-order human direction is 'self-actualisation' (Goldstein, 1940) or the 'actualisation of potential' (Rogers, 1959): achieving the best that is within us (Ryff & Singer, 2008). This is a tendency towards increased differentiation, complexity, and coherence (Greenberg, Watson, & Lietaer, 1998): *heterostasis* (a drive towards growth and change), as opposed to the Freudian emphasis on *homeostatis* (a drive towards balance, consistency, and the status quo) (Goldstein, 1940; Maslow, 1968; Rogers, 1959).

This highest-order direction towards growth is closely associated with a movement towards *authenticity* (Bugental, 1981; Rogers, 1961). This is about existing as the people that we really are: being intensely 'alive' (Ryan & Deci, 2001). It is also closely connected to the Jungian and transpersonal concept of *individuation* (e.g., Assagioli, 1965). This is 'a movement towards wholeness by means of an integration of conscious and unconscious parts of the personality' (Samuels, 1986, p. 102).

Autonomy/control

Autonomy features as a highest-order directions in nearly all the taxonomies presented in Table 6.1, and is viewed as the highest-order direction in several theoretical models (e.g., Angyal, 1941; Powers, 1992). Autonomy can be defined as 'being the perceived origin or source of one's own behavior' (Ryan & Deci, 2002, p. 8). This has been equated with a direction towards self-organisation and integrated functioning (Deci & Ryan, 2000). It is also similar to viewing 'control' as a highest-order motivating force (e.g., Grawe, 2004; Powers, 1992; Shapiro & Austin, 1998), or 'freedom' (de Beauvoir, 1948), which can be defined as 'the ability to make choices; to move around; to be independent; to feel unrestrained and unconfined' (Brickell & Wubbolding, 2000, p. 294). Control, in this context, is not about controlling others, but about being in control of our being in the world – and, for Powers, our perceptions. Here, then, it has been argued that we have a basic direction towards feeling in charge of our lives, not to be dominated and determined by others or things – even if it might bring us pleasure. This would explain many people's responses to Nozick's experience machine (see above), and is a point frequently made by *Star Trek's* Captain Kirk, who is willing to leave (or even destroy) civilisations that promise eternal happiness, but at the price of enslavement. Research provides some support for the importance of autonomy to wellbeing, showing that the two are closely associated (Reis, Sheldon, Gable, Roscoe, & Ryan, 2000; Sheldon, Ryan, & Reis, 1996).

From the philosophy of Nietzsche to contemporary psychology, 'power' has also been proposed as a highest-order human direction (McClelland & Burnham, 2008). To some extent, this goes beyond autonomy and control over the self, towards influencing others and the world around us.

Competence/self-worth

Competence can be defined as 'feeling effective in one's ongoing interactions with the social environment and experiencing opportunities to exercise and express one's capacities' (Ryan & Deci, 2002, p. 7). It is similar to 'self-worth' or 'self-esteem' (e.g., Brickell & Wubbolding, 2000; Maslow, 1987), which are widely hypothesised in the social psychological field to be powerful motivating forces (e.g., Mezulis, Abramson, Hyde, & Hankin, 2004). Competence is also closely related to achievement (McClelland & Burnham, 2008), which, as a highest-order direction, may be a particular trigger for virtuous and vicious cycles (see Chapter 4, this volume). Again, there is good evidence to support the association between feelings of competence and wellbeing (Reis et al., 2000; Sheldon et al., 1996).

Relatedness

Along with these 'self-oriented needs', it is hypothesised in each of the taxonomies that human beings have a fundamental direction towards interpersonal relatedness: for attachment, connectedness, affiliation, intimacy, or love (e.g., Baumeister & Leary, 1995; Bowlby, 1979; Glasser, 1965; McClelland & Burnham, 2008; Stern, 2004). Fromm (1957), for instance, writes, 'The deepest need of man … is the need to overcome his separateness, to leave the prison of his aloneness' (p. 14). This relatedness is the third of the basic needs in self-determination theory, and is defined as 'feeling connected to others, to caring for and being cared for by those others, to having a sense of belongingness both with other individuals and one's community' (Ryan & Deci, 2002, p. 8). Research suggests that this desire for relatedness may be the most powerful of human directions (Pöhlmann, 2001). Altruism and giving to others could also be seen as a component of this basic human striving (Pöhlmann, 2001) (see Box 5.1). An abundance of research shows that the achievement of relatedness is closely associated with wellbeing (see Mearns & Cooper, 2018; Reis et al., 2000; Sheldon et al., 1996). To the extent, however, that the desire for approval from others might be considered a means towards relatedness, this highest-order direction has also been conceptualised as the source of many psychological problems (see humanistic therapies, Chapter 11).

Safety

Although it is not made explicit in more contemporary psychological and therapeutic approaches, Maslow (1987) considered *safety* to be a basic human direction. This can include shelter from the elements, physical safety from others, and freedom from threat and psychological harm. More broadly, a desire for safety can be seen as underpinning all avoidance goals (see Chapter 5). It can also be seen as including a desire for stability, certainty, and order (Flanagan, 2010).

Physiological directions

From a therapeutic perspective, it may also be important to consider basic physiological directions as highest-order: for instance, for air, food, water, warmth, and sleep (Maslow, 1987). This may be helpful, for instance, when we consider somatically-related conditions such as anorexia, where there may be a conflict between the client's desire for control and their basic physiological striving for food. Physiological directions may also play an important role in trauma-related difficulties, where the body's instinctual, automatic drive towards survival may 'take over'.

Meaning and purpose

Although a highest-order direction towards meaning and purpose only features in the human givens taxonomy in Table 6.1, it is considered by many existential philosophers and therapists to be the most fundamental human desire (e.g., Frankl, 1967; van Deurzen, 2009). From this existential perspective, what we strive for most in our lives is to have a reason for why we are here and doing the things that we do. Other desires, like happiness, may be important but, from this standpoint, they are a means towards meaning and purpose, rather than highest-order direction in themselves. Support for this perspective can be seen in cases where 'people are quite willing to endure pain, deprivation, and other adverse events if there is some meaning such as a purpose or justification or an increase in self-worth' (Baumeister, 1991, p. 233). In the words of Nietzsche, 'He who has a *why* to live can bear with almost any *how* (in Frankl, 1984, p. 97).

If meaning and purpose are equated with direction, then to a great extent this existential perspective can be seen as the philosophical underpinnings of the present text (which is not surprising, perhaps, given my own existential background). That is, that the highest-order human direction is *to move in a direction*, and that this directionality is superordinate to any particular directional object: whether pleasure, autonomy, or relatedness. In other words, we are striving beings, and it is this desire to strive that sits atop of the structural hierarchy. We can strive for pleasure, or for mindfulness, or to win at Monopoly, but what is most fundamental in all these processes is that desire to move forward in some way.

Individual differences in highest-order directions

In each of the theories reviewed above, it tends to be assumed that highest-order directions are generalisable across cultures and individuals. Maslow (1943, 1987), for instance, argues that the basic, highest-order needs are universal, even if their manifestations are more culturally specific. Similarly, Glasser (1965) states, 'no one seriously disputes that in all cultures and in all degrees of civilization men have the same essential needs' (p. 9).

In recent years, however, this assumption has been seriously disputed. For instance, it has been argued that the needs, wants, and desires of people in Eastern and Western cultures vary, with the former tending to strive more for harmony and social integration, and the latter placing greater emphasis on individual autonomy and competence (Lago, 2005). Even within Western civilisation, Sorokin has argued that different meaning systems have dominated at different times: the *sensate* (a striving for physical and material pleasure); the *ideational* (a striving for ascetic, spiritual ends); and the *idealistic* (which 'combine an acceptance of concrete sensory experience with a reverence for spiritual ends', such as the Renaissance) (Sorokin, 1962, in Csikszentmihalyi,

2002, p. 220). It has also been argued that highest-order desires can vary across gender, with men placing more emphasis on autonomy and women valuing relatedness (Jordan, Walker, & Hartling, 2004). There may also be variations over the life course (Freund, 2007; Jacobsen, 2007), with people striving for what may be most normative at each age (e.g., excitement in one's 20s, family in one's 30s, and television box sets from one's 40s onwards).

There are also typologies which suggest that highest-order directions vary at the individual level. For instance, McClelland and Burnham (2008) argued that there were three basic human needs (see Box 6.1), and that people could be categorised according to the one that is most dominant. Similarly, Allport argued that there were six types of people, defined by their principal life goals (Allport, 1961, in Jacobsen, 2007). These were the *theoretical person*, whose goal is to discover truth; the *economic person*, whose goal is to use things and create profit; the *aesthetic person*, who is oriented towards form and harmony in things; the *social person*, who focuses on cultivating love and affinity with others; the *political person*, who seeks power; and the *religious person*, who seeks unity with something behind the everyday world.

Idiographic highest-order directions

Although the above models assume that individuals vary in their highest-order directions, they still assume that the highest-order directions that do exist are consistent across people. A yet more idiographic approach is the assertion that different individuals have different highest-order directions, and that the nature of these directions may vary from person to person (and may be 'given' to us, see Web Resource 6.1). So, from this perspective, one person's highest-order directions may be to feel excited, to feel free from anxiety, and to experience financial security, while another's may be to experience belongingness, to have excitement, and to experience passion in their lives. Silberschatz (2017) advocates such a position, arguing that 'individual needs or goals vary considerably' (p. 2). Hence, 'Patients who share the same diagnosis often differ in a variety of substantive ways' (p. 2). This emphasis on the individual uniqueness of human directions is also the essence of the pluralistic approach to therapy (Cooper & Dryden, 2016; Cooper & McLeod, 2007, 2011; Chapter 1, this volume), which draws from the pluralistic philosophical assumption that 'individuality outruns all classification' (James, 1996, p. 3).

An absence of highest-order directions

A very different viewpoint from the ones summarised in Box 6.1, and again associated with an existential perspective, is that, ultimately, there are no highest-order directions (Camus, 1955; Heidegger, 1962; Sartre, 1958). Sartre (1996), for instance, states that 'life has no meaning *a priori*. Before you come alive, life is nothing, it's up to you to give it a meaning, and value is nothing else but the meaning that you choose' (p. 264). In terms of the present framework, what this means is that, while we can go up the vertical hierarchies, we can never get to the 'top'. That is, to a point that is fixed and stable, to which the question 'Why?' yields an answer of ultimate, intrinsic value. This is illustrated in Figure 6.7, with the arrows ascending from pleasure, competence, and safety into a void. So, for instance, we might say that you are reading this book to become a better therapist, and you want to become a better therapist to help people more effectively, and you want to help people because it gives you a sense of relatedness to others. But so what? What is the ultimate meaning or value of this relatedness?

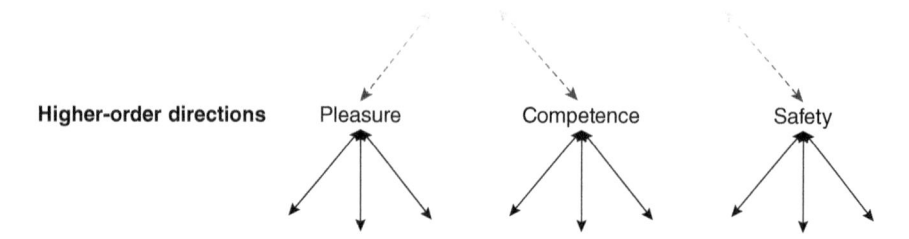

Figure 6.7 An absence of highest-order directions

For existentialists like Camus (1955), this lack of ultimate purpose makes our lives 'absurd'. Like the mythological figure Sisyphus, who is condemned – for all eternity – to push a boulder up a hill only to watch it roll back down again, we strive and struggle without any ultimate reason for doing so. Yet Camus, like his fellow existentialists, does not see this as a reason for despair or demoralisation. Rather, he argues, we can live our lives 'without appeal' (p. 64), engaging deeply in the whirlwind of everyday activity, all the while acknowledging its lack of ultimate foundation. Csikszentmihalyi (2002), the positive psychologist, expresses something similar when he states: 'It is one thing to realise that life is, by itself, meaningless. It is another thing entirely to accept this with resignation. The first fact does not entail the second any more than the fact that we lack wings prevents us from flying' (p. 215).

Discussion: 'Let a thousand highest-order directions bloom'

As we have seen in Table 6.1, across a range of different theories and frameworks, eight highest-order directions have been proposed. No doubt, this taxonomy could be refined and reduced further, and it may be that some of these directions are subordinate to others or vary in their intensity across individuals. Here, further research is required.

From a therapeutic standpoint, however, perhaps a question of greater importance than the empirical one is an ethical one (see Chapter 1). For even if science could show that one direction, *in general*, was of a higher order than the others, most therapists would still want to respect the particular highest-order directions that a client claimed as their own? That is, if a client said that what they wanted most in life was happiness, or intimacy, or faith, few therapists would want to dispute this. Indeed, to do so would be to go against the ethical principle of *autonomy*: a respect for the client's right to be self-governing (British Association for Counselling and Psychotherapy, 2018). More broadly, as the philosopher Berlin (2003, p. 11) states, the basis of a democratic society is *value pluralism*: that people are allowed to establish their own ends, without any one highest-order direction being imposed on us all. As Berlin writes, 'To force people into the neat uniforms demanded by dogmatically believed-in schemes is almost always the road to inhumanity' (Berlin, 2003, p. 19).

The research and theory discussed in this part of the chapter, then, may be very helpful in identifying the kinds of highest-order directions that clients may have. But, ultimately, we may need to leave unanswered the question of whether any one direction, or set of directions, is the highest-order one for all. In other words, we can have many different theories of what clients are striving for, and these may be helpful in formulating an understanding of their lives, but, as therapists, we have an ethical duty to 'make the world safe for disagreement' (Rescher, 1993, p. 5). This means being open to whatever highest-order directions our clients have – provided they do not impede the highest-order directions of others (see Chapter 9, this volume).

QUESTIONS FOR REFLECTION

- Starting with a basic direction (like completing this book), construct for yourself a vertical hierarchy indicating how you are doing it (i.e., lower-order directions) and what it is for (i.e., higher-order directions). Now add to that structural diagram one example of equifinality (where one goal has multiple means towards it) and multifinality (where one means is able to achieve multiple goals).
- What do you consider are your highest-order direction(s): the one(s) that other directions lead to (for instance, pleasure, relatedness)? To what extent do you think that everyone else has the same highest-order direction?
- Red pill or blue pill: Which would you choose to take?

FURTHER READING

Ford, M. E. (1992). *Motivating humans: Goals, emotions, and personal agency beliefs.* Newbury Park, CA: Sage. Integrates a range of models and understandings of goal processes, proposing Motivational Systems Theory.

Mansell, W. (2005). Control theory and psychopathology: An integrative approach. *Psychology and Psychotherapy: Theory, Research and Practice, 78*(2) 141-178. doi:10.1348/147608304 X21400. A concise summary of control theory and its potential contribution to therapeutic thinking and practice.

Michalak, J., Heidenreich, T., & Hoyer, J. (2004). Goal conflicts: Concepts, findings, and consequences for psychotherapy. In W. M. Cox & E. Klinger (Eds.), *Handbook of motivational counseling* (pp. 83-97). New York: John Wiley. A valuable review of theory, research, and practice on goal conflicts.

Powers, W. T. (1973). *Behavior: The control of perception.* Chicago, IL: Aldine. The original perceptual control theory text. Very detailed in places, but essential reading for those interested in this approach.

7

EFFECTIVENESS

Better ways of getting to where we want to be

This chapter discusses:

- The importance of *vertical coherence* within a structural hierarchy: that lower-order directions are *effective* means of achieving higher-order ends.
- The reasons why lower-order means may be *ineffective*, and the links between this and psychological difficulties.

In Chapter 3, the question was raised as to why a directional being would fail to actualise its directions. That chapter provided a provisional answer to this question. However, the structural model presented in Chapter 6 provides the basis for developing a much richer and more comprehensive answer. As we saw here, there are two types of links between directions: vertical ones and horizontal ones. And, as has been argued, both need to be 'coherent' for optimal psychological functioning (Sheldon & Kasser, 1995). This chapter focuses on *vertical coherence*, and horizontal coherence will be examined in Chapter 8.

Vertical coherence, or *effectiveness* (Brown, 2008), refers to the extent that a lower-order means is able to bring about a higher-order goal. As Sheldon and Kasser (1998) write, 'an action system is optimally configured when purposes at higher levels of the system are readily served by behavioral competencies at lower levels of the system' (p. 1319). If I want to reduce my levels of anxiety, for instance, it is effective for me to go out for a run. Nearly every time I do it, I feel calmer and more relaxed afterwards. On the other hand, ruminating on the thing that I am worried about – albeit an intelligible strategy to try to resolve my worries – is almost always ineffective. It does not reduce my levels of anxiety; if anything, it makes them worse. Indeed, in object relations terms, we could say this behaviour is not only ineffective but 'self-defeating' (Greenberg & Mitchell, 1983). To use the analogy of travelling, ineffective strategies are like trying to get from London to Rome by boarding a flight to Bucharest (Alsleben & Kuhl, 2011). We take ourselves in the wrong direction, and then may have to spend time and effort getting ourselves back on track.

Alongside effectiveness, we might also talk about the 'efficiency' or 'inefficiency' of particular means of actualising our directions (Dryden, 1999; Powers, 1992). A lower-order means, for instance, may be able to actualise a higher-order direction at some point, but if it takes a considerable amount of time and effort to do so, then it may not be a particular profitable approach. In perceptual control theory terms, efficiency can be operationalised as the amount of effort required to reduce a given amount of error (between perception and reference standard).

In support of the hypothesis that vertical coherence is associated with optimal functioning, Sheldon and Kasser (1995) found that people who rated their strivings as more helpful in taking them towards desired futures – self-acceptance, intimacy, and societal contribution – had greater positive affect, vitality, and self-esteem. They also scored higher on a scale of self-actualisation. Similarly, reviewing the evidence, Diener and Lucas (1999) stated that 'people with high SWB [subjective wellbeing] are those who have developed effective strategies for meeting their needs within the constraints of cultural expectations and life circumstances' (p. 224).

'That's so rank', grinned Logan, sitting back in his chair, 'I knew she'd never go with me.' Logan is a second client that will be discussed in this book. Seventeen years old, pale skin, with blond hair shaved at the sides and fading into a longer top, Logan was referred to counselling by his GP for a range of anxiety problems. Most days, Logan would be late for college because of his morning 'rituals', such as repeatedly checking he has closed his front door and walking particular routes through his estate. Being with Logan was like being next to a dynamo – constantly moving, whirring, and active – but he also had a gentleness and honesty that was endearing, particularly when he let his 'ghetto' persona drop.

Logan was desperate to overcome his various anxieties and get on with his life – he wanted to train as an architect and produced beautiful, delicate pencil sketches that he would sometimes bring to sessions – but when he recounted his week at the start of each counselling session, the issue that seemed to concern him most was his difficulties in finding a girlfriend. Here, we might hypothesise that Logan, like many of us, has a highest-order desire for relatedness, and establishing a relationship with a young woman seemed a potentially effective means of trying to actualise this. However, what he then did to actualise this goal seemed less effective. For instance, he described how, when he went to parties, he and his closest friends tended to cluster around a television screen, playing *Grand Theft Auto* (*GTA*) or other console games, with a vague hope that the young women there would be interested and impressed. And, in the few instances that he did directly talk to young women, Logan described how he went into 'jokey' mode, teasing them about their clothes or make-up, or making fun of how they danced. For Logan, this was a genuine and intelligible way of trying to get closer to the young women around him. However, through discussing it in therapy, Logan was beginning to recognise that it was not having the desired effect on the young women around him. What Logan and his counsellor started to discuss, then, was more effective strategies for reaching his higher-order goals. 'You know,' the therapist said to Logan, 'maybe– it works with your mates, but maybe those women don't like it when you tease them. Maybe you could try a more in depth conversation.'

'About what?' said Logan.

'Maybe– I don't know,' said the therapist, 'maybe about you? About them? Being honest. I can see that's such a– you're really good at connecting, Logan, when you tell me about what's really going on. Even when you talk about your anxieties. And also, maybe, you know, listening to where they're at.'

The different strategies that Logan might use to establish relationships with women are illustrated in Figure 7.1. On the left, Figure 7.1(a), are his relatively ineffective strategies, presented as thin lines. On the right, Figure 7.1(b), are those that may be more effective in helping him reach his higher-order directions.

Logan's door-checking ritual provides a second example of vertical incoherence, but within the more intrapersonal domain. Logan, we might hypothesise, has a highest-order direction towards feeling safe and, as part of that, wants to reduce his levels of anxiety. So when he starts to feel anxious because he is not completely sure that he closed his front door, his strategy is to return to his flat and check it. Such 'safety-seeking behaviour', again, is intelligible, and effective in reducing short-term anxiety ('Phew, I did lock the door'), but ineffective in the long-term because it increases his

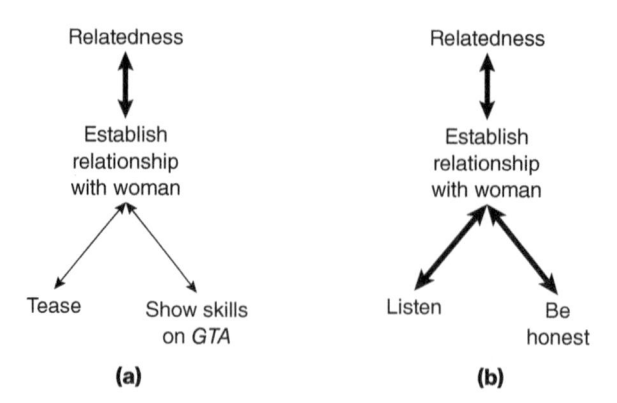

Figure 7.1 (a) Ineffective and (b) potentially effective means of progressing towards higher-order wants

Note: Line thickness indicates effectiveness of means

reliance on reassurance-seeking behaviours (Moorey, 2014). By contrast, if Logan tried to 'stay with' his anxiety and not act on it – through, for instance, a CBT programme of 'exposure and response prevention' – Logan might learn that the anxiety jangling within him will dissipate of its own accord and 'safety behaviours' are not required.

Vertical incoherence means that, at times, people may behave in ineffective, inefficient, and self-defeating ways. However, as we have seen with Logan, this does not contradict the basic principle of intelligibility (Chapter 2): that there are reasons why people do the things that they do. As people, it can be argued, we are always striving to do our best, but doing our best is not always the best thing that we can be doing. Brown (2008) makes a similar point when she writes, 'all persons make attempts to solve the problems of their existence, but that not all strategies work as well as others' (p. 286).

How is it, then, that a being whose actions are intelligible and oriented towards higher-order desires and goals can end up adopting ineffective strategies?

LACK OF AWARENESS OF HIGHEST-ORDER DIRECTIONS

A first possibility, flagged up when discussing the awareness phase of the directional arc (Chapter 3), may be that a person simply does not know what their higher-order directions are; and, without that knowledge, they may be less able to get there. Does Logan, for instance, know that he wants relatedness in his life? Yes and no. He is aware that he gets very lonely at times, and that he loves spending time with his friends, but he also finds it difficult to consciously acknowledge – to himself and to others – that he really longs for deeper connections with others: both male and female. Without that awareness, Logan still strives for relatedness: it is, after all, a deeper, embodied direction. But the lack of conscious recognition means that Logan is less able to muster his intelligence, his skills, and his willpower to achieve this highest-order goal.

Research and clinical experience suggests that many people may not have a strong sense of their highest-order directions (e.g., di Malta, Cooper, & Oddli, 2018; Steger, Frazier, Oishi, & Kaler, 2006). In addition, as we saw in Chapter 5, what they believe they want may not actually be what they want. When Logan was asked at assessment what he wanted in his life, for instance, his immediate response was to raise his eyebrows with a 'knowing look', as if to intimate 'I want sex'. Through therapy, however, it soon emerged that Logan was actually very nervous about sex, had found it a fumbling and disheartening experience, and was much more concerned about approval from – and relatedness with – his friends. However, by consciously setting himself 'sex' as his primary objective, Logan was mobilising himself towards self-attributed goals that did not really bring him satisfaction, and neglecting those implicit goals that really could have enhanced his wellbeing.

LACK OF AWARENESS OF EFFECTIVE MEANS

A second reason people may not use effective strategies is simply because they do not know what those strategies are. Why should we expect Logan, for instance, to know that the young women he is trying to get close to may be more likely to respond to listening and conversation than teasing? No one has told him that; and given that his friends respond positively to his teasing (as he does), it is not unreasonable of him to assume that the young women he meets will respond similarly. Equally, there is no reason why he should know that checking and re-checking his front door is likely to make his compulsive behaviour worse. In fact, the strategy that is most likely to be effective (learning to bear his anxieties) is also the most counterintuitive.

Such an analysis is relatively consistent with cognitive-behavioural thinking, which uses 'psychoeducation' to teach clients effective strategies for actualising their directions (see Chapter 13). But how does it fit with a more humanistic perspective, with its emphasis on the client as an active self-healer (Bohart & Tallman, 1999)? One way of reconciling this is to suggest that, at the highest orders, directions are likely to reflect an organism's intrinsic sense of what is most maintaining and enhancing: the *organismic valuing tendency* (Rogers, 1959). In other words, intuitively, we probably do sense what brings us relatedness, competence, or pleasure – and no 'expert' can ever tell us what this is. However, as one goes down to more practical, 'in-the-world' means and strategies, there is less reason why an organism should 'know' what is the best way of acting. As the humanistic psychologist Sheldon (2001) writes, 'innate motivational tendencies carry little information about what to do – the specific direction of behavior depends on the past learning, the person's current situation, and the person's self-perceptual skill'. He goes on to write:

> Although the non-specificity of the basic motives may be quite functional because it provides many degrees of freedom for individuals to adapt to particular environmental circumstances, this lack of specificity or structure may also represent a point of vulnerability. In other words, it provides ample room for us to 'go wrong' in our motivated behavior (from a well-being or developmental standpoint), without clearly realizing it. (p. 31)

This means that, to develop effective means of actualising our highest-order directions, we need to develop accurate knowledge of both our inner and outer worlds. Logan, for instance, needs to learn that the more he tries to avoid his anxiety, the stronger it becomes; and he also needs to learn that real young women, out there in the world, may not be particularly impressed by his skills at *GTA*. Therapies like CBT encourage us to develop a greater understanding of intrapersonal dynamics, while others, such as reality therapy (Glasser, 1965) or interpersonal therapy (Stuart & Robertson, 2012), try to help us gain a more realistic understanding of others and the world outside (see Chapter 13).

Not only may we be missing the critical information that we need to actualise our highest-order directions, we may also be misinformed. As with Logan, for instance, we may believe that x will lead to y, when actually it leads to its opposite: $-y$. Such misinformation may emerge for a host of reasons: for instance, because people have told us the wrong things (for many years I was terrified of visiting Switzerland because my dad had told me, when I was four years old, that the Swiss imprison you for dropping litter), because we have made erroneous assumptions, or because we want to protect ourselves from emotional pain. As an example of the latter, Yalom (1980) describes how people may develop a belief in an 'ultimate rescuer' to defend themselves from the fear of death.

CHILDHOOD EXPERIENCES

As with my perceptions of Switzerland, a particularly pervasive and powerful source of inaccurate knowledge – and, consequently, ineffective means of actualising our highest-order directions – may be childhood experiences. Silberschatz (2017) gives the example of a female client who grew up with an extremely narcissistic father who 'needed his children to always see things his way' (p. 5). Consequently, the client 'developed the pathogenic belief that in order to maintain a relationship – particularly with a man – she needed to subjugate herself and her wishes' (p. 5). Here, what we see is a client who has learnt to see, and act towards, her world in a particular way. And, as a child, this was quite accurate: the client's father was a narcissist, and therefore she probably did need to subjugate herself to him to receive the higher-order relatedness that she wanted. But the inaccuracy comes from carrying over this belief from the past to the present: of assuming that people in her current world are the same as her father. As an intelligible being, there is every reason why she should make this assumption – after all, what else can you draw on if not your past – but it is nonetheless inaccurate to her present circumstances.

Note, as with this example, that although the client's 'pathogenic' belief is at the core of her difficulties, it is only problematic because it shapes her means of trying to actualise a higher-order direction. If, for instance, the client did not want relatedness in her life – say, for example, that all she wanted was to be the world's greatest marathon runner – then her assumptions about men would be unlikely to affect her wellbeing. So the inaccuracy of her cognitions only matters because it mediates how she goes about striving towards her highest-order desires and goals. From the present perspective (and somewhat in contrast to cognitive theory), wrong beliefs *per se* are not the problem. The problem is when we have the wrong beliefs for actualising a particular goal.

SOCIALISATION

As was suggested in Web Resource 2.2, society may be increasingly bombarding us with information about what we want, and how we should go about getting it. Television shows like the *X-Factor*, for instance, teach us that fame is a worthy and 'normal' highest-order direction. No wonder, then, that when I ask my 13-year-old daughter Shula what she wants to do in her life, she simply says 'be famous'.

'Famous for what?' I ask.

'Dad,' she replies irritably, 'it really doesn't matter. Just famous.' (And I suspect that having this book dedicated to her isn't going to count!)

Meanwhile, makeup tutorials on YouTube teach girls that happiness comes from a well-applied blusher; and boys, like Logan, learn that gaming brings popularity and success.

Such socialisation is not problematic in itself. I know from my eldest daughter, Maya, for instance, that the process of putting on makeup can be intrinsically rewarding and creative – something that does genuinely bring her happiness. Indeed, as I argued in Chapter 2, even our highest-order directions may be inseparable from the world around us. But the problem comes where a person is socialised into adopting means that, for them, do not actually help them actualise the intended higher-order direction. Logan, for instance, smokes cannabis with his friends because he has 'learnt' that it brings pleasure and relaxation, but actually it does not. It makes him more anxious and on edge. Here, Logan has become ineffective at progressing towards his highest-order goals because he is doing it in ways that, while potentially effective for other people, do not work for him. This is consistent with the theory and research on extrinsic goals (see Chapter 5) and the person-centred view that psychological difficulty arises when we act towards external values rather than our own intrinsic sense of what is right for us (e.g., Rogers, 1961).

COGNITIVE ERRORS

Sometimes, the reason that we adopt ineffective strategies is less to do with our knowledge of the world around us, and more to do with the way that we think about it.

Take, for instance, Logan's choice of smoking cannabis. As we have seen, in reality, it makes him feel more anxious. However, when he reflects on this experience – deciding, for instance, on whether to meet his friends again for a smoke – what is most salient (alongside his socialised belief that he enjoys it, see above), is his memories of a few brief moments of intense 'high', and also his feeling of accomplishment and relief as he 'comes down'. This tendency to overestimate peak and end states when evaluating an experience is just one example of 'irrational', 'dysfunctional', 'distorted', or 'erroneous' thinking, which has been a principal focus of cognitive psychology and the applied field of cognitive and rational emotive behaviour therapy (REBT) (e.g., Beck et al., 1979; Dryden, 1999). Note, as with other ineffective strategies, 'irrational' here does not mean that such thinking processes are unintelligible or non-intentional (Dennett, 1987). Rather, the claim is that they are: (a) unhelpful for the person in achieving their higher-order goals (i.e., ineffective), (b) illogical, and (c) inconsistent with the empirical reality (Dryden, 1999, 2014).

We will explore the rationale behind irrational thoughts later on in this chapter. However, much of it can be understood in terms of the use of *heuristics* in our thinking processes. A heuristic is a cognitive shortcut, 'a simple procedure that helps find adequate, though often imperfect, answers to difficult questions' (Kahneman, 2011, p. 98). In effect, heuristic thinking involves 'jumping to conclusions': inferring patterns and order when actually the reality is much more complex. So, for instance, when Logan reflects on his experience of being stoned, he quickly averages the peak and the end experiences to work out what it is like, rather than carefully and systematically surveying the whole of his experience. In many instances, this would not be a bad way of estimating what his experience is like. However, as in this case, there can often be a sizeable gulf between estimation and reality, and this can lead the person to adopt strategies that are not effective at actualising their higher-order directions.

As with this 'peak–end rule', heuristic strategies tend to use the most salient, immediate, and easily accessible features of a situation or experience to judge the whole. So we don't think deeply about a situation and 'look behind the scenes'. Rather, we work on the principle of WYSIATI: What You See Is All There Is (Kahneman, 2011). Examples of such heuristics include:

- *Going on appearances.* We base our decisions on how things look. So, for instance, we think that someone who smiles at us is 'nice and friendly', without considering the many 'behind the scenes' reasons why they may be smiling.
- *Stereotypical thinking.* Attributing features to a whole group of individuals, based on common (and usually superficial) characteristics.
- *Availability heuristic.* Our judgements are influenced by the ease with which things can be brought to mind. If we have seen a friend die of bowel cancer, for instance, we may overestimate the likelihood of this event for ourselves.

- *The focusing illusion.* Things that are in our mind take on greater importance and significance than they might otherwise have. This may be at the root of many anxiety-related vicious cycles, where we worry about something, it looms larger in our mind, and we worry more.
- *Affect heuristic/emotional reasoning.* Our judgements are influenced by the emotions that we experience. When we feel tired, for instance, we may assess a colleague as more irritating than when we are in a relaxed state of mind.
- *Over-optimism.* We can be overly confident of the outcome we are hoping for, because it is so present in our mind, and consequently under-plan: 'I'm sure it will just work out.'
- *Framing effects.* Our judgements are shaped by the context within which something is presented. For instance, we are more likely to choose a meal that is '95% fat-free' than '5% full of fat'.
- *Over-estimation of rare events.* Unlikely, but thrilling, possibilities – like winning the lottery – can seem more likely because of their salience. Equally, negative rare events (like losing all the back-ups for one's files) can seem more likely than they actually are.
- *The sunk cost fallacy.* We may keep working towards a goal, even though it is a 'lost cause', because we are so aware of the effort we have already put in (and less aware of the wasted effort to come).
- *Loss aversion.* Losses may be weighed more heavily than gains, because of the salience (for evolutionary reasons, perhaps) of threat (Kahneman, 2011; Layard, 2006).

From a cognitive psychology perspective, everyone uses such heuristics to some degree. Indeed, it has been suggested that human beings are natural 'cognitive misers' (Taylor, 1981); without such short-cuts in thinking, it would be impossible to consider all the things we need to on a daily basis. Moreover, as research shows, rational, deliberate thinking is hard work – there is evidence of it drawing upon mental resources ('ego depletion'; Vohs & Baumeister, 2004; see Web Resource 7.1), such that, in some circumstances, the benefits of getting the right answer may be outweighed by the costs of further calculations (Dennett, 1987). However, from the standpoint of cognitive therapy, an over-dependence on such simplistic, 'primitive' thinking processes ('System 1', as opposed to the more rational, effortful, and conscious 'System 2'; Kahneman, 2011) may be a key factor in the aetiology (i.e., development) and maintenance of psychological problems. Within a specifically therapeutic context, cognitive and REBT therapists have particularly focused on the following, interrelated distortions (illustrated with quotes from Logan):

- *Overgeneralisation.* Drawing a general rule on the basis of isolated experiences: e.g., 'There's no point trying to talk to people at my college about stuff – I started opening up to my tutor yesterday and he was really busy'.

- *Arbitrary inference.* Drawing conclusions in the absence of evidence: e.g., 'Women find me really attractive when they see me doing well on *GTA*'.
- *Selective abstraction.* Taking a negative detail out of context without considering the 'bigger picture': e.g., 'I messed up so bad when I got out of the car and started shooting [on *GTA*]. People at the party thought I was such a dope'.
- *Magnification/minimisation.* Errors in evaluating the significance of an event: e.g., 'I went up to Jeannie at the party and she told me to "stop taking the piss" – I think she was just making a big deal out of it: I was being cool'.
- *Catastrophising/awfulising.* Magnifying how terrible an outcome is. 'Jeannie walked off after a bit and didn't come back. Honest. It was just the worst. I felt SO bad'.
- *Either/or (dichotomous) thinking.* Placing experiences in one of two opposing categories: e.g., 'I need people to see me as "sorted", because otherwise they'll think I'm a complete twat'.
- *Personalisation.* Taking things personally: e.g., 'I'm sure Jeannie left the party because of me'.
- *Should statements/musturbation.* Telling yourself that things have to be a certain way: e.g., 'I must have a girlfriend to be valued by my friends' (Beck et al., 1979; Dolan, 2014; McCormick, 2012; Neenan, 2000; Palmer & Neenan, 2000; Reinecke & Freeman, 2003).

To some extent, all these forms of distorted and heuristic thinking might be considered a manifestation of one fundamental miscalculation: *delay discounting* (Correia et al., 2011). This is where we underestimate the value of longer-term benefits (Klinger & Cox, 2011), and instead over-value such short-term rewards as cognitive ease and lack of effort. This may be because short-term rewards feel more immediate, visceral, and salient; or because longer-term rewards, being further off, feel less certain, tangible, and specific (Correia et al., 2011). Either way, by under-prioritising longer-term directions and over-prioritising shorter-term ones, we may essentially end up with 'what we paid for': pleasure or ease in the short-term, but a lack of a more sustained and longer-term actualisation of goals.

CHRONIC INEFFECTIVE STRATEGIES

Whatever their source, what makes ineffective strategies so potentially problematic is not their ineffectiveness *per se*. If, for instance, Logan tried impressing women with *GTA*, realised that they were not particularly impressed by it, and then went on to try something else, then his initial approach – however irrational – might not be too problematic. So the key issue is that Logan keeps on using a strategy that is not working: he is failing to be sufficiently equifinal or plastic. Here, then, we can refer to the ineffective strategy as *chronic*. That is, it has become an automatic, 'default' strategy, triggered across a range of contexts and generally operating at an unconscious level (Bargh, 1990; Moskowitz, 2012).

But why might ineffective strategies become chronic? One explanation may be that our natural cognitive miserliness means that we shy away from the mental work of developing new strategies to reach our goals (Dolan, 2014). Hence, even if our strategies are not working, we may be reluctant – consciously or unconsciously – to expend effort to change or to see things in a different way. If Logan, for instance, wanted to develop a new – and potentially better – way of attracting young women, he might need to go through a period of in-depth reflection, reconsider his current strategies, and look at what he could do differently in future. Affectively, too, he might need to face such feelings as shame and despair, in acknowledging he was getting things wrong. In many ways, then, it may be tempting for Logan, or for any of us, to keep going with our default, 'tried-and-trusted' approach – however ineffective it might be – rather than seeking something new. This may be particularly the case if we do not have any idea of where else to start from, or if we do not even know whether 'better' possibilities exist.

CONTEXTUAL FACTORS

In this section, we have focused primarily on the psychological factors that may make people more or less able to actualise their higher-order directions through lower-order means. However, as discussed in Chapter 2, directional processes are never 'internal' alone: they are always in relation to a world. This means that no means, in themselves, are ever wholly 'effective' or 'ineffective'. Rather, their adequacy 'can be judged only with reference to a particular situational environment' (Caspar, 1995, p. 66). Were it the case, for instance, that the young women who went to Logan's parties did actually care about *GTA* – and admired people who did well on it – then playing it at parties might be an extremely effective means for Logan to reach his goals. To a great extent, then, effectiveness comes down to 'fittedness': to what extent are our strategies suitable for the particular environment that we are in?

Even with the most fitted strategies, however, the degree to which we will actualise our directions remains highly dependent on our contexts (Grawe, 2004). As a young child, for instance, Mei wanted to feel safe at school, and the way she tried to achieve this was by disconnecting, emotionally, from those around her. Given the racism that she encountered, this was probably a highly effective, fitted strategy. However, she still did not feel as safe as she wanted to (and had a right to), because her context continued to be threatening and discriminatory. This point is critical because it means that, when we look at ways of helping people to actualise their directions, we also need to consider change at the social and political level as well as at the intrapersonal one. We will explore this more fully in Chapter 16.

CONCLUSION

Based on the structural model of directionality introduced in Chapter 6, this chapter has argued that one of the main reasons why people may fail to actualise their highest-order directions is because their means for doing so are ineffective. This may be due to a lack of awareness, learning the wrong things from parents or society, or because of an over-reliance on cognitive short-cuts. These processes would not be problematic if the person could revise and adjust their strategies in more effective directions, but if they are chronically attached to ineffective strategies, psychological difficulties may result. We should not forget, however, the importance of contextual factors in determining, ultimately, whether a strategy is effective or not.

In Chapter 1, I stated that the aim of this book was not to create a new and improved brand of therapy, but to describe a conceptual framework that can integrate together many different therapeutic approaches. I hope that this is becoming clearer in the present chapter. That is, that although the terminology may be new – with, for instance, 'directions', 'effectiveness', and 'structural hierarchies' – what is being drawn on and brought together are pre-existing concepts from the therapeutic field. However, rather than opposing these concepts – contrasting, for instance, the role of childhood experiences (from a psychodynamic approach) against cognitive errors (from a CBT approach) – what is being proposed is a means of aligning them. That is, helping clients find better ways of getting to where they want to be might involve analysing early relational learnings, and it might also involve identifying cognitive errors: a stance of *both/and*, rather than *either/or*.

QUESTIONS FOR REFLECTION

- To what extent do you think that ineffective means towards goals accounts for people's psychological difficulties?
- Identify a higher-order direction in your life and the means through which you try to actualise it. Being honest with yourself, how effective is this strategy? Are there better ways in which you could be doing it?

FURTHER READING

Kahneman, D. (2011). *Thinking, fast and slow*. London: Penguin. A best-selling, highly-accessible analysis of irrational thinking processes.

8
SYNERGIES ARE GOOD

This chapter discusses:

- *Synergetic* relationships: where the actualiaston of one direction facilitates the actualisation of another.
- *Dysergetic* relationships: where the actualisation of one direction impedes the actualisation of another.
- *Rogue goals*.
- The sources of dysergetic relationships between directions.

As we have seen, across similar levels in a directional structure, multiple desires and goals may exist. Riediger (2007) suggests three types of relationships between goals – *interference, facilitation,* and *independence* – and this is largely consistent with other theorising in this field (e.g., Little, 1983). Interestingly, research here suggests that goal interference and goal facilitation are independent dimensions, rather than opposite ends of a single pole (e.g., Boudreaux & Ozer, 2013). That is, two directions can both facilitate each other and interfere with each other. For instance, 'eating nice food' may help someone towards their goal of 'happiness', but it might also work against the latter goal by being a fattening pursuit.

SYNERGIES

A facilitative relationship between directions means that 'the pursuit of one goal simultaneously increases the likelihood of reaching another goal' (Wiese & Salmela-Aro, 2008, p. 490). This has also been termed 'horizontal coherence' (Sheldon & Kasser, 1995, p. 532), 'positive spillover' (Wiese & Salmela-Aro, 2008), or 'goal alignment' (Ford, 1992). In the language of the wider social sciences field, it is synonymous with *synergetic* relationships (Corning, 2003), and is also termed *non-zero-sum* (Wright, 2000), 'win–win', or 'cooperative' relationships (Axelrod, 1984) (see Chapter 9, this volume). We saw an example of a synergetic relationship between directions in Chapter 6, where relatedness with Saul also brought Mei sexual pleasure and intellectual stimulation. Operationally, we can say that a synergetic relationship exists between Direction x and Direction y if the means of actualising Direction x facilitates the actualisation of Direction y, and/or vice versa. This also means that either Means x (the means towards x), or Means y, is *multifinal*.

Because of its pan-disciplinary usage, the term *synergy* will be adopted to refer to such mutually beneficial inter-directional relationships (Corning, 1998). The term comes from the Greek 'sun' (together) and 'ergon' (work), and is commonly understood as the principle that the whole is greater than the sum of its parts (Corning, 2003; Katz & Murphy-Shigematsu, 2012). Synergy, then, can be defined as 'the interaction or cooperation of two or more organizations, substances, or other agents to produce a combined effect greater than the sum of their separate effects' (*English Oxford Living Dictionaries*). Striving towards x brings more of y, and/or vice versa, so that the combined $x + y$ is more than the sum of striving for either in isolation. Corning (2003) refers to synergies as 'nature's magic', in that they create 'something out of nothing'. If you can do things in synergetic ways – if, for instance, getting your hair cut also means getting to offload your problems to your hairdresser also means getting a decent cup of coffee – then you are getting something more than if each direction was in isolation.

Synergetic relationships between directions can be *synchronic* or *diachronic*. A synchronic relationship is one in which the synergy happens at one time, as in the above example of getting your hair cut. A diachronic synergetic relationship unfolds over time, so that the actualisation of one direction now helps the actualisation of another direction at a later point. For instance, to calm himself down, Logan starts to learn basic mindfulness techniques in therapy. And this has the added advantage that, when he goes to parties, he is now slower and more thoughtful when he talks to young women.

Given that a synergetic relationship between goals, by definition, leads to a greater overall actualisation of directions, it seems reasonable to assume that intrapersonal synergies will be associated with greater psychological wellbeing. Several authors within the therapy field have proposed such a hypothesis (e.g., Berne, 1961; Cooper & Cruthers, 1999; Elliott & Greenberg, 1997; Epstein, 1994; Hermans, 2001; Stone & Winkelman, 1989; Vargiu, 1974). Epstein (1994), for instance, writes, 'good adjustment is fostered by fulfilment of ... basic needs in a synergistic, harmonious manner' (p. 716), and he goes on to state, 'The task of therapy is to ... promote synergistic (rather than conflictual) need fulfilment' (p. 717). Psychological researchers, too, have argued that 'harmony and integrated functioning among one's goals are essential for subjective well-being' (Emmons, 1986, p. 1065). Indeed, Seligman (2002, p. 257) suggests that human beings may have an innate capacity to experience positive affect in the presence of win–win relationships.

Some research supports this view. For instance, Wiese and Salmela-Aro (2008) found that participants who perceive their family goals as facilitating their work goals experience greater satisfaction in these domains. However, to date, the majority of studies have found limited evidence of a significant relationship between inter-directional facilitation and wellbeing (Riediger, 2007; Sheldon & Kasser, 1995; Wiese & Salmela-Aro, 2008). What does seem clear, however, is that the more synergetic a person's goals, the more they tend 'to engage in goal directed actions' (Riediger & Freund, 2004), including commitment to therapy (Michalak, Heidenreich, & Hoyer, 2011). This is consistent with Ford's (1992) view that people are more motivated when an action leads to multiple positive outcomes. What is also interesting to note is that horizontal coherence is significantly correlated with vertical coherence (Sheldon & Kasser, 1995). In other words, people whose goals are working together also seem more effective at working towards their goals.

DYSERGIES

The opposite of synergetic relationships between directions is what can be called *dysergetic* relationships (Cooper, 2012; Corning, 2003). This is widely termed *goal conflict*, and can also be described as 'interfering', 'blocking', 'competing', or 'win–lose' relationships between goals (Austin & Vancouver, 1996; Michalak & Grosse Holtforth, 2006; Powers, 1973; Wiese & Salmela-Aro, 2008). Here, 'a goal that a person wishes to accomplish interferes with the attainment of at least one other goal that the individual simultaneously wishes to accomplish' (Michalak, Heidenreich, & Hoyer, 2004,

p. 84): that is, the person's directions are self-defeating (Snyder & Taylor, 2000). As we saw with Mei (Figure 6.2), for instance, her desire for relatedness (through establishing a relationship with Saul) runs against her desire for stability (through maintaining a relationship with Rob). If she progresses towards greater relatedness, she gets less stability; and if she stays with her stability, she makes less progress towards relatedness (at least in the short term). Operationally, we can say that a dysergetic relationship exists between Direction x and Direction y if the means towards Direction x impedes the person's movement towards Direction y, and/or vice versa. We could also say that it is a situation in which no single act can advance both plans at the same time (Miller et al., 1960).

In a dysergy, then, the 'whole' (Direction x + Direction y) is less than the sum of the individual parts. Here, it is not just that they are different or pointing in opposite directions. Indeed, oppositional relationships can be 'productive' as well as 'unproductive' (Rescher, 1993): for instance, two individuals enjoying a game of poker. Rather, in a dysergetic relationship there is a loss of overall benefit, so that the putting of the two directions together makes less overall benefit than if the directions were acting on their own. If Mei, for instance, had two separate lives, she could enjoy passion and excitement with Saul *and* enjoy security with Rob. But she cannot: the two separate Meis are inescapably one. And getting one thing means not getting the other. If you had two separate lives, what things would you do that are too dysergetic to do now?

Dysergies might be between two approach directions (for instance, wanting both Rob and Saul), two avoidance directions (for instance, fearing rejection but also fearing stagnation), or an approach and avoidance direction (for instance, wanting to be loved by others but fearing a loss of self) (Grawe, 2004).

In many instances, this dysergetic relationship may be considered *incidental*. That is, Direction x gets in the way of Direction y, but it does not mean to: Direction x is not specifically intending to be obstructive. Rather it is a 'side effect' (Caspar, 1995) or 'unintended consequence' of the means towards Direction y. So, for instance, to achieve his goal of looking 'cool' to his friends, Logan smokes cannabis, which has the unintended consequence of undermining his goal of relaxation. However, conflicts between directions can also be *deliberate*. This is a more malevolent form of intrapersonal conflict, in which Direction x specifically intends to control, defeat, or annihilate Direction y. For instance, 'part' of Logan wants to feel better about himself: more self-reassuring and compassionate. But another 'part' meets any surfacing of that direction with derision and ridicule: 'I'm so soft, man', he says, 'You can see me. I'm such a fool.' While the former type of intrapersonal conflict is like two colleagues wanting different things, the latter is like a war, with two forces deliberately trying to wrench control from the other.

An understanding that people's goals can come into conflict stretches right back to Plato and his 'tripartite theory of soul': that we have a logical part, a spirited part, and an appetitive (pleasure-oriented) part (Braude, 1991; Rowan, 1990). It has also been present from the earliest days of psychology. In 1890, for instance, William James (1981) wrote that:

> I am often confronted by the necessity of standing by one of my empirical selves and relinquishing the rest. Not that I would not, if I could, be both handsome and fat and well dressed, and a great athlete, and make a million a year, be a wit, a *bon-vivant*, and a lady-killer, as well as a philosopher; a philanthropist, statesman, warrior, and African explorer, as well as a 'tone-poet' and saint. But the thing is simply impossible. The millionaire's work would run counter to the saint's; the *bon-vivant* and the philanthropist would trip each other up; the philosopher and the lady-killer could not well keep house in the same tenement of clay. Such different characters may conceivably at the outset of life be alike *possible* to a man. But to make any one of them actual, the rest must more or less be suppressed. (p. 295, emphasis in the original)

The hypothesis that dysergetic relationships can exist between directions is also intrinsic to many models of therapy. Conflict, for instance, is at the heart of psychoanalytic theory, defined as 'Opposition between apparently or actually incompatible forces' (Rycroft, 1995, p. 25). Person-centred theory, too, revolves around the presence of conflicting drives – *actualisation* versus *self-actualisation* (Rogers, 1959) – and models of intrapsychic conflict have also been developed in cognitive (e.g., Mansell, 2005), integrative (Grawe, 2004), and existential approaches (e.g., Spinelli, 1994). As Mansell et al. (2013) state, therapies as seemingly diverse as person-centred counselling and exposure therapy can be seen as involving essentially the same process: that of helping clients to become more aware – and resolve – conflicting directions. We will explore this much more fully in Part II of this book. Web Resource 8.1 gives a summary of the main directional conflicts that have been hypothesised to exist.

The hypothesis that follows on from this – that conflict between directions is a source, if not *the* source, of psychological distress – is also pervasive across both the psychological literature on motivation (e.g., Cavallo & Fitzsimons, 2012; Mansell, 2005; Michalak et al., 2004; Miller et al., 1960; Riediger, 2007) and in the wider psychotherapeutic field (e.g., Carey, 2006; Cooper, 2003; Ferrucci, 1982; Grawe, 2004; Greenberg et al., 1993; Lebow, 2008b; Vargiu, 1974). Indeed, Powers (1973) writes that 'Since the time of Freud and no doubt for much longer than that, inner conflicts have been recognized as a major cause of psychological difficulties' (p. 265). Powers goes on to state:

> Unresolved conflict leads to anxiety, depression, hostility, unrealistic fantasies, and even delusions and hallucinations. In fact, as I have come to realize what inner conflict means in terms of this feedback model, I have become more and more convinced that conflict *itself*, not any particular kind of conflict, represents the most serious kind of malfunction of the brain short of physical damage, and the most common even among 'normal' people. (p. 265, emphasis in the original)

Given the pervasiveness of inter-directional conflicts, it is important to note here that Powers (1973) identifies unresolved (or what we might term 'chronic', as per chronically ineffective strategies, see Chapter 7, this volume) conflicts as the source of psychological distress, rather than conflicts *per se*. Sundae or sorbet for dessert: delicious-but-fattening versus healthy-but-bland? In most cases, I can make a fairly quick decision on this and move on. But if this conflict remains chronic – if, for instance, I am consistently torn between my desire for food and my desire to lose weight – then this conflict starts to become more problematic.

On this basis, we might also predict that unconscious conflicts are more likely to be more problematic than conscious ones, because the individual has less capacity to mobilise resources to resolve them (Kelly, Mansell, & Wood, 2015). If, for instance, my direction towards food is really a means towards achieving comfort, but I am not aware of the latter, then the drive towards food may be more persistent because I cannot work on finding other ways of meeting that higher-order want.

In addition, conflicts between higher-order directions are likely to be more problematic than those at lower levels (Kelly et al., 2015). Should I have a glass of red wine or white? Such lower-order conflicts are unlikely to become a source of serious problems because neither direction is particularly pervasive – it is very context-specific (Miller et al., 1960) – and neither direction is particularly important to me. But should I drink alcohol to numb my feelings or try to be healthier? This seems a more likely source of psychological difficulties because both directions, as higher-order desires and goals, have an influence across my life. As this example suggests, more distress may also be associated with stronger opposition between the directions and where the total abandonment of either direction is felt to be impossible (Miller et al., 1960). This may particularly be the case if both directions are avoidance, because the person is 'trapped' with no way of escaping both threats.

While, as we saw, the evidence linking synergetic relationship to wellbeing is mixed, there is an abundance of evidence to show that goal conflict is associated with psychological difficulties (Austin & Vancouver, 1996; Cox & Klinger, 2002; Emmons, 1986; Emmons & King, 1988; Karoly, 1999; Kelly et al., 2015; Riediger, 2007; Riediger & Freund, 2004). Summarising the research, Michalak and colleagues (2011) wrote: 'most studies reveal a relation between intrapsychic conflicts and people's psychopathological status' (p. 98). In a recent meta-analysis, Kelly and colleagues (2015) found significant associations between goal conflicts and outcomes in 78 out of 83 studies. They concluded that the detrimental consequences of goal conflict were 'significant and wide-ranging', and included:

> [I]ncreased levels of psychological symptoms, for example anxiety, depression and negative affect; negative effects on subjective well-being factors such as life satisfaction and self-esteem; disruptive effects on self-regulatory variables like goal progress or perceived likelihood of goal success; physical effects including somatic

symptoms, physician visits, pain symptoms and physical illnesses; and negative consequences in applied contexts, for example, reduced job satisfaction and greater job-related exhaustion. (p. 226)

However, as Michalak et al. (2011) caution, 'because of the correlational nature of the majority of the presented results, a causal hypothesis that intrapersonal conflicts lead to psychopathological symptoms cannot yet be verified' (p. 98).

A number of reasons can be proposed for why dysergies between directions are likely to have pathogenic effects. First, and perhaps most obviously, where conflict exists, people are impeded – by definition – from actualising higher-order directions. Mansell (2005) likens such conflict to 'two different air conditioning systems operating in the same room, one set at 20°C and the other at 30°C' (p. 147). So, here, neither air conditioning system is able to approach or achieve its goal.

In addition, like two people in the same room trying to regulate according to different temperature goals, the very existence of an internal conflict may evoke feelings of turmoil, confusion, frustration, vacillation, mixed emotions, and disintegration in a person, and may leave them feeling exhausted and drained of resources (Berrios, Totterdell, & Kellett, 2015; Karoly, 1999; Miller et al., 1960). Research suggests that it may also have an immobilising effect, increasing levels of rumination and reducing direction action (Emmons & King, 1988). This latter explanation is supported by research by Boudreaux and Ozer (2013), which showed that individuals with greater levels of goal conflict were less successful in achieving their goals, but the ones that they were less successful in achieving were not necessarily the ones in conflict. This suggests that the impact of directional conflict may be less on the specific directions being impeded, and more in terms of a general impact on the person's ability to actualise their directions.

Here, we might also suggest that the degree of distress associated with directional conflict will be related to the degree to which a person strives to overcome the conflict itself – a *secondary direction* (see Chapter 5). If a person, for instance, feels that they should be conflict-free and consistent, then they may experience greater failure, frustration, or disappointment when their directions come into conflict. By contrast, if they are accepting that, at times, they will have competing desires and goals, then they may experience less negative affect at these times. Here, an existential perspective on therapy (e.g., Spinelli, 1994), which starts from the assumption that 'dilemmas' may be intrinsic to human existence, may be a particularly useful way in to addressing this distress (see Chapter 12).

Rogue goals

What is the experience of directional conflict actually like? In some instances, whether incidental or deliberate, it may feel like an argument going on in our heads, for instance:

'Go on, go up to Jeannie and say "Hi". What's the worst that's going to happen?'
'No way man, she'll think I'm a twat.'
'So what? At least give it a try.'

Here, both desires are present in Logan's head at once: they are able to converse and interact. As with synergies, we can term this conflict *synchronic*. An alternative form of intrapersonal dysergy, however, may be where different directions 'take over' the person at different periods of time: *diachronic* conflict. Here, then, the person becomes dominated by Direction x (the 'active goal'; Bargh & Huang, 2009), and then by Direction y, and then by Direction x again, and there may be very little actual dialogue between the competing directions. As Logan, for instance, starts to smoke cannabis, his direction towards getting 'wasted' takes over completely, and competing desires – like wanting to be healthy or more active – become silenced. But then, once he comes out of it, his desire to be healthy takes over and he berates himself for getting stoned: 'I'm such an idiot'. Such a form of internal oscillation is also evident when Logan gets anxious. Here, when he's panicking about whether or not he has locked his front door, other concerns – like being warm and chatty to his mates – get pushed to the back of his mind. But once he is relaxed again, he cannot understand at all his previously 'obsessive' behaviour.

A more extreme form of this dysergy is when one direction is consistently dominant, forcing to the background other, non-compatible directions. For instance, Irving and Cannon (2000) conceptualise eating disorders as a process in which the desire for thinness takes over from every other direction that the person may have. They write, 'The tenacity of individuals diagnosed with anorexia is legendary; weight goals become a focal point around which the individual's life revolves; the individual pursues weight goals with a rigid persistence that is physically and emotionally exhausting' (p. 269).

Diachronic conflict has been conceptualised in different ways across various forms of therapy – although it is always viewed as problematic. In cognitive analytic therapy, for instance, it is referred to as 'living at one end of a dilemma' (McCormick, 2012), psychosynthesis talks about being 'held prisoner by a subpersonality' (Ferrucci, 1982), and existential therapists write about the person being taken over by 'daimonic' functions (May, 1969a). Powers's perceptual control theory uses the term *arbitrary control* (Mansell, 2005; Powers, 1973), which is defined as 'Attempts to make behavior conform to one set of goals without regard to other goals (and control systems)' (Powers, 1973, p. 271) (or, indeed, without regard to the conflict that is caused) (Mansell et al., 2013). Arbitrary control can be likened to 'tunnel vision', 'selective attention', or 'goal myopia'. At its extreme, it can be considered akin to *dissociative identity disorder*, whereby the person develops two or more distinctive 'personalities' – embodying different directions – that become active at different times.

Grawe (2004) uses the term 'attractors' to describe the particular states that we can get drawn into: deep valleys along which our directions can end up running. For him, these are associated with specific neural activation patterns – as the adage goes, 'cells that fire together wire together' – and he sees psychotherapy as a process of destabilising 'disorder attractors' and overwriting them with new therapeutic experiences.

We might also term these autonomous, single-minded goals which take over the system as *rogue goals*, with evidence suggesting that this 'hijacking' of the individual's executive functioning can happen unconsciously (Marien et al., 2012). Rogue goals act unrelentingly in their own interest, irrespective of whether it is helpful or not for the person-as-a-whole. It is the ultimate in what Bargh and Huang (2009) call 'the selfish goal' (see below); and what Koestler (1967) describes as 'cognitive holons running riot'. Koestler (1967) writes:

> There is a whole gamut of mental disorders in which some subordinate part of the mental hierarchy exerts its tyrannical rule over the whole; from the relatively harmless infatuation with some pet theory ... to the clinical psychoses in which large chunks of the personality seem to have 'split off' and lead a quasi-independent existence. (p. 266)

So a client shouts at their partner, even though they know that this makes things worse, or they take drugs, or they 'just can't help having affairs', or they say 'no' when they know they need to say 'yes', or 'yes' when they know they need to say 'no'. All these instances, and many more, are examples of where specific client goals 'go rogue': acting in ways that actualise their one direction, but to the detriment of many others.

One reason why rogue goals may emerge is because 'Having a goal sensitizes a person to respond to goal-related cues, thus drawing the individual's perceptions, memories, thoughts, dreams, and actions back to the goal pursuit' (Klinger & Cox, 2011, p. 25; Riemann & McNally, 1995). This can create a vicious cycle where, as the goal becomes more salient, the person becomes more sensitive to relevant cues, thus enhancing the salience of that goal, *etc.* For instance, as Logan starts to worry more about how he is looking to others, so he becomes more aware of their glances towards him. This then increases his concerns about how he looks, leading to more 'paranoia' (as he describes it). In addition, the more we become fixated in one direction, the less interested we may become in other goals – or less confident about our ability to achieve them. Hence, again, our attention may be drawn back to the rogue goal as our principal source of interest and capability. In these respects, then, lower-order goals can become autonomous, 'in the sense that the organism strives after them even in circumstances in which they are no longer means to basic [i.e., highest-order] goals' (Woodfield, 1976, p. 151).

SOURCES OF DYSERGY

As with ineffective goals, we can ask why dysergetic goals might arise within an individual.

The inherently conflictual nature of human being

From a range of therapeutic perspective, such dysergies may be seen as emerging from the inherently conflictual nature of human desires. Freud, for instance, believed that human beings' highest-order desires stood in diametrical opposition to each other: for instance, the life force and the death force (Marcuse, 1966). CBT, too, sees conflicting desires – in this case, between short-term heuristics and long-term rationalism – as inherent to the human system (Kahneman, 2011), as does existential philosophy and therapy (e.g., Jaspers, 1932; van Deurzen, 1998). For van Deurzen, one of the givens of existence is that we will always be pulled between the poles of different *dilemmas* – for instance, between a desire for relatedness and a desire for independence – for which there is no possibility of resolution. From a psychological standpoint, Bargh and Huang (2009) also see dysergy as a consequence of the natural human state, which 'comprises of many, often-conflicting goals' (p. 140). For Bargh and Huang, our goals are inherently 'selfish', and 'will single-mindedly pursue their agenda independently of whether doing so is in the overall good of the individual person' (p. 131).

From the standpoint of other therapeutic perspectives, however, it is not inevitable that directional conflicts with arise. In particular, humanistic approaches view the organism as an inherently integrated whole, that has the capacity to function in non-conflictual, coherent ways (e.g., Rogers, 1959). Here, conflict arises through the introjection of external values and meanings.

The structural model proposed in Chapter 6 may be a useful means of trying to draw these different perspectives together. If we start by considering human beings' highest-order directions (Table 6.1), then the 'natural' degree of conflict would seem to vary by the particular combination that we are considering. The desire for autonomy and the desire for relatedness, for instance, would seem to have a high potential for conflict, whereas the desire for autonomy and the desire for competence would seem to be more naturally synergetic. With any of these directions, however, the issue of whether or not they come into conflict will be determined by the means through which the individual attempts to actualise them. If the desire for competence, for instance, is actualised through developing skills as a specialist in some field, it may closely support the desire for autonomy. If, on the other hand, it is actualised through striving to earn the approval of others, it may compromise the need for independence much more profoundly. In support of this perspective, Zaleski (1987) found that conflicts are more prevalent across shorter-term goals (which would typically be of a lower order), compared with longer-term ones (which would typically be of a higher order).

Individual factors

So what determines whether people will adopt synergetic or dysergetic means to actualise their highest-order directions? All else being equal, and with conscious awareness and deliberation, there is evidence that people will tend towards adopting synergetic strategies (Chun et al., 2011, see Web Resource 17.2). This makes intuitive sense. Given, for instance, the choice between three pairs of shoes – (a) stylish but uncomfortable, (b) unstylish but comfortable, and (c) stylish and comfortable – few people would not choose (c), the synergetic option. At the same time, however, this capacity to choose in synergetic ways may require a relatively high level of abstract thinking, and there may be many times when a more single-minded focus on achieving one particular goal, as above, dominates. In this case, synergetic means may be as much serendipitous as anything else.

In addition, there may be personal differences in the extent to which people tend towards synergetic or dysergetic means of actualising their highest-order directions. Research shows, for instance, that people vary in their levels, or need, for self-consistency (e.g., Altrocchi, 1999); and it is interesting to note that people with a more stable and consistent self-structure experience lower levels of maladjustment and neuroticism. This may relate to metagoals (see Chapter 5). For instance, a person with a secondary goal of 'I need to focus on this task now, and not worry about its impact on anything else' may end up with more dysergies than someone who believes it is always important to view things from a wider perspective. To what extent do you concern yourself with the development of dysergies in your life? How might this relate to your actual levels of internal conflict?

At an individual level, the development of dysergies may also be related to power imbalances within a person's directional structure. If some directions are very dominant – for instance, due to the internalisation of authoritarian voices – it may lead to the subjugation and disowning of other directions (Stone & Winkelman, 1989), with the potential for greater dysergies as 'the repressed' 'return'. When Logan's desire to avoid his anxiety, for instance, comes to the fore, it pushes all other directions outside his awareness. Hence, when these subjugated directions return, they may act in ways that are oblivious – or even counter – to the previously dominant need. So Logan tries to form relationships by smoking cannabis with his friends, which then brings his anxiety back to the fore. In addition, although we may all experience rogue goals to a certain extent, some people – due, for instance, to the dominance of heuristic cognitive processes – may be more likely to switch backwards and forwards between conflicting directions.

Limited resources

The emergence of dysergetic directions can also be seen as the consequence of contextual factors: specifically, scarcity in a person's context (Cavallo & Fitzsimons, 2012; Kelly et al., 2015; Marcuse, 1966; Michalak et al., 2004; Riediger & Freund, 2004). Empirical evidence supports this hypothesis, showing that when people report on conflicting goals, a 'great majority' are due to 'limited resources' (Boudreaux & Ozer,

2013, p. 441). This is an individual-level equivalent to social psychology's 'realistic conflict theory', which holds that 'limited resources lead to conflict among groups' (Aronson, Wilson, & Akert, 1999, p. 486). It can be described as follows:

> [O]ur wants are often in tension with each other ... because we inhabit an environment in which the achievement of one want frequently necessitates the subjugation of another. A person in a context of limited financial resources, for example, might only be able to achieve their desire for financial security by suppressing their desire for excitement and stimulation: for instance, by taking a job in a fast food restaurant. Alternatively, in that environment, the person may be able to actualise their desire for stimulation by forming a musical group with their friends, but then they might have to compromise their desire for financial security. (Cooper, 2006, p. 88)

Here, the term 'resources' is used in the widest possible sense: not just economic and social goods, but anything in the person's context which they might need to fulfil their directions, such as love, respect, time, and mental energy. For instance, 'positive regard' (Rogers, 1959) might be understood as a contextual resource, and 'conditional positive regard' as:

> [A] case in which the social world has essentially pitted the need for relatedness against the need for autonomy. The children are thus in the uncomfortable position of being controlled, or having to relinquish autonomy (and thus not be who they really are) in order to gain parental love. (Deci & Ryan, 2000, p. 249)

The argument that limited contextual resources force dysergies between a person's directions is a critical one for the present text, as it forms a key 'bridge' between psychological and sociopolitical theories of wellbeing and change. Mei's conflict as a child, for instance, between feeling close to others and feeling good about herself, was a consequence of the very real racism that existed in her social world. Similarly, in his economically-deprived context, Logan struggles to find meanings in his life that also actualise his desire for healthiness or creativity. Like many of our clients, then, Mei and Logan require more than just psychological work to achieve a greater level of wellbeing. They require real, in-the-world, sociopolitical transformation: less racism, less economic deprivation, more opportunities for all.

CONCLUSION

In this chapter, it has been argued that one of the main reasons why people do not actualise their directions is because they have desires and goals pulling in opposing directions. Psychological wellbeing, then, comes from finding more synergetic ways of actualising directions. In Part II of this book, it will be argued that this is the underlying premise of many of our counselling and psychotherapeutic approaches. However, what is less well recognised in our field is that, to a great extent, these dysergies emerge due to limited social resources. Hence, to create a world in which people can actualise their highest-order directions requires more than just individual-level, therapeutic change. It means creating a world in which more resources exist for more people more of the time.

QUESTIONS FOR REFLECTION

- Consider three or four of your most important directions. To what extent are each of them synergetic or dysergetic with the other directions? What are the implications of this for your psychological wellbeing?
- What are your rogue goals?
- To what extent do you agree or disagree with the argument that, for many people, psychological wellbeing requires social change?

FURTHER READING

Mansell, W. (2005). Control theory and psychopathology: An integrative approach. *Psychology and Psychotherapy: Theory, Research and Practice, 78(2)*, 141-178. doi:10.1348/147608304 X21400. A valuable summary of control theory and its potential contribution to therapeutic thinking and practice.

Michalak, J., Heidenreich, T., & Hoyer, J. (2004). Goal conflicts: Concepts, findings, and consequences for psychotherapy. In W. M. Cox & E. Klinger (Eds.), *Handbook of motivational counseling* (pp. 83-97). New York: John Wiley. A useful academic review of theory, research, and practice on goal conflicts.

Powers, W. T. (1973). *Behavior: The control of perception*. Chicago, IL: Aldine. The essential control theory text.

9

FROM INTRAPERSONAL TO INTERPERSONAL LEVELS OF ORGANISATION

Playing to win-win

This chapter discusses:

- The transposition of the concepts of directionality, dysergies, and synergies to interpersonal levels of organisation.
- *Non-zero-sum* games, as developed in *game theory*, and how this can develop our understanding of synergies and dysergies.

To this point, it has been argued that a person's context – including their interpersonal and social relationships – plays a crucial role in determining how, and whether, a person will actualise their directions. However, this analysis remains focused at the individual level, in terms of how the actualisation of a person's directions are shaped by their context. By contrast, in this chapter, we will look at how the whole framework, and the concepts developed so far, can be transposed to a range of interpersonal levels: dyadic, family, community, national, and global. So the focus turns to *interpersonal directionality*, *interpersonal synergies*, and *interpersonal dysergies*. No doubt, much could also be said about effective and ineffective strategies at the interpersonal level (see Chapter 7). However, for reasons of space, the principal focus here is on horizontal coherence and incoherence alone.

LEVELS OF ORGANISATION

Within the field of individual counselling and psychotherapy, as in this book, there is a tendency to start with the person as the organising unit of analysis. On the other hand, disciplines like sociology or politics tend to start with more macro *levels of organisation* (Koestler, 1967) – like classes, communities, or society as a whole – and understand individual processes in terms of these wider social 'fields' (Mindell, 2014). From a Marxist perspective, for instance, individuals' desires and behaviours may be understood in terms of the power and interests that flow 'through them' (Smail, 2005). Within the therapeutic field, couples, groups, or family therapists may also start with more macro units of analysis: seeing, for instance, the 'family system' (Gurman, 2003), or the 'group-as-a-whole' (Foulkes, 1984), as the principal operating entity, rather than its individual components. Here, individual difficulties may be viewed as a product of dysfunction within the larger family system (Lebow, 2008a). That is, fields are seen as creating and organising us as much as we organise them (Mindell, 2014).

Certainly, a focus at the macro level alone cannot explain many micro-level processes and variations. While it may be true, for instance, that girls in Western society are socialised to desire thinness, this does not hold for everyone. Some girls may be quite happy being larger. Conversely, however, 'Collective actions … cannot be reduced down to individual intentions' (Gibbs Jr, 2001, p. 113). This is because once individuals collect together they form relationships and interconnections – synergies and dysergies (see below) – that make them 'greater than' the individual parts alone. Lewin (1947) writes:

> There is no more magic behind the fact that groups have properties of their own, which are different from the properties of their subgroups or their individual members, than behind the fact that molecules have properties which are different from the properties of the atoms or ions of which they are composed. (p. 8)

FROM INTRAPERSONAL TO INTERPERSONAL LEVELS OF ORGANISATION

Just as water, then, has very different properties from hydrogen and oxygen alone, so a collection of two or more people is not simply the additive effects of their individual characteristics. A couple, for instance, has its own 'personality', habits, and friendship network – evolving over time – and these are more than just the sum of its individual parts. 'Posh and Becks' is more than Victoria Adams and David Beckham in isolation; 'Brangelina' was more than Brad Pitt and Angelina Jolie alone. Indeed, the contemporary tendency to hybridise couples' names into a single identity highlights the Gestalt-like unity of such a higher-level entity.

Koestler's (1967) concept of a *holarchy* may be a useful way of conceptualising these different levels of organisation. For Koestler, each organising unit (or what he termed a *holon*), sits within an 'open-ended' hierarchical structure, with lower- and higher-level units that can range from sub-atomic quarks to the omniverse (see, for instance, Figure 9.1). Here, higher-level organising units are 'made up' of lower-level units. So, for instance, the individual is made up of goals, the family is made up of individuals, and the community is made up of families. But because the higher-level units are formed through the relationships between the lower-level units, they are never simply reducible to them. This means, then, that at each level, the holons can be considered a functioning whole – self-regulating and semi-autonomous – with none more 'real' or significant than the others.

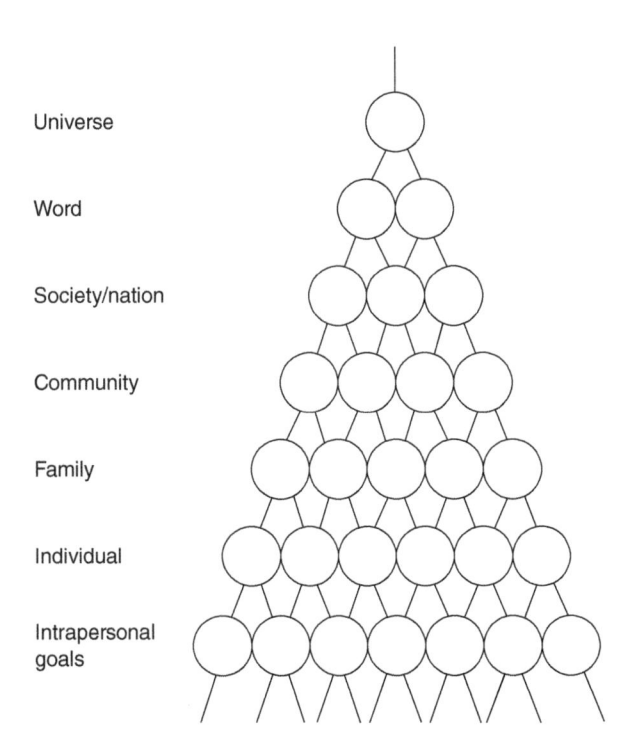

Figure 9.1 An illustrative holarchy

INTERPERSONAL DIRECTIONALITY

Just as individuals have desires, intentions, and goals, so too do higher levels of organisation (Malle et al., 2001; Mindell, 2014). A couple, for instance, might be striving to buy their first home, or a social class might be fighting to control the means of production. Within the therapy and psychology field, there has been a particular focus on the way in which small groups (such as therapy groups) can have a 'will', 'drive', and 'common purpose' of their own (e.g., Bion, 1961; Foulkes, 1984) and behave in the light of particular 'needs' (Houston, 1993). As at that individual level, these can be conscious or unconscious (Mindell, 2014).

Theorists and researchers have also described how small groups can move through a sequence of stages – such as 'forming', 'storming', 'norming', and 'performing' (Tuckman, 1965), or 'induction', 'goaling', 'change', and 'termination' (Burlingame & McClendon, 2003) – which have many parallels with the phases of the direction arc (Chapter 3, this volume). The family has also been described by therapists as a goal-oriented system (e.g., Lebow, 2008a): for instance, striving to create, and maintain, a particular 'phantasy' of what it is, despite the actual experiences of individual members (Laing, 1967). Within the organisational field, too, practices have developed which emphasise particular phases of the directional arc, in particular feedback. This includes the use of 'PDSA' cycles (Plan–Do–Study–Act) and the 'Agile Method', where iterative cycles of testing and adjustment are carried out before changes are disseminated more widely.

Critically, as with all aspects of these organising units, this *we-intentionality* (Gibbs Jr, 2001) cannot be reduced down to the intentionality of its constituent members. An example of this is the way that when two people dance together, their movement co-evolves in a highly interactive and indetermined way (Gibbs Jr, 2001). Here, intention is not simply in each dancer's head; rather, it interactively emerges through the process of being together (Gibbs Jr, 2001). Another example is: 'John and Jeremy' want to buy their first home, but this 'dyadic desire' is not simply the sum of John's desire plus Jeremy's desire. They are a couple, with a particular, distinctive vision that they have created together for their home, and a way of striving towards it that has emerged from their relational dynamic.

One of the particular reasons why directionality, at the interpersonal level, is irreducible to individual directionality is because of the way that one person's directions interact and shape those of another person. John, for instance, wants to buy a minimalist loft conversion by the sea, and because one of Jeremy's highest-order desires is for John to get what he wants, Jeremy wants this loft conversion too. But John gets frustrated when Jeremy wants what he wants – he wants Jeremy to make his own mind up – and so he starts going off the idea of a loft conversion and starts thinking about a bungalow in the countryside. This is one thing that Jeremy really does not want, but the more he pushes back against John, the more adamant John becomes. Finally, they agree on a semi-detached house in a seaside town. Here, the directionality of 'John-and-Jeremy' as a couple emerges as a complex web of their interacting, individual directions. It cannot be reduced to either alone.

INTERPERSONAL DYSERGIES

In Chapter 8, we saw how the actualisation of higher-order directions can be understood in terms of dysergies and synergies between lower-order directions. Similarly, as suggested by Figure 9.1, we can think of a directional structure at each of the other levels of organisation: with, for instance, lower-order, individual directions nested within higher-order, dyadic, family, or group etc. directions (Miller et al., 1960). This means that relationships within higher levels of organisation can also take one of three forms – synergetic, dysergetic, or independent – with higher-level directions actualised to the extent that their lower-level directions are pulling together, rather than apart.

The dynamic between Mei and Rob illustrates how directions between two individuals can be dysergetic, to the detriment of the overall dyad (see Figure 9.2). Mei desperately wants excitement and passion in her life, but Rob's priority is for 'down time'. If Mei and Rob were independent entities, these different directions would not be a problem. But as a couple, who have been committed to the sharing of time and space together, a push from one party has an inevitable influence on the other. So Mei feels dragged down by Rob's 'laziness'; and Rob might feel that his pursuit of pleasure is continually interrupted by Mei's busyness. As with dysergies at an intrapersonal level, then, Mei and Rob are like two thermostats in a room, each trying to regulate the same activity according to different standards. The result is a problematic relationship, and consequently two dissatisfied individuals.

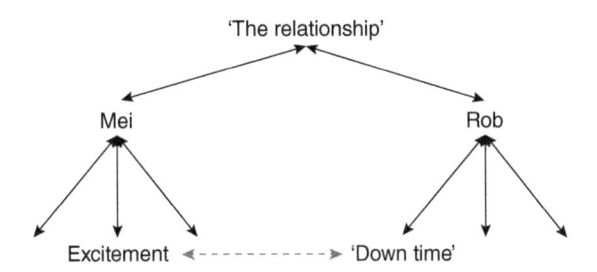

Figure 9.2 Dysergetic interpersonal relationship

Such dysergies can also be seen in therapy groups (Slavson, 1957) or in family systems where, for instance, two members form a coalition against a third (Kaslow, Dausch, & Celano, 2003). A father and son, for example, strive to maintain their sense of camaraderie by teasing the mother for being 'stupid', thereby undermining her desire for self-worth. Racism can be understood as a manifestation of a similar dysergy at the community level: one group actualising its desires (for instance, for self-worth) through the undermining of another's. And, of course, war – the social ill that causes an abundance of misery, terror, and loss (Layard, 2006) – can be considered the most macro form of dysergetic relating. Here, one nation's directionality is specifically aimed at overpowering and controlling the directionality of another.

In these latter examples, we can see parallels to the deliberate forms of conflict discussed in Chapter 8. And if directionality is understood as the essence of human being, then deliberate attempts to sabotage or suppress it in others is, perhaps, the most malevolent of human actions. This compares with its more incidental form. Mei and Rob, for instance, pull each other in different directions, but they do not intend to deliberately block the other's direction; rather, it is a by-product of their striving for their own goals.

To complicate matters further, we can also consider dysergies *between* levels. For instance, Mei may decide, in relationship to Rob, to do exactly what she wants. But this then has a detrimental effect on the actualisation of their relationship – and, consequently, on her. In this respect, we could conceptualise the conflict between intrinsic and extrinsic directions (see Chapter 5) as a dysergy across levels: with the individual's desires pulling against those of their family, or society. A cultural more that boys should not cry, for instance, may run against the individual's own desire for emotional expression, or a cultural value for genital mutilation may fundamentally undermine an individual's highest-order directions towards safety, autonomy, and self-worth (Deci & Ryan, 2000). Within organisations, we also often see a conflict between what a company or institution wants and an individual's personal goals (Powers, 1992). For instance, an individual may have a desire to be original or creative in their work, but the organisation needs them to complete more mundane tasks.

This means that we cannot conceptualise the individual's directions in isolation from the directions of those around them. And, indeed, at times, people may face a choice between actualising individual-level directions and contributing to the actualisation of a greater whole. For instance, at a personal level, Mei might want to leave Rob and Olivia to live with Saul, but this would have serious detrimental consequences for her family as well as for Saul, and perhaps their wider social network. Furthermore, because Mei herself is part of these higher-level organising units – the family or the social network – she herself will lose out if the larger group loses out. Hence, in parallel with intrapersonal processes, there is a complex balance to be found between actualising one's individual directions and actualising those of the larger whole. In group therapies, this may be a particular focus, where members learn to negotiate the tensions between the group needs and their own individual needs (Bion, 1961; Paul, 2012).

Moreover, as at the individual level, interpersonal conflicts may become increasingly intensified with reduced levels of resources and possibilities (Powers, 1992). In an affluent society, for instance, people may be able to follow their own interests and directions without having a particularly detrimental effect on others. But in a

FROM INTRAPERSONAL TO INTERPERSONAL LEVELS OF ORGANISATION

more poorly resourced context, the actualisation of one person's individual needs may directly take away from the possibilities of others. If, for instance, I try to get my client to be seen more quickly by the National Health Service (where resources are very limited), I know that another person will be disadvantaged (Kagleder, personal communication, 17 April 2018). By contrast, if our NHS was very well funded, then there would be resources to see my client more quickly without the need to de-prioritise anyone else.

INTERPERSONAL SYNERGIES

Relationships at higher levels of organisation may also take more synergetic forms. Here, 'two people [or groups, etc.] have arranged their relationship in such a fashion that one person's advantage is the other person's advantage rather than one person's advantage being the other's disadvantage' (Maslow, 1971, p. 200). Such synergies can also be seen in Mei and Rob's relationship. For instance, as depicted in Figure 9.3, Mei wants to nurture Olivia in a supportive, loving, and caring family, as does Rob. Through working together on this, they have both been able to actualise this desire in a way that neither could do so fully on their own.

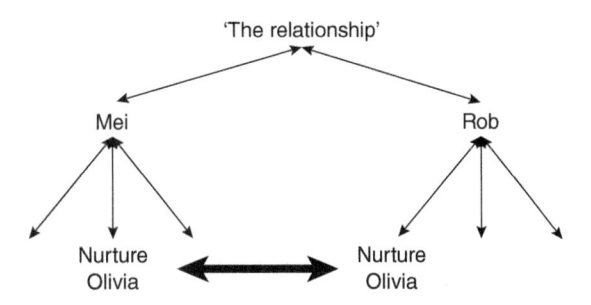

Figure 9.3 Synergetic interpersonal relationship

These synergies may also exist at the level of the group. From a group analytic perspective, for instance, Slavson (1957) writes that:

> The basic integrating force that assures the survival and achievement of ordinary groups is what has been described as *synergy*. By synergy is meant the drive, purpose, aim and effort common to and congruent in all the individuals constituting a group or mass of people. The cementing ties, the coherence in these groups, is the personal homogeneity of their members and/or of their interest or goal. (p. 169)

For Slavson (1957), however, it is this synergetic organisation that is missing, by definition, in therapy groups, with each patient acting as an individual, for his or her individual ends, rather than for a common group aim.

At the wider community level, Maslow (1971) also describes social arrangement in both traditional and contemporary cultures that are high and low in synergy. An example of the former is the Kalahari Ju/'hoansi hunter-gatherer community, in which spiritual healing energy (*n/om*) is shared out among the group (Katz & Murphy-Shigematsu, 2012). Unlimited in supply, the activation of this energy in one member of the community is seen as stimulating *n/om* in others. Katz and Murphy-Shigematsu (2012) also point to self-help groups – such as Alcoholics Anonymous – as a paradigmatic form of synergistic community (somewhat in contrast to Slavson, above), in which members benefit from both providing and receiving support. By contrast, Maslow points to the college grading system in the USA as a dysergetic system, in which a higher grade for one student necessarily entails a lower grade for another.

As at the interpersonal level, systems can be seen as 'good' to the extent that they are synergetic rather than dysergetic. Synergetic systems increase the overall actualisation of highest-order directions – that is, more people (or families, or groups, or communities) get more of what they want more of the time – whereas dysergetic systems decrease it. In this way, as Maslow (1971) suggests, the synergy principle 'opens up the way for a supracultural system of values by which to evaluate a culture and everything within it', because it 'furnishes a scientific basis for Utopian theory' (p. 199).

Here, for instance, actions like communication, tolerance, and compassion can all be considered 'good' things because, through their synergetic potential, they can increase the 'net' actualisation of directions across the system. Acting compassionately, for instance, helps some people feel good because they experience the pleasure of reaching out, and it helps other people feel good because they experience the pleasure of being helped and supported in their lives. By contrast, actions like intolerance, racism, and homophobia are 'bad' because they reduce the net actualisation of directions. Homophobia, for instance, reduces the capacity of its many victims to feel good about themselves without actualising anything of positive or enduring worth for anyone else. Understanding society in these terms, we can begin to develop a robust argument for why values and actions such as compassion and altruism are the basis for a thriving society. Not because they are simply 'nice' or 'kind', but because they are the best way of all us getting more of what we want.

This perspective on social wellbeing can be considered a modified version of utilitarianism, which holds that 'The *rightness* of an action is to be judged by the contribution it makes to the increase of human happiness or the decrease of human misery' (Urmson & Ree, 1989, pp. 318–319, emphasis in the original). Here, however, the rightness of an action, or of a society, is judged more broadly: in terms of its contribution to the actualisation of highest-order human directions, whatever they may be. So this may be happiness, but it may also be autonomy, relatedness, or whatever highest-order directions are unique to the individual (see Chapter 6). This is similar to Powers's definition of an affluent society as one in which many people have achieved their goals; to Snygg and Combs's (1949) statement that 'The good society satisfied need' (p. 198); and to Rescher's (1993) *Principle of Benevolence*, which holds that 'A world in which people have what they want is a better world than one in which they do not, provided there is no harm to what they [or others] want' (p. 129). Hence, while a utilitarian position holds that 'the greatest happiness is the right guide to public policy' (Layard, 2006, p. 114), from the current perspective, public policy should be oriented to the greatest actualisation of all higher-order directions. We shall explore the practical implications of this in Chapter 16.

This valuing of synergetic relationships can be seen, albeit implicitly, in the many forms of therapy that focus on person-to-person dynamics, as well as those that work with two or more clients consecutively. For instance, one of the principal aims of interpersonal therapy is to help clients improve their interpersonal relationships and to reduce levels of conflict (Stuart & Robertson, 2003). Similarly, transactional analysis uses the concepts of *complementary* and *crossed transactions* to help clients improve their interpersonal functioning (Stewart & Joines, 1987). Complementary transactions are those in which people respond from the ego-state to which they were addressed. For instance, Mei talks to Rob as an Adult ('I'd really like it if you could help me take the kids out'), and Rob responds from Adult to Adult ('I've just got to do something for five minutes and then I will'). By contrast, crossed transactions are those in which the ego-state addressed is not the one that responds. For instance, Mei talks to Rob from Adult to Adult, but Rob responds from Adapted Child to Controlling Parent ('You're always telling me what to do...' [feeling: 'it's not fair']). In complementary transactions, we can see a basic synergetic relationship: the two parties matching, and building on, each other. However, crossed transactions involve a basic dysergy: one form of communication undermines the other. Similarly, couples therapy aims to help clients develop conflict management skills (Meneses & Scuka, 2016); family therapies aim to help clients develop cohesive, yet flexible, family structures and functioning (Kaslow et al., 2003; Lebow, 2008a); group psychotherapies all strive to address interpersonal foundations of pathologies (Dies, 2003); and mediation practices strive to help clients move from *win–lose* to *win–win* relationships.

NON-ZERO-SUM GAMES

To develop a deeper understanding of processes at interpersonal levels of organisation (and, in Chapter 16, back to intrapersonal levels), we now turn to *game theory* and its concept of *non-zero-sum games*. Game theory 'is the study of strategic interdependence – that is, situations where my actions affect both my welfare and your welfare and vice versa' (Spaniel, 2015, p. 1). Game theory is used in such fields as economics and political sciences, and involves the development of mathematical models of conflict and cooperation. It provides a helpful – albeit somewhat mechanistic – language for deepening an understanding of synergies and dysergies.

In game theory, *zero-sum games* are those in which the 'fortunes' of each 'player' are inversely related. This is a 'win–lose' or a 'draw–draw' interaction, in which any gains in one party are mirrored by the losses of another (Wright, 2000). A classic example of this might be a game of poker between two players. If I win £3, the other player loses £3, and vice versa. So the total 'gain' is constant, or 'zero sum', in the sense that the minuses and the pluses always cancel each other out. In a zero-sum game, synergies and dysergies are not possible: there is no slackage, no room for allowing more (or less) optimal outcomes overall. And in a truly zero-sum game, where there are no advantages whatsoever to more equal outcomes (including, for instance, a moral sense of fairness), then there is no reason for people not to engage in direct competition.

In reality, however, most real human interactions are *non-zero-sum*. These are 'games' in which the total amount of benefit is not constant: where there is the possibility for 'win–win' and 'lose–lose' outcomes, as well as various degrees of 'win–lose'. Non-zero-sum games are synonymous with a potential for synergy (Wright, 2000), and Corning (2003) describes synergy as the 'hidden key' in game theory modelling: the difference between the zero and the non-zero of a game.

One reason why most real 'games' may be *non-zero-sum* is because any situation is likely to involve a variety of directions. For instance, it is true that, in terms of purely monetary gain, my victory at poker is mirrored in my partner's losses. But if, for instance, we both also desire excitement from playing poker together, then a longer game (say, two hours) would be more synergetic than a shorter one (say, five minutes). Most games are also non-zero-sum because the majority of human interactions continue over time, and this means that any immediate outcomes are just one part of a more complex, dynamic, non-linear network of consequences. For instance, even if my partner and I were playing for purely monetary gain, if I won £3000 from them rather than £3, they might refuse to play poker with me again, or skill themselves up so that they won the next time (or, if in the Wild West, shoot me), so there is no simple cancelling out of gains and losses. And, of course, any two-person game is embedded in a wider social network which then, as discussed above, may be affected by – and effect – lower levels of organisation. If I win £3000 from my friend, for instance, other friends may refuse to play poker with me – so again, the overall gains and losses in utility may be varied. And if we think about this in the context of multiple people and multiple levels of organisation with multiple desires and goals, it seems unlikely that there will ever be a real-life situation in which the overall 'sum' remains zero.

Within game theory, the classic scenario that has been used to explore non-zero-sum games is the *prisoner's dilemma game* (Axelrod, 1984; Wright, 2000). This takes the following form:

> Two criminals, A and B, are arrested and imprisoned. They are in solitary confinement so that they cannot talk to each other. If they both stay silent (i.e., 'cooperate' with each other), the police will not have enough evidence to prosecute them, but they can get them on a lesser charge, and each will go to

prison for one year. However, the police offer each criminal the opportunity to 'defect' (i.e., admit the crime), with the promise that if they do so, then they will be set free (and their partner will get three years in prison). However, if both criminals defect – and admit to their crime – then they will both receive a two-year sentence. So what should each criminal do? (https://en.wikipedia.org/wiki/Prisoner%27s_dilemma)

To help explore such dilemmas, game theorists often use *payoff matrices*, with different numbers representing different 'wins' or 'losses' for 'different players'. The payoff matrix for the above game, in terms of years imprisoned, is displayed in Table 9.1 (with scores preceded by a minus sign to indicate that more is worse). This shows the different combinations of moves, and the payoffs for A and B if each makes the choice to cooperate with, or betray, the other. The 'payoff' for A is in the bottom left of the square cells, and for B in the top right of the cells. So, for instance, in the top left-hand cell, we can see that if B cooperates and A cooperates, A will get one year in prison and B will get one year in prison; and in the top right-hand cell, we see that if A cooperates and B betrays, A will get three years in prison and B will get no years in prison. What this matrix also shows, as a non-zero-sum game, is that the total payoff varies from cell to cell: from -2 (A and B both stay silent) to -4 (A and B both betray each other).

Table 9.1 Payoff matrix for the classic prisoner's dilemma game

A \ B	B cooperates (stays silent)	B betrays (defects)
A cooperates (stays silent)	-1 years / -1 years	0 years / -3 years
A betrays (defects)	-3 years / 0 years	-2 years / -2 years

Note: The 'payoff' for A is in the bottom left of the square cells, and for B in the top right of the cells

Although this payoff matrix refers to a specific, imaginary situation, we can apply it to many real-life scenarios. For instance, imagine that Mei and Saul are both deciding on whether to ask the other out, and the payoff in this vignette is in terms of 'psychological suffering' (Table 9.2). Here, if Mei asks Saul out but Saul says nothing, she feels awful (a -3 of embarrassment), and the same goes for Saul. If neither of them say anything, on the other hand, they both lose out pretty badly in terms of missing a potential romance (-2). The 'winning' scenario, then, is if they both take the plunge, and both experience just a wince of discomfort, but feel better because the other has done the same.

The payoff matrix given here is just one of an infinite variety of zero-sum and non-zero-sum matrices that might exist; and scores can be positive as well as negative. For

Table 9.2 Payoff matrix for Mei and Saul dating

Mei \ Saul	Saul asks Mei out	Saul says nothing
Mei asks Saul out	-1 / -1	0 / -3
Mei says nothing	-3 / 0	-2 / -2

instance, in the above scenario, we might suggest that if both Saul and Mei ask each other out, then both will gain +5, or perhaps +10 or even +100,000. And it may also be that different participants have different gains or losses with different combinations (Spaniel, 2015). For instance, Mei might feel deeply humiliated by asking Saul out (-5), but Saul actually quite enjoys it as it gives him a sense of bravado (+2). And while Mei might find it torturous not going out with Saul (-10), and yearns to have more time with him (+10), Saul might be more diffident about it (±1). However, in zero-sum games, the total scores in all cells of the matrix will be equivalent; whereas in non-zero-sum games they will vary, with the most synergetic solution being the cell with the highest total score.

In some instances, synergetic solutions may be compatible with each person's immediate self-interest (i.e., the cell in which they score the highest). Supposing, for instance, that Mei and her girlfriend, Sasha, are deciding whether or not to go out on a Friday night (see Table 9.3). Both of them will feel bored and alone if they stay in (-2 'pleasure' each), but even worse if they end up going out on their own (-4 'pleasure' each). However, if they both go out together, they will really enjoy themselves (+7 'pleasure' each). Here, both Sasha and Mei, individually, are better off going out than staying in, and this win–win solution also gives the best overall outcome (+14).

Table 9.3 Payoff matrix for Mei and Sasha's evening in/out

Mei \ Sasha	Sasha stays in	Sasha goes out
Mei stays in	-2 / -2	-4 / -2
Mei goes out	-2 / -4	7 / 7

However, what is so fascinating about the kind of payoff matrix in the prisoner's dilemma game is that, for both players, their immediate rational self-interests – when considered in isolation – lead to sub-optimal outcomes overall (Axelrod, 1984). If A, for instance, considers their best move in relation to each of B's possibilities (in game theory terms, the *dominant strategy*), then they might think the following: 'If A stays silent, then I am better off betraying them (0 [years in prison]) than staying silent (-1); and if B betrays me, then I am also better off betraying them (-2) than staying silent (-3); so I should choose to betray.' The exact, same logic holds for B. However, if both A and B act in terms of their immediate, rational self-interest, then the outcome for both (-2 each) is worse than if they had chosen to act with regard for the other (-1 each).

Put another way, in game theory terms, the *Nash equilibrium point* in the prisoner's dilemma game – the 'position in which neither side can then independently change its strategy without ending up in a less desirable position' (Fisher, 2008, p. 18) – is not the optimal solution. The Nash equilibrium in this game is the 'betray–betray' option: and once at this point, neither side can independently move without making things worse for themselves. Yes, this is a trap, and means that neither can achieve the optimal solution.

To summarise, then, in the prisoner's dilemma game, if both parties act according to their immediate self-interest, the outcome is worst for all (Axelrod, 1984; Rapoport, 1960). This is a *lose–lose* outcome, and this can be seen as 'an abstract formulation of some very common and interesting situations' in the real world (Axelrod, 1984, p. 9). For instance, my partner and I are having an argument, and we both know that the way to resolve this is to communicate to the other in a more tender way, rather than with hostility. Yet this co-hostility is the Nash equilibrium point: if I move towards a softer position, and she does not, I lose out (I feel humiliated), and vice versa. Even though, then, we are better off moving out of our positions, it is not easy to do so (Fisher, 2008). Another personal example, on a larger scale: if I get on to a crowded underground train, it is not in my personal interests to move down the carriage. I have to walk more and end up further from the door. However, if everyone else also acts according to the same individualistic logic – hanging round the train doors rather than moving down the carriage – then everyone loses out: fewer people can get on to the trains. Similarly, Rapoport (1960), writing in the 1960s, described the arms race as a scaled-up version of the prisoner's dilemma game. Country A and Country B have the choice to arm or not arm, and both countries might think that, by arming, they can gain security in relation to the other nation. But the problem, of course, is that if Country A spends money on arms, then this motivates Country B to do the same, and vice versa.

What we also see in these examples, and as touched on above, is that, in reality, most 'games' are played out numerous times. And the more extended the time period, the more non-zero-sum they become. If, for instance, the prisoner's dilemma game is played only once, then the difference between dysergetic and synergetic solutions would not be that great (from -2 to -4). But if the game were played ten times or a thousand times, then the differences between the most and least synergetic approaches could be vast. Moreover, as a game extends over time, so the strategy that a person adopts in one round has the capacity to impact back on them in subsequent rounds. Person A, for instance, may get away with betraying Person B if they play just one round of the prisoner's dilemma game, but if they play this game ten or a thousand times, Person B will quickly learn that they are better off betraying back – to the detriment of Person A and the dyad overall. Again, then, with more time comes the potential for more or less synergetic configurations.

At this point, what may be obvious to the reader (and, hopefully, of interest) is the parallels between game theory at the interpersonal level and the intrapersonal processes explored earlier in the book. Just as goals, for instance, can go rogue (Chapter 8), so we can see how people can end up acting in terms of immediate self-interest, even if it is to the detriment of the greater whole. At an intrapersonal level, we can envisage people as constantly getting stuck in Nash equilibrium points, where they know what is going to be most helpful overall but cannot get out of their ruts because of the immediate costs. Logan, for instance, knows that he is better off seeing himself in a more positive light: quietening his critical voice and giving more space and acceptance to his vulnerability. But his vulnerable side is terrified of coming out its bunker and facing the full force of the critical voice; his critical side is terrified of giving ground and letting his vulnerabilities overwhelm. So relationships, at an intrapersonal level, remain betray–betray, neither side risking a more cooperative stance. As we begin to explore ways of forming more synergetic interpersonal relationships, then, we can also begin to consider the implications for intrapersonal relating.

CONCLUSION

In this chapter, we have seen how the structural model of directionality, developed at the individual level (Chapter 6), can be extended to interpersonal levels of organisation. From dyads to nations, it has been proposed that collections of individuals can have directions – irreducible to the directions of their individual constituents – which can function in synergetic or dysergetic ways. Game theory has been used to develop this analysis, and later on in this book we will look at what has been learned from it in terms of facilitating synergetic functioning (Chapter 16). At this stage, however, perhaps the most important 'take away' point from this chapter is that the structural model developed in this book can be – and has been – effectively transposed to different levels of organisation. This suggests that it is a robust and replicable structure. It also suggests that this framework has the potential to account for a wide variety of phenomena: from individual to group to societal actions.

QUESTIONS FOR REFLECTION

- Consider one of your closest interpersonal relationships. What are the synergies in this relationship for you and what are the dysergies?

- Identify a current situation which involves you and someone close to you having to make a decision (for instance, whether to go on holiday together, or whether to talk about a difficult issue). See if you are able to develop a payoff matrix for it. What is the Nash equilibrium point? What is the solution with the greatest overall benefit?

FURTHER READING

Axelrod, R. (1984). *The evolution of cooperation*. New York: Basic Books. Classic, very readable text detailing the outcomes of the prisoner's dilemma tournament and what it can teach us about human conflict and cooperation.

Koestler, A. (1967). *The ghost in the machine*. London: Pan. Dated, but a very valuable text introducing such key concepts as holons and the holoarchy.

The Evolution of Trust (http://ncase.me/trust/) Excellent online game theory tutorial.

PART II
RESOURCES FOR AN INTEGRATIVE PRACTICE
Putting the elephant back together

This part of the book reviews the four principal approaches to individual therapy, and shows how their theories and practices can be understood within the theoretical framework outlined in Part I. That is, I hope to show that, underneath the differences in theories, concepts, and practices, each of these approaches understands clients in directional ways: as agentic beings who come to experience psychological difficulties because their directions conflict with each other, or because their means of actualising their higher-order directions are ineffective. Hence, each approach strives to help clients become better at actualising their higher-order desires and goals: by developing more synergetic internal configurations, and by finding more effective ways of progressing towards what they want. Here, therapy is essentially a process of 'restructuring the goal hierarchy and identifying alternative means of goal attainment' (Michalak et al., 2004, p. 93).

Moreover, in different ways, each of these therapies strives to help clients embed these new ways of being as 'habits', so that they become a natural and non-effortful part of the client's life. In terms of the four stages of competence (Gordon Training International, 2016), this can be understood as a movement from 'unconscious incompetence' at achieving certain goals to 'conscious incompetence', followed by 'conscious competence', and finally 'unconscious competence'.

Clearly, as we will see, differences exist across each of these orientations. Each posits different highest-order directions and also conceptualises core conflicts in different terms. However, from the standpoint of contemporary value pluralism (see Chapter 6), there would be serious ethical problems in attempting to claim that any one of these highest-order directions, or core conflicts, is the universal concern for all clients for all times. Hence, within a contemporary therapeutic framework, it would seem quite possible – if not ethically necessary – to allow these different perspectives to co-exist: as 'resources' that different therapists can draw on at different times in response to clients' particular interests, issues, and preferences.

As we will also see, one of the principal ways in which the therapeutic approaches differ is that some are more insight-oriented, while others are more focused on planning and actions (Grawe, 2004). On the left bank of the Rubicon are the 'clarification-oriented' approaches which focus on clarifying motives and forming clear intentions; on the right bank of the Rubicon are the 'mastery-oriented' approaches which focus on realising intentions and acting with volition. However, as with Grawe's (2004) use of the Rubicon model, the directional arc helps us to see how these differing foci can be conceptualised as part of a single process: only at different phases (Figure II.1). Here, psychodynamic, humanistic, and existential approaches tend to focus on the awareness and evaluation phases, with the existential approaches particularly focused on the moment of intent. Cognitive and behavioural approaches then focus more specifically on the post-intentional phases: planning, action, and feedback.

Viewed in this way, incompatibilities across the approaches tend to dissolve. Rather, different approaches can be seen as being more or less helpful to different clients at different points in time, depending on what they might need and want to help them along their directional trajectory. A client, for instance, who wants to work out what they really want in life may be most helped by an awareness- and evaluation-focused therapy, while a client who wants specific plans to help them achieve specific goals may be much more helped by a planning- and action-focused approach. And, for some clients, and with sufficient time in therapy, each (or some) of these phases may be an important part of the therapeutic work: space to recognise and work out what they want; support for committing to and planning particular actions; and then encouragement to take action, review, and terminate as and when appropriate.

For Grawe (2004), 'therapists should be experienced in moving around on both banks of the Rubicon landscape' (p. 300). However, given that training programmes tend to be based around specific orientations (at least in the UK), and that therapists

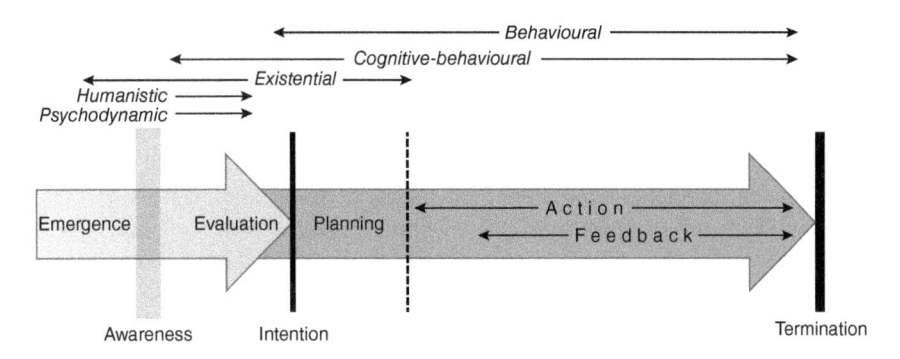

Figure II.1 Foci of different therapeutic approach along the directional arc

may have preferences for one bank or the other, it does not seem essential that all counsellors and psychotherapists are equally competent in clarification- and mastery-oriented practices. Rather, from a pluralistic standpoint (Cooper & McLeod, 2011), what would seem important is that therapists have an awareness of where their own skills are, and the ability and humility to recognise when an onward referral may be appropriate. Nevertheless, recognising the different ways in which different approaches can help clients progress along the directional arc may be an essential knowledge base for all therapists: helping us to recognise what might be possible, and the different skills and understandings that we may want to develop for the future.

In addition, from the present framework, an understanding of the sociopolitical landscape surrounding the field as a whole may be an important addition to a therapist's set of competencies, as developed in the politically-informed approaches to therapy (see Box II.1).

BOX II.1
Politically-informed approaches

Politically-informed approaches to therapy are orientations, theories, methods, or frameworks that understand – and strive to address – clients' problems in the context of the 'mechanisms and structures of power and control within society' (McLeod, 2013, p. 503). These approaches have been particularly well developed in the American counselling psychology field (e.g., Enns & Williams, 2013; Toporek, Gerstein, Fouad, Roysircar, & Israel, 2006). They include feminist therapies (e.g., Brown, 2008; Chaplin, 1988), multicultural approaches (e.g., Enns & Williams, 2013), LGBT- (lesbian, gay, bisexual, transgender) affirmative practices (Barker, 2017), and anti-discriminatory practices (Lago & Smith, 2010), as well as the newly-developed *Power Threat Meaning Framework* (Johnstone & Boyle, 2018). They may be applied as 'stand-alone' therapies, integrated into other therapeutic practices, or viewed as 'meta-level' frameworks for the therapeutic field as a whole. These

(Continued)

approaches are generally less well developed and prevalent than the four approaches described in this Part of the book. However, they are strongly aligned with the present framework – and make a critical contribution to its development – because of their consideration of the social, cultural, and political factors that can stop people from actualising their directions.

This may be through a number of processes. First, sociopolitical factors may undermine the self-efficacy of people from marginalised groups, so that they do not have the confidence to move from desires to intentions to planned actions (see Chapter 3). From a feminist therapy perspective, for instance, it might be argued that Mei has been socialised to believe that she needs a man – Rob, Saul, or whoever – to achieve happiness and self-worth, and that she cannot achieve this on her own. Most importantly, perhaps, it may also be in terms of the actual, 'external' barriers that are put in the way of marginalised groups, in terms of prejudice, discrimination, and social inequalities, and that prevent them from actualising their directions. For instance, Logan, who is from a working-class background, is likely to struggle much more to actualise his desire to be an architect than someone from an affluent background. His sense of demoralisation and hopelessness at achieving this goal – and, arguably, his turning to drugs as an alternative means towards experiencing 'fulfilment' – is not just about internal inefficiencies and dysergies, but about real economic barriers in the world he inhabits. In addition, it could be argued that people from minority and oppressed groups are laden with a host of extrinsic, self-inconsistent desires, goals, and expectations – much more so than for members of the dominant majority, who set their goals for themselves. As we have seen, for instance, young women in Western societies may be socialised into goals around thinness and beauty (Irving & Cannon, 2000), goals which, from a feminist perspective, may be seen as serving patriarchal interests by weakening women and diverting their attention from real political inequalities.

On this basis, politically-informed approaches propose a number of strategies for helping to support all clients to actualise their directions. These include:

- Helping clients to develop insight into how their problems may have been shaped by social, cultural, political, and economic factors (such as racism, poverty, gender roles, or refugee status) rather than pathologising or 'psychologising' their difficulties.
- Celebrating diversity: encouraging clients to accept, express, and prize their uniqueness (including their unique desires and goals).
- Therapist self-reflexivity: ensuring that internalised prejudices towards clients from marginalised groups can be bracketed.
- Therapist cultural competence: actively developing a knowledge and awareness of the experiences of clients from particular marginalised groups, and the challenges that they face.
- Working to build an egalitarian, collaborative relationship with clients in which clients feel empowered to voice – and actualise – their desires and goals.
- Therapist awareness of how power and cultural dynamics may be enacted in the therapeutic relationship (e.g., older male therapist talking down to a young female client).
- Supporting clients to initiate, and be involved in, political change in their own lives and communities.

- Therapist engagement in political activities that challenge social injustices and inequalities.
- Developing services to support specific marginalised groups, such as refugees or survivors of domestic violence. (Ballinger, 2017; Barker, 2010; Ivey & Brooks-Harris, 2005; Lago & Smith, 2010; McLeod, 2013)

Further discussion of politically-informed approaches to addressing emotional distress can be found in the *Power Threat Meaning Framework* (Johnstone & Boyle, 2018)

10

PSYCHODYNAMIC APPROACHES WITHIN A DIRECTIONAL FRAMEWORK

Change through awareness

This chapter discusses:

- The psychodynamic model of human being, oriented around unconscious conflicts.
- Psychodynamic perspectives on the highest-order directions: life, death, and relatedness.
- Core conflicts within the psychodynamic approaches: id versus ego.
- Key elements of psychodynamic practice, as viewed through a directional lens: free association, interpretation, and analysing the resistance.

The psychodynamic approaches are a family of therapies, rooted in the work of Freud, that aim to help clients develop a greater awareness and understanding of the unconscious forces determining their thoughts, feelings, and behaviours. Psychodynamic therapies have been shown to be effective for a range of psychological problems, including depression, anxiety, and personality disorders (Barber et al., 2013). In this chapter, we will primarily focus on the classical psychodynamic approach. However, variants of psychodynamic therapy, such as the Jungian approach or contemporary relational psychoanalysis, can also be very much understood in terms of directionalities, synergies, and dysergies.

MODEL OF THE HUMAN BEING

As the name suggests, at the heart of the psycho*dynamic* approaches is an understanding of human beings in terms of directional phenomena, such as 'instincts', 'drives', 'needs', 'wishes', and 'desires' (Samuels, 1986). *Instincts* form the basis for classical Freudian theory, and can be defined as innate biologically determined drives to action (Rycroft, 1995, see Web Resource 3.2). Instincts have been conceptualised as having four parts: a biological source, a supply of energy, an aim, and an object (Rycroft, 1995). In contrast to the present framework, classical psychoanalytic theory tends to emphasise the causal role that these forces have in determining human behaviour – choice and free will being illusory. However, the concept of instincts *per se* is not dissimilar from the embodied directionality described in Chapter 2: an organised, mobilising, bodily responding to the world in a meaningful way.

An understanding of human experiencing and behaviour as intelligible – however random, accidental, or irrational it may seem to be – is also at the heart of a psychodynamic approach. Indeed, Freud's very *raison d'être* was to show 'the sense of symptoms' (Freud, 1962, p. 296). That is, that 'even the delusional ideas of the insane would certainly be found to have a sense if only we understood how to translate them' (Freud, 1962, p. 296). In the classic case of 'Little Hans's, for instance, Freud argues that his seemingly irrational phobia of horses actually stemmed from a fear that his father would punish him, through castration, for sexual desires towards his mother (Freud, 2002). Hans's avoidance of horses, then, can be understood as an intelligible – albeit problematic – attempt to achieve a particular (avoidance) goal.

As with Little Hans, psychodynamic theory particularly focuses on how clients' pasts shape their present behaviour and experiences, including within the therapeutic relationship itself. In terms of the present framework, this can be understood as the way that people establish particular means towards higher-order desires and goals – based on certain experiences and beliefs – and how those means can then become outdated and ineffective – but chronically activated – within the present context (see Childhood Experiences, in Chapter 7). Within the psychodynamic field, this is primarily in relation to interpersonal assumptions and behaviours. Contemporary attachment-based psychodynamic therapists, for instance, refer to internal working models: chronic expectations about the self, significant others, and the relationship between the two (Curtis & Hirsch, 2003). Mei's early relationship with her mother and her teachers, for instance, has led her to assume that others will criticise and undermine her. Hence, to attain her higher-order goal of safety, she assumes that she needs to be very cautious in how she relates to others. To open up, assumes Mei, would be to leave herself vulnerable to hurt and attack. Feminist psychodynamic therapists refer to such patterns as *chronic strategies of disconnection* (Jordan, Kaplan, Miller, Stiver, & Surrey, 1991). These are means that we have developed to keep 'safe' from interpersonal hurts (for instance, putting up a façade, not expressing our wants, becoming compliant), but which stop us from fulfilling a highest-order desire for relatedness (Cooper & Knox, 2018).

Central to the psychodynamic approaches, however, is also the assumption that the majority of these processes operate at an unconscious level (Barber et al., 2013). That is, that people are generally not aware of the directions underlying their experiences and behaviour, or the beliefs that mediate them. More than that, though, it holds that people actively *repress* (that is, render unconscious) 'unacceptable' impulses or ideas as a means of reducing levels of anxiety (see below; Rycroft, 1995). In terms of the present framework, this can be understood to mean that, at times, people will experience desires that threaten other higher-order directions (in particular, safety) and hence will strive to push those former desires away.

Within psychodynamic theory, repression is hypothesised to be just one of several 'defence mechanisms' that may be used to try to keep unacceptable directions at bay (Magnavita, 2008). Other mechanisms include *regression* (returning to an earlier level of functioning), *projection* (seeing our negated desires in another), and *sublimation* (transforming our desires into socially acceptable aims, such as making art). As with repression, each of these can be seen as intelligible means – albeit unconscious ones – of striving towards a higher-order goal of safety.

Within psychodynamic theory, these defences can range from primitive mechanisms (such as somatisation, regression, dissociation, denial, and acting out) to more mature ones (such as sublimation, compensation, and the use of humour), and the application of primitive mechanism is seen as a principal antecedent of psychological difficulties. Essentially, this is the 'law of unintended consequences': the individual strives to protect themselves from anxiety and threat but does so in ways that make matters worse in other areas of their lives. We might hypothesise, for instance, that Logan smokes cannabis to repress the anxiety he experiences in the world: a consequence of his rock-bottom self-confidence. This does, temporarily at least, achieve this goal. But, in doing so, he anesthetises himself, and therefore makes it more difficult for him to actualise other important directions in his life, such as a sense of self-worth and creative expression. In addition, from a psychodynamic standpoint, because the defended-against directions are unlikely to go away (the 'return of the repressed'), they may continually threaten to 'break through' to the surface: creating anxiety and a sense of threat. And if they do break through, unmediated by conscious control, they may be expressed in chaotic and highly destructive ways: rogue goals (see Chapter 8). So when Logan's anxiety does surface, he feels desperate, terrified, and out of control: 'I just don't know what hit me, it's like I'm sucked into a whirlpool.'

From this psychodynamic standpoint, we cannot get rid of socially unacceptable wishes and desires, and therefore defence mechanisms will always be required. However, what we can do is to move from more primitive and unconscious means of defending against them, to more mature and constructive strategies. For instance, rather than trying to deal with his anxiety through smoking cannabis, Logan might take up a sport, like basketball, through which he can 'run off' some of his anxiety. Or he might develop skills to assertively express his anxiety, so that he is able to get some support for it. In terms of the present framework, what we have here is essentially the development of more effective, longer-term strategies for achieving our highest-order directions, and ones that are less damaging to – that is, dysergetic with – other higher-order directions.

HIGHEST-ORDER DIRECTIONS

Freud's theory went through a number of changes, much of it based around the nature of human beings' higher-order desires and the means by which these are achieved. However, the desire for pleasure – or, more precisely, the desire to avoid pain and displeasure, through gratifying instinctual tensions – is always central to Freud's thinking. In his earlier theory, this is expressed through the 'libidinal' drive (and later, the 'life instinct'), with Freud also positing an aggressive drive (later connected with a 'death instinct') (Wolitzky, 2003). This latter 'drive to return to the inanimate state' (Rycroft, 1995) was particularly taken up by Klein and her followers, who charted the means by which the child's destructive impulses are expressed (Greenberg & Mitchell, 1983). However, the death instinct, as a highest-order desire, is contested by many in the psychodynamic field (Schwartz, 2012); it can be understood as a means towards a higher-order desire of pleasure (through the extinction of all excitation) or as the consequence of goal-directed activities being frustrated (Curtis & Hirsch, 2003).

Within contemporary relational approaches to psychodynamic theory, and particularly attachment theory, the emphasis is much more on relatedness as the highest-order direction (Curtis & Hirsch, 2003; Schwartz, 2012). However, from an evolutionary attachment perspective, it might be argued that this focus on attachment, in itself, is a means towards a higher-order goal of safety and survival.

CORE CONFLICT

Within the psychodynamic field, inner conflict is considered 'inevitable and ubiquitous' (Wolitzky, 2003, p. 30) – Freud (1962) believed that mental life was 'interlaced'

INTRODUCTION: RESOURCES FOR AN INTEGRATIVE PRACTICE

with contradictions and polarities. As suggested above, this is primarily conceptualised as a conflict between the desire for immediate gratification (though, for instance, sex and aggression) and the desire to behave within socially-sanctioned parameters. However, it is important to note that, from a psychodynamic perspective, the latter is not seen as independent from the desire for pleasure or aggression, but as an outgrowth of it (Wolitzky, 2003). That is, we learn that, to genuinely achieve pleasure in the world, we often need to conform to the wishes of others or delay gratification. In this respect, then, the core psychodynamic conflict is similar to the basic conflict between short-term and long-term directions (see Chapter 5), but all aiming towards the same highest-order goal.

In Freud's (1923) 'structural model', this conflict is conceptualised in terms of the battle between *id, ego*, and *superego* (see Figure 10.1). Here, the id's desire for unadulterated, hedonistic gratification (the *pleasure principle*) comes up against the superego's desire for moral and socially sanctioned behaviour, with the ego being that part of the person that is attempting to mediate between these two powerful forces in relation to the external world (the *reality principle*; Magnavita, 2008). Here, the intrapsychic conflict is specifically conceptualised as being deliberate, rather than incidental (see Chapter 8), with the ego working to silence and control the id's desires.

A classic example of this is given in Figure 10.1, which we can think about in relation to Mei. She has strong sexual desires towards Saul – her libidinous id – but at the same time wants to 'behave well' to gain social acceptance: she cannot, for instance, simply pounce on Saul by the water cooler. So her ego manages the tension by repressing her feelings. But the problem, here, is the unintended consequences: by pushing down her sexual desire she also cuts herself off from her body, deadens herself, and perhaps even starts to somatise (for instance, through physical ailments).

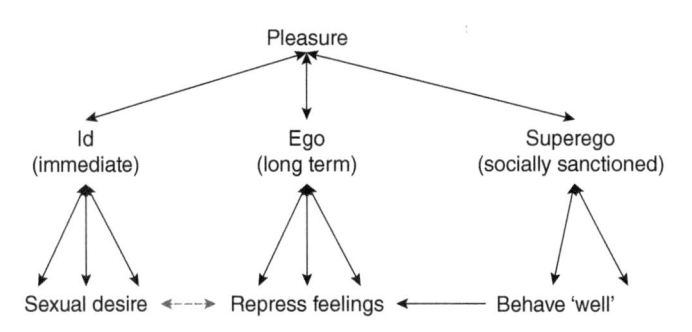

Figure 10.1 Psychodynamic structural model

In terms of core conflicts, Klein's developmental theory provides a useful way of conceptualising the relationship between different highest-order desires. In the 'paranoid-schizoid' position, there is a black-and-white splitting between the 'good' and the 'bad' object, but as the child matures, they move to the 'depressive position', in which the good and the bad can be conceptualised as existing in the same entity (Segal, 2014). In this respect, we can think of the child as moving from a phase in which conflicting directions towards the same object are expressed serially (i.e., diachronic dysergies, see Chapter 8) to a phase in which they are able to experience these conflicting directions in parallel (i.e., synchronic dysergies). For instance, rather than shifting between desperately wanting their mother and desperately wanting to push her away, the child may come to a position where they see the mother as someone they both love and hate. As the name suggests, this 'depressive' position means accepting the loss of both idealised goal-objects; but it is also more realistic, and allows for the possibility of more synergetic configurations to emerge. For instance, the child may then be able to move to a position of 'I want my mother's love, but I also need to get it in a way that does not leave me feeling abandoned.'

PRACTICE

In terms of the directional arc (Chapter 3), the focus of the psychodynamic approaches is particularly on the initial phases of emergence and awareness (or what can also be termed 'insight'). Here, the therapist's task is to 'help the person surmount his or her "defences" in order to discover what he or she really intended' (Bruner, 2001, p. x). This might involve tracing back from behaviours, emotions, dreams, and symptoms to help clients identify what those higher order desires might be. For instance, through a psychodynamic analysis, Mei might start to recognise that she is very avoidant of real intimacy, because she is so afraid of getting hurt, but also that she desperately yearns for relatedness with others. Through such insight, she can then review whether she really wants to continue behaving in this way, or whether there would be more utility for her in allowing closeness with others. In addition, insight, in itself, may fulfil a higher-order need for clarity and control (Grawe, 2004).

As an approach which hypothesises that these desires are pushed – deliberately and forcefully – far back into the unconscious, it tends to hold that space, time, and therapist expertise are required to bring these directions to the fore.

Free association

To help clients develop insight – and to develop the skill of doing this on their own (Caspar, 1995) – the 'first rule' of psychodynamic therapies (Bailly, 2012) is to invite clients to *free associate*: that is, to report whatever comes into their heads, without censorship or conscious deliberation (Magnavita, 2008). Through doing so, there is a greater possibility that the client's genuine desires, intentions, and goals – as well as other experiences, beliefs, and emotions – will emerge; free from the ego's conscious agenda. Here, the role of the psychodynamic therapist is to listen to the client 'with evenly hovering attention', and without judgement, interruption, or personal agendas coming in. Gradually, through this process, the client may come to reveal – and recognise for themselves – more of their directions. 'I like it here', Logan might say, early on in psychodynamic therapy, 'I like talking to you'. Later on, as he feels freer to talk, he might reveal deeper, less socially acceptable desires. 'Sometimes, I just don't want to tell you anything', 'It just flit through my mind that what would happen if I got angry and thought about breaking things?'

Interpretation

In psychodynamic therapies, the therapist supports this process of developing insight through the well-evidenced practice of *interpretation* (see Williams, 2002). This can be defined as 'a verbal intervention, which makes something that is unconscious conscious and by doing so offers a new formulation of meaning and motivation' (Yakeley, 2014, p. 35). In this respect, psychodynamic interpretations are particularly concerned with identifying the unconscious wishes, desires, and intents that are implicit in a client's experiences, behaviours, and symptoms. And, of course, classical Freudian practice was particularly interested in detecting the censored and forbidden wishes that were expressed – in heavily disguised and symbolic form – in a client's dreams (Freud, 1962).

This process of interpretation may be *reconstructive*, whereby clients' experiences or behaviours are linked to their pasts (Yakeley, 2014). With Mei, for instance, a therapist might say, 'I wonder if you fear being honest and open with Saul because you experienced so much pushing away as a child'.

On the other hand, the interpretation may be *transferential*, whereby it focuses on the here-and-now relationship between therapist and client (Yakeley, 2014). As suggested above, from a psychodynamic perspective, clients' beliefs, expectations, desires, and means towards those desires may be displaced onto – and enacted within – the therapeutic relationship; hence this relationship itself can be a focus for the interpretative work. In the following dialogue, for example, a psychodynamic therapist invites Mei to track back from her in-therapy behaviour to her higher-order desires and means.

THERAPIST I wonder if, when you arrive late at the sessions, what you are trying to tell me is that you don't really care about the therapy. It's not important to you. Yet I also sense it really is.

MEI I get– Maybe there's a bit of a rebellious part of me. I don't try and be late, but if I am running late I think I don't have to be a 'good girl', turning up on time all the time.

THERAPIST You don't want me to see you as a good girl?

MEI There is something maybe about saying, 'get off', 'leave me alone', 'I don't need you'.

THERAPIST It's really important for me to know that you don't need me?
MEI Yes, something like that. 'Back off'. It doesn't feel safe.
THERAPIST You want to feel safe. And to do that you feel you need to push me away. But I also wonder what the consequences are of doing that to people....

Here, we can also see how the therapist invites Mei to consider what the implications of this strategy might be in terms of her relationship with others. For instance, at some level, is she trying to communicate to Saul and Rob that she really does not need them?

More broadly, from both a psychodynamic perspective and the present framework, we can consider each act of the client within the session as a directional one: striving to actualise some form of desire or goal. What is Mei trying to do, for instance, when she tells me, with a half-grimace, that she and Rob have not had sex for two years? Is she trying to communicate how bad her life is? Is she wanting me to know that sex is important to her? Is she trying to amuse me and get me to like her? Psychodynamically, many of these in-session directions will be at an unconscious, implicit level. Hence, as May (1969a) writes, the task of the therapist is to be conscious, as best they can, 'of what the intentionality of the patient is in a particular session' (p. 247), and to help the client develop an awareness of this.

To facilitate this process of analysis, psychodynamic therapists – particularly of the more classical type – tend to be cautious about disclosing their own directions: their agenda, preferences, or opinions (Jones, 2014). The goal, here, is to be a 'blank canvas' – to manage and bracket off 'countertransferential' feelings – such that the client's own directionality can be seen in the clearest possible light. In addition, such 'analytical neutrality' is advocated as a means of respecting the uniqueness and individuality of clients, and their right to find their own answers in their own way – without the therapist taking sides (Wolitzky, 2003).

Analysing the resistance

'Every patient who comes to treatment wishes both to change and to remain embedded in his or her old world', state Curtis and Hirsch (2003, p. 81). *Resistance* is the psychodynamic term for that latter force: 'the opposition encountered during psychoanalytical treatment to the process of making unconscious processes conscious' (Rycroft, 1995, p. 158). This resistance might be against the process of free association, or it might be towards the therapists' interpretations. Either way, in terms of the present framework, we can understand resistance as a means towards a higher-order goal – in most cases, perhaps, safety – which runs into conflict with other higher-order directions: for instance, greater wellbeing, through more insight and awareness. Logan, for instance, wants to feel better, and he knows that he has to talk about things in therapy to achieve this. But when the therapist asks him about his early childhood, he starts to experience a quiver in his stomach: a sense of threat. And so, to re-establish feelings of safety, he ignores the therapist's question, or perhaps criticises what they say: 'I just don't know', he answers irritably. This resistance, then, can be understood an intelligible, agentic behaviour – the 'wisdom of the resistance' – but it is also a pathogenic one: because it sacrifices higher-order, longer-term directions for more short-term, immediately important ones (see Chapter 5). If the therapist can help the client see this – without provoking further opposition, for instance through open questions and minimal encouragers (Mahalik, 2002) – then this may help the client find more synergetic and effective means of progressing towards their higher-order goals.

BOX 10.1

Cognitive analytic therapy

Cognitive analytic therapy (CAT) is a contemporary psychodynamic model that also draws on cognitive-behavioural insights. It specifically understands human beings as existing within a nexus of interpersonal intentions and meanings (Dunn, 2014; Ryle, 1990). Here, mind is conceptualised in terms of goal-directed sequences of planning, acting, and sensitivity to feedback, all the time perceiving and interpreting (or misinterpreting) the intentions of others. Consistent with the present framework, CAT understands psychological difficulties in terms of fixed and inflexible ways of acting, and an absence of the self-reflectivity needed to identify more effective ways of acting. CAT also identifies three particular patterns of behaviour and thinking that can stop us moving forward in our lives. Traps are vicious cycles of thinking, feeling, and behaviour that confirm the negative assumptions driving them. For instance, Logan believes that he will fail in his life, he gives up easily, and thereby proves to himself his original assumption. Dilemmas are 'false dichotomised choices of thinking, feeling and acting neither of which work' (Dunn, 2014, p. 366). Logan, for instance, believes 'If I'm not in absolute control of my feelings, then everything will burst apart'. Consequently, he tries to quash all feeling; but in doing so, he generates a whole set of unintended consequences that take him further, rather than closer, to his higher-order goal of feeling safe. Finally, snags are 'the sabotaging of appropriate intention due to negative beliefs about self and other' (p. 366). In terms of the present framework, these are ways that we deliberately stop ourselves from actualising certain highest-order directions because we fear that its achievement will undermine another, more implicit, direction (i.e., a horizontal conflict). At some level, for instance, we might hypothesise that Logan sabotages his own success because he fears that, if he did succeed, he would no longer know who he is. 'I've been a failure all my life,' says Logan, 'at least I have the comfort of knowing who I am.'

CONCLUSION

With their focus on wishes and desires, their assumption that all human experiencing is meaningful, and their understanding of psychological difficulties in terms of intrapsychic conflicts, the psychodynamic approaches fit well with the current framework. Furthermore, these approaches make a distinctive contribution to this framework in a range of ways:

- An appreciation of the unconscious nature of many desires, intentions, and goals.
- The understanding that directions may deliberately fight against other directions – not just incidentally divert from them.
- An understanding of the value of insight – through free association, interpretation, and analysis of the resistance – as a means of helping clients find more effective and synergetic ways of actualising their desires.
- The development of a 'neutral' therapeutic stance, such that the client's directions may most clearly be seen.

QUESTIONS FOR REFLECTION

- Think of a client you are currently working with (perhaps one that you are experiencing as challenging). What unconscious directions may be underpinning their actions in therapy? (That is, what are they really trying to do with you?). Is there a way that, helpfully, you could facilitate their awareness of this?

---- FURTHER READING ----

Bateman, A., Brown, D. and Pedder, J. (2010). *Introduction to psychotherapy: An outline of psychodynamic principles and practice* (4th ed.). London: Routledge. Clear and comprehensive introduction to psychodynamic theory and its application to practice.

Lemma, A. (2015). *Introduction to the practice of psychoanalytic psychotherapy.* (2nd ed.) London: Wiley-Blackwell. Popular, in-depth introduction to the psychodynamic field.

Howard, S. (2017). *Skills in psychodynamic counselling and psychotherapy.* London: Sage. Practical, concise guide to psychodynamic methods.

11

HUMANISTIC APPROACHES WITHIN A DIRECTIONAL FRAMEWORK

Helping directions unfurl

This chapter discusses:

- The humanistic model of human being as growth-oriented and agentic.
- Humanistic perspectives on highest-order directions: actualisation.
- Core conflicts within the humanistic approaches: actualisation versus social approval.
- Key elements of humanistic practice, as viewed through a directional lens: space to talk, unconditional positive regard, empathy, emotion-focused work, facilitating internal and external dialogue.

Humanistic therapies are a family of counselling and psychotherapeutic approaches that emphasise human beings' capacity to 'grow' and to develop their potential (Cain, Keenan, & Rubin, 2016a). They are relatively well supported by the empirical evidence, particularly for depression (Elliott, Greenberg, Watson, Timulak, & Freire, 2013). The approaches emerged in the 1940s and 1950s, initially in the USA, through the works of such founding fathers as Maslow, Rogers, and Bugental. Rogers's (1951) person-centred approach is probably the most widely practised of the humanistic therapies, particularly in the UK. Other therapies that are generally agreed to fall within the humanistic umbrella are Gestalt therapy (Perls et al., 1951), focusing (Gendlin, 1996), emotion-focused therapy (Greenberg et al., 1993), and psychodrama (Moreno, 1946) (Cain, Keenan, & Rubin, 2016b). A range of other therapies can also be considered to be broadly consistent with the humanistic stance, including transactional analysis (TA; Berne, 1961), reality therapy (Glasser, 1965), and psychosynthesis (Assagioli, 1965).

MODEL OF THE HUMAN BEING

As a field which is rooted in existential and phenomenological philosophy (see Chapter 2) – and which emerged as a reaction to the mechanistic behaviourist and psychoanalytic models of its day – humanistic approaches hold a fundamentally directional understanding of human being. Here, people are understood as wanting, motivated, intentional beings, who strive – consciously or unconsciously – towards the satisfaction of their 'fundamental desires' (Bugental, 1981; Maslow, 1987; Rogers, 1951). Rogers (1951), for instance, writes, 'one of the most basic characteristics of organic life is its tendency toward total, organized, goal-directed responses' (p. 487); and he describes behaviour as the 'goal-directed attempt of the organism' to satisfy its experienced needs (Rogers, 1959, p. 222). Humanistic practices like Gestalt therapy, reality therapy, and transactional analysis (TA) also place directional constructs – such as 'needs', 'wants', and 'psychobiological hungers' – at the core of their models (Clarkson, 1989; Sills, 2014).

An explicitly teleological understanding of human being – 'persons as future-oriented processes' (Bohart, 2001, p. 100) – is also evident across the humanistic field (see, for instance, Maslow, 1987). A principal goal of psychosynthesis, for instance, is to cultivate in clients 'the ability to purposefully direct psychological energies … in line with our highest values, deepest aspirations and a sense of meaning. … [That is] what deeply matters to us, "what makes our heart sing"' (Sieroda, 2012, p. 333). This is, perhaps, most evident in TA's concept of *life scripts* (see Web Resource 11.1).

Maslow's (1987) understanding of human motivation – in terms of 'means' and 'ends' – comes particularly close to the vertical hierarchies described in Chapter 7 of this book. He writes:

> We want money so that we can have an automobile. In turn we want an automobile because the neighbours have one and we do not wish to feel inferior to

them, so we can retain our own self-respect and so we can be loved and respected by others. Usually when a conscious desire is analyzed we find that we can go behind it, so to speak, to other, more fundamental aims of the individual. (p. 47)

An understanding of people as agentic, creative beings – whose 'direction' emerges from 'within' (Rogers, 1961) – is also central to humanistic approaches (Bohart & Tallman, 1999). Therapeutically, this means that clients are conceptualised as active agents who make therapy work, rather than as passive recipients of therapeutic techniques and interventions (Bohart & Tallman, 1999). This claim is supported by research which shows that 'clients make the single strongest contribution to outcome' (Bohart & Wade, 2013, p. 219). It has been estimated, for instance, that client factors, such as their levels of motivation, involvement in, and hope for therapy as well as their life events and external circumstances, account for almost 90% of therapeutic change (Bohart & Wade, 2013; Cooper, 2008).

Relatively uniquely, humanistic therapies (and in particular the person-centred approach) see people as having a natural tendency towards greater *self-healing*. That is, we tend to 'self-right' and move towards a resolution of our issues (Bohart & Tallman, 1999). Rogers, for instance, writes that the client is the one 'who knows what hurts, what directions to go, what problems are crucial, what experiences have been deeply buried' (Rogers, 1961, pp. 11–12). This self-healing, however, is not conceptualised as a conscious, deliberative process. Rather, it is seen as an organismic tendency that will unfurl under the right conditions (see below). Rogers sees this natural, self-healing process as a movement towards greater self-awareness, self-liking, trust in one's self, and towards more intrinsic goals (Rogers, 1961). In support of this latter claim, research has shown that people do tend to shift towards intrinsic goals over time (Sheldon, Arndt, & Houser-Marko, 2003). More broadly, research shows that people can progress towards greater levels of wellbeing with even very minimal or placebo interventions (Bohart & Tallman, 1999; Cooper, 2008).

In terms of the present framework, this self-healing process can be conceptualised as a natural movement towards more effective and synergetic directional configurations (see Chapters 7 and 8). Indeed, Ryan and Deci (2004), like Jung, see the 'true self' as being 'integrative' in nature and serving a 'synthetic function'. For instance, as Logan starts to reflect on his use of cannabis, so he begins to consider – and move towards – ways of dealing with his anxiety that do not have such detrimental consequences. 'Maybe', he says, 'I could try out kick-boxing.' A natural self-healing tendency seems a reasonable claim: as we have argued, all else being equal, there is little reason why people would choose ineffective strategies over effective ones, or dysergetic means over synergetic ones. And, as cited above, there is some evidence to support a general tendency towards multifinal strategies (Chun et al., 2011). However, as we have seen, ineffective and dysergetic strategies have multiple payoffs – such as avoiding cognitive effort – that may make the starting balance far from 'equal'. In addition, as argued

HIGHEST-ORDER DIRECTIONS

For humanistic psychologists like Goldstein (1940) and Rogers (1980), there is one highest-order motive in human beings: *actualisation* (see Figure 11.1). This can be defined as 'the inherent tendency of the organism to develop all its capacities in ways which serve to maintain or enhance the organism' (Rogers, 1959, p. 196) – that is, to develop its potential (Cain, 2002). As indicated in Figure 11.1, this might involve actualisation of the organism's creative capabilities, or its capacity for relatedness, or any other of the potentials that the organism has. Drawing from Kierkegaard, Rogers (1961) also describes this basic striving as 'to be that self which one truly is' (p. 166). This is similar to Maslow's (1987) description of self-actualisation: 'the desire to become more and more what one idiosyncratically is, to become everything that one is capable of becoming' (p. 64). Note, however, that for Maslow, this need is one among several, rather than an all-encompassing, highest-order direction.

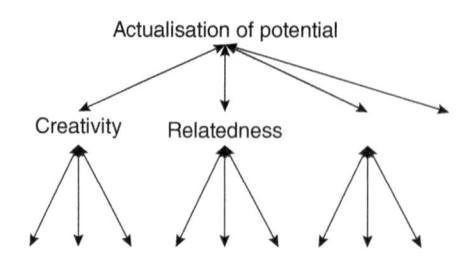

Figure 11.1 Humanistic structural model

For both Rogers (1959) and Maslow (1968), a basic distinction is made between those directional tendencies that serve to maintain the organism and those that serve to enhance it. Maslow refers to the former as *D-needs* (i.e., deficiency needs) and includes such 'lower-level' needs as food and physical safety. By contrast, he refers to self-enhancing directions as *B-needs* (i.e., being needs), which would include such 'higher-level' needs as autonomy, beauty, and purpose. D-needs operate on *homeostatic* principles: the person experiences a deficiency, and seeks to compensate for it, such that they can return to a state of equilibrium (cf. perceptual control theory, Box 6.1). By contrast, from a humanistic standpoint, B-needs operate on a different, *heterostatic* set of principles. Here, desires do not become satiated; rather, the person strives to fulfil them more and more. This distinction between deficiency-oriented and growth-oriented desires has many parallels with the avoidance/approach dichotomy, discussed in Chapter 5 of this book.

Although, as we have seen, the humanistic approaches posit a single, universal highest-order direction (actualisation), the non-specificity of this direction means that it can be actualised in a multiplicity of ways. In this respect, humanistic approaches tend to put particular emphasis on the uniqueness of each person (Cain, 2002). As Maslow (1987, see above) states, to actualise is to become more and more what one idiosyncratically is. This is also consistent with the fundamental values of humanistic therapies, which, like the present framework, 'believe that people have the right, desire, and ability to determine what is best for them and how they will achieve it' (Cain, 2002, p. 5).

CORE CONFLICT

Within the humanistic field, as with other approaches, psychological difficulties are primarily conceptualised in terms of conflicts between two fundamentally opposing forces. Indeed, humanistic psychologists have developed a concept of synergy that is very close to the present model. Maslow (1971) writes:

> I have found the concept of synergy useful for the understanding of intrapersonal psychodynamics. Sometimes this usefulness is very obvious, as in seeing integration within the person as high synergy, and intrapsychic dissociations of the ordinary pathological sort as low synergy, i.e., as a person torn and set against himself. (p. 202)

For humanistic psychology, the most basic conflict is between intrinsic, authentic directions and those that are considered extrinsic to a person's genuine experiences and desires (see Chapter 5). Billy Elliot wants to be a ballet dancer, but his coal miner father forbids it, and sends him to the gym to learn boxing. Maslow (1968) states: 'The primal choice, the fork in the road ... is between others and one's own self' (p. 52). Rogers (1951, 1959, 1961), in his classic person-centred model of development, argues that human beings come into the world with an innate tendency to positively value experiences which maintain or enhance the organism (the 'actualising tendency', see above). Through encountering the judgements of others, however, they come to introject certain beliefs about how they should experience the world, and therefore strive to act in ways that boost their approval from others and their sense of 'self' but which are not truly self-maintaining or self-enhancing (the 'self-actualising tendency'). Similarly, Fromm (1942, 1961, 1965, 1991), like other advocates of a humanistic psychoanalytic and Marxist perspective (e.g., Marcuse, 1966), argues that human beings, within a capitalist socio-economic context, come to develop false and synthetic needs, and are alienated from their genuine human motivations and desires.

As I have argued previously, however, this model is not entirely cogent, as it does not explain where those 'non-actualising' directions come from (Cooper, 2013). That is, if the actualising tendency, as Rogers (1959) posits, is the sole highest-order direction, why would an individual come to act in non-actualising ways? As Klinger (2013) suggests, then, extrinsic desires need to be understood as 'subgoals in a chain leading to something of intrinsic value' (p. 33). That is, approval from others must lead to the fulfilment of higher-order goals – like self-esteem, relatedness, or safety – which then lead up to a highest-order movement towards actualisation. This is consistent with TA's assertion that we have an innate hunger for *strokes* ('units of recognition' from others, such as smiles or verbal affirmations) – they do not just materialise from outside (Berne, 1961). Within the humanistic therapies, then, the core conflict may be best understood as being between a 'self-actualising' direction and all other directions within the organism (Cooper, 2013). This is illustrated in Figure 11.2, where the desire for approval (as, for instance, a means of gaining self-esteem) is pitted against the other desires within the individual. Here, then, we can envisage the young Billy Elliott who wants to actualise his potential for creativity through dance but who is also pulled to be valued and approved of by his family. Framed in this way, the desire for approval is part of the overall actualising tendency, but one that may 'go rogue' and come to dominate and block other desires (Angyal, 1941). Fortunately, with Billy Elliot, it does not.

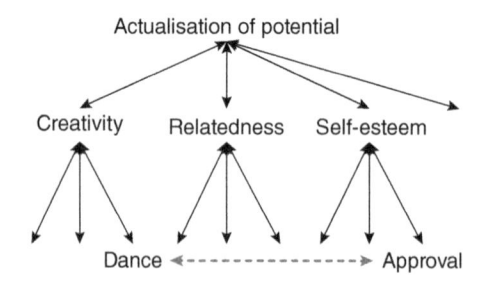

Figure 11.2 Conflict between the desire for approval and other organismic directions

In TA, which combines elements of the above model with psychodynamic thinking, the core conflict is characterised as a struggle between three 'ego states': *Parent* ('behaviours, thoughts and feelings copied from parents or parental figures'), *Adult* ('behaviours, thoughts and feelings which are direct responses to the here-and-now', cf. the ego) and *Child* ('behaviours, thoughts and feelings replayed from childhood') (Berne, 1961; Stewart & Joines, 1987, p. 12). The Parent ego state is then further divided into the 'Controlling Parent' (cf. the superego and the critic) and the 'Nurturing Parent', with the Child ego state divided into the 'Free Child' (cf. id) and the 'Adapted Child' (cf. EFT's 'experiencer'). We can associate each of these ego states with particular directions:

- Adapted Child: to fit in with others' expectations
- Free Child: to act naturally and spontaneously

- Adult: to respond effectively to the actual here-and-now situation
- Controlling Parent: to criticise and dominate
- Nurturing Parent: to care and protect.

Given that people in relationships will act from different ego states, this sets up the possibilities for conflicts between people as well as within them (see Chapter 9). In TA terms, this typically involves *crossed transactions*, where Person A's direction towards Person B clashes with Person B's direction towards Person A. For instance, Person A wants to criticise and control Person B (from Controlling Parent to Adapted Child) but Person B wants to talk to Person A as Adult-to-Adult.

PRACTICE

As we have seen, humanistic approaches tend to attribute psychological difficulties to horizontal conflicts, which are relatively high up in the directional structure. In terms of the directional arc, this can be conceptualised as a focus on the evaluation phase (albeit non-conscious, rather than conscious, evaluation), and particularly the way that certain, emerging desires are blocked from further actualisation. Humanistic practice, therefore, tends to focus on helping clients become aware of – and actualise – their blocked desires: to feel, and be, more 'authentic'. Here, lower-order, concrete directions (or, in process terms, planning and action phases) tend to be less of a focus. Indeed, to the extent that higher-order directions are seen as difficult to access and identify, an overly-keen focus on planning and action phases may be seen as simply reinforcing extrinsic, inauthentic, and superficial directions.

Space to talk and dialogue

Humanistic approaches, as discussed above, tend to assume that clients have a natural movement towards more effective and synergetic configurations. Hence, as with the psychodynamic practice of free association, a primary focus of much humanistic work, particularly in the person-centred field, is on providing clients with an unencumbered 'space' in which they can focus on their problems, such that reorganisation can begin to take place (e.g., Rogers, 1942). Key competencies for humanistic therapists, then, are the ability to be active and attentive listeners (Egan, 1994), who can 'bracket' their own views and assumptions, such that clients can work towards their own solutions. This has been described as a 'non-directive' stance (Rogers, 1961) and is not dissimilar from the psychodynamic practice of free association. Equally, however, therapists are also encouraged to be present to their clients in collaborative, empathic, and 'congruent' ways, helping clients to 'tell their story' (Egan, 1994) and to further support reflection and reconfiguration. Bohart and Tallman (1999) write:

Most fundamentally, the therapist provides an opportunity for dialogue with another intelligent being. Through dialogue, clients are able to think out their problems more productively, experience aspects of their problems they need to experience to learn from and about them, and explore neglected aspects of their experience that might provide solutions. (p. 19)

BOX 11.1

Solution-focused therapy

Solution-focused therapy (SFT), or solution-focused brief therapy (SFBT), is an integrative approach that is particularly well-alligned with the present framework. It combines a humanistic view of human being with a CBT focus on techniques and here-and-now change. Here, the client is viewed as a 'resilient, skilled, imaginative, idiosyncratic problem-solver', who has the resources and competencies to generate solutions to their problems in 'creative' and 'flexible' ways (Macdonald, 2014; O'Connell, 2012).

Establishing clear goals, based on SMART principles (see Chapter 14), 'is one of the most important aspects' of SFT (Tarragona, 2008, p. 179). One of the best-known ways of trying to clarify the client's goals is to ask the miracle question. 'Suppose that one night while you were asleep, there was a miracle and the problem was solved. How would you know? What would be different?' (Hoyt, 2003, p. 380). SFT also uses scaling to help clients set small, identifiable goals. Here, clients are asked where they are on a scale from 0 ('the worst') to 10 ('the best it could be') on a particular dimension or goal, and then what would look different if they moved up one level (or how might they achieve that). For instance, 'Logan, you've said that you like yourself 2 out of 10 at the moment. If this went up to 3, what would you notice, what would it feel like?'

Rather than focusing on how or why problems have come about, SFT encourages clients to focus on the times when they have managed their problems ('exceptions'), and to look at how these ways of acting may be repeated. For instance, an SFT therapist might invite Logan to think about when he does feel good about himself:

LOGAN   'It's in the mornings when I- when I get up for college. First thing. I just feel that energy.

THERAPIST   What happens at those times?

LOGAN   It's when- everything is ready and organised. I've got my college books ready, my clothes laid out. I feel on top of things.

THERAPIST   So are there ways that you could follow those principles in other areas of your life?

In structural terms, we might see this as times when the vertical hierarchy is working well: when clients are actualising their higher-order directions in effective ways. The basic rules of living that SFT tries to communicate to clients, then, is that: 'If it ain't broke, don't fix it', 'Once you know what works, do more of it', and 'If it doesn't work, don't do it again; do something different' (Hoyt, 2003, p. 379). In terms of the present framework, this is about directly identifying, and then embedding as habits, these more effective means towards goals. In addition, by encouraging clients to envision positive solutions and outcomes, SFT methods can be seen as enhancing hope and the perceived attainability of goals.

Unconditional positive regard

From a humanistic standpoint, providing clients with 'unconditional positive regard' is an essential part of this therapeutic process (Bozarth & Wilkins, 2001; Rogers, 1959). In the terms of the present framework, this is essential because it can help to undo the conflict that is hypothesised to exist at the core of the client's difficulties. That is, clients have come to block certain directions because the actualisation of these directions would run against the client's desire for approval. But, if clients can experience approval for whatever they think or feel, then there is no reason for them to block any other directions. Logan, for instance, starts to talk in therapy about wanting to look after his health, and initially he is very timid of doing so: he feels ashamed and embarrassed that he is concerned about it. But as he does so, and as the therapist responds with warmth and acceptance rather than ridicule, so he begins to acknowledge this desire more fully himself. Tentatively, he also discloses that he is worried about his foreskin being tight and painful, and the therapist encourages him to talk this through with his GP. Here, through the experience of unconditional positive regard, Logan is increasingly enabled to actualise this direction towards health – he is freed from his concerns about disapproval.

Providing clients with unconditional positive regard can also be seen as a direct means of helping clients to experience relatedness: one of the most commonly posited highest-order directions (see Table 6.1).

But does unconditional positive regard mean accepting everything the client does? What if they wanted to kill someone? These are questions often asked by students on humanistic therapy trainings, and the structural model outlined in Chapter 6 can help to clarify what unconditional positive regard means. Here, acceptance is about accepting the highest-order directions that clients have: that their strivings for relatedness, self-esteem, or safety are always inherently 'OK'. And it is also about accepting that a client's lower-order directions are intelligible attempts to actualise these higher-order directions. As Caspar (1995) writes, 'The key to real acceptance is the insight that every instrumental behavior ultimately serves a superordinate human need. Needs on the highest level are always human and acceptable, even if extremely problematic means are used to realize them' (p. 239). However, as Caspar suggests here, this does not require us to accept every lower-order means that a client adopts to actualise these higher-order directions. We might consider it wrong, for instance, for Logan to tease the young woman at his party and, as his therapist, we might even tell him so. But we can still accept, and prize, his desire to achieve for himself a greater relatedness, and also see the intelligibility in how he is striving to do this.

Empathy

Empathy is, perhaps, the most universal of the humanistic practices, and has the clearest association to positive therapeutic outcomes (Elliott, Bohart, Watson, &

Greenberg, 2011). In terms of the present framework, to empathise with a client is to align oneself with their directions, and to reflect this back to them. So this may be a reflection of feelings, or thoughts, or other aspects of experiencing, such as perceptions. But it is also about picking up on where clients are trying to go to: what Bohart (2001) refers to as 'future-directed empathy'. For instance, picking up from Chapter 6:

THERAPIST So you're saying that you know, now, totally what you what.

MEI Yes, it's brilliant.

THERAPIST To be with Saul?

MEI What? Umm… No. Really no. I mean, I know he's lovely and sexy and everything. And it was amazing being with him. But no. He's *so* messed up. Two days with him– you just couldn't miss it. And he's got another lover, and complicated, and ambivalent…. No, we ended that, and I need to talk properly to Rob now and work out where we're going. And then make my life something. That's really what I need to do.

THERAPIST So it's about making something now of your life? Being more decisive?

In each case, the therapist's responses here focus on where Mei is wanting to go (though only the latter was accurately empathic). This contrasts with more present-centred responses, for instance, 'You had a really amazing time with Saul, you'd experienced it as just so tender'. Future-directed empathic responses are a bit like passing a football to where a teammate is running to (as you should), rather than where they are currently at. Its aim is to connect with the other person in their forward-moving, directional being, rather than as a static object.

As with psychodynamic practices (see Chapter 10), empathising with a client's direction also means sensing the essence of what they are trying to communicate to us here-and-now: the *implied message* (Pascual-Leone, Paivio, & Harrington, 2016). That is, what is my client really wanting to say to me? What do they want me to know? An example of the opposite may help to illustrate this. A few months ago, I was sitting in a hotel lobby, eavesdropping on a conversation between two of the bar staff. The younger man was talking in a soft and croaky voice, and seemed intent on telling his older colleague how awful their manager had been to him. As I understood it, this manager had been telling the young man that he should speak louder and more assertively, and the younger man was giving his older colleague a long, elaborate, and vitriolic account of how the manager should never have spoken to him like that: 'It's just the way my voice is', he raged. At the end of the monologue, the older man responded with the words 'You know, Strepsils would be really good for that'. Listening in, it seemed to me that the older man had entirely missed the direction of the younger man's narrative. What was the young man wanting? It seemed affirmation, support, a confirmation of the manager's reprehensibility. What he got instead was health advice. If the younger man's direction had been 'I really don't know what to do about my voice and I want to some advice', then the older man's response might have been entirely empathic. But he had crossed the younger man's direction (a dysergetic interpersonal relationship, see Chapter 9) rather than aligning himself with it: in TA terms, a crossed transaction.

Interestingly, the end of this story is that the younger man just carried on with his narrative anyway and did not seem particularly fazed by the older man's empathic failure. Perhaps it was all that he expected, perhaps he was not really listening to the older man anyway, or perhaps the older man had a much more empathic understanding of the younger man's direction than I did. Whichever way, the point here is that, as therapists, we should try to seek out the *red thread* (Bugental, 1976) of the client's concerns. 'This is the essence of what they are trying to tell us, their real concern or concerns, the thing or things that are presently most significant for them' (Mearns & Cooper, 2018, p. 146). It is what they want us most to know.

BOX 11.2

Motivational interviewing and systematic motivational counselling

Motivational interviewing (MI) is a well-evidenced form of humanistic therapy developed in the 1980s by Miller and Rollnick (2012). It combines the person-centred 'core conditions' with a more directive and action-oriented stance. It was primarily developed for people with drug and alcohol problems to try to support the process of change (McLeod, 2013). In terms of the present framework, motivational interviewing can be seen as mainly focusing on the evaluation phase of the directional arc, helping clients to increase the value of 'change goals' (e.g., getting clean from drugs) over 'non-change goals' (e.g., remaining in the addiction). It does this by providing clients with an opportunity to talk through this dilemma but, in contrast to a non-directive person-centred perspective, it encourages them to see the value of change. In addition, motivational action encourages clients to move on from awareness and evaluation to intention, planning, and action: through, for instance, action reflections, which reflect back to clients the potential concrete steps forward that they have directly or obliquely mentioned (Resnicow, McMaster, & Rollnick, 2012). At the heart of motivational interviewing is also the process of 'rolling with the resistance'. This involves accepting the client's reluctance to change, and exploring it, rather than pressuring them to act differently. From a humanistic standpoint, 'resistance' might be best understood as a means that clients adopt to reach a higher-order goal of autonomy.

Systematic motivational counselling (SMC; Cox & Klinger, 2011d) is an intervention that was also developed for alcohol and drug use, and it has many similarities to MI (Cox & Klinger, 2011c). Although SMC is less well known, its underpinning theory is particularly close to the present framework. Its focus is on improving clients' abilities to reach their goals, resolve internal conflicts, disengage from inappropriate goals, and move to approach goals over avoidance goals (Cox & Klinger, 2011c). At the heart of SMC is the use of tools to identify and assess clients' goals, and these will be discussed in Chapter 14 of this book.

Emotion-focused work

'One of the most distinguishing features of humanistic therapies is their emphasis on the importance of emotions' (Cain, 2002, p. 10). This is particularly true for *emotion-focused therapy* (EFT; Elliott et al., 2004; Greenberg et al., 1993): a contemporary, well-evidenced synthesis of person-centred and Gestalt approaches that centres around the expression and processing of emotions. Consistent with the present framework, this emphasis is not aimed at venting or catharsis of emotions *per se* (Kennedy-Moore & Watson, 1999). Rather, it can be understood as a means of helping clients to connect with their organismic, unconscious, highest-order directions (Custers, 2009): providing important information about their 'priorities' (Pascual-Leone et al., 2016). From a humanistic standpoint, as we have seen, directions are generally seen as residing outside conscious awareness – particularly when they are blocked. But emotions, as argued in Chapter 4, can be considered a 'royal road' to a person's genuine directions; and this is a viewpoint particularly emphasised within the humanistic approaches (e.g., Goldstein, 1940; Greenberg et al., 1993; Rogers, 1951). So a person, from this perspective, might think x, or say y, but when they feel z, this is telling us something really fundamental and 'truthful' about where it is that they are trying to get to. From a humanistic standpoint, then, it may not be particular productive to ask a client such as Logan what he really wants. He may not know it, and he may be too threatened to admit its existence. Rather, then, invite Logan to explore his feelings – something more visceral, more concrete – and through this process, his higher-order directions may emerge:

THERAPIST So how is it– You said last Saturday: you didn't go to the party that evening and I wonder how that was? Knowing that others were… were there?

LOGAN It's alright– I– it's a bit bored perhaps. I guess. Bit of a sad twat.

THERAPIST Sad?

LOGAN It's alright you know but… yeah… sad. Alone. Sad fucker.

THERAPIST So there's a sadness there. You feel sad and feel like you're a– you feel sad?

LOGAN Yeah. A bit… I guess a bit ashamed. I don't want other people to see I'm a sad, lonely fuck. [Logan stares into the distance, tears slowly forming in his eyes.]

THERAPIST Can you stay with that for a bit… [silence]. There's something– that sadness. [Silence. Logan is bent over, his tears gently dripping onto the floor.] Logan, I can see that you've really touched something raw. Something really sad.

LOGAN It's– I just don't want to be on my own again….

As we can see in this example, through giving Logan space and encouragement to talk about his feelings – and, perhaps more importantly, to activate them in the here-and-now – the humanistic therapist helps him begin to connect with higher-order directions: in this instance, a desire for relatedness with others. And, as part of the therapeutic work, the therapist can help him increasingly differentiate and identify what his feelings are about (Pascual-Leone et al., 2016). As with all forms of awareness work (see Chapter 3) this then allows clients to stand back from their immediate feelings and reactions, identify what they want, and establish more effective and synergetic ways of actualising this. Greenberg et al. (1993) state:

> [I]n order for people to behave adaptively, they, in addition to becoming aware of their feelings, must also identify the need associated with the feelings, realize that this need has not been recognized or met, and utilize skills to meet the need appropriately. It is thus recognition of primary adaptive emotions, acknowledgment of the need with which they are associated, and the use of appropriate means to meet the need that are important in guiding adaptive action. (p. 76)

In this respect, within emotion-focused therapy, the final stage of therapeutic work with emotions – having encouraged clients to focus on them, intensify them, and symbolise them – is to 'establish intents'. This involves focusing on what the client is wanting, needing, and their goals, and then helping them plan and take action in the world (Greenberg & Paivio, 1997).

Focusing

Closely related to this emotion-focused work is the humanistic practice of *focusing* (Gendlin, 1996; Krycka & Ikemi, 2016; and see Chapter 2, this volume). Here, clients are encouraged to directly engage with their bodies' 'own knowledge or implying of what is needed now' (Hendricks, 2002, p. 243). This is their *felt sense*: the emerging, forward-moving, 'bodily sense of some situation, problem or aspect of one's life' (Gendlin, 1996, p. 20). It is the 'edge' of their experiencing (Cornell, 1996). Here, clients might be encouraged to ask their felt sense questions like 'What do you need?' 'How would things look if it were resolved?' 'What actions need to be taken?' (Leijssen, 1998, p. 139). Clients might also be encouraged to notice the felt senses that are evoked by considering different possibilities. Cornell (1996) gives the example of a client, Matt, who was living in Chicago but felt an urge to live elsewhere. His therapist invited Matt to bring his awareness into his body (i.e., to 'focus'), to imagine staying in Chicago, and then to notice his feelings. Matt reported a heavy feeling in his arms and legs, and a sense of stagnancy in his stomach. Then he was encouraged to imagine moving away from Chicago and again notice what he felt in his body. This time, he felt a tingling, excitement, and lightness. While, previously, Matt had attempted to identify the best way forward through making a list of pros and cons for each choice, this connecting with his felt senses revealed a deeper insight into his directions, as embodied. Cornell reports that Matt did, soon after, relocate to the new town, and 'never regretted his move' (p. 55).

Facilitating internal dialogue

Methods for facilitating 'internal dialogue', which is widely used in the humanistic field, are also closely aligned to the current framework. Indeed, they may be the *sine qua non* of developing more synergetic intrapersonal configurations. They have been incorporated into such humanistic practices as psychodrama, Gestalt therapy, psychosynthesis, emotion-focused therapy (Elliott & Greenberg, 1997; Greenberg et al., 1993), and voice dialogue (Stone & Winkelman, 1989). They have also spread to non-humanistic approaches, such as the constructivist 'dilemma-focused intervention' (Feixas & Compañ, 2016). In internal dialogue, clients are encouraged to talk from one 'part' of the self to one or more other 'parts'. Most commonly, this is through *chair work* – a well-evidenced therapeutic intervention (Greenberg & Dompierre, 1981; Greenberg et al., 1993; Perls et al., 1951). Here, clients move from one chair to another to personify different 'parts' of the self. However, many other methods may also be used to facilitate such dialogues, including guided visualisations (for instance, imagining that the different parts of the self are different organisations; Cullen & Russell, 1989), art work, and sand tray methods (see Cooper & Cruthers, 1999).

Internal dialogue work is typically initiated when a client articulates two or more conflicting 'I-positions'. This may be expressed in terms of opposing desires. For instance, a client might say, 'On the one hand, I want to x, but another part of me wants to y' (Greenberg et al., 1993, p. 188), or describe a part of themselves that does want to change and a part of themselves that does not (Feixas & Compañ, 2016). From a humanistic standpoint, a conflict that may be particularly salient is between something that the client genuinely wants to do (i.e., an intrinsic desire) and another thing that they feel that they should do (i.e., an extrinsic desire). For instance, Logan might say, 'I sometimes feel that I just want to hang out in the kitchen with my mum but my mates– I just feel that that would be such a naff thing to do.' Closely related to this, as described above, humanistic therapists have particularly focused on conflicts in which part of the self (the 'inner critic' or 'top dog') judges, or berates, the person (the 'experiencing self' or 'underdog'). For instance, 'I'm such an idiot', 'I should never have done that', 'I'm a waste of space' (Greenberg et al., 1993; Perls et al., 1951).

Once the different I-positions have been identified, internal dialogue work proceeds by inviting clients to speak as each I-position, and to begin to listen to what the other I-positions are saying. For instance, a client who says to themselves that they are useless might be encouraged to elaborate on that: 'What is it that is useless about you?' They might then be encouraged to hear that from the other I-position: 'So how is it to hear that?' 'What would you want to say in response?' Here, as in the above section, a crucial aspect of humanistic practice is helping clients to express their underlying feelings from one I-position to another (Greenberg et al., 1993). For instance, 'I just feel so angry with how useless you are?' 'It really hurts when you talk to me like that?'

Through such emotional expression, clients can then begin, as above, to identify – and affirm – the higher-order directions behind their I-position (Nir, 2008). This has been described as the 'core' of that position (Vargiu, 1974), and it is an essential element of the internal dialogue work (e.g., Elliott et al., 2004; Greenberg et al., 1993). Vargiu (1974) states:

So the first step is to establish clear and open communication. One can then focus on what the two sides want from each other (always keeping in touch with the feelings involved), and from the expressed wants, trace the reasons, the 'whys' for those wants, and then the needs behind those reasons [i.e., the higher-level directions]. (p. 73)

Similarly, Beahrs (1982) writes:

Contacting each part of the individual in a respectful manner, we can find out what each wants and believes and from this how things are going wrong. Just as in international diplomacy, progress is more likely to result if the unique needs of all parts are given adequate attention and respect. (p. 9)

So, for instance, a client who identifies a 'victim' part of himself may connect with the deep sadness associated with this part, and from here see its profound longing for comfort and attention. Here, the role of the therapist can be to listen for the associated directions, and to guide the client to express them directly to the other I-position (Elliott et al., 2004).

An extended example of this internal dialogue work comes from Elliott et al. (2004), describing two-chair dialogue with a client called 'Lynn'. Lynn wants to be herself and express what she feels (the 'experiencer'), but she feels that that would make her a mean person (the 'inner critic'). Lynn is encouraged to speak as her critic: 'you're no good, what comes out of your mouth is senseless...' (p. 226); and then to say how it feels to receive this as her experiencer: 'I feel sad and afraid' (p. 228). The therapist then encourages Lynn to say what she, as the experiencer, wants from the critic: 'I want you to like me for who I am and what I feel' (p. 228). Later in the work she says, 'I want your comfort and love and understanding' (p. 234). The assertiveness of the experiencer now leads to a 'softening' in the critic: 'I'm sorry. (crying).... Your feelings are important to me, and, yes, you do count, and I'm sorry. I didn't mean to step all over you. I want you to feel loved' (p. 234). Now the therapist invites the critic to express how it is feeling and what it wants: 'I'm sorry for being demanding. I was just protecting you. I'm afraid to let you go.... I'm afraid you are going to abandon me' (p. 234).

As is evident in this work, at the core of the critical I-position is a desire that is benevolent – or, in Vargiu's (1974) terms, 'good' (p. 82) – and this allows for the emergence of a final phase in the internal dialogue work, which is a negotiation between the different parts towards a more mutually beneficial solution. At a minimum, this may involve a 'compromise' between the different parts (i.e., a reduction in conflict), but, optimally, a 'win–win' solution (Nir, 2008). Lynn's critic, for instance, asks that her experiencer listens to her, and in return she promises to 'stand aside' and give the experiencer some space (Elliott et al., 2004). In another example, a conflict between a client's 'worker' side and her 'exhausted' side is resolved by the promise, from 'worker' to 'exhausted', that she can have some rest time; and from 'exhausted' to 'worker' that she can catch up on some of her work (Emmerson, 2006). Importantly, too, in this example, both sides agree that they will try to talk openly, and with respect for each other, in the future. Hence, the endpoint of this internal dialogue work 'is a clear understanding of how various feelings, needs, and wishes may be accommodated and how previously antagonistic sides of the self may be reconciled in a working relationship' (Greenberg et al., 1993, p. 193).

In terms of the present framework, what is being described here is a shift from dysergetic to more synergetic internal configurations, through establishing less conflictual means of actualising higher-order directions (see Chapter 8). Lynn wants to protect herself – a legitimate, higher-order direction – and her means towards doing this is self-criticism (perhaps on the logic that, if she gets in the criticism first, others won't be able to). But her self-criticism runs against other higher-order directions, such as her desire for self-worth. Through internal dialogue, the damaging effects of this lower-order strategy become apparent, and what also becomes apparent is the higher-order want that her self-criticism is trying to achieve. This then empowers Lynn to stand back from this chronic, lower-order strategy and to find ways of actualising this higher-order direction that may be less dysergetic with other directions.

Facilitating external dialogue

Within the humanistic therapies, and particularly EFT, clients may also be encouraged to uncover – and take forward – higher-order directions through 'empty chair work' with a significant figure in their lives (Elliott et al., 2004). This aims to help clients resolve 'unfinished business' – that is, to complete the Gestalt cycle (see Chapter 3) – by providing them with an opportunity to express their needs and wants to the other, as imagined. An example of this comes from session 11 of EFT with a female client in her mid-forties, who was working through feelings of anger and betrayal towards her mother (Greenberg, Korman, & Paivio, 2002). The therapist encourages the client to 'bring mother here' and 'say something to her'. The dialogue proceeds as follows (abridged, and with annotations removed):

CLIENT   I (Sob), I can't, I can't believe what you did to me. (Sighs). I can't believe that you did that to me. That you put me in that situation. That was worse than, than death.
THERAPIST   Tell her, 'I'm angry at you.'
CLIENT   'I'm angry at you for that. How could you behave so despicably?...
THERAPIST   That's good. Say more to her.
CLIENT   I was just a ... sad, lonely sixteen-year old, and where was my mother? Nowhere. You didn't come. You didn't care....
THERAPIST   Mm-hmm. Tell her what you want from her.
CLIENT   I want you to recognize what you did – I want you to see how much I suffered when I was sixteen. And I want you to say you are sorry....
THERAPIST   Tell her what you needed when, when you said I was furious when you didn't come to me when I needed you. What did you really need? What would you have liked then for yourself?

CLIENT   I would have liked her to care. I would have liked you to show that you cared and to show that you were a strong presence behind me ready to support me through this. (pp. 518–519)

As we can see here, a central part of this empty chair work is helping the client to access, and communicate, her higher-order desires towards her 'mother'. As we have seen, however, from a humanistic standpoint, this first requires the client to access and experience her emotions at a level of intensity (e.g., Therapist: 'That's good. Say more to her'), so that the directions being expressed are genuine, organismic ones, rather than more superficial cognitive conceptualisations.

In the example of empty chair work above, the client is then invited to enact the role of the mother, and she says from this position that she is sorry for what she did and asks the client for forgiveness. The client is then asked how she is feeling now.

CLIENT   I just feel so sad for me as a young mother. I was so alone and so needed someone to love me. But I was not bad, unworthy. Actually, I was very courageous, my mother just couldn't cope. (p. 520)

As with all humanistic work, what we see here is that, through connecting with her higher-order directions, the client comes to see the intelligibility of her experiences and behaviours. Lower-order means (like 'being cold to my mother'), in isolation, may feel unintelligible to clients, and generate secondary feelings like shame, confusion, or self-doubt ('Why am I always such a bitch to my mother?'). But if clients can come to see the highest-order directions that these experiences and behaviour are intended to lead to (directions which themselves are always intelligible), then these negative secondary feelings can begin to dissolve.

BOX 11.3

Reality therapy

Reality therapy, developed by Glasser (1965) in the 1960s, is another form of humanistic therapy with a particular proximity to the current framework. Based extensively on Powers's control theory (see Box 6.1), it starts from the assumption that human beings are purposive and intelligible: they are striving to meet a set of highest-order needs (see Table 6.1). Here, unmet needs are seen as leading to frustration and, as with Powers's control theory, people will tend towards behaving in ways that 'close the gap' (Brickell & Wubbolding, 2000). However, as with the present framework, it is also hypothesised that people may get certain payoffs from staying in a miserable state: for instance, not having to express anger, avoiding having to work on problems, being the focus of help from others, and, in particular, not having to face up to reality. Hence, a central focus of reality therapy (as with existential approaches, see Chapter 12) is in encouraging clients to take responsibility for their lives. This is defined as 'the ability to fulfil one's needs, and to do so in a way that does not deprive others of the ability to fulfil their needs' (Glasser, 1965, p. 13).

(Continued)

To help clients take responsibility and find better ways of fulfilling their needs, reality therapy uses the principles of 'WDEP'. This has many parallels to the directional arc (Brickell & Wubbolding, 2000):

- W = Wants – helping clients to clarify what they actually want and need. A reality therapist, for instance, might ask Mei, 'So you want to start "getting on with your life". What does that actually mean?'
- D = Doing and direction – helping clients to look at the actual directions in which their behaviour is taking them. For instance, 'You've been looking for courses in journalism now Mei, and planning to retrain. Where are you wanting to go with that?'
- E = Evaluation – helping clients to work out whether what they are doing is actually getting them to where they want to be, and whether their goals are realistic and satisfying. For instance, 'So you've decided to finish things with Saul. And you're going to talk to Rob about changing your life. Is that definitely what you want?'
- P = Planning – helping the client make a plan of action that can get them closer to where they want to be. For instance, 'So let's think about what you want to say to Rob now. You've said you want to be totally honest with him. How are you going to do that?' In reality therapy, the therapist may also try to directly teach the client better ways of fulfilling their needs.

CONCLUSION

Humanistic approaches – with their agentic, dynamic understanding of human being – are closely aligned to the present framework. Some of the distinctive contributions that they make are:

- The hypothesis that human beings have a natural, inherent tendency towards more effective and synergetic configurations – and, therefore, the value of simply providing clients with space to talk and dialogue.
- The hypothesis that a core intrapsychic conflict is between the desire for approval and other directions – and, therefore, the value of an unconditional acceptance in the therapeutic relationship.
- Highlighting the value of focusing on affective and embodied responses in therapy as a means of accessing higher-order directions.
- The development of methods for facilitating intrapersonal and 'interpersonal' dialogue as a means of accessing underlying, higher-order directions.

QUESTIONS FOR REFLECTION

- Think of a client you are currently working with (perhaps one that you are experiencing as challenging). What hidden potentials, or strengths, might they be striving to develop? What stops them from doing so? How might you help them actualise this potential more fully?

FURTHER READING

Cain, D., Keenan, K., & Rubin, S. (Eds.). (2016). *Humanistic psychotherapies* (2nd ed.). Washington, DC: American Psychological Association. Comprehensive, contemporary, and definitive collection of chapters on key humanistic approaches.

Elliott, R., Watson, J. C., Goldman, R. N., & Greenberg, L. S. (2004). *Learning emotion-focused therapy: The process-experiential approach to change*. Washington, DC: American Psychological Association. Accessible guide to emotion-focused practices.

12

EXISTENTIAL APPROACHES WITHIN A DIRECTIONAL FRAMEWORK

Choosing to choose

This chapter discusses:

- The existential model of human being as choice-making, meaning-creating, and towards-the-future.
- Existential perspectives on highest-order directions: meaning and nothingness.
- Core conflicts within the existential approaches: dilemmas and tensions.
- Key elements of existential practice, as viewed through a directional lens: meaning-oriented practices, facilitating choice, and facing limitations.

Existential therapies are a particularly diverse set of practices that are based on existential philosophical insights (Cooper, 2017a). They include meaning-centred therapies (e.g., Frankl, 1984), daseinsanalysis (based on the later writings of Heidegger; Boss, 1963), and contemporary existential-phenomenological approaches (Spinelli, 2015; van Deurzen, 2012a). Data is more limited for the effectiveness of these approaches, but the contemporary meaning-centred approaches have shown good evidence of positive benefit (Vos et al., 2014).

MODEL OF THE HUMAN BEING

As discussed in Chapter 2, to a great extent the ontological basis for the present model is drawn from existential philosophy. This is, in particular, its understanding of human being as directional: intentional, meaning-creating, and towards-the-world (e.g., Bugental, 1987). Frankl, for instance, writes, 'man possesses a positive vector, a natural bent towards an objective goal in transcendent space' (cited in Bulka, 1982). Similarly, Heidegger's philosophy starts with an understanding of human being in terms of our '*pre*theoretical intentional acts', 'operative in such everyday lived experience as work, talk, self-concern and faith' (Guignon, 1993, p. 81). That is, before consciousness, before splits between mind and body, or self and world, there is an intentional being stretching towards its world. Hence, existential approaches understand human beings as fundamentally future- and purpose-oriented (e.g., Spinelli, 1994, 2006; van Deurzen & Kenward, 2005). It is not just that human beings have possibilities; but that we are our possibilities (Sartre, 1958). Here, agency also plays a critical role, with a non-deterministic understanding of being that emphasises the human capacity for choice. At the core of existential approaches is also the assumption that human experiencing and behaviour – even at its extremes – is far more possible to understand than is generally supposed (Laing, 1965). In his classic work, *The divided self*, for instance, the existential psychiatrist Laing (1965) shows how psychosis can be understood as an intelligible phenomenon: a desperate attempt by the person to withdraw from reality, and thereby 'preserve a being that is precariously structured' (p. 77).

As with the humanistic approaches (see Chapter 11), the existential therapies primarily understand psychological distress in terms of people's alienation from their authentic, genuine realities. However, as approaches which tend to understand being as fundamentally in-the-world (see Chapter 2), this authenticity is understood more as an acceptance of worldly 'givens' – such as death, anxiety, and freedom – rather than as some 'inner' honesty or congruence (Yalom, 1980). And, from this existential standpoint, these givens are by no means palatable. Yalom (2008), for instance, writes that 'Our existence is forever shadowed by the knowledge we will grow, blossom, and, inevitably, diminish and die' (p. 1). In this respect, existential therapies, as with the present framework (see Chapter 4), hold that psychological difficulties emerge in the discrepancies between 'self' and 'reality', and particularly where people have unrealistic expectations about their lives. This might involve a denial that deterioration and death, as above, come to us all (Heidegger, 1962); or a fantasy that a 'brave new world of sublime and enduring well being' is just around the corner (van Deurzen, 2009, p. 71). In terms of the TOTE cycle (Box 6.1), we can see that the problem here is that, if I hold a reference value like 'I must be youthful', then I am going to experience increasing disappointment as my 'testing phase' reveals greater discrepancy with my external condition. And, of course, any 'operations' here are doomed to fail because the situation, ultimately, is unalterable. For Wolfe (2008), disordered anxiety is this refusal to accept the existential reality of our situations. Our directions remain forever unactualised because, rather than revising our reference standards, we are constantly striving for something that we cannot have.

Consistent with this, as with the present framework, psychological difficulties are understood by many existential therapists as a disruption, blocking, or frustration of a person's inherent directionality (Bulka, 1982). This may be at the emanation and evaluation phases, in terms of not being able to recognise, or prioritise, deeper purposes, meanings, and values (e.g., Frankl, 1986). Or it may be at the intention phase, in terms of not taking these purposes forward: of failing to choose and then act. With this disruption, from an existential standpoint, comes a stunted, inauthentic state of being: living a half-life rather than one that is fully vibrant, vivid, and real. Hence, as with the present framework, the aim of many existential therapies is to help clients find ways of actualising their higher-order directions: for instance, discovering and realising meaningful goals (Wong, 1998).

HIGHEST-ORDER DIRECTIONS

Existential philosophers and therapists tend to take one of two positions on the issue of human beings' highest-order directions. On the one hand, as discussed in Chapter 6, are those existentialists that hold that there are no highest-order, ultimate directions. Rather, from this perspective, all desires and goals are ultimately ceilingless: contingent, arbitrary, and unattached to anything intrinsically meaningful (see Figure 6.7). Holzhey-Kunz (2014), for instance, writes:

> [S]omeone who suffers from a sense of meaninglessness or complains of a loss of meaning does not simply yet have to find the meaning and has not temporarily lost it, but is being confronted with the truth that we indeed mostly dwell in meaning-contexts without really being secure in meaning because all meaning is fragile and 'behind' all meaning 'bare being' always lurks in its facticity that is devoid of all meaning. (p. 39)

On the other hand, there are those existential therapists who see meaning and purpose itself as the highest-order direction. Frankl (1984), for instance, argues that the 'will to meaning' is the one driving force behind all human behaviour; and that

Adler's will to power, Freud's will to pleasure, and Maslow's self-actualising drive are all 'derivatives' of it (Frankl, 1988) (that is, lower-order means towards its achievement, see Figure 12.1).

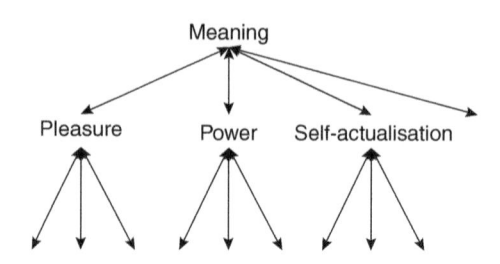

Figure 12.1 Existential structural model: Meaning-centred

As can be seen in Web Resource 6.1, however, for Frankl, there is no universal set of means towards this highest-order goal. Rather, each individual has their own, unique, pathways towards a meaningful life.

This focus on meaning means that, in contrast to most other therapeutic approaches, highest-order directions are not only conceptualised in biological or psychological terms (e.g., safety, self-esteem, relatedness), but also in more conceptual, philosophical ones (e.g., truth, goodness, faith). In other words, 'abstract' principles and values (van Deurzen, 2002) are seen as having as much capacity to orient human beings' experiences and behaviours as more basic biological and psychological wants. Mei, for instance, believes passionately in being a good friend to others, and much of her behaviour – for instance, spending hours on the phone at night providing 'counselling' to her close friends – could be understood as a means towards this end. This is not to say that existential therapists deny the importance of biological or psychological desires, but they see the human being – as lay-philosopher and ethicist – as having the potential to prioritise their purposes and values over more prosaic biological wants (Frankl, 1998). We see this most tragically evident, perhaps, in the suicide bomber, who is willing to sacrifice their very life for something that they passionately believe in.

CORE CONFLICT

As with the psychodynamic and humanistic approaches, many existential therapists have suggested that human beings are embedded within a web of 'tensions' or 'dilemmas' (Spinelli, 2001, 2015; van Deurzen, 2012a; Wahl, 2003). 'Human existence', writes van Deurzen (2002), 'is a struggle between opposites' (p. 52). In contrast to the psychodynamic and humanistic approaches, however, these tend to be viewed in more idiographic (i.e., individual) terms: for instance, a client's tensions may be between control and surrender, giving and receiving, or apathy and concern (Spinelli,

2015; van Deurzen, 2002). In fact, somewhat like Freud, van Deurzen (2002) does suggest that these polarities can be understood as variations of a basic, primordial opposition between 'life and death' (p. 54), but this is not central to van Deurzen's theory. The existential-humanistic therapist Schneider (1999) also proposes a basic tension: between a desire for smallness, limits, and containment (*hyperconstriction*) and a desire for expansion, growth, and forward movement (*hyperexpansion*). In many respects, this maps onto the distinction between avoidance and approach strivings, respectively (see Chapter 5).

In contrast to the humanistic approaches, however, the existential approaches also put particular emphasis on the inevitability of tensions, conflicts, and dilemmas (van Deurzen & Adams, 2011). From this standpoint, it is in the very nature of human existence to be pulled in different directions by competing directions; and to assume that we can overcome such conflicts is to set up another unrealistic metagoal that may bring further frustration and disappointment (van Deurzen, 1998). Spinelli (2001) writes, 'what existential therapy does *not* attempt is to seek to direct some means of balancing, integrating, improving or changing the lived experience of these tensions' (p. 12, emphasis in original). Rather, the aim of existential practice is to help clients come to terms with their tensions, to meet them resiliently, and to learn to live within this web rather than striving to escape it (for instance, by attempting to forge synergies). An existential therapist, then, might place less emphasis on helping Mei to resolve her conflicted loyalties to Saul (excitement) and Rob (security), and more on helping her to accept that she has these competing desires within her.

PRACTICE

As with the psychodynamic and humanistic approaches, the existential therapies tend to focus on the earlier phases of the directional arc – emanation, awareness, and evaluation – rather than concrete planning and action. However, the existential emphasis on human freedom means that there is also a particular focus on the intent phase of the arc: that is, choosing. From an existential perspective, and somewhat in contrast to a humanistic perspective, intent is not seen as naturally and effortlessly flowing on from emergence, awareness, and evaluation. Rather, it is seen as something that the person must actively do: a 'leap of faith' that requires courage and commitment, and which could always be otherwise (Tillich, 2000).

Existential practices are also similar to psychodynamic and humanistic practices in that a principal focus of the work is on the creation of a facilitative therapeutic relationship, through which clients can explore their lived-experiences (Correia et al., 2018). However, within these approaches – and, particularly, the meaning-centred therapies – there may also be an explicit focus on helping clients to identify, and actualise, their highest-order purposes, meanings, and values. This contrasts somewhat with the psychodynamic approaches, in that the focus tends to be less on the client's past and more on their meanings to be fulfilled for their futures (Frankl, 1984).

Meaning-oriented practices

What the existential therapist does, writes van Deurzen (2002), 'is to help the client to trace back her original intention, her deepest sense of what is important to achieve in her life' (p. 144). In other words, 'What ultimately matters in existential work is to determine what it is that really matters to the clients' (2012a, p. 125). This is, essentially, a process of helping clients to 'clarify' their highest-order directions: their ultimate projects, meanings, and values (Iacovou & Weixel-Dixon, 2015). As with the psychodynamic and humanistic approaches, this may be through active listening and dialogue. But existential approaches have also developed a range of 'meaning-oriented' practices, which are well-evidenced in the clinical research field (Thir & Batthyány, 2016; Vos et al., 2014) and are specifically aimed at helping clients gain a greater sense of meaning and purpose.

In classic logotherapy, one of the most commonly used therapeutic methods is *Socratic dialogue* (Frankl, 1984, 1986). Here, the therapist enters into a dialogue and debate with the client and 'poses questions in such a way that patients become aware of their unconscious decisions, their repressed hopes, and their unadmitted self-knowledge' (Fabry, 1980, p. 135). Such a practice may be relatively challenging, directive, and didactic, but it has the aim of helping the client identify what is genuinely meaningful and of value to them: that is, their highest-order wants. For example:

THERAPIST Mei, so what is it– you're thinking about journalism?
MEI Yes. It's– it was always where I wanted to go. What Rob and I talked about.
THERAPIST So what... why journalism? What does it mean to you?
MEI It's– I love that discovery. That finding out about– Definitely for music. But maybe other things too. I love that immersion and that passion and that discovery and then communicating that passion. It's something about being passionate and communicating passion.

More contemporary meaning-centred therapists have developed a range of further methods, exercises, and questions to help clients identify their highest-order desires, values, and purposes (e.g., Cooper, 2017a; Schulenberg, Hutzell, Nassif, & Rogina, 2008). For instance, clients might be asked:

- 'Select one word which best expresses the meaning you would like life to have?'
- 'Write the epitaph which you would prefer for yourself?'
- 'If you were able to decide your future, what would be an ideal life situation for you three or five years down the road?'
- 'If you only had a year left to live, what would you prioritise most?'

We will explore other methods for facilitating this much more fully in Chapter 15.

Recent years have also seen the development of a range of structured meaning-centred therapy groups, primarily for people with life-limiting illnesses (e.g., Breitbart et al., 2010), which have shown good evidence of efficacy (Vos et al., 2014). Such groups focus on helping clients to identify potential meanings and purposes in their lives – despite their diagnoses – using a mixture of therapeutic techniques: for instance, psycho-educational input, discussion, reflective experiential exercises, and homework (Cooper, 2017a). Group participants, for instance, might be introduced to a range of potential social sources of meaning (such as friendships or communities) and asked to consider the importance of these meanings in their own lives (Vos, 2015). Alternatively, they might be invited to construct a 'lifeline': visualising their lives from birth to present, and then thinking about the goals they can work towards within their potentially time-limited futures (Lee, 2008) (see Chapter 15).

Facilitating choice

As indicated above, the aim of existential meaning-oriented work is not just to help clients clarify their highest-order directions, but also to help them find ways of bringing their lives into alignment (Bugental, 1978). As well as emergence, awareness, and evaluation, then, this requires the phase of intending: making the choice to put preferences into action (Schneider & Krug, 2010). From an existential standpoint, such choices require the courage to stand by one's own convictions (May, 1953), and to face the anxiety of diving into an uncertain and unpredictable future. Anxiety, as discussed in Chapter 4, can be conceptualised as the experience of certain directions being threatened and, from an existential standpoint, we can attempt to avoid it by not 'crossing the Rubicon': by not attempting to actualise such desires in planning and action. For instance, if I fear that I might fail at a training programme, I can always avoid that fear by not attempting to apply. But, through such actions, we fail to actualise many of our highest-order directions. Moreover, some desires will always be carried over into intentions and actions whether we want to or not – even if it is the avoidant intention not to have any intentions. So, we cannot choose not to choose. Rather, it is a question of whether we make choices consciously, deliberately, and in the most optimal (i.e., effective and synergetic) ways, or whether we allow our choices to be reactive, chaotic, and pulling us in multiple competing directions.

So how do existential therapists strive to facilitate this choice-making process? Here, we can identify three main strategies (Correia, Cooper, & Berdondini, 2015).

First, therapists can help clients to acknowledge that they do have freedom, responsibility, and the capacity to make a choice. That is, that they have the capacity to choose whether or not to translate their desires into actions, and that no one can make or do this for them. For instance:

MEI   I do need to talk to Rob about all of this. Tell him what I want to do.
THERAPIST   How will you do that?
MEI   Maybe if Rob– he's so– he's always sitting there, watching TV. He's so difficult to talk to.
THERAPIST   Yes, I really get that. But you– That's you who has to make that happen, isn't it? You need to say to Rob 'Let's talk'.

Second, therapists can help clients become more conscious of the ways in which they might evade making choices. For instance, clients might become apathetic, fatalistic, or, like Mei, comply to external wishes and demands (Correia et al., 2015). With Mei, for instance, a therapist might say:

I wonder if– you know, it is maybe difficult to get Rob to talk. But I wonder if sometimes that's an excuse, that you use, for not having to raise stuff with him. Like, 'Oh, I can't talk about this because Rob is watching TV'. Maybe it's also about you avoiding things?

Third, existential therapists might help clients think of what they specifically need to do to help them move from wish to action. This then moves towards planning and strategies, such as implementation intentions (see Box 3.1).

Facing limitations

As with making choices, existential therapists may try to help clients face up to the existential limitations of their situation through encouraging them to acknowledge these limitations, and to be more aware of the ways in which they might try to evade them. Here, for instance, in a continuation of the above dialogue, the therapist helps Mei to consider whether she has unrealistically high expectations of how interpersonal difficulties can be dealt with:

MEI   I just– it is really hard talking about these things. I think that's what puts me off. I don't like upsetting Rob. Or people. Generally, I don't like it when people get upset.
THERAPIST   Yes, it's true. He– people maybe do get upset when we tell them things that are difficult to hear. But I wonder if– that's kind of one of the givens of life. Things aren't always easy. People do get upset. And we can avoid that – or face that and do stuff despite.

CONCLUSION

Of all the therapeutic approaches, the existential therapies are probably most explicitly aligned with a directional understanding of human being. Their therapeutic practices also work directly with helping clients acknowledge, and actualise, their highest-order purposes and desires. In this respect, the emerging evidence base in support of meaning-centred practices is encouraging for the present framework.

Some of the unique contributions that an existential perspective make to the present framework is that they:

- Identify overly-high expectations – particularly about life – as a potential source of psychological difficulties.
- Propose that purpose itself is a highest-order direction.
- Recognise that our highest-order directions may be conceptual, philosophical, and ethical as well as psychological and embodied.
- Conceptualise people's directions in highly idiographic terms.
- Understand that, ultimately, there may be no highest-order directions.
- Emphasise the inevitability of conflicts and the importance of coming to accept the inherently dysergetic nature of existence.
- Detail a number of strategies to help people identify their highest-order directions.
- Focus on the intent phase of making a choice and how this can be facilitated in clients.

QUESTIONS FOR REFLECTION

- How sympathetic are you to the view that, ultimately, there are no highest-order human directions – everything is ultimately arbitrary?
- Think of a client you are currently working with. What is the key tension in their life? Do you think it would be more helpful to focus on ways of resolving that tension, or to focus on ways of accepting the unresolvability of that tension?

FURTHER READING

Cooper, M. (2017). *Existential therapies* (2nd ed.). London: Sage. Reviews the different schools of existential thought and practice.

Frankl, V. E. (1984). *Man's search for meaning* (revised and updated ed.). New York: Washington Square Press. One of the most influential existential texts, detailing Frankl's experiences in the death camps and the logotherapeutic, meaning-centred approach that evolved through it.

van Deurzen, E. (2012). *Existential counselling and psychotherapy in practice* (3rd ed.). London: Sage. Classic introduction to a contemporary existential approach.

Vos, J. (2018). *Meaning in life*. London: Palgrave. Comprehensive new introduction to meaning-centred theory and practice.

13

COGNITIVE-BEHAVIOURAL APPROACHES WITHIN A DIRECTIONAL FRAMEWORK

Effective strategies for life

This chapter discusses:

- The cognitive-behavioural model of human being as learner.
- Core conflicts within the cognitive-behavioural approaches: short-term ease versus long-term benefit.
- Key elements of cognitive and behavioural practice, as viewed through a directional lens.

The cognitive-behavioural therapies (CBTs) are a family of relatively structured, directive therapeutic practices that aim to bring about psychological improvements by directly influencing thinking, behaviour, or both. They are the best-evidenced and best-researched of all the psychological therapies (Hollon & Beck, 2013), with findings indicating that they can bring about significant improvements in depression, anxiety disorders, and a wide range of other psychological problems.

MODEL OF THE HUMAN BEING

Although classic behaviourism adopted a relatively mechanistic and un-agentic view of human beings – with behaviour determined by external forces (e.g., Watson, 1925) – contemporary CBT approaches are based on a much more active conceptualisation of human being (Bandura, 2001; Bandura & Locke, 2003; Beck et al., 1979; Reinecke & Freeman, 2003). In his highly influential paper, 'Social cognitive theory: An agentic perspective', for instance, Bandura (2001) describes human beings as intentionally and purposively striving to 'make desired things happen' (p. 2). That is, to achieve their 'goals' (p. 8). Similarly, with respect to practice, Moorey (2014) states that the first theoretical assumption of cognitive therapy is that 'The person is an active agent who interacts with his or her world' (p. 244).

In contrast to the psychodynamic approaches, the cognitive and behavioural therapies primarily focus on conscious intentions, thoughts, and activities (Moorey, 2014). However, they acknowledge that thoughts can be outside awareness – though not entirely sealed off to the person's own understanding.

As we have seen in Chapter 7, cognitive and behavioural approaches can be conceptualised as understanding psychological difficulties in terms of ineffective means of achieving higher-order directions. Cognitively, this involves irrational thinking processes, which reduce the person's ability to effectively respond to their circumstances. Behaviourally, this may be more a case that the person has not learnt the skills or abilities to turn intentions into effective plans and actions: lacking, for instance, social skills, assertiveness, or the methods to effectively organise their daily activities. As we have seen, however, both cognitive and behavioural difficulties can also be seen in terms of horizontal dysergies: that a person's desire for cognitive ease, or to act in ways that feel safe, undermine their capacity for more growth-enhancing directions. 'Ultimately', then, as Grawe (2004) writes, 'cognitive therapy is about modifying conflictual intentions' (p. 90). However, it is so taken for granted that one side of the conflict (the irrational side) is the 'wrong' one that 'in cognitive problem formulation one usually does not speak in terms of conflicts but only in terms of problematic assumptions representing only one side of the conflict' (p. 90).

HIGHEST-ORDER DIRECTIONS

For early behaviourists, the principal drivers of human behaviour were the experiencing of pleasure and the avoidance of pain. Within the contemporary cognitive-behavioural literature, there is less explicit discussion of highest-order directions, though some associated with the approach continue to emphasise the primacy of pleasure and happiness (e.g., Layard, 2006).

CORE CONFLICT

In the psychodynamic approaches, we might conceptualise the core conflict as being between a lairy drunk (id) and an aggressive police officer (superego), with a rational-minded social worker (ego) desperately trying to mediate in between. In the humanistic approaches, it is between a free-spirited child and a critical, controlling parent who is worried about what the neighbours think. In the existential approaches, it is between two disputants who cannot – and will not – agree. In the CBT approaches, we might liken this core conflict to an argument between two roommates: one a sensible, hard-working student (who still knows how to enjoy themselves) and the other a lazy slob who has never really developed the skills or confidence to make the most of their life. The slob is always looking for the 'route of least resistance': does not really want to go out, to make an effort, or to learn how to do things better. And, underneath it all, the slob is actually pretty depressed and anxious. Depressed because they are not doing much, and anxious because the more they just sit in, the scarier the outside world gets.

PRACTICE

Cognitive-behavioural practice draws on a wide variety of methods and techniques, particularly in its more eclectic forms (e.g., multimodal therapy; Lazarus, 2005). However, these therapies are relatively unique in that they focus primarily on the later stages of the directional arc: planning, action, and the effective use of feedback. Within the more cognitively-oriented approaches, however, evaluation may also be a major focus, in terms of weighing up more, and less, helpful approaches to thinking. Awareness, in terms of recognising one's highest-order directions, is less commonly a focus of CBT. However, it may be there in such techniques as 'upward questioning' (see below). In addition, in behavioural activation (BA) and acceptance and commitment therapy (ACT), a contemporary 'third wave' form of behavioural intervention, highest-order directions are termed *values*, and there is a particular emphasis on helping clients align the behaviours accordingly (Boorman, Morris, & Oliver, 2012). As with the concept of equifinality, ACT also encourages clients to develop *psychological flexibility*, such that they are less rigid in their views of how the world is and how things must be done (Baer & Huss, 2008). ACT is also relatively unique among the CBTs in that it focuses on the intent phase of the directional arc, inviting clients, as the name suggests, to commit to behaviours that are linked to their highest-order values (Boorman et al., 2012).

Goal setting

In contrast to psychodynamic, humanistic, and existential approaches, goal setting is integral to most cognitive-behavioural approaches to therapy (e.g., Dryden, 2018; Grey et al., 2018). Antony and Roemer (2003), for instance write that behaviour therapy focuses on identifying 'key problems and realistic goals' (p. 192), selecting treatment strategies that can facilitate the achievement of these goals. This goal-oriented approach is consistent with an emphasis on the 'post-intent' phases of the directional arc. Here, it is assumed that clients have crossed over the Rubicon and have specific goals that they want to achieve in their lives: the question, then, is how they achieve them. This contrasts with the more insight-based therapies, where it is assumed that getting to the Rubicon may be a major therapeutic achievement in itself.

Consistent with the psychological evidence (see Chapter 5), CBT tends to emphasise the setting of specific, concrete, and measurable goals. Treatment goals for health anxiety disorders, for instance, might be:

- Decreased disease conviction
- Decreased health-related worry
- Decreased bodily checking. (Taylor & Asmundson, 2004)

Importantly too, and consistent with the present framework, CBT also emphasises the setting of realistic goals. Hence, for instance, with a health anxious client, it would not be appropriate to set a goal of 'not having aches and pains' or 'being worry-free'. Rather, as with a broader CBT approach, the aim is to move away from 'black and white' thinking (e.g., 'If I'm not worry-free, then I will be consumed with anxiety')

BOX 13.1

Problem-focused approaches to therapy

Within the counselling and psychotherapy field, there are a number of 'problem-focused' approaches to helping that fit closely with the current framework, and have some evidence of effectiveness (e.g., D'Zurilla & Nezu, 1999; Neenan & Palmer, 2000; Pinsof, 2005). These approaches, which tend to combine CBT methods and structure with a broadly humanistic sensibility, encourage clients to directly identify current problems in living (the 'presenting problem'), and then to develop or acquire a series of strategies for overcoming them, which is often broken down into manageable, small steps (Lopez et al.,

2000). In terms of the present framework, this can be characterised as identifying obstacles to higher-order goals, and then developing the knowledge and skills to remove these obstacles, both in relation to the presenting problem and for the future.

Probably the best known of these is Egan's problem-management approach (Egan, 1994; Egan & Reese, 2019), which emphasises action as a means towards 'valued outcomes' (i.e., highest-order goals). Egan breaks this therapeutic process down into three stages, closely paralleling the directional arc. The first, 'reviewing the current situation'/'problem definition' invites clients to tell their story, identify and challenge their 'blind spots' to seeing the situation clearly and moving ahead', and then finding the areas that they can work on to make a positive difference in their lives ('leverage'). In stage two, 'developing the preferred scenario'/'goal setting', clients work on developing a range of possibilities for a better future (cf. evaluation), translate these possibilities into viable goals, and then commit to a programme of constructive change (cf. intent). Finally, stage three 'Determining how to get there'/'action planning', invites clients to brainstorm strategies for action, choose the strategy, or strategies, that best fits the environment and resources, and then develop a step-by-step plan for achieving each goal (Egan, 1994; Wosket, 2012).

As part of these latter two stages, a range of different techniques are proposed by Egan (1994). In particular, clients may be encouraged to brainstorm the various options and means to achieve these options, and weigh them up with a written 'balance sheet' of pros and cons. This latter decision-making method takes a range of forms across the therapies, such as motivational interviewing's 'decisional balance sheet' (Miller & Rollnick, 2012), motivational counselling's 'decisional matrix' (Cox & Klinger, 2011c), and the 'decision-fostering intervention', whereby group participants evaluate and prioritise options, justify their choices to other members of the group, finalise them, and then plan how they will act (Grosse Holtforth & Michalak, 2012). Once action is initiated in these therapies, feedback is used throughout the therapeutic process to evaluate the client's progress. In this way, the therapeutic transition involves 'moving from the current to the preferred scenario by implementing the plan' (Egan, 1994, p. 39).

A similar set of steps is proposed by Neenan and Palmer (2000; Palmer & Neenan, 2000) in their sequential model of practical problem solving: problem-identification ('What is the problem?'), goal-selection ('What outcome(s) do I want?'), generation of alternatives ('How do I reach those goals?'), consideration of consequences ('What are the pros and cons?'), decision-making ('What's the most feasible solution?'), implementation, and evaluation ('What happened?', 'How successful was it?' and 'What can be learnt?'). Here, as with other problem-focused therapies (e.g., Egan, 1994; Pinsof, 2005), an eclectic mix of cognitive, behavioural, emotive, and imagery-based techniques are proposed. In addition, some specific, practical problem-solving strategies are outlined, such as 'planograms', in which the obstacles are visually mapped out on a notepad or whiteboard.

Although problem-focused approaches to therapy fit well with the current framework, this is primarily with regard to the later, post-intentional phases of the directional arc. By contrast, these approaches do not particularly focus on the emergence of desires and may not provide sufficient opportunity for clients to connect with their higher-order, less conscious directions. They also construe the change process in a relatively linear manner and may not fully fit the complex, cyclical, and intermeshed nature of people's actual directions.

towards a greater appreciation of shades of grey (e.g., 'It would be good to experience less worry, but I can also bear a certain amount'). This is not dissimilar from the existential emphasis on realistic expectations.

Chapter 14 presents a more extended and integrative discussion of goal setting in therapy.

Cognitive methods

Cognitive methods are 'a set of techniques that are designed to alleviate emotional distress by directly modifying the dysfunctional cognitions that accompany them' (Reinecke & Freeman, 2003, p. 245). In the classic cognitive model, beliefs (B) are seen as mediating the relationship between an activating event (A) and its emotional consequences (C). So, for instance, Logan goes to a party (A), and feels low (C) because he thinks that no one wants him there (B). As discussed, the present framework is slightly different, in that it also recognises the role of directions ('D') in this process. In other words, B ('no one wants me here') only leads to C (sadness), because Logan wants to be liked and approved of (D). (Were it the case, for instance, that Logan genuinely did not care about being liked, then the belief that no one wanted him at the party would have little emotional consequence).

However, the role of D can be considered implicit within the cognitive framework – or, perhaps, as so obvious as not needing mentioning. Moreover, as discussed in Chapter 6, beliefs play a critical role from the perspective of the present framework, because they mediate between higher-order and lower-order directions. Hence, interventions which strive to make beliefs more rational and attuned to the real world should, in terms of the present framework, be extremely useful means of helping people act more effectively towards their higher-order desires and goals.

Cognitive therapists tend to adopt a relatively active, questioning, didactic stance – though not always (see Box 13.2, The method of levels). They use a wide range of techniques and methods, but most of these essentially involve helping clients identify dysfunctional thoughts, establish more functional alternatives, and then implement those more functional ways of thinking. This might involve:

- Questioning the evidence: exploring with clients whether certain beliefs (for instance, 'I can't make friends') are really true. *Collaborative empiricism* – drawing on the evidence to see if certain beliefs are true or not – is at the heart of many cognitive techniques.
- Psychoeducation: teaching clients about different psychological processes and problems (e.g., the panic cycle) and how it may relate to clients' experiences.
- Inviting clients to keep a diary of automatic irrational thoughts (for instance, 'If a woman ignores me at a party, it proves they hate me') and to identify rational

alternatives (for instance, 'If a woman doesn't talk to me at a party, it's probably because she's involved with something else').
- Scaling: inviting clients to rate particular experiences, emotions, or perceptions (for instance, 'On a 1 to 100 scale, how popular do you think you are with your friends') to help them get away from all-or-nothing thinking.
- Cost-benefit analysis: encouraging clients to directly consider what they gain and lose from maintaining certain beliefs or behaviours. This may take the form of assessing the long-term and short-term benefits of their assumptions, and may also involve offering feedback and psychoeducation (for instance, on the health risks of alcohol) to support clients towards more effective choices. (Antony & Roemer, 2003; Beck et al., 1979; Correia et al., 2011; Dryden, 1999; Kellogg & Young, 2008; Reinecke & Freeman, 2003).

Within the third-generation CBTs, particular compassion-focused therapy, there may also be a focus on helping clients to reconsider shaming, blaming, pathologising, and stigmatising beliefs about themselves, and instead to view themselves in more compassionate and normalising ways (Gilbert & Irons, 2014).

Another widely used method in cognitive therapy, of particular compatibility to the present framework, is called the *downward arrow* technique (Kellogg & Young, 2008). Essentially, this involves asking clients 'why?' questions about key beliefs and feelings (Mansell, 2005) to identify the underlying thoughts and potentially dysfunctional assumptions. For instance:

THERAPIST   Why does it bother you so much, Logan, that that woman at the party didn't seem interested in talking to you?
LOGAN   I dunno. I guess it maybe means that she doesn't like me.
THERAPIST   And why is that a problem? What does it mean to you?
LOGAN   Because if she doesn't like me, probably none of the girls like me. They think I'm an idiot.
THERAPIST   And that bothers you because…?
LOGAN   …It's so shameful. I'm a total idiot to my mates.
THERAPIST   And if that did happen, why would that be so bad?
LOGAN   I'd just be on my own, every day. Would be totally wretched.

As can be seen here (and somewhat confusingly), this downward arrow technique essentially equates to going up the vertical hierarchy in the structural model of directionality (see Chapter 7). Starting from everyday beliefs and concerns, it tracks back to what is really important to the client, and what they might perceive as being under threat. This process has also been termed 'laddering up' (Feixas & Compañ, 2016) or 'value laddering' (Little, 2011).

The reverse of this process is that clients may also be encouraged to 'ladder down' (or 'act laddering'; Little, 2011): to explore the subordinate implications of a particular way of thinking (i.e., an 'upward arrow' technique). This means asking clients 'How?'

questions (Mansell, 2005). For instance, with Logan, a therapist might ask, 'It's important for you to make people like you, so how do you go about doing that?' Within the personal construct field, there is also 'dialectical laddering': reconciling two lower-order approaches in a higher-order integration or synthesis (Feixas & Compañ, 2016). This, then, is essentially finding more synergetic ways of being in the world: for instance, 'Logan, how could you approach parties in a way that both helps you feel safe and gets you closer to people?'

An extension of these up and down laddering methods, developed in Self–System Therapy, is termed *psychological situation analysis* (Vieth et al., 2003; see Chapter 5, this volume). Here, clients are first asked about their goals in a particular situation, then how they tried to attain them, and then whether these strategies worked or not. This would seem the most direct method of helping clients reflect on the effectiveness of their means towards higher-order goals (Chapter 7), and can then serve as the basis for identifying more effective strategies.

BOX 13.2

The method of levels

The *method of levels* (MOL) is a form of CBT directly derived from Powers's (1973) perceptual control theory (Box 6.1) (Carey, 2006, 2008; Mansell et al., 2013; Powers, 1992).

As with the present framework, MOL associates psychological difficulties with conflicts between 'control systems' (i.e., across vertical hierarchies). Hence, it strives to provide opportunities for clients to 'redirect their awareness to higher levels where reorganization can eliminate the conflict they experience' (Carey, 2006, p. 63). For Powers (1992), however, this needs to be more than just a cognitive recognition of conflict, or reconfiguration. Rather, along humanistic lines (see Chapter 11, this volume), he argues that clients need to experience their conflicts *in situ* to be able to resolve them.

Unlike most forms of CBT (and closer to the humanistic stance of Powers himself), MOL emphasises that clients have the capacity 'to get themselves better': that is, to bring about more synergetic reconfigurations at the highest levels of their control hierarchy (Carey, 2006). Hence, and fairly uniquely among the CBTs, MOL adopts a relatively non-directive stance. Here, the emphasis is on providing clients with space to talk openly about their problems, and supporting them through respect, trust, and optimism (Mansell et al., 2013). Indeed, Mansell et al. (2013) suggest that therapists do not even need to direct their clients' attention towards problem areas, as awareness will naturally move to the place in the system where there is the biggest error, in an attempt to correct it. However, MOL therapists will also engage with their clients from a stance of intense curiosity (for instance, asking what they might mean when they use various words), and upward laddering questions (see above) may be used to help 'nudge' their clients' attention to higher levels (Carey, 2006).

In addition, MOL therapists listen out for *disruptions* in the client's narrative. These are times when a client might look away, or smile to themselves, or comment on their speech ('That sounds so stupid'), which, from an MOL perspective, are indicators that the client has shifted to a higher level of control. Here, the MOL therapist will follow up with such questions as 'What made you smile?' or 'What came into your head just then?' to explore the client's perceptions and experiences at these higher levels. For instance:

MEI So I-I said to Rob about the journalism course. About doing that. About wanting to travel more [Mei winces].

THERAPIST [Softly] I noticed- you winced just then. You're face tightened up. I wonder- What happened at that point?

MEI It's just-It's really hard for me to just put things out there: 'I want this.'

THERAPIST So there's something about... finding it really hard to say what you want. Is the wince-like almost someone is going to slap you in the face if you say it?

Behavioural methods

In contrast to the cognitive methods, the behavioural techniques focus directly on changing clients' in-the-world actions: that is, trying things out in the real world. Although this is very different from the insight-orientation of the psychodynamic, humanistic, or existential approaches, the phase model of directionality helps us see that, actually, these approaches are by no means incompatible; they are just focused on different phases of the directional arc. As well as planning and carrying out actions, feedback is also essential to the behavioural therapy process: reviewing the effectiveness, or otherwise, of particular actions and evaluating their utility.

As with the cognitive therapies, there is a wide variety of behavioural techniques, most of which are well supported by the empirical evidence. *Behavioural experiments* are a behavioural method that is also closely linked to the cognitive therapies (e.g., Beck et al., 1979; Bennett-Levy, Butler, Fennell, Hackmann, Mueller, & Westbrook, 2005). Essentially, they are planned experiential exercises through which clients can test the validity of their beliefs about themselves, others, and their world (Bennett-Levy et al., 2005). Logan, for instance, believes that women like him better if he makes sarcastic comments. Here, a CBT therapist may encourage Logan to actually survey the women he knows to see if this is really true. He might also be encouraged to canvass their views on what they find attractive about men; or, perhaps more boldly, what they like and do not like about him. Such in-the-world experiments could help Logan move away from his unrealistic expectations and assumptions, and instead let him start to engage with the real world in a way that may help him more effectively get to where he wants to be.

Another widely used set of behavioural methods, adopted primarily when clients are experiencing anxiety, is *exposure* techniques (Marks, 1978). Here, anxiety is purposefully evoked in clients through confrontation with a situation that produces fear. This may be *in vivo* (i.e., in reality), in imagination, or through virtual reality (Antony & Roemer, 2003), and is often done in a graded way: from the least anxiety-evoking situation to the most anxiety-evoking one. For instance, a behaviour therapist might encourage Logan to practise leaving his house and stopping himself from returning to check his front door ('response prevention'). No doubt, Logan will experience anxiety when he does this, but if he can 'stay with' that anxiety rather than trying to quell it through his compulsive checking, he can learn that the anxiety will naturally subside of its own accord. Now, in terms of the present framework, Logan has acquired a means of attaining a higher-order goal (safety) that is less dysergetic with other higher-order goals (such as getting on with life and meeting people).

Another set of behavioural methods – with particularly good evidence of effectiveness for depression (Jacobson et al., 1996) – involve helping clients to restructure their daily activities to be more positively rewarding. This *behavioural activation* is perhaps the purest method of facilitating the planning and action phases of the directional arc: directly encouraging clients to plan, and do, more things that will help them achieve more of what they most fundamentally want. And although its focus is on the very practical, day-to-day activities at the lower levels of the structural model, these actions are essential to achieving any higher-order goals (Mansell et al., 2013). This approach begins by assessing what clients currently do in their day-to-day activities, and how that leads them to feel (O'Carroll, 2014). Here, for instance, Logan might begin to recognise that he feels particularly low when he is in his room on his own. Then, closely connected to the present framework, clients are invited to assess their 'values' (see above): that is, their higher-order directions, and their valued behaviours. The therapist then works with the client to develop a *personalised behavioural activation plan* (that is, a daily schedule of activities) based around what they find positively rewarding. For instance, having recognised that he is happier spending time with friends, and that he likes to be a 'good person', Logan may start to schedule in more social time during his day. Spending some time volunteering in a youth club might be another way that Logan would restructure his day to experience more positive reward. As well as providing more positive experiences, such encouragement to plan and act may help clients develop their self-confidence, a critical step in then feeling capable of actualising other directions (see Chapter 3).

Behavioural methods may also involve training clients in skills that help them, more effectively, to actualise their directions. Typically, these will also involve opportunities for practice and feedback, so that the clients can hone these skills and embed them in their everyday, habitual repertoires. Problem-solving training, for instance, involves teaching clients specific skills in defining their problems, generating potential solutions, weighing up these solutions, selecting a solution, implementing it, and then evaluating its effectiveness (Antony & Roemer, 2003; see also Box 13.1). Clients may also be taught breathing exercises and applied muscle relaxation (Öst, 1988), which can help them progress towards a desired state of relaxation. Alternatively, they may be taught social and communication skills, for instance, through role-plays or through observing an expert communicator (Antony & Roemer, 2003). In *fixed-role therapy,* from the personal construct approach, clients specifically play out a new character and behaviour in order to practise and develop a new repertoire of means towards goals (Fransella & Winter, 2012).

One form of interpersonal skills training of particular relevance to the present framework is *assertion* or *assertiveness training* (Sanchez, Lewinsohn, & Larson, 1980). A key component of this is learning to be clear and direct with others about what we do want, as well as what we do not want. For instance, Mei's therapist might encourage her to look at ways of communicating more clearly to Rob what she wants in her life, and how she feels towards him, and then to role-play this in the therapeutic context. For instance, 'Rob, I really love you. And the first part of our relationship was amazing. But I feel that, these days, we're wanting really different things in life. What do you think? Should we be together or apart?' In terms of the present framework, the basic principle here is that the best way of getting our interpersonal desires met is by communicating them to others in clear, direct, and non-critical ways. We may assume that others know what we want (e.g., 'Rob just wants to slob out') but, as we have seen in Chapter 7, this may be an erroneous cognition and ineffective in helping us move forwards. From an assertiveness training standpoint, 'aggressive' (e.g., 'Rob, I'm going to move on in my life because you're a lazy slob') and 'passive-aggressive' forms of communication (e.g., 'Rob, I know that you're really unhappy with our relationship and so I'm going to try and move on') may also be relatively ineffective in helping us get what we want. Assertiveness training may be particularly helpful for women and other marginalised groups who have been trained to prioritise the desires and goals of others (Chaplin, 1988; McCormick, 2012).

Behavioural therapists, particularly in inpatient settings, may also use *contingency management procedures*, in which clients are directly rewarded for behaviours that are viewed as being constructive and effective (Correia et al., 2011). For instance, people recovering from drug addiction may be rewarded with tokens or vouchers for opioid-negative urine specimens. These methods have shown positive impacts and can be seen as ways of directly influencing the evaluation process: creating 'alternative reinforcers' that add weight to the 'change' rather than the 'sustain' side of the decisional balance.

BOX 13.3

Interpersonal psychotherapy

Interpersonal psychotherapy (IPT) is an empirically-supported treatment for depression, which aims to alleviate clients' suffering through improving their here-and-now interpersonal relating (Stuart & Robertson, 2003). It is informed by psychodynamic thinking (in particular, interpersonal psychiatry; Sullivan, 1953), but has the focused, technique-based, time-limited structure of the cognitive-behavioural therapies. As with attachment theory, IPT conceptualises people as having a highest-order desire for relatedness and social

(Continued)

support (either through a close interpersonal relationship or their wider social nexus), and psychological difficulties as the failure to actualise this, often due to poor patterns of communication (i.e., ineffective means) (Howard, 2014). Hence, the role of the therapist is to 'assist the patient to appreciate that his or her communication is not effective – i.e., that it is not effectively achieving the patient's goal of meeting his or her attachment needs' (Stuart & Robertson, 2003, p. 31). Once this is achieved, the interpersonal therapist aims to help the client find – and establish – more effective means of communication.

Communication analysis, a central IPT technique, invites clients to describe, in detail, a recent difficult exchange, as if it were viewed through a video camera. The therapist then helps the client to analyse it in detail, looking at how their communication style – for instance, ambiguous communication, defensiveness, failing to communicate affect, or assuming that the other can read their mind – may have negatively impacted on the interaction (Howard, 2014; Stuart & Robertson, 2003). Role-plays may also be used to help clients to see their way of interacting more clearly, and to rehearse more effective forms of communication.

In IPT, communication analysis and skills training draw on the 'communication theory' of Kiesler (1996) and others, which is closely linked to attachment theory (Stuart & Robertson, 2003). This holds that we have characteristic styles of communicating along three dimensions – dominance, affiliation, and inclusion – and that these styles evoke complementary responses in others, which may then reinforce the original styles of communicating. More specifically, dominant forms of communication are seen as evoking submissive responses (and vice versa), affiliation as evoking affiliation, and inclusion as evoking inclusion. Here, problems are seen as occurring where a client's chronic communication style evokes responses that do not meet their highest-order desire for relatedness. 'Consider, for example, an individual who communicates a desire for care in a hostile fashion. Rather than eliciting a response which is high in affiliation, this kind of communication is almost certain to evoke a response from others which is low in affiliation – in essence, potential care providers are driven away by the hostility' (Stuart & Robertson, 2003, p. 24).

This model can help us make sense of some of the difficulties Logan experiences. He wants relatedness, but his relatively submissive and non-inclusive forms of communicating are more likely to evoke dominant and non-inclusive responses back, which then reinforce his passivity and non-inclusivity. Here, an interpersonal therapist might encourage Logan to recognise this ('metacommunicative feedback'), and to practise engaging with others in a more affiliative and inclusive way. Psychoeducation and direct encouragement might also be part of this: 'Logan, if you want others to like you, you need to show them that you like them. I know you're shy, but others can feel very shy too. Maybe you need to take a lead.'

Although IPT does not focus on the therapeutic dynamic *per se*, a closely related intervention for depression, Cognitive Behavioral Analysis System of Psychotherapy (CBASP; McCullough Jr, 2006), does. Here, the therapist uses the client–therapist relationship to help identify and modify (where appropriate) the client's characteristic style of relating. For instance, Logan's therapist might notice that, in response to Logan's passivity, they are becoming more and more dominant in the relationship, and are becoming increasingly irritated by Logan's behaviour. Rather than acting out a complementary dynamic, however, the therapist would strive to maintain a more neutral, non-complementary stance, and also to reflect on the dynamic with Logan (i.e., metacommunicate). Again, then, the focus of this interpersonal work is on helping clients to see how their means of trying to actualise their highest-order directions may be ineffective, and on helping them to establish more effective strategies.

Affective methods

Within the third-wave CBTs, like dialectical behaviour therapy (DBT), clients may also be taught skills to improve their emotion regulation capabilities (Dimeff & Linehan, 2001). From this perspective, individuals who experience psychological difficulties, in particular borderline personality disorder, may have a nervous system that is easily aroused, and lack the skills to regulate it once this happens. In other words, external stimuli evoke fast and extreme responses, impairing the client's ability to process information in the service of longer-term goals. In terms of the present framework, this can be understood as bodily strivings (for safety, perhaps, in particular) going rogue, such that the attainment of other higher-order goals becomes undermined. When Logan, for instance, feels criticised by his dad, his anger rises in a flash and he lashes out: 'You're an arsehole yourself. You've done nothing in your life. You're a waster.' Here, then, clients may be trained to identify and label their emotions, and taught techniques to reduce, or tolerate, them: for instance, distracting themselves, visualising themselves in a 'safe space', or adopting a 'helicopter view' to see the bigger picture (Baer & Huss, 2008).

As part of this, or used as a therapy in its own right, clients may also be taught mindfulness skills (Mardula & Larkin, 2014). This can help clients to develop the ability to detach themselves from rogue emotional drivers, and to return to more 'centred', measured states of mind. In addition, mindfulness, like other third-generation CBTs, encourages clients to develop an 'acceptance' of what is: an open, compassionate relationship to the present moment. As with the existential approaches, then, the focus here is less on getting closer to our goals through establishing more effective strategies, and more on doing this through lowering our expectations and standards for how things 'should' be.

CONCLUSION

Although classical behavioural psychology tended to view human beings in relatively non-agentic terms, contemporary CBT approaches – particularly as translated into therapeutic practice – are highly compatible with the present notion of clients as directional and intelligible. The particular contributions of the cognitive-behavioural therapies to the present framework are:

- Identifying the problems caused by vertical conflicts: when people are not effective at actualising their higher-order directions.
- Recognising how short-term thinking strategies can interfere with long-term wellbeing.
- Highlighting the importance of the planning, action, and feedback phases in actualising directions.
- Establishing well-evidenced techniques for helping clients to identify helpful thoughts.
- Establishing well-evidenced methods for helping clients to plan helpful activities.
- Establishing well-evidenced methods for helping clients to try out, and monitor the success of, particular means of actualising their directions.

QUESTIONS FOR REFLECTION

- Think of a client you are currently working with. How good are they at getting the things they most fundamentally want in life? What might they do to become more effective?

FURTHER READING

Beck, A. T., Rush, A. J., Shaw, B. F., & Emery, G. (1979). *Cognitive therapy of depression*. New York: Guilford Press. Classic text detailing the fundamentals of cognitive therapy.

Dryden, W. (2018). *Flexibility-based cognitive behaviour therapy*. London: Routledge. Details an approach to CBT that is closely aligned to a pluralistic, goal-oriented framework.

Mansell, W., Carey, T. A., & Tai, S. J. (2013). *A transdiagnostic approach to CBT using methods of levels therapy*. London: Routledge. A brief, accessible introduction to the methods of level approach (Box 13.2). For a more detailed introduction, see Carey (2006).

PART III
DIRECTIONAL PRACTICES
Riding the elephant

In Part II of this book, we reviewed a number of methods that can facilitate the process of identifying, and working with, higher-order directions. This included free association, interpretation, internal dialogue work, meaning-oriented practices, and an unconditional acceptance of all of a client's highest-order desires. Here, in Part III, we develop this analysis further, and consider a range of specific, trans-orientation methods that may be able to facilitate these processes.

14

GOAL-ORIENTED PRACTICES

This chapter discusses:

- The potential value, and challenges of, working with goals in therapy.
- Tailoring goal-oriented practices to individual clients.
- The use of goal-based tools.
- Practical considerations when working with goals in therapy.
- The kinds of goals that it may be most helpful to set with clients.

'So, Mei, do you have a sense of what your goals are for therapy? How do you think therapy might be able to help you?' Flashback to the assessment session, and Mei is looking quizzical.

'If I knew that', she eventually responds, 'I wouldn't be here. Aren't you supposed to know?' She smiles.

I smile back, somewhat embarrassed. 'OK, sorry, let me try to put this another way. Like, if we get to– say, six months down the line. Where would you like to be? What would you like to change in your life?'

'Um,' replies Mei, 'OK, I guess I'd like– I want things to be sorted with Rob. No, I guess – that's probably unrealistic. I want to know what I want to do about my marriage. I want to be clear. Not have it running around my head all the time.'

'So being clear about what you're doing with Rob.'

'Or not doing... And, definitely spending less. I really need to cut down.'

From a directional standpoint, *goal-oriented practices* have the potential to serve as key tools in facilitating counselling and psychotherapy; indeed, goal development and pursuit may be considered a therapeutic practice in itself (Lopez et al., 2000). Goal-oriented practices can be defined as therapeutic activities which explicitly discuss or explore the client's treatment objectives. This includes: *goal setting*, 'the process of identifying and establishing goals – generally at the start of therapy' (Cooper & Law, 2018a, p. 3); *goal tracking* (or *goal monitoring*), 'the evaluation of clients' progress towards their goals, generally through some kind of individualized outcome measure' (p. 3); and *goal discussion*, or *metatherapeutic communication about goals* (Cooper, Dryden, Martin, & Papayianni, 2016; Papayianni & Cooper, 2018), in which 'client and therapist collaboratively talk about the goals for therapy' (Cooper & Law, 2018a, p. 4).

Goals have been used in therapy for several decades (Jacob et al., 2018), reaching back to the work of Charlotte Buhler (Michalak & Grosse Holtforth, 2006), and goal setting is one of the most commonly used behaviour change techniques (Epton et al., 2017). However, they are controversial (see, for instance, Rowan, 2008), and while some approaches – like CBT, interpersonal therapy (IPT), and pluralistic therapy – consider them to be integral to therapeutic practice, others – like psychoanalysis – consider them to be anathematic to the therapist's work (Grey et al., 2018).

Goal-oriented practices may be relatively formal: for instance, goal setting as part of a structured assessment interview, as with Mei above. Alternatively, they may be relatively informal and spontaneous, emerging naturally in the therapeutic dialogue. For instance, several sessions into the therapy, Logan comes to therapy particularly tired and demoralised.

LOGAN 'What– What are we doing here? I don't know what... the work is about. What's the point?'

THERAPIST 'I guess– When we started, we said that we'd focus on trying to help you overcome your anxieties.'

LOGAN   'Yes, but, I'm not really sure that's the– What's most important to me right now. There's– are we going to look at some of the stuff from my past?'
THERAPIST   'So– OK– Do you want to spend some time on that?'

To some extent, goal-oriented practices are specifically related to the intentional and post-intentional phases of the directional arc (Figure 3.1). That is, it is only once a client has intended to act in a particular way that explicit goals become relevant. However, it is important to remember here the conceptual distinction between life goals and therapy goals (Chapter 5), and that 'micro' cycles of goal-oriented activities may be taking place, without explicit, conscious links to higher-order goals. What this means is that, even if clients have not got – or are not aware of – specific life goals, they have still come to therapy for a purpose. And that, in itself, is a goal-directed act. For instance, they may have come to therapy because they want 'time to reflect', or 'to get some advice', or simply 'to feel better'. So, from a directional standpoint, there are always goals at some level, and the aim of goal-oriented practices is to make these more explicit.

VALUE OF GOAL-ORIENTED PRACTICES

Although the value of goal-oriented practices have yet to be comprehensively tested in therapy (see, for instance, Sheldon, Kasser, Smith, & Share, 2002), wider psychological research indicates that goal setting and monitoring has a reliable, positive impact on progress towards those goals, in the small to moderate range (Epton et al., 2017; Harkin et al., 2016; Locke & Latham, 2002; Schunk, 1990). Indeed, Locke et al. (1981) write, 'The beneficial effects of goal setting on task performance is one of the most robust and replicable findings in the psychological literature' (p. 145). This may be particularly true for males, Asian individuals, and for those of a younger age – though it is not clear why (Epton et al., 2017). Goal-oriented practices may be therapeutically helpful for several reasons (di Malta et al., 2018; Egan, 1994; Locke & Latham, 2002).

First, and most basically, goal-oriented practices – and particularly goal setting – provide clients with an opportunity to recognise what their directions are (Ford, 1992), and to reflect more deeply on them. That is, it supports the awareness phase of the directional arc (see Chapter 3): facilitating introspection and a greater insight into higher-order directions (di Malta et al., 2018). For instance, one client stated:

> Even though I knew they were the things I wanted, it was all jumbled up in my head so to actually write it down on paper and see what I want to do and how I want to improve myself made it a bit easier or it just clarified it a little. (di Malta et al., 2018)

Second, closely related to this, through talking about their goals, clients may also then become clearer about their problems and challenges.

Third, goal setting may energise clients (Locke & Latham, 2002), stimulating them to progress from the evaluation phase of the directional arc to intent, planning, and action (Egan, 1994). Goal setting requires clients to make a specific, 'public' statement of intent, and, in doing so, their tendencies to procrastinate or avoid goal-directed behaviours may be surmounted. Indeed, research indicates that this public element of goal setting is an important contributor to its effects, as is setting goals on a face-to-face basis, rather than online (Epton et al., 2017; Harkin et al., 2016).

Fourth, by seeing how they have progressed, goal setting and goal monitoring may also help to boost clients' 'sense of achievement, recognition, and accomplishment' (Latham & Locke, 1979, p. 72). This may then lead to a range of higher-order outcomes, such as feelings of excitement or enhanced self-esteem, as well as an increased sense of self-efficacy.

Fifth, and closely related to this, goal setting and goal monitoring may enhance persistence in goal-directed behaviours, extending effort over time (Locke et al., 1981). This may be because a lack of goal progress cannot simply be ignored (the 'ostrich problem'; Harkin et al., 2016), because of receiving incentives and 'micro-rewards' along the way (in terms of seeing goal progress) (Dolan, 2014), and because of the 'public' commitment that has been made to achieving the goal.

Sixth, goal-oriented processes may engender hope and positive expectations about goal achievement (Locke & Latham, 2002). This may be because: it instils greater self-efficacy (as above); a positive image for the future is called to mind; a potentially overwhelming problem is broken down into achievable steps; it conveys a belief in clients that they can change their lives; and, through goal monitoring, clients can see any progress that they are making. Mackrill (2010) writes, 'Focusing on client goals encourages clients to look forwards'. He adds, 'When a therapist focuses on a client's goals, the therapist implicitly emphasizes that existence involves a person having dreams, hopes, and desires' (p. 98).

Seventh, goal setting – and particularly goal monitoring – may focus effort, providing a 'target' and directing attention to the specific objectives being sought (di Malta et al., 2018; Locke et al., 1981). In therapy, it may be easy for clients and therapists to wander 'off topic'. Goal-oriented practices remind clients of the key issues they want to work on, and can help to bring them back on track. As one client stated, 'Instead of drifting along through life getting from day to day – surviving but not living, setting goals and working on achieving them focused my life in ways that nothing else had' (Feltham, Martin, Walker, & Harris, 2018, p. 74).

Eighth, some clients may feel that having goals creates a safer, more predictable structure for therapy. One client stated: 'I quite like knowing what I'm in for' (di Malta et al., 2018).

Ninth, goal-oriented practices may help clients feel more empowered – and therefore more confident in reaching their goals – by being 'constructed' (as with the present framework) as choice-making, intelligible beings, who have the potential to act upon their worlds (Cooper & Law, 2018a). Mackrill (2010) writes, 'Focusing on goals and tasks in psychotherapy is also an implicit way of drawing attention to a client's agency. ... [T]he client is not just thrown into the world; the client is also a thrower, a mover and a shaker in the world of things and people' (pp. 101–102).

Tenth, and closely related to this, goal-oriented practices may help clients feel better about themselves. It sends a clear message to them that 'their individuality and uniqueness are highly valued, and that their distinct perspective is considered an important contribution to the therapy process' (Elliot & Church, 2002, p. 252).

Eleventh, goal-oriented practices can help to ensure that clients and therapists have a shared understanding of the goals of the therapeutic work, a factor which is known to correlate with positive therapeutic outcomes (Tryon, 2018; Tryon & Winograd, 2011). Put conversely, difficulties can emerge in the therapeutic work when clients and therapists have different understandings of what the purpose of the therapy is. For instance, a client might be wanting advice, while a therapist might be wanting to provide the client with a space to reflect. Here, goal setting and goal discussion can help to bring these issues to the fore, and provide a forum in which clients and therapists can establish more mutually agreeable and 'aligned' (McLeod, 2018a) goals (or, if not, identify alternative ways in which the client might be helped). Consistent with this, research shows that clients are more likely to engage in therapy, and follow through with the therapists' suggestions and recommendations, if their goals for the treatment are accommodated (Miller et al., 1997).

With respect to shared understandings, therapists may feel that they already have a good sense of what clients want from therapy. However, research suggests that, in many instances, this may not be the case, and reflect therapists' over-confidence. Swift and Callahan (2009), for instance, found that in only about a third of cases did clients and therapists match on the same two goals for therapy, in about half of cases they matched on one, and in around 10% they matched on neither. For instance:

> [O]ne client indicated that her goal for treatment was to learn to cope with her recent divorce and loss of contact with her son because of restricted visitation rights. On the other hand, that client's trainee therapist reported that the goal for treatment was to help the client overcome symptoms of post-traumatic stress disorder related to a car accident. (p. 234)

In addition, research shows that most clients do want goals to be set for therapy. A survey of around 300 lay-people, for instance, found that approximately six out of ten expressed a preference for goals to be set, two out of ten did not want goals, and two out of ten said that they did not mind (Cooper & Norcross, 2015). Research on goal setting with young people also found that around 70% agreed that having goals helped them to stay on track, and a similar percentage found it easy or very easy to set goals (Pender, Tinwell, Marsh, & Cowell, 2013).

Finally, discussing and eliciting clients' goals for therapy may have an important ethical dimension. McLeod and Mackrill (2018) write:

[A]voidance of clarification around client goals could be regarded as an ethical breach, as it would make it impossible to know whether the direction and focus of therapy was congruent with the client's views. That is, some kind of explicit checking-out of therapeutic goals is a necessary aspect of respect for client autonomy. (p. 27)

CHALLENGES AND LIMITATIONS OF GOAL-ORIENTED PRACTICES

There are also important challenges and limitations to goal-oriented practices. Perhaps the most obvious one is that clients, particularly at the start of therapy, may not know what their goals are. In one study, around 40% of clients experienced uncertainty about identifying their goals. One client, for instance, said: 'It's nice that I was asked my opinion on something… but it kind of put me in the spotlight a bit and I was just there, like… "I don't know, whatever you think is best"' (di Malta et al., 2018). In terms of the directional arc (Figure 3.1), the problem here is that goal setting 'speaks to' clients at the intention phase. That is, it assumes that clients have already committed – or are close to committing – to a particular end. If, indeed, clients have been through the awareness and evaluation phases of the directional arc, then this is not a problem. But if the client is still trying to recognise and evaluate what they want, then goal setting may be premature.

Closely related to this, the goals that clients articulate (if at all) will only ever be their conscious, 'self-attributed' ones; and, as we have seen, these may bear little relationship to their implicit motives – the ones that seem more closely connected to their real-world behaviours (see Chapter 5). Mei's direction towards Saul, for instance, is an intangible, embodied yearning – towards something 'warmer-closer-clearer-freer' – not something that she can consciously articulate. Hence, as with Mei, the goals that clients are able to put into words may be a vast over-simplification of their complex, dynamic, fluid strivings. As one client put it, in relation to therapeutic goal setting:

> I'm working with– like a big tangled mess, and I didn't know where to start with it, so I didn't want to set out with, 'Right, this is what I want to focus on,' because I wasn't sure that that might actually be the correct thing to focus on. (di Malta et al., 2018)

Furthermore, as Hoffman (2009) states, 'Many clients based their initial treatment goals largely on their preconceived ideas about psychotherapy. Often these are inaccurate, such as the depictions of the psychotherapeutic process found in mass media portrayals' (p. 49). So a client, for instance, may see the goal of therapy as uncovering a past trauma that can help them overcome their panic attacks, because this is what they have seen on *The Sopranos* or *In Treatment*.

There is a danger, then, that goal-setting and goal-monitoring practices can actually divert clients away from higher-order, more intrinsic directions. Based on the research (see Chapter 5), this may particularly be the case where clients have less awareness of their internal bodily states and are less concerned with self-consistency.

Another potential problem with goal-oriented practices is that it may make clients feel judged and pressurised, and that they have failed themselves or their therapists if they are not showing 'good' goal progress. One client said that they were hesitant of setting goals 'because if I fail them, then I'll feel worse about myself, whereas if I don't set goals then I can be surprised by my progress' (di Malta et al., 2018). Goal-oriented practices may be experienced by clients as emphasising attainment, striving, and doing over a more 'authentic' state of being, or of not fitting how they perceive themselves.

Closely related to this, clients may feel that their problems, or their way of being in the world, cannot be articulated in goal-related terms (di Malta et al., 2018). One client, for instance, stated that the main issues in their life were too broad to be simply represented as goals (di Malta et al., 2018). Along these lines, clients may feel that formulating their difficulties in terms of goals is diminishing. Another client stated, 'I just feel – it's almost like a checklist. It's almost, like, if it's something so easy to just, like, cross it off' (di Malta et al., 2018). As here, clients may also experience goal-oriented practices as mechanistic (di Malta et al., 2018).

TAILORING GOAL-ORIENTED PRACTICES

From the standpoint of a directional framework, then, goal-oriented practices have the potential to be very helpful in therapy, but they also have the potential to be unhelpful. A key factor here is likely to be how they are done. Specifically, goals which are allowed to emerge – and evolve – flexibly, through therapist–client dialogue and collaboration, may be most helpful. By contrast, goals that are 'pinned down', early on in therapy, with little discussion, exploration, or follow-up dialogue may be of least help (di Malta et al., 2018; Michalak & Grosse Holtforth, 2006). As one group of service users stated:

> [T]he goal setting process needs to be an ongoing conversation, with either party feeling able to bring up the goals to discuss and adjust again whenever they feel it is appropriate. Goal setting can't simply be a 'set and forget' process if it is going to be successful. (Feltham et al., 2018, p. 82)

This means that clients should not be pressurised to set goals too early on, and should be reassured that it is 'OK' if they do not have clear goals at the start (di Malta et al., 2018; Feltham et al., 2018). Similarly, goal-oriented processes which allow for complexities and subtleties to emerge may be more helpful than those that expect simple, one-dimensional objectives. In support of this, Oddli, McLeod, Reichelt, and Rønnestad (2014) found that, although highly experienced psychotherapists did practise in a range of goal-oriented ways (for instance, ensuring that what happened in therapy was meaningful and relevant), they did not explicitly discuss goals with their clients. Rather, goal-oriented work was 'processual' and 'nonlinear'. They write:

> By accepting the complexity, ambivalence, conflicting goals, and resistance, the psychotherapists revealed a nuanced and complex understand of the forces of change, and did not resort to a straightforward description of goals to which the client had to commit. (p. 261)

This is consistent with the findings that experts in a particular field tend to use *forward-driven strategies*, whereas novices use *backward-driven strategies* (Bédard & Chi, 1992). In the former, the individual works on the immediate problems given, without specific regard to the goal. By contrast, with the latter, the individual starts with goals, and then work backwards to the problems given. This raises some interesting challenges to goal-oriented practices, although it does not, in itself, show that forward-driven strategies are more effective. Rather, it suggests that when people have sufficient knowledge in a particular field (such as experienced therapists), they may be more willing to risk launching into particular ways of working without an explicit focus, with the knowledge and confidence that it typically produces good outcomes. By contrast, having an explicit direction may be more important to novices in a field, who do not have a more intuitive sense of where they should be going.

In addition, research suggests that clients may benefit more from goal-oriented practices when therapists help them to set appropriate goals: for instance, realistic, manageable, and specific goals (di Malta et al., 2018; see below). For instance, as one client put it, 'She's kind of helping pick out a book on a book shelf essentially, and which one and where it is'.

Ultimately, however, the helpfulness or unhelpfulness of goal-related practices may be dependent on the individual client; and we have already seen how clients differ markedly in their desires, or readiness, to use goals in therapy. From the perspective of a directional framework, goals may be particularly useful for clients who are already at the intentional phase of the directional arc: clients who have a sense of what they want but need the motivation and focus to move into planning and action. On the other hand, clients who are at – or want to stay within – the awareness and evaluation phases may have less need for specific goal-oriented practices. In addition, goal-oriented practices may be more helpful to clients who value structured, focused, and action-oriented ways of living their lives, while clients who want to just 'be', or who want to move towards a less task-focused and pressurised way of living, may find goals less helpful. Some clients may also be put off by the language of goals (Egan, 1994), or lack the cognitive capacity to be able to articulate them (Jacob et al., 2018).

GOAL-BASED TOOLS

Goal setting and monitoring may be facilitated through the use of goal-based tools. These are handwritten, or digital, questionnaires and procedures that allow clients to set out one or more goals for therapy, and then to rate their progress towards these goals on a regular basis. There are several self-report goal-based tools that have been shown to be reliable and valid (Lloyd, Duncan, & Cooper, 2018). These include:

- *Goal Attainment Scaling* (GAS) (Kiresuk & Sherman, 1968; Kiresuk, Smith, & Cardillo, 1994): the most widely-adopted approach to measuring goal progress in therapy. Goals for therapy are identified, and then expected outcome levels for each goal are set, with ratings at the end of therapy. It is time-consuming to train in and apply with clients but gives a rigorous assessment of outcomes against expectations.
- The *Motivational Structure Questionnaire* (MSQ)/*Personal Concerns Inventory* (PCI) (Cox, 2000; Cox & Klinger, 2011a): clients describe their concerns in different areas of life, identify goals for each concern, and then rate each goal on a number of dimensions, including 'chance of success' and 'when it will happen'. The MSQ was developed as a key part of systematic motivational counselling for clients with addiction issues (see Box 11.2). It is relatively time-consuming to administer but gives a very in-depth and comprehensive goal assessment. It can also be used to analyse intergoal relationships (i.e., synergies and dysergies; Cox & Klinger, 2011c). The PCI is a modified and abridged version of the MSQ that is designed to be simpler and more user-friendly.
- *Personal Project Analysis* (Little, 1983): as with the MSQ and PCI, this is an in-depth procedure for eliciting and appraising goals. It also has a 'cross-impact matrix' that can be used to assess synergies and dysergies between directions. It is widely used in psychological research and can be applied within a clinical setting. A digital version of this tool is available.
- The *Goals Form* (Cooper, 2015b): a simple, easy-to-use measure in which up to seven goals for therapy are established – typically at a first assessment session – and then rated on a 1 (*not at all achieved*) to 7 (*completely achieved*) Likert-type scale. It is practical and flexible, with the capacity for session-by-session use. Simplicity of procedures, however, means that the goal-setting procedure may be less comprehensive and in-depth.
- *Goal-Based Outcome Measure* (Law & Jacob, 2015): a goal progress measure designed specifically for use with children, young people, and their parents/carers. Clients, and/or their parents, identify goals and then rate them on a session-by-session basis. As with the Goals Form, it is designed specifically for use within a clinical context, but simplicity may come at the cost of less in-depth analysis.

In addition to these *idiothetic* tools (which combine the individual [idiographic] identification of goals with general [nomothetic] ratings of progress) there are also wholly nomothetic tools, in which clients can rate progress on a series of pre-established goals (e.g., Bern Inventory of Treatment Goals; Grosse Holtforth & Grawe, 2002). There are also tools, such as the Striving Instrumentality Matrix and the Computerized Intrapersonal Conflict Assessment, which are specifically designed to assess the degrees of synergy and dysergy between different directions (see Michalak et al., 2011). Projective tools, such as the Thematic Apperception Test, are also available (Murray, 1943). These are designed to identify and evaluate implicit (rather than self-attributed) directions through the interpretations that people make of ambiguous stimuli (such as pictures).

Research with Goal Attainment Scaling (see above) suggests that clients may experience greater improvements, and find the therapy more satisfying, when such an instrument is used (Smith, 1976). This seems to be particularly the case when the client is actively involved in the goal-setting process (Willer & Miller, 1976). In addition, as we have seen, research shows that people make better progress towards goals when those goals are physically recorded and rated. This may be because it reminds them of what their goals are, and makes them feel more accountable for progressing towards them (Harkin et al., 2016). As one client stated, 'it's really helpful to have it written down on paper. Maybe you don't really acknowledge it until you actually see it' (di Malta et al., 2018). Using goal-based forms is also a way of making goal-monitoring processes more public and less private, which is another factor that has been associated with greater goal progress (Harkin et al., 2016). The use of goal-based instruments is also consistent with wider trends towards 'routine outcome monitoring' in counselling and psychotherapy services, such as NHS England's Improving Access to Psychological Therapies programme (Clark, 2011). In support of these developments, meta-analyses indicate that providing therapists with feedback on client progress brings about positive improvements in outcomes, as compared with treatment as usual (Lambert & Shimokawa, 2011). This is especially the case for clients who are at risk of poorer outcomes, or who may drop out of therapy (Lambert & Shimokawa, 2011).

In addition to these self-report goal-based tools, there are also goal identification instruments that are completed by the clinician or researcher. Potentially, these can be incorporated into therapeutic assessment and practice. One example of this is the *plan formulation method*, in which 'clinical judges' review session transcripts, identify (among other things) goals, and then these goals are rated for relevance to the case (Silberschatz, Curtis, & Nathans, 1989, see Web Resource 15.1). Another example is the Adult Intentional and Motivational Systems (AIMS; Wadsworth & Ford, 1983), which specifically aims to develop individual goal hierarchies (see Chapter 6, this volume). Here, participants are first interviewed about what they want out of life, their recent day-to-day activities, what they seek in seven different domains of life (for instance, leisure, personal growth), and additional goals and areas of satisfaction. Working from the transcriptions of these interviews, coders then seek to identify the participants' goals, and to set these out on a matrix consisting of seven life domains by four 'goal levels' (from 'Short-term specific' to Long-term very broad'). Coders also worked to draw arrows between goals that seem to have a means–end relationship (e.g., the short-term, leisure goal of 'going for a run' may lead to the longer-term, personal growth goal of 'being healthy'). Research suggests that this process produced reliable and valid matrices of the participants' goals; and one that the participants, themselves, considered very accurate.

PRACTICAL CONSIDERATIONS IN WORKING WITH GOALS

Goals for therapy can be set primarily by the therapist or by the client. However, it is generally recognised that best practice involves a collaborative process (e.g., Feltham et al., 2018), whereby 'client and therapist engage in a discussion about what goals to work toward in psychotherapy and how to work toward them' (Tryon, 2018, p. 88). In this respect, as Grosse Holtforth and Michalak (2012) state, therapy goals should be distinguished from both 'naïve treatment concerns presented by the patient' and 'treatment goals defined exclusively by the therapist' (p. 449).

Working collaboratively means that, at times, therapists will need to put to one side their own sensibilities about what clients need and trust their clients' own articulation of their goals (Duncan et al., 2004). Duncan and colleagues give the example of a client, Sarah, whose goal was to be a cheerleader but whose status as a mentally ill residential patient, and whose daily activity of watching TV and eating snack foods meant that her therapist could not accept this. Duncan et al. report that the therapy floundered until the therapist started to accept, and engage more, in Sarah's explicitly stated goal. As they started to talk more about cheerleading, and watched cheerleading contests on TV, the interactions became more vibrant and Sarah took a more active role in her community: organising a cheerleading squad for the local basketball team.

As we have seen above, however, clients can find it helpful to be guided by their therapists in this work (di Malta et al., 2018). Here, therapist expertise can lie in knowing strategies for bringing clients' highest-order – and most salutogenic – desires to the fore (see Chapter 15). This is a skilled and complex ability: as we saw with Mei, for instance, directly asking a client 'What are your goals for therapy?' may not be particularly productive. And, indeed, research shows that simply asking people to list their goals is often ineffective (Koestner et al., 2002): clients may feel put on the spot, or not know what their goals are, or feel ashamed to directly say what they want. Goal discussion, then, is an essential precursor to goal setting, and indirectly asking clients about their wants and goals may be the best way of stimulating this process. Some 'openers' might be:

- What did you hope would be different in coming here?
- What did you want to change about your life?

- Where would you like to be by the end of therapy?
- How will you know that counselling has been helpful?
- What would a future look like without the problem?
- What one word would you use to describe what you want from therapy?

(Duncan et al., 2004; Lazarus, 1981; McLeod & McLeod, 2011; Miller et al., 1997; O'Connell, 2012)

As with the Personal Concerns Inventory (see above), in establishing goals, it may be helpful for therapist and client to begin by surveying the different domains of the client's life – for instance, relationships, work, and leisure – and seeing where there are areas of dissatisfaction (Lopez et al., 2000). This, in itself, may also help to identify whether the client's goals are just in a limited number of domains, or more evenly distributed across a diversity of categories (Little, 2011).

McLeod and Mackrill (2018) suggest that many clients and therapists may find it facilitative to talk about goals as a journey. This metaphor might involve invoking 'places and destinations, modes of transport, companions on a journey, taking time out to rest, bends/forks in the road, and so on' (p. 21). For instance, a client might be asked 'Where do you want this therapy to take you?' and 'How shall we go about getting there?'

Although it is often helpful to set goals towards the beginning of therapy, these may be revisited and revised as the therapy progresses. This might be at regular review points; when difficulties or ruptures arise in the therapeutic work; or when particular goals have been achieved, to a sufficient extent, and there is a need for new directions (or bringing the therapy to an end). In addition, the focus of goal discussion and setting may just be on a particular session, rather than the therapeutic work as a whole (Papayianni & Cooper, 2018). In other words, rather than asking clients the question 'Where do you want to go through therapy?', the question may simply be 'Where do you want to go today?'

HELPFUL GOALS

In terms of guiding clients, a particularly valuable role for therapists, as identified above, may be in helping them identify and establish salutogenic goals. Based on the analysis presented in this book, the following considerations can be suggested.

Higher-order goals

Generally, clients should be encouraged to set goals that reflect (or are aligned with, see below) their highest-order directions: those things that are most fundamentally important to them (for instance, 'Develop my self-confidence,' 'Deepen my connections to others'). However, this needs to be balanced against setting goals that are specific and achievable. Higher-order goals are also likely to be those of most importance and urgency to the client but, as we have seen, some important goals – where they are very short-term, extrinsic, or dysergetic – may be unhelpful foci for the client.

Intrinsic goals

As indicated above, clients' goals should be directly related to their higher-order desires and values. This means intrinsic goals, – rather than goals that are contingent on the attitudes or actions of others (i.e., extrinsic goals, Michalak & Grosse Holtforth, 2006). Clients who are oriented towards intrinsic goals are likely to be more committed to those goals, take greater ownership of them, and experience them as more appealing (Egan, 1994).

Effective goals

A client's goals need to be credible ways of actualising their highest-order directions, rather than inefficient or indirect strategies, so it may be important to reflect with clients on what those goals are for ('laddering up', see Chapter 13), and whether they will really help the client get there. If a client, for instance, says that her goal is to lose weight because she wants to be happier, some discussion is needed about the effectiveness of this goal, and whether it will really help her get to where she wants to be.

Synergetic goals

Goals should be supportive of other therapeutic goals, or at least not in conflict with them (for instance, 'I want more time on my own', when the client has already stated 'I want to be closer to my partner') (Cox & Klinger, 2011d). Therapists should be particularly mindful of rogue goals (see Chapter 8), where the client's stated objective seems to endanger many other wants in their lives. An example of this might be a client who wants to get fitter, but where time spent at the gym is damaging their family, relational, and work life. Generally, Ford (1992) suggests that clients should strive for *goal balance*, where they are pursuing a broad number of goals through a range of strategies, rather than being too focused in any one area.

Longer-term goals

As we have seen throughout this book, many psychological difficulties may relate to the prioritisation of very short-term goals over medium or longer-term ones. It may be helpful, therefore, to encourage clients to look towards longer-term objectives as well as short- and medium-term plans, so that there is a focus beyond immediate obstacles or rewards. At the same time, however, clients' goals need to be realistically attainable (see below). Again, then, it may be important that clients strive for goal balance, where they are pursuing a range of short-, medium, and long-term goals (Ford, 1992).

Approach goals

As we saw in Chapter 5, research suggests that it is generally better for clients to be oriented towards positive, promotion goals (for instance, 'Increase my social networks'), rather than negative, prevention goals (for instance, 'Stop feeling so alone'). The latter may be particularly problematic if all of a client's goals are avoidant rather than approach (Caspar, 1995): essentially, this means that they are asking the therapist to help them 'go nowhere' (Mackrill, 2011). For Elliot and Church (2002), then, therapists should be 'discussing the ineffective and potentially problematic nature of avoidance goals [with clients], and working to reframe these goals in terms of approaching positive possibilities' (pp. 249–250). Similarly, where clients want to reduce 'unhealthy negative emotions', such as anxiety, it may be helpful to refocus them on increasing 'healthy positive emotions', such as concern (Dryden, 2018).

Realistic goals

Clients' goals need to be achievable within the therapeutic time frame. Goals that are based on unrealistically high expectations should be challenged, especially when these are expectations of feelings or other metagoals that may fuel vicious cycles (for instance, 'I want to feel calm all the time') (Dryden, 2018). Equally, therapists should challenge goals that are unrealistic because they are dependent on others, or the world, doing something (for instance, 'I want my girlfriend to stop criticising me all the time') (Dryden, 2018). These should be reframed in terms of what the client themselves can do (e.g., 'I want to feel confident to challenge my girlfriend when she criticises me'). Therapists should also be mindful of the number of goals that clients are setting: are there too many to be realistically achieved (or too few to be sufficiently challenging)? If, as the work proceeds, it becomes apparent that clients' goals are unattainable, it may be important to support them in the process of disengaging.

'Small steps' goals

Although, ultimately, clients should be aiming towards higher-order, longer-term goals, in many cases, the importance of being realistic means that it may be most therapeutically beneficial to set smaller subgoals with clients. These are objectives that they can succeed in, one step at a time. This process, also referred to as 'goal stepping' (Snyder & Taylor, 2000) or 'goal laddering' (Cox & Klinger, 2011c), can help boost clients' self-efficacy (Ford, 1992; Michalak & Grosse Holtforth, 2006), and hence their ability to achieve subsequent goals, in a virtuous cycle (see Chapter 4). For instance, if a client wants to develop relatedness in their life, an initial goal might be to join a club, followed by a goal of forming a friendship, followed by a goal of sharing more personal narratives. Research suggests that this process of breaking down superordinate goals into more manageable tasks is experienced by clients as helpful: facilitating both a sense of achievement and relieving pressure (di Malta et al., 2018). In support of this, a group of service users write:

> While it is wonderful to hear that a client has big ambitions, you won't be able to help your client sprout wings and fly to the moon! The great thing is, we as clients know this, and mostly we think this is ok; it is not your role to get us to some huge or unobtainable milestone. What clients tell us is important is the discussion and deliberation to understand together why this may be unobtainable and to work together to agree what may be a more realistic goal. (Feltham et al., 2018, p. 79)

Given such perspectives, Ford (1992) suggests that the best approach to goal setting may be to have a 'strategic emphasis on attainable short-term goals combined with a periodic review of the long-term goals that gives meaning and organization to one's short-term pursuits' (p. 99).

Challenging goals

While clients seem to benefit from realistic, small steps, therapists should also bear in mind the psychological research that difficult goals tend to lead to greater overall progress (see Chapter 5). For instance, a client whose goal is to cut down to six units of alcohol a day might be encouraged to consider whether four units might be a better objective. For Ford (1992), this is the 'optimal challenge principle': working with clients to set goals that are difficult but still attainable.

Specific goals

As also discussed in Chapter 5, goals that are specific, clearly-defined, concrete, verifiable/measurable, and simple (e.g., 'Talk back to my bully at work'), may be preferable to goals which are vague, abstract, and complex (e.g., 'Be assertive'). In part, this might be because they are easier to monitor. However, the specificity of goals needs to be weighed against their relative order (see above). Also, goals that are too specific may lack flexibility and make it difficult for the client to revise their goals to a more meaningful, or realistic, objective.

Process-focused goals

Finally, goals that extend over time (for instance, 'enjoy my final year at college') rather than a single endpoint (for instance, 'get a good final grade') may support a more ongoing sense of wellbeing and be less pressurising. As Miller et al. (1960) write:

> [S]uccessful living is not a 'well-defined problem,' and attempts to convert it into a well-defined problem by selecting explicit goals and subgoals can be an empty deception ... [I]t is better to plan towards a kind of continual 'becoming' than

towards a final goal. The problem is to sustain life, to formulate enduring Plans, not to terminate living and planning as if they were task that had to be finished. (p. 114)

CONCLUSION

Within the project and performance management fields, it is often stated that people should develop SMART goals (Specific, Measurable, Assignable, Realistic, and Time-related). However, it is worth bearing in mind that the focus of much of the work on goals is on profit and productivity maximisation rather than psychological wellbeing (e.g., Latham & Locke, 1979). As we have seen in Chapter 5, the achievement of goals *per se* does not necessarily mean that people will actualise more of their higher-order directions and therefore achieve greater wellbeing. A person, for instance, might achieve a well-defined goal of increasing their earnings by £5,000 within a year but such extrinsic goal achievement is not actually associated with greater happiness. Hence, when it comes to therapy, goals need to be more than SMART. They need to be... (At this point, I was hoping to come up with a compelling new acronym for what goals in therapy should be. Unfortunately, after many hours on acronym generator programs, the best I could come up with was 'HEALS CRISPS': Higher-order, Effective, Approach, Longer-term, Synergetic, Challenging, Realistic, Intrinsic, Small steps, Process-focused, and Specific. Sorry!)

QUESTIONS FOR REFLECTION

- Which of your clients do you think might benefit most from goal-oriented practices? Why is that?
- What kinds of goals do you think might be most helpful for clients? Do you agree that they should meet the HEALS CRISPS criteria? (And can you come up with a better acronym!)

FURTHER READING

Cooper, M., & Law, D. (Eds.). (2018). *Working with goals in counselling and psychotherapy.* Oxford: Oxford University Press. A wide-ranging collection of chapters on all aspects of goal-oriented therapeutic work.

15

WORKING WITH DIRECTIONS IN COUNSELLING AND PSYCHOTHERAPY

This chapter discusses a range of further therapeutic methods that emerge from a directional framework:

- Therapeutic methods for helping clients to identify their higher-order directions: descriptive, creative, experiential, and relational.
- Formulation based on a directional framework.
- Integration in practice: a summary of methods for different phases of the directional arc.

HELPING CLIENTS TO IDENTIFY HIGHER-ORDER DIRECTIONS

If psychological wellbeing comes from actualising our highest-order directions, then helping clients to develop an awareness of these directions is likely to be an important element of the therapeutic work. As Mansell et al. (2013), for instance, write, 'the core mechanism of any effective therapy is the degree to which it can help a person focus on a present moment perception in order to develop awareness of the associated higher-level goals' (p. 53). Through this process, clients can develop a greater sense of what they really want in life, and therefore the means that they need to adopt to get there. It can also help them address the higher-level conflicts that, from a methods of levels perspective, are the critical ones that need addressing (Carey, 2008). Of course, this process of identifying higher-order directions is closely associated with goal-oriented practices (see Chapter 14), and may be a precursor to it, or a part of the ongoing therapeutic work. However, while goal-oriented focus primarily on conscious, self-attributed directions, the methods in this chapter rely 'not only on rational information processing, but also on imaginative and emotional processing' (Willutzki & Koban, 2011, p. 439).

To facilitate this review, we will focus on four different kinds of direction-elicitation methods: descriptive, projective, experiential, and relational (Cooper & Cruthers, 1999). Methods from each of these domains may be combined in a variety of ways.

Descriptive methods

Descriptive methods are those practices in which clients are helped to express their higher-order directions in verbal or written form (Cooper & Cruthers, 1999). Verbal prompts, here, may be similar to those used to set goals. For instance:

- What are the things you most want in life?
- What are your deepest desires?
- What do you value most in life? (Egan, 1994)

A focus on desired future possibilities may be a particularly useful way in to elicit higher-order directions. For instance:

- Who would you like to see yourself as being in the future?
- What would you like to be doing in the future that you are not doing now? (Egan, 1994)

From an existential perspective, this process may also be facilitated by helping clients consider future limitations, in particular death. For instance, in the appropriate situation, it might be possible to ask a client, 'If you knew you only had one year left to live, what would it be most important for you to do?' Such methods are supported by evidence that, faced with these situations, people tend to connect more deeply with their own personal values when compared with the broader values of the society in which they are immersed (Martin, Campbell, & Henry, 2004).

Creative methods

Creative methods are those techniques in which clients are encouraged to express their higher-order directions through expressive media. For instance, a client might be asked to draw an image that represents something they want deeply in their life, or they might be invited to find an object to symbolise the person they want to become (Carrell, 2001).

Life lines (Carrell, 2001), or *time-lines* (McLeod & McLeod, 2016), are a creative method with evidence of effectiveness (Lee, Cohen, Edgar, Laizner, & Gagnon, 2006). Here, clients are invited to draw a horizontal line across the centre of a page, with 'birth' marked on the left of the line and 'now' towards the right. Clients and therapists then work together to 'fill in' life events and turning points along the line. After this, there is then an opportunity for clients to depict their desired future at the right-hand end of the line: where they ideally want things to go.

Guided visualisations are another creative method that can be used to help clients identify their higher-order desires and hoped-for futures. For instance, a client could be asked, 'Can you picture your ideal life? What would it look like? What would you be doing? How would things be?'

Ferrucci (1982), who comes from a psychosynthesis background, suggests the following visualisation. It builds on the descriptive exercise of inviting clients to write down what the main purposes in their lives are. Next, they choose the one that seems most salient at the present time. The client is then invited to close their eyes and to allow an image to emerge that symbolises that purpose to them. They are then invited to imagine seeing it at the end of a long, clear path, on the top of a hill, and to visualise, on both sides of the path (but not blocking the path), the presence of various forces (such as situations or persons) that will try to stop them reaching that purpose. Clients are encouraged to visualise themselves slowly proceeding on the path, feeling the pull of the various obstacles but willing themselves to the top. Once there, they are invited to enjoy it and to reflect on how it feels to achieve their purpose.

Lazarus (1981) suggests another visualisation called the *deserted island fantasy technique*, which he often uses as an assessment tool. Here clients are invited to imagine being whisked off to a deserted island, with or without a companion, where they can choose to spend their time however they like. For Lazarus, this can reveal some deep insights about what clients want, and also how they feel that they can get what they want. For instance, one client said, 'You said there's lots of food? Good, I'd have an orgy – food and sex, not necessarily in that order' (p. 106). Diagnostically, however, what is also interesting about this exercise is how clients relate to their wants or believe that they can be actualised. For instance, a client's response might be 'God, I'd feel absolutely raw and unprotected in that situation' or 'Knowing me, I'd say that my moodiness would ruin everything. Here is a perfect chance to have a great time, but I'd blow it' (p. 106). Here, then, clients are not just revealing their higher-order directions, but also their relationship to them.

Another method, part of the *Elaboration of Positive Goal Perspectives* (EPOS) intervention module (Willutzki & Koban, 2011), invites clients to generate images of an ideal future, irrespective of what might be realistic or not. The *5-year question*, the centrepiece of the module, is as follows:

> Imagine that I met you in five [or three or ten] years from today and up to then everything has turned out well in your life. You have reached certain personal goals that were important for you, and many other things went just the way you wanted. Where am I meeting you, what are you doing [in 5 years], and how do you feel? (p. 443).

The therapist then explores the imagery with clients, encouraging them to continue describing it 'in the present': for instance, 'I am sitting in a café in France', rather than 'I would be sitting in a café in France'. Once the visualisation is concluded, both clients and therapists listen to a recording of the session, and in the next meeting they move on to setting concrete and specific goals (Willutzki & Koban, 2011).

Creative methods may also involve helping clients to identify higher-order directions that are projected into their dreams, art work, or pre-existing fantasies about the future. For instance, Beitman, Soth, and Bumby (2005) discuss therapeutic work with clients' *expectation videos*: defined as their mental plans and images of future possibilities. Here, clients might be asked to describe problematic (for instance, overly-pessimistic) expectation videos, to 'let them go', and to generate instead a future vision where they have achieved everything they want. Clients might also be invited to write down their 'future autobiography'.

Another creative method that may help clients identify higher-order directions is by asking them to identify others who embody the characteristics that they desire. McLeod and Mackrill (2018) give the following example, which also includes the use of a timeline:

> Tom was 15 years of age and had lost his way at school. He had started to skip classes and avoided completing homework. Worried about his progress, his mother persuaded him to make an appointment with the school counsellor. Following an initial exploratory meeting, the counsellor asked Tom if he would be interested in joining a 9-week *school-to-work* group that was starting after the vacation. Tom agreed to give it a try. 'School-to-work' comprised a small group of students, was highly participative and experiential, and was oriented around the idea of identifying possible selves (i.e., what do you want to do/ be when you leave school?) and identifying a plan for how to become that

person. A key activity involved finding images of adults doing things that were appealing to the young person, and then talking about the characteristics and attributes of people in these roles. Other helpful activities included making contact with adults in the community who represented 'possible future selves'; and constructing a timeline that connected up their present situation with their hoped-for future work role, and specified tasks, roadblocks, and decision-points on that journey. All this was extremely helpful for Tom, who was able to map out a direction in life that included both his ideal possible self (being a professional footballer) as well as other options. While being a highly goal-oriented intervention, the group leaders did not use words such as 'goals' or 'objectives', but instead created activities and exercises that concretized these concepts at an experiential level. (pp. 22–23)

Another creative method that may be particularly engaging for young people in identifying goals – and means towards those goals – is called *goal maps* (Eames & Denborough, 2017). Here, young people are invited to draw a sports pitch, such as a football field, and to write down a goal at the top near the goal net. Uniquely, the young person is then invited to draw on the map the 'team players', who have, or can, help them achieve that goal – for instance, friends, teachers, and youth workers – and to diagrammatise the process of passing the ball forward until they score. This approach, then, encourages young people to think about ways that their directional processes are supported by – and embedded within – a wider social network. In this method, young people are also first asked to depict how goals have been scored in the past, to help build confidence. Then are they encouraged to think about how goals might be achieved in the future.

Experiential methods

Experiential methods are those in which clients dramatise their particular directions and the dynamic between them. Probably the most common form of this is two-chair work (see Chapter 11).

Cullen and Russell (1989) propose an interesting group exercise called the 'Circle of wants'. In this, participants are asked to make a long list of wants and then identify five that are the most important to them. The person then goes into the centre of the group and other group members are assigned one of the wants. The 'wants' are all asked to speak at the same time, to yell and scream what they want in role, and the person gets to experience what it is like to be at the centre of that – all those conflicting desires. After some time of experiencing this, the person in the centre is invited to start 'managing' the different 'wants': for instance, telling some to be quiet and encouraging others to take a more dominant role. As well as recognising the different directions, this exercise is about developing the capacity to stand back from different directions and learning to coordinate them from a 'centred' place.

Relational methods

Relational methods are those that use the therapeutic relationship itself to help clients identify their higher-order directions. As Grawe (2004) writes, the therapeutic relationship can be viewed as a 'diagnostic instrument' (p. 105) for identifying a client's underlying motivations, and the dynamics between them. Here, the therapist can be asking: 'What does this client seem to want from me?' 'What are they pulling me to do?' 'How do they want me to be?' 'How do they want me to see them?' (Caspar, 1995, p. 150). This can be conceptualised as the client's unconscious *plan* for therapy (Silberschatz, 2017). For instance, Mei's warmth, her use of humour, and her deference gives a sense that she really wants to be liked by her therapist. Logan, on the other hand, seems to want certainty from his therapist, and also a sense of being respected – of being seen as a 'man'. As Yalom (2001, p. 52) suggests, there may also be times when it is appropriate for therapists to directly ask these questions to clients: 'What do you want from me, here, now?'

In trying to sense what the client wants from their relationship, a therapist may find it useful to consider the desires that emerge in their relationship with particular clients: their 'countertransference'. As we saw in Box 13.3, characteristic styles of relating may evoke complementary responses. My feeling of warmth towards Mei, for instance, suggests that Mei may be seeking affiliation, while the therapist's sense of frustration and irritation with Logan at times suggest that Logan may be seeking dominance and certainty in others. And, in terms of heightening awareness, it may be important that the therapist does not simply 'act into' the client's desires – as proposed in CBASP (see Chapter 13). A therapist, for instance, who consistently points out to Logan how he is looking for certainty in others may be more useful in enhancing his awareness of this desire than a therapist who simply takes control.

Higher-order directions, and conflicts between them, may also be revealed in the difficulties, ruptures, and frustrations that arise in therapeutic work. For instance, the therapist's feeling of frustration with Logan seems to relate to some disparity between Logan's explicit therapeutic goals and something more intrinsic and unconscious. Logan's explicit goals for therapy are to overcome his anxieties, and he says repeatedly that he wants to change. And yet, in many instances, Logan will spend long periods in therapy 'bragging' about friends of his who have done such-and-such, or how 'nasty' he is. Here, as well as his explicit directions, Logan seems to have an implicit and unacknowledged direction towards boosting his self-worth in the eyes of others. Given how dysergetic this may be with his more explicitly-stated directions, this seems an important issue to discuss with him.

DIRECTIONAL FORMULATION

The process of *formulation* also closely links to goal setting (Chapter 14), as well as the identification of higher-order directions (see above). In formulation, 'the therapist and client co-create a story or narrative that describes and explains the issues the person wants help with' (Law, 2018, p. 168). Formulation typically takes place in the first few sessions of therapy, and aims to guide the therapeutic methods used (Johnstone & Dallos, 2006). However, it may be preferable to consider it in terms of the verb-like 'formulating' – or 'progressive hypothesising' – rather than as a static, noun-like thing. In other words, it is an 'interactive, vibrant and live activity' (Dallos, Wright, Stedman, & Johnstone, 2006, p. 167) that is increasingly refined over the course of therapy (Caspar, 1995).

In developing a formulation, it is important to consider that clients are likely to come to therapy with their own 'client formulation' of the problem (Beitman et al., 2005). Mei, for instance, attributes her problems to not having the confidence to ask for what she wants; Logan wonders if there is something 'wrong' with the 'wiring' in his brain. Hence, as argued from a pluralistic standpoint, it may be preferable to think of this process as *co-formulating*: therapist and client working together to make sense of the issues that the client is experiencing (Cooper & McLeod, 2011; McLeod & McLeod, 2016). At the same time, as we have suggested throughout this book, clients may have little awareness of their higher-order directions, or the dynamics between them. Co-formulating, therefore, should not just rely on the client's verbal self-report or explicit client–therapist dialogue. Rather, the therapist should draw on a range of other sources of information, such as observations of the client's behaviours, styles of communication, and expressed emotions, as well as their own countertransferential response to the client, to help build up the most accurate picture.

Directional or *goal-based formulations* 'refer to understandings of clients and their problems that are based on a teleological, purpose-oriented understanding of self' (Cooper & Law, 2018a, p. 4). It is a non-diagnostic approach, based around trying to understand a client's directions, their relationship to them, and the relationships between them (Caspar, 1995). Drawing on the framework developed in this book, three key questions to consider are:

- Which higher-order direction(s) is my client struggling to actualise?
- Are there ways that my client is trying to actualise their higher-order directions that are ineffective?
- What conflicts between directions might underpin my client's difficulties?

Based on the answers to these questions, we can then go on to consider how our clients might reconfigure their ways of being in the world so that they can actualise their directions more fully.

Mei, for instance, seems to be struggling to experience the intimacy, excitement, and passion that she wants in her life. More than that, she seems to lack a sense of meaning: that her life has some purpose and value. In part, this seems to be because she is also wanting stability in her life, and because she wants others (Olivia, Rob) to be happy. However, it also seems to be because Mei has a powerful desire to please others – perhaps for relatedness, perhaps for self-worth – and this does not seem to be such an effective means towards her higher-order ends. Instead, it seems to mean that people take her for granted: getting her, ultimately, less of what she actually wants. Here, then, is a potential point of therapeutic 'leverage': if the therapist can help Mei move away from trying to please others and/or towards more effective strategies for achieving relatedness and self-worth, she may feel better in her life. Closely related to this, at times, Mei's difficulties in getting what she wants seems to come down to a lack of assertiveness. Rather than proactively trying to sort things with Saul, for instance, she tends to wait for him to approach her; and the same things tends to happen with Rob, and also her mother. This is intelligible, in terms of trying to avoid rejection, shame, or interpersonal hurt, but it is a short-term strategy without any real long-term value: if she is going to be rejected by Saul, for instance, it will happen at some point. We have, then, a second point of therapeutic leverage closely related to the first: helping Mei to become more assertive and move from avoidance of interpersonal issues to proactively tackling them.

Logan, like Mei, seems to be struggling to achieve the relatedness and sense of purpose that he wants in his life. However, the directional conflicts for Logan, and his ineffective strategies, are quite different. At a very basic level, Logan's strategies for developing connections with people, particularly young women, are not good at getting him the intimacy he wants. Similarly, his use of cannabis seems to be worsening his anxiety – except in the very short-term – rather than making it better. Closely connected to this, Logan's compulsive behaviours, like his door checking, bring very short-term reassurance, but at the cost of greatly enhanced long-term anxiety. A principal focus of the therapeutic work with Logan, then, is likely to be on helping him to stand back from short-term, temporary 'gains', and to try to act in ways that are of longer-term, ongoing benefit.

In working to develop such directional formulations, there are a range of other questions that can be asked, as developed in this book:

- At which phase(s) of the directional arc is my client having the greatest difficulties (awareness, evaluation, intention, planning, action, feedback, termination)?
- Which aspect(s) of the directional process is my client struggling to actualise (a sense of direction, attainability, progress, achievement, appreciation)? What might my client's emotions suggest about this?
- What are the characteristics of my client's most important directions, and how salutogenic are they (e.g., intrinsic versus extrinsic, approach versus avoidance)?
- What might my client be trying to achieve through their symptoms and emotions? (Caspar, 1995)

- What are the beliefs, perceptions, and misperceptions that form the vertical links between the directions? (Goldstein, 1990)
- Could my client's lack of actualisation, in fact, be caused by external factors? Are there actually any points of therapeutic leverage?

In developing an understanding of our client's highest-order directions – and those that are not being actualised – it may be useful to consider the literature, as summarised in Table 6.1. We may also find it helpful to consider more generic understandings of the directions and future expectations associated with any particular diagnosis our client might have. Beitman et al. (2005), for instance, suggest the following:

- Mania: 'I feel very powerful. If I imagine something, I can accomplish it.'
- Alcohol abuse: 'With alcohol I do not have to feel awful emotions. I cut off a painful future possibility. Getting drunk is more reliable than people at making me feel good.'
- Paranoid personality: 'If I trust anyone, I will be hurt. Others will take advantage of me.'
- Borderline personality: 'My feelings control me; I must escape them by running away or hurting myself. Eventually I will be abandoned.' (p. 72)

Structural diagrams (see, for instance, Figure 6.1) may be helpful in developing – and discussing – a clearer and more coherent formulation of a client's difficulties. These might be drawn out on a sheet of paper or on a whiteboard, or with self-sticking notes that can be moved over a board or wall (Caspar, 1995). This diagrammatic process is as the heart of Caspar's (1995) *plan analysis*, and his book of this title provides an excellent, comprehensive introduction to formulation from a directional perspective. In Caspar's structural diagrams, plans are formulated in the imperative (for instance, 'avoid aggressive conflicts'), with lines joining higher- and lower-order directions. Caspar suggests the use of two-ended arrows to indicate conflict, and dashed lines to indicate where one direction leads to the neglect of another. 'Frame boxes' are also used so that non-instrumental information can be included (for instance, health conditions, or the quality of the client's relationships). In developing structural diagrams, however, therapists can use whatever systems of representation they wish. For instance, the effectiveness of particular means could be represented by thicker or narrower lines (as per Figure 7.1), or different kinds of directions (for instance, intrinsic versus extrinsic or approach versus avoidance) could be represented by different colours. Figure 15.1 presents an example of a detailed plan formulation, as developed by Caspar. This is relatively complex and is a prototypical plan (for clients with psychosomatic problems) rather than one for an actual client, but it gives an idea of what a fully developed structural diagram might look like.

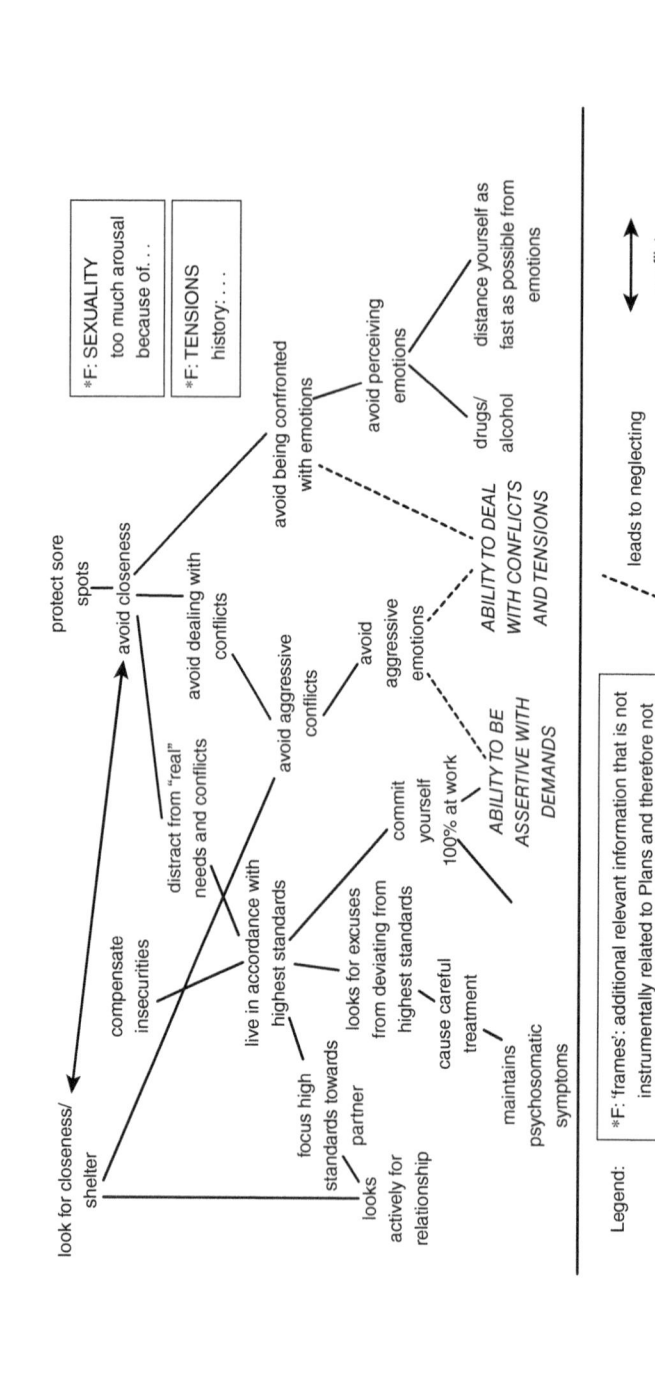

Figure 15.1 Plan formulation (Caspar, 1995, p. 82)

In contrast to a more collaborative co-formulation, Caspar (1995) suggests that a full plan analysis should be conducted 'away from' the client. He writes that, from experience, it may be asking too much of clients to speak extensively about hypothetical plans, and that it can also become an intellectual defence from real change. While this might be seen as reflecting an unwillingness to be open with the client, Caspar writes that 'the issue of power in the therapeutic relationship can not simply be dealt with by teaching a patient our vocabulary and concepts at any price' (p. 241). However, he does suggest that therapists might share parts of the directional structure with clients, and may discuss it with them using non-technical language (e.g., avoiding terms like 'plans', or 'functions', or 'directions'). For instance, Figure 15.2 presents an example of a simplified structural diagram, which might be developed in collaboration with a client like Mei. Such a diagram could help a client to both make sense of their difficulties and see possible ways forward in their lives. For instance, with Figure 15.2, a therapist might draw an additional line from 'Music, journalism, "doing things for me"' to 'Self-worth', suggesting to Mei that perhaps she could achieve this higher-order desire in a more synergetic way.

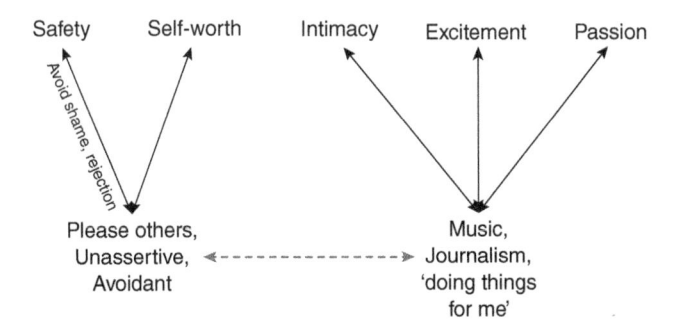

Figure 15.2 Simplified structural diagram for Mei

In support of this approach, Caspar (1995) reports that a therapeutic approach based upon plan analysis led to significant improvements over client-centred therapy or 'broad spectrum' behaviour therapy. Similarly, Silberschatz, Curtis, and Nathans (1989), using the 'plan formulation method', found that therapists whose activity was closer to a pre-defined map of the client's plan showed more positive changes (see Web Resource 15.1).

INTEGRATION IN PRACTICE: A SUMMARY OF METHODS

Through goal setting and directional formulation, therapists and clients can begin to build up a picture of the particular methods that may be most helpful for particular clients. From a directional standpoint, as with a pluralistic one (Cooper & Dryden,

2016; Cooper & McLeod, 2011), any therapeutic method has the potential to be of value (assuming that the therapist has had the necessary training). However, as discussed previously in the book, different methods are likely to be more or less helpful at different points in the directional arc. If the issue, for instance, is that the client does not know what they want from life, then awareness- and evaluation-focused methods may be most helpful. If, on the other hand, they are clear about what they want but do not know how to get there, then intention-, planning-, and action-focused methods may be most appropriate. Suitable methods for each of these phases, based on the analysis in Part II of this book, are summarised below.

Awareness-focused methods

These methods are likely to be the starting point for any therapeutic intervention: helping clients to recognise what it is that they want in life, and how they are trying to get there. They are also ways of helping clients to understand how their difficulties may have arisen: the conflicts and the ineffective methods that they have adopted. Awareness-focused methods may be particularly helpful for clients who want insight into their goals, difficulties, and challenges. Methods include:

- Free association/Space to talk and dialogue
- Emotion-focused dialogue: intensifying, differentiating, symbolising
- Empathic understanding
- Upward questioning
- Goal clarification and goal setting
- Focusing
- Interpretation
- Analysis of the resistance/transference
- Meaning-oriented practices and exercises
- Facilitating internal dialogue
- Facilitating external dialogue
- Noticing disruptions.

Evaluation-focused methods

Evaluating different directions, and the strategies that are used to actualise them, is at the heart of virtually every therapeutic approach. It is the process of helping clients work out how best to move towards where they want to be. Strategies include:

- Space to talk and dialogue
- Interpretation/analysis of resistance and transference
- Problem-focused methods (e.g., decisional balance sheets)
- Socratic dialogue (as per CBT)

- Cost-benefit analysis/Decisional matrix
- Motivational interviewing
- Facilitating internal dialogue: recognising and resolving internal conflicts
- Facing limitations
- Psychoeducation
- Thought and moods diaries
- Behavioural experiments
- Identifying and challenging unrealistic expectations.

Intention-focused methods

These methods aim to help clients move from knowing what they want to making a commitment to action:

- Identifying and facilitating choices
- Motivational interviewing
- Facing limitations
- Supporting social change activities
- Highlighting client's strengths.

In addition, mindfulness and mentalisation-based techniques can be seen as helping clients to stand back from potentially unhelpful intentions, allowing them to choose either to not act or to act in different ways.

Planning-focused methods

Planning-focused methods aim to help clients identify the most effective ways of actualising their intentions. They include:

- Problem-focused methods
- Behavioural activation
- Psychoeducation
- Psychological Situation Analysis: asking clients about the effectiveness of particular methods
- Skills training
- Developing implementation intentions
- Mentally rehearsing planned activities.

Action- and feedback-focused methods

These methods invite clients to try out their planned activities, to review how they get on, and, ultimately, to break old habits and embed the more effective actions as new ones. They include:

- Behavioural experiments
- Exposure techniques
- Behavioural activation
- Skills training
- Role play
- Goal monitoring
- Communication analysis and training
- Assertiveness training
- Inviting clients to test out potentially effective actions in the therapeutic relationship itself (e.g., being assertive, repairing ruptures), and receiving feedback from the therapist
- Learning through modelling (e.g., watching a video of an expert communicator).

DISCUSSION

There are numerous methods, then, that can be used to facilitate client change within different phases of the directional arc. For some clients, work will be focused on just one main phase; other clients will work across several phases; and, probably, in most cases, clients will be working on multiple phases of multiple directions at different points in time. In some sessions, for instance, Mei may be free associating or upward laddering to develop a greater awareness of what she wants from life and what stops her getting there. In others, she may be practising her assertiveness skills to develop actions and gain feedback. For some clients, it may be preferable to focus on one direction, or one phase, at a time; other clients may benefit from moving backwards and forwards between multiple directions and phases. However, the divisions between phases are not likely to be rigid or clear. A client, for instance, might talk about awareness, evaluation, and planning all in one sentence, or test out behaviours that involve intention, planning, and action.

Of course, the particular methods that therapists adopt will be dependent on their particular training and experience. No one can be skilled in all the therapeutic strategies listed above (let alone those not listed), so a therapist will only ever be able to draw on a selection of these methods. In addition, the choice of particular methods should be shaped by the client's particular preferences and goals, as well as their feedback on what they are experiencing as helpful and unhelpful. Methods should also vary by the content of the difficulties that the clients are contending with. For instance, a client who is dealing with relational problems may be more suited to interpersonal or psychodynamic methods; a client who has lots of irrational thoughts may be more suited to CBT. However, the framework developed in this book shows how methods from very different orientations can be brought together into a coherent whole. Rather than having to make forced choices between different therapeutic practices, this model shows how methods from very different traditions are – and can be – aligned. And while therapists can not be skilled in every method going, they do highlight the value of therapists being 'interactionally flexible' (Caspar, 1995): that is, as with other aspects of wellbeing, having the capacity to adopt equifinal means towards the same goal (of helping the client). Caspar (1995) writes: 'The more possible ways of proceeding a therapist can choose from, the higher the probability that he or she can achieve the favorable main effect with a maximum of favorable and a minimum of unfavorable side-effects' (p. 214).

BOX 15.1

Therapists' directions

'Before seriously considering herself a counsellor,' write Munro, Manthei, and Small (1989), 'each person should critically and honestly examine her own motivations for taking on the responsibilities of helping another person' (p. 19). They go on to write that a counsellor's reasons for helping are 'seldom entirely pure and altruistic' (p. 19). In support of this analysis, Hill and colleagues (2017) found that nearly all psychotherapists derived 'self-oriented' meanings through their work. Most typically, these were 'enjoyment and feeling fulfilled', 'personal, intellectual, and emotional growth', and 'connection and intimacy'. Therapists did also have other-oriented meanings: 'help others or alleviate suffering' and 'make a better world'. However, even here, we can still ask what these might 'ladder up' to. For instance, is alleviating suffering in others a means towards a higher-order goal of establishing relatedness?

Of course, it is no bad thing *per se* that therapists' work is based on a range of self- and other-oriented directions. What may be important, however, is to develop an awareness of what these are: that is, to understand our own desires, goals, and agendas. And, through this, to try to ensure that this does not take precedence over the client's own directions in the therapeutic work. It may be, for instance, that we have a desire to be liked, and that working as a therapist is partly a means of gaining 'strokes' from clients. With some clients this may not be too much of a problem. If, however, we are working with a client who needs to learn to express their anger, then it may be dysergetic to where the client needs to go. In addition, research suggests that therapists may have a tendency to project their own directions onto those of their clients (Kivlighan, 2002). Again, then, therapist directional awareness may be important to allow clients' own directions to come to light. Consistent with this, a review of the psychotherapy research suggests that the therapist's management of their countertransference is a 'promising and probably effective' element of the therapeutic relationship (Steering Committee, 2002).

CONCLUSION

This chapter has focused on therapeutic practices, derived from a directional perspective, which form a framework for the theories and methods discussed in Part II of the book. Building on Chapter 14's discussion of goal-oriented practices, it has reviewed ways of helping clients identify higher-order directions, discussed the development of directional formulations, and looked at strategies for integrating a range of methods into a directional approach.

In a sense, successful therapy, if it can happen (see Web Resource 15.2, Why therapies fail), comes down to having an effective, and synergetic, plan for approaching plans: a *metadirection* (or metaplan; Miller et al., 1960). What would this look like? What is the most salutogenic direction for therapists and clients to take towards the client's directions? Being able to stand back from specific directions and develop a greater awareness of them would seem an essential first step here, allowing clients and therapists to see how the client's directions might be configured more synergistically and effectively. And, for therapists, knowing methods for facilitating their actualisation – as listed above – would seem important. Honouring each higher-order direction, and taking it seriously, would also seem to be key to the development of more synergetic relationships: a 'multidirectional partiality' (Boszormenyi-Nagy & Krasner, 1986). At the same time, there is a need for a critical – albeit still respectful – attitude towards the strategies by which clients are striving to fulfil their higher-order directions, and an equifinal openness towards alternative means. In addition, it may be essential that both therapists and clients have realistic expectations about the extent to which particular directions might be actualised, and the rate of change. Too high expectations and a vicious cycle of demoralisation and failed goals may rapidly ensue. This means, then, that therapy may be most effective if goals are approached in a measured way, rather than pursued frenetically.

Through such a metadirectional stance, clients may not only be able to make best use of therapy, but also to take away from therapy – that is, internalise – a more facilitative stance towards their own directions (Mackrill, 2010). Through therapy, for instance, Mei learnt that it was 'OK' for her to have desires and goals, and that it was generally fairly effective – rather than shame-inducing – for her to express these to others. However, she also learnt that she was responsible for taking these directions forward: if she waited for others to do what she wanted, she could be waiting a very long time. Logan, too, learnt that he needed to take more time to weigh up his different desires, and that short-term gains (in terms of immediate anxiety reduction) were often associated with long-term costs. Like Mei, he also developed more confidence in identifying and trusting his own sense of his higher-order directions. He could know what he wanted, outside the wants of others. At the same time, however, Logan learnt in therapy that his default, natural strategies for achieving things (like attracting women by teasing them or improving himself through self-criticism) were not always the most effective ones. Rather, he needed to be open to new learnings about how to progress towards his higher-order goals.

QUESTIONS FOR REFLECTION

- Which of the creative methods for identifying higher-order directions do you think might be most useful in your work with clients? Consider trying one on yourself to see how you find it.
- Consider developing a directional formulation, perhaps with a diagram, for a client you are currently working with. In what ways is this helpful, and not helpful, for your therapeutic work?
- Which set of methods do you feel most skilled at in helping clients to actualise their directions (e.g., awareness-focused methods, planning-focused methods)? Which skills would you most like to develop for the future?

FURTHER READING

Caspar, F. (1995). *Plan analysis: Towards optimizing psychotherapy*. Bern: Hogrefe & Huber. A valuable and unique text that details a directional approach to formulation.

McLeod, J., & McLeod, J. (2016). Assessment and formulation in pluralistic counselling and psychotherapy. In M. Cooper & W. Dryden (Eds.), *Handbook of pluralistic counselling and psychotherapy* (pp. 15-27). London: Sage. Details the use of the timeline map, as well as other assessment practices from a pluralistic, directional perspective.

16

DEVELOPING INTERPERSONAL SYNERGIES

This chapter discusses:

- A range of strategies for building synergies at interpersonal levels of organisation.
- The role of limited resources in restricting the development of synergies.
- Common change processes at the intrapersonal and interpersonal levels.

In Chapter 9, we looked at how the directional framework could be extended to the interpersonal level, drawing extensively from game theory. In this chapter, we look at how it is possible for people, within non-zero-sum games, and over time, to move from dysergetic to more synergetic interpersonal configurations – particularly when it is not in their immediate self-interest? This is relevant to the successful facilitation of dyadic, family, and group therapies. More importantly, perhaps, it is essential to the development of a 'better' society: in which more people are able to actualise more of their higher-order directions being more of the time.

In many respects, the question being asked in this chapter is an interpersonal version of the intrapersonal question: How can we help clients change in therapy (when it is often not in their immediate self-interests)? In the game theory field, one main way that researchers have studied this question is by setting up 'tournaments' using the prisoner's dilemma paradigm (see Chapter 9). Here, different computerised strategies play against each other under different conditions (Axelrod, 1984). This chapter explores the findings of this research, and also considers what we might learn from it about common processes of intra- and interpersonal change.

SEEING THE 'BIGGER PICTURE'

To be able to strive towards synergies at interpersonal levels of organisation, we need to know that a synergetic solution is available and that it gives a better overall outcome than following immediate self-interest (cf. the intrapersonal phases of awareness and evaluation). When I first played the prisoner's dilemma game against my son Zac (who was about 7 years old at the time), he instinctively betrayed me every time: the apparent 'quick win' (see Table 9.1). It was only after losing at the game a few times when playing it as a 'round robin' (in which three or more players play several rounds against each other), that he realised that the cooperative strategy had overall better outcomes. Now, he consistently chooses to cooperate, and giggles at his grandmother (my mum), who has not grasped this principle, and usually chooses to betray – always ending up last in a round robin tournament.

To make a synergetic choice, however, a person must also have the cognitive complexity to recognise that the other is not a passive, inanimate 'object', but an agentic subjectivity of their own. In other words, they need the capacity to *mentalise*: to see that the other is acting towards, and responding to, them, as a directional being, just as they are to the other (i.e., an I–Thou stance). This is why, in the prisoner's dilemma game, the strategy of betraying the other, in the long term, is doomed. Because it fails to take into account that the other is an intelligible being who will respond to such a strategy by themselves choosing to betray. As Rapoport (1960) put it, then, the tragedy of human beings in society is to play a non-zero-sum game as if it were a zero-sum game: to think that the other will simply succumb to loss when we win rather than recognising their capacity for reaction, retaliation, and impact.

Synergetic choices, then, require the ability not just to conceptualise the mind of the other, but to be able to 'see up' to a higher level of organisation – a 'helicopter view', the 'bigger picture' – and to recognise that one's outcomes are always embedded within a more complex, non-linear, reciprocal whole. In the prisoner's dilemma game, 'there is no best strategy independent of the strategy used by the other player' (Axelrod, 1984, p. 15): the strategies and outcomes of each player are fundamentally intertwined. Moreover, by seeing up a level, the focus becomes the directionality of the more macro unit – the dyad, group, or society – rather than individual-level directions. In this respect, by definition, the dysergies are transcended and individuals act towards the good of the greater whole. This process can be seen in some relationship therapies, where partners are encouraged to focus on, and actualise, their potential as a couple rather than on their individual desires and goals (Lantz & Gregoire, 2000).

What does this mean in terms of developing a better, more synergetic society? First, it may be important that children are taught the importance of empathy: the capacity to stand in the shoes of another and see the world as they see it. This may be at school (for instance, in personal, social and health education [PHSE] classes), through modelling from their parents, or through other forms of learning (see, for instance, Sornson, 2013). It also means helping children, as well as adults, to be more mindful of the long-term implications of actions for society as a whole and not just short-term individual gains. Axelrod (1984) refers to this as 'enlarging the shadow of the future' (p. 126). Globally, a key example here is climate change, where countries acting solely in terms of national self-interest risk total environmental devastation. We can see, here, parallels with an intrapersonal over-prioritisation of short-term directions (see Chapter 5). Mindell (2014) also makes the point that, in overcoming interpersonal conflicts, we need *metacommunicators*: people who can stand outside the 'turbulent storm' and see both sides. In other words, as a society, we need people who can hold the 'bigger picture' when others, perhaps inevitably, can see only their own way. Mediators, as discussed above, may have a valuable role to play here; so too leaders (see below).

MOTIVATION TO DEVELOP SYNERGIES

In some non-zero-sum games, as we have discussed in Chapter 9, the synergistic solution is compatible with a player's immediate interests. In others, such as the prisoner's dilemma game, played over time, they are not compatible with a player's short-term interests, but they are with their long-term interests. If this is the case, then knowledge of these solutions should orient the person towards them. However, in other cases, the synergistic solution may be tangential to a person's interests, or even actively contrary to them. For instance, supposing I am working on a research project that is struggling for funds. I want to be involved in the project, but also know that I am the least critical team member, and therefore that it makes most sense for me to withdraw. Such withdrawal is not in either my immediate or long-term interests, but it is the 'right' thing to do because – in those circumstances – it maximises the overall wellbeing of the group.

In such situations, then, synergetic solutions may require people to be actively motivated towards achieving them: to be striving to create a greater good. This is, in Levinas's (1969) terms, a genuine willingness to give to the other: a generosity of spirit. In terms of the present framework, we can think of this as having a higher-order direction towards synergetic solutions: to want to create the best at higher levels of organisation, even if it may be to the detriment of the individual's own desires and goals. As Powers (1992) points out, cooperation is a standard just as any other, and that '[i]n order to cooperate, a person must deliberately choose cooperation as a goal' (p. 104).

Closely related to this, synergistic solutions require people to *take responsibility* for creating them. That is, not only having the desire to create synergies, but also moving through intention to action. Fisher (2008), from a game theory perspective, writes about the *Tragedy of the Commons*: when everyone thinks it is OK for them to do their own thing – and no one is willing to try to coordinate efforts – with the result being that everyone loses out. For me personally, for instance, it is a hassle to take my plastic bags to the supermarket; I would rather just pay a few pence for one when I get there. And probably many other people feel the same way. But unless someone is willing to take responsibility for acting in a different way, and helping others to do so, then we all face a major ecological crisis.

So why is it that one person in a crowd may be willing to stand up and say 'no'? If we go back to expectancy–value theory (see Chapter 3), it may partly be about cooperative outcomes being really important to them, and partly also about having the belief in their self-efficacy to bring it about (Bandura, 2001). Holding a sense of responsibility, however, seems to be a third critical factor – and one that is less well theorised. This goes beyond thinking 'I want this' and 'I can do it', to 'I should do it' (or perhaps 'I know that if I don't do this, no one else will'). This is an externally-oriented direction, but it is not extrinsic in the sense of striving for social approval and reward (see Box 5.1). Rather, it about taking responsibility for actualising directions at a higher level of organisation. Again, then, this raises the issue of leadership: someone who can stand above any one individual desire or perspective and personify the possibilities for synergy of the group as a whole (Slavson, 1957).

TRUST

Why does my mum choose to betray – and thereby lose – at the prisoner's dilemma game? The essence of it seems to be that she does not trust us. Her expectation seems to be that we will betray her, and therefore she chooses to betray us as a means of 'protecting' herself – getting the best payoff possible – in the 'circumstances'. What my mum does not tend to realise, however, is that the rest of us are, in fact, willing to cooperate with her by choosing to stay silent. More than that, what she does not seem to realise is that, by betraying others, she then creates the conditions in which others will choose to betray her: a downward, dysergetic spiral. For people to move from dominant to synergetic solutions, therefore, they need trust in the other; and this is one of the most important learnings from the game theory field (Wright, 2000). Fisher (2008) writes, 'If we could find ways to trust each other, we could then find win–win solutions to many of our most serious problems' (p. 129). This is something that is also recognised in the fields of relationship and couples therapy, and in mediation. For instance, Boszormenyi-Nagy, Grunebaum, and Ulrich (1991) write that trust is a 'crucial requirement for viable, close relationships' (p. 28). In a world where levels of trust seem to be receding (Layard, 2006), this issue may be of particular contemporary importance.

Trust may be a lot easier to break down than to build up. Once we know, for instance, that my mum is going to betray us, and we have betrayed her, it becomes very difficult for either party to trust that the other will start to act in a more cooperative way. Similarly, in relationships, or between communities or nations: once distrust sets in, the 'costs' of trying to be cooperative – and risking betrayal, humiliation, and ridicule – become higher and higher. In game theory terms, the Nash equilibrium point becomes increasingly entrenched: that is, there is more and more of a risk that attempting to forge a cooperative solution will lead to betrayal and loss.

So how can trust be rebuilt? Most likely, it needs small commitments from each side. As I have written previously:

> Synergies are like an arch bridge, they cannot be built up one side at a time. Rather, they require both sides to be prepared, and to trust and have faith that the other side will be ready to meet them. Once the synergy is established, like the setting of a keystone in the arch bridge, they can be extremely strong; but until that time, they are highly vulnerable to collapse. (Cooper, 2016, p. 590)

Game theory suggests that the capacity to forgive is an essential quality here (Axelrod, 1984). Famously, in the original round robin tournament of the prisoner's dilemma game, in which numerous computerised strategies played against each other, the overall winner was a strategy called TIT FOR TAT (Axelrod, 1984). This was one of the simplest strategies. It consisted of 'cooperating on the first move and then doing whatever the other player did on the previous move' (p. 13). So TIT FOR TAT started from a position of 'trust', and would quickly get back on track with a position of 'trust' (i.e., cooperating), if the other player started to act in more cooperative ways. TIT FOR TAT did not bear grudges. Indeed, under conditions in which players may be more prone to miscommunication and error, a strategy of TWO TITS FOR A TAT (that is, only defecting if the other player defects twice) may be most profitable overall. In addition, the winning TIT FOR TAT strategy was not 'envious', in the sense that it did not act 'nasty' if it was defeated by other particular strategies (Axelrod, 1984). In fact, remarkably, TIT FOR TAT never once scored better in a single bout than its 'opponent'

(Axelrod, 1984). So 'it won the tournament not by beating the other player, but by eliciting behaviour from the other player which allowed both to do well' (Axelrod, 1984, p. 112). Hence, overall, it achieved the highest points.

Game theory also suggests that making a credible commitment can be an important means of building up trust (Fisher, 2008). Essentially, this means demonstrating that we really are committed to acting in a cooperative way by creating – and making explicit – losses for ourselves if we were to defect. So if I make my commitment to acting cooperatively very public, putting myself in a position where my reputation will be damaged if I betray, then the other may see my offer of cooperation as more believable and trustworthy. Similarly, if I 'burn my bridges' – that is, make it clear that I have no way back to a strategy of defecting – then, again, the credibility of my move may be enhanced.

The success of TIT FOR TAT suggests that, generally, a stance of trust towards the world – until you have reason not to – seems to be most beneficial, across all levels of organisation. This accords with a humanistic worldview, in which people are seen as essentially 'constructive and trustworthy' (Rogers, 1961). It is also consistent with the view of human being outlined in Chapter 6 of this book: that there is nothing intrinsically 'bad' or malevolent about our higher-order directions.

COMMUNICATION

As game theory makes clear, one of the principal ways of establishing trust is through communication. In our family, we play two different versions of the round robin prisoner's dilemma game. In one, we are not allowed to talk to each other; in the other, we are. Almost invariably, the overall levels of cooperation – and scores – are higher in the latter version. 'Right,' says Zac, 'So you say "cooperate" and I absolutely, totally promise I will too.' I look him straight into his eyes, 'You promise?' He nods eagerly. 'No pocket money next week if you don't', I say, invoking a credible commitment. He laughs. Very tentatively – 1... 2... 3... – I take the risk of giving him the benefit of the doubt: 'Stay silent', I say. He does too. A sigh of relief. Now I trust him. We cooperate for the rest of the round. This is consistent with findings from the game theory field, which show that cooperative choices can as much as double when communication is introduced (Rapoport, 1960), while misunderstandings increase the levels of defections (Axelrod, 1984).

So why does communication help to build trust and lead to a greater likelihood of win–win solutions. First, without communication, it is very easy to build up negative 'fantasies' of the other, and what they are 'up to'. Communication brings us down to reality: it can help us understand what the other is really striving for, their highest-order, non-malevolent desires and goals. Second, communication can help us feel that the other is more honest and open and, in seeing that, we may feel that they are more reliable and less likely to cheat us. Third, when the other starts to communicate, we get a more humanised sense of them as real, genuine people. Hence, we may be more willing to act in cooperative and caring ways. Fourth, communication allows people to develop, together, more sophisticated and more mutually beneficial coordination strategies (Fisher, 2008). Through the free flow and exchange of information, people can work creatively together to generate synergistic solutions (Katz & Murphy-Shigematsu, 2012). Finally, when channels of communication are open, it can help people feel that they are more in control of the situation and less at the mercy of the other. Hence, they may be more willing to take risks. If I know, for instance, that I can come back to my son and 'have a go' at him for betraying me, I may be more willing to risk trusting him than if I feel I have no possibility of response.

Given these factors, it seems reasonable to hypothesise that some forms of communication may be more likely to bring about trust and synergetic solutions than others. More specifically, while a very basic form of communication – such as information exchange – may go some way to demystifying the other, a style of communication that is honest, humanising, negotiative, open, and ongoing may be most suited to the development of synergetic relating. This is *dialogue* (Bohm, 1996; Buber, 1947), in which the communicating parties are both *receptive* and *expressive* to the other (see Cooper, 2015a; Cooper et al., 2012; Mearns & Cooper, 2018).

Receptivity means that each person 'takes in' the other. This is a listening, attentiveness, or curiosity: a putting to one side of assumptions and preconceptions and an openness to the other and their directions as something new, different, and unknown (Cooper, 2009; Cooper & Spinelli, 2012; Schmid, 2006). It is also a stance of deep acceptance and confirmation of the other, even if there is disagreement, tension, or conflict (Cooper & Ikemi, 2012). In relation to the present model, such receptivity particularly involves an openness to the other's directions: an attunement to and acceptance of where it is that they are wanting to go.

Expressivity, on the other hand, is a willingness to be genuine and transparent in the encounter: again, particularly, with respect to our desires and goals (i.e., being assertive). It is a commitment to sharing all of oneself, including those aspects of being that might be more withheld in everyday life: such as one's vulnerabilities, hidden qualities, or implicit experiences, the 'wordless depths' (Buber, 1947, p. 42). In focusing terms, this is about sharing at the edge of one's awareness: the implicit understandings and feelings that one is just touching upon (Gendlin, 1996). Expressivity is also about communicating clearly – a quality of winning strategies in the prisoner's dilemma game. TIT FOR TAT, for instance, simply says, 'I'll keep on being nice to you as long as you are nice to me' (Axelrod, 1984, p. 55). The immediacy of 'retaliation' also heightens the clarity of the TIT FOR TAT strategy. There is no room for doubt: nasty behaviours will not be tolerated (Spaniel, 2015). Here, also, we can see how clarity builds trust: 'You know what I am going to do. Even if it hurts you, I told you that it was coming.'

At the dyadic level, this focus on improving relating through dialogue is at the heart of couples therapy. This holds that 'When couples are in distress, a major cause and/or causality is communication' (Evans, 2012, p. 584). Hence, the aim of therapy with the couple 'is to assist them to establish constructive communication patterns' (Evans, 2012, p. 584). Similarly, in family therapy, problems are understood in terms of impaired and inconsistent means of communication, with a focus on developing clearer methods of talk (Kaslow et al., 2003). Individual therapies, such as interpersonal therapy, also work on helping clients to improve their lives through improving their communication skills (Stuart & Robertson, 2003; and see Box 13.3, this volume). Here, there may be a particular emphasis on learning to communicate more transparently (Rogers, 1959) and through moving away from more dishonest and 'ulterior' forms of communication (Stewart & Joines, 1987) in which people communicate one want at the overt level, but another at the implicit level.

At a wider, social level, what this points to is the importance of developing communication skills and *emotional literacy* (aka emotional intelligence) in our children and young people (Goleman, 1996). Emotional literacy means that children can recognise their feelings – and thereby their directions – and communicate these to others. It means, for instance, children developing the ability to say 'I felt angry when you teased me. I don't want you to do that again', rather than acting it out or perpetuating cycles of shaming and violence. And it also means children learning to empathise with the feelings and directions of others, so that they are able to see where another is coming from – and going to.

ESTABLISHING AGREEMENTS

When Zac and I decide to cooperate on the prisoner's dilemma game, we make an agreement. It is not written down, and there is nothing that formally binds us to it, but it is a statement of agreed actions that, in some way, facilitates our cooperation: the concrete in our bridge. This agreement, in a sense, is one form of the 'social contract' that operates at all levels of organisation – between partners, companies, nations – that allows people to function in more synergetic ways (Spaniel, 2015). Indeed, we could think of the law as one extended social contract that supports us all, at least to some extent, to meet our needs in ways that minimise dysergies with the needs of others. Fisher (2008) writes that the secret to getting out of mistrusting, dysergetic positions may be for the parties to 'find some way of agreeing to coordinate their actions and for all parties to stick to it' (p. 22).

Why might agreements facilitate synergies? First, by having to establish a specific set of 'rules', all parties are pushed to talk together until they can identify a synergetic solution. Second, the agreement keeps the shared strategy in memory. This helps all parties to stick to it and thereby not slide down into dysergetic spirals. Third, because clear rules exist, people know what to expect, and can therefore trust more: they do not need to waste energy on 'What if?' scenarios (Kagleder, personal communication, 17 April 2018). Fourth, in some cases, such as the law, sanctions may help to keep mandated behaviour in place. Sanctions also enhance the credibility of the commitment: if I know you know that you will be punished for breaking the agreement, I may be able to trust you more.

BEING NICE

As with TIT FOR TAT in the prisoner's dilemma round robin tournaments, there was 'a single property which distinguishes the relatively high-scoring entries from the relatively low-scoring entries. This is the property of being *nice*, which is to say never being the first to defect' (Axelrod, 1984, p. 33). That means avoiding unnecessary conflict for as long as the other does (Axelrod, 1984). Axelrod goes on to report that each of the eight top-ranking entries were nice, and that they did particularly well when playing against other nice strategies. In other words, two nice strategies – synergistically relating to each other – can 'earn' enough between themselves to make up for more mixed encounters with 'nasty' strategies. Moreover, once in the majority, nice strategies are also relatively 'stable': in the sense that they continue to do well in a round robin tournament even if a few nasty strategies 'invade'. This is because, although the nasty strategies may win out in single bouts against the nice strategies, their combined scores are much lower than in nice–nice matches (Axelrod, 1984). Interestingly, however, the reverse is not true: that is, just a small number of nice strategies can 'invade' the nasty strategies and start to 'take over' (Axelrod, 1984). Hence, although synergies may be difficult to establish, they also have a certain hardiness. Like roots pushing up through concrete, 'cooperation can emerge even in a world of unconditional defection' (Axelrod, 1984, p. 68).

This 'niceness' parallels a stance of *unconditional positive regard* or *non-judgmental acceptance*: where we value the experiences of another in an unconditional way (Rogers, 1959, see Chapter 11). In family therapy terms, it involves the therapist holding a stance of *multidirected partiality*: valuing all the different voices within the family (Boszormenyi-Nagy et al., 1991). '[T]his principle of inclusiveness', writes Boszormenyi-Nagy, 'has to be linked to the therapist's determination to discover the humanity of every participant – even of the family's "monster member"' (p. 418). Through such a stance, the therapist can help the client – whether individual, couple, or family – to develop more caring and compassionate attitudes to themselves and others. And, through this, to enhance their capacity for synergetic functioning.

However, it is not only that 'niceness' lays the basis for synergetic relating; it is also, perhaps, the quintessentially synergetic act in itself. This is because it is not just the 'recipient' of niceness that benefits. Rather, niceness – as caring, compassion, and reaching out to the other – is also, in many instances, rewarding for the 'giver' (Cantor & Sanderson, 1999) (perhaps as a means towards the higher-order direction of relatedness). Sheldon and Schmuck (2001) write that communal goals – like volunteering work and political activity – can be deeply satisfying to the person. They suggest that 'the source of individual happiness lies in caring for something greater than yourself' (p. 221). Consistent with this, research suggests that there is a 'positive relationship between volunteering and subjective well-being, and altruistic behaviour promotes subjective well-being' (Stoll, Michaelson, & Seaford, 2012, p. 29). Indeed, based on a comprehensive review of the research, 'Give...' was cited as one of five key ways to psychological health and wellbeing (the other four being 'Connect...', 'Be active...', 'Take notice...', and 'Keep learning...'; Aked et al., 2008). This suggests, perhaps, that niceness has enormous potential as a source of greater social wellbeing, and that teaching people to care about the welfare of others (and the rewards that they can get from it) could be of considerable social value (Axelrod, 1984).

RECIPROCATION

As a strategy, TIT FOR TAT is nice, but it is not naïve or gullible (Axelrod, 1984). Should it be betrayed, then it will punish the other for its defection, giving a clear and simple message that it cannot be taken advantage of. In other words, it has a quality of 'provocability' (Axelrod, 1984). Here, again, we see resonances with assertive behaviours: 'I have my directions. You have yours. I will do my best to help you move in your directions, but you must also let me move in mine. If not, there will be consequences.'

CELEBRATING DIVERSITY

Moving on from game theory, the celebration and prizing of diversity can be seen as a further means by which synergies can be enhanced. In many respects, this is an extension of being nice: valuing and prizing the other whatever their otherness, that is, whatever their higher-order desires and goals (provided that it does not impinge on the directions of others). This can also be considered a 'radical democratic pluralism' (McLennan, 1995, p. 91), in which the other is allowed to be in their own way. Diversity, however, also maximises benefits because it provides opportunities for each of us to develop and grow. Through encountering different cultures, different types of people, different ways of being, we can all discover different means towards our ends. Indeed, if growth and discovery are considered to be highest-order directions in themselves (see Chapter 6), then the encountering of diversity implicitly brings with it a deep sense of fulfilment. Certainly, diversity and difference can also be frightening; and there are also higher-order directions towards safety and control. However, if such aversions to encountering difference are considered avoidance goals, then, as with all avoidance goals, their actualisation may ultimately do more harm than good to the greater whole.

Celebrating diversity may also mean creating a society in which multiple forms of 'good' exist (Powers, 1992; Walzer, 1983). In our contemporary Western world, success tends to be judged by only a very few criteria, such as money, physical appearance, and employment status (Cooper, 2016). This means that there are only a small number of avenues by which people can achieve, and that we are constantly thrown up against one another to attain a sense of self-esteem. Imagine a small group of people where there is only one criterion for success, say attractiveness. Here, one person 'wins' and everyone else loses. Now imagine the same group where there are many different criteria for 'success', say attractiveness, fitness, friendliness, creativity, kindness, intelligence, and articulateness. Here, by creating diverse forms of 'good', there is the potential for many more people to experience a sense of self-worth. This is, in the words of Walzer, a 'complex egalitarian society'. Small inequities may still exist, but because each exists in different 'spheres of competence and control' (p. 17), they are not compounded or reinforced.

CREATIVITY

Closely related to the celebration of diversity is the fostering of creativity, which can also be seen as having a high synergetic potential (Maslow, 1971). This is not only because creativity can be understood as a natural expression of the authentic, actualising individual (Maslow, 1971; Rogers, 1961), but because creativity is an inherently heterogenic force (i.e., facilitative of diversity). Creativity generates new possibilities, new domains, and new areas for growth. Through creativity, society has the capacity to branch outward, to differentiate and grow. By doing so, it creates new means that people can adopt towards their goals, and the conditions by which larger number of human beings can succeed.

In societal terms, what this points towards is the importance of a world which values arts and crafts: where people are working to produce – and exchange – things that have been forged through their own, unique skills and experience (Cooper, 2016). One person develops their expertise in dance, another in textile designs, a third in digital software. As we move towards the increasing mechanisation of mundane tasks, there is the possibility of creating a world in which each person can be recognised for excellence in their own field – and without impinging on the self-worth of others. Here, in contrast to the system of industrial mass production, the worker is no longer a 'crippled', 'alienated' appendage of the commodities that they produce (Fromm, 1961). Rather, their work may be a free and unalienated expression of their authentic being.

EQUALITY

In *The spirit level*, Wilkinson and Pickett (2010) present compelling evidence that equality is not only better for the disadvantaged members of society, but for everyone. Societies with the greatest *income inequality* – that is, the gap between its richest and poorest members (such as the USA and the UK) – have the greatest physical health, mental health, and social problems, such as violence. In other words, equality seems to be a basic condition that is necessary for the development of synergetic solutions. 'The evidence shows that reducing inequality is the best way of improving the quality of the social environment, and so the real quality of life, for us all' (Wilkinson & Pickett, 2010, p. 29).

Why is that? In part, it may be because, as the research shows, inequality reduces trust (Wilkinson & Pickett, 2010), which is essential for the development of synergies (see above). To some extent, this may be because, through the creation of subgroups within a society (for instance, by class, gender, or race), 'in-group' and 'out-group' dynamics are likely to form. It may also be because those that are disadvantaged will feel that the advantaged members of society have got something 'over' on them, and the advantaged members of society may feel that the disadvantaged members are trying to 'take' something from them. This can create psychological stress for both parties: the stress of feeling that you cannot actualise your directions (and the helplessness, hopelessness, and envy that also goes with it), and the stress of 'status anxiety', that something is going to be taken from you (Wilkinson & Pickett, 2010). In addition, if some members of society feel disadvantaged – that is, their reference standards are not met by their reality – then their focus is likely to be on trying to meet expectations at a personal level, rather than higher-level social concerns. In essence, we might liken this to a game of prisoner's dilemma in which one party – the advantaged – has already started off with a nasty move. The natural 'move' of the disadvantaged, then, may be to betray too, with a consequent spiralling down into dysergetic conflict.

Inequalities may also lead to a loss in overall wellbeing because 'most of us share a desire to live in a society where fairness is the operative norm' (Corning, 2011, p. 5). This higher-level direction towards social equity, in the form of the 'Golden Rule' (see Web Resource 1.1), is found in virtually every society, stretching back to early hunter-gatherer cultures as well as in primate species (Corning, 2011). It is still operative today. For instance, a recent UK survey found that around 80% of people thought that the gap between the richest and poorest was too large, with just 1% feeling that it was too small (Curtice, 2016). Indeed, around 90% of British people expressed a preference for reasonable levels of wellbeing for everyone, as compared with higher overall levels of wellbeing but with some people high in wellbeing and others low (Dolan, 2014). Research also suggests that people will, and do, sacrifice self-interest to make things fairer (Rabin, 1993). Consistent with this, in the prisoner's dilemma game, participants seem to experience mutual cooperation as the most personally satisfying outcome, with neuroscientific evidence linking it to the stimulation of reward areas in the brain (Rilling et al., 2002).

In addition, in terms of maximising overall benefit, equality makes sense because the worth of something is likely to be greater to someone who does not have that thing than to someone who does (Layard, 2006). Ten pounds, for instance, may mean very little to a millionaire, but for someone begging on the street, it could buy considerable (albeit temporary) happiness. Furthermore, as the research on risk averseness suggests, the misery brought about by disadvantage is of greater magnitude than the happiness brought about by advantage (Kahneman, 2011).

Closely linked to this discussion is the issue of power. In terms of the present framework, power can be defined as the capacity of an individual or group to actualise its directions over and above the directions of others. In control theory terms, this can be considered arbitrary control at the interpersonal level (Powers, 1973): the attempt by one person (or group) to control the behaviour of another person (or group) without reference to that other's directions. However, for Powers, such attempts are always, ultimately, doomed to fail, because (as suggested in Table 6.1) people have a highest-order desire to control their own lives (Powers, 1973). He writes:

> There is only one way I can see for fallible, ignorant human beings to live in accord with their own real natures and that is to discard forever the principle of controlling each other's behavior, dropping even the *desire* to control other people, and seeing at every level the fallacy in the logic that leads to such a desire. Whatever system concept we adopt in the effort to reach the conflict-free society, it must contain one primary fact about human beings: they cannot be arbitrarily controlled *by any means* without creating suffering, violence, and revolution. (pp. 281–282, emphasis in original)

At the social and political level, then, this analysis points towards the value of *deep democracy* (Mindell, 2014). This is a form of power whereby all the different voices within the system are respected, valued, and 'encouraged to express themselves completely' (p. 42). Here, as with Boszormenyi-Nagy et al.'s (1991) multidirected partiality, there is a recognition that even the most disavowed and feared parts of the system are necessary in making up the whole. For Cornish (2012), synergy, by definition, involves '*power with* (as opposed to *power over*)', whereby 'people commit themselves to one another in collective interdependent partnership, mutually affecting and enhancing one another, building or increasing power through reciprocal nurturance and cooperation' (p. 244, emphasis in original). Cornish writes that 'Empowerment promotes a synergistic environment' (p. 246) and, concomitantly, synergies promote empowerment. In fact, to a great extent the concepts of synergy and empowerment – and, indeed, equality – can all be considered synonymous.

LIMITED RESOURCES

As we have seen, within any non-zero-sum game there is the possibility for greater or lesser degrees of synergy. However, as suggested earlier, the extent to which people are motivated to cooperate or compete is likely to be very dependent on the 'payoffs' involved, and this is determined by the context in which the interaction takes place.

If Player A, for instance, risks '-10' for cooperating, they may be more likely to betray than if they only risk '-2'. And given that people tend to weigh losses more heavily than gains (Kahneman, 2011), the lower the overall 'payouts', the more likely that people may come to compete against each other. Desperation kicks in; the fear of losing out; more primitive behaviours come to the fore: 'every person for themselves'. The greater the environmental stressors, then, the more that synergetic, mindful solutions may retreat, with dysergetic, chaotic, rogue directions coming to dominate (Corning, 2011). In this way, different social orders are likely to create very different potentials for synergetic relating (Shaw & Colimore, 1988).

In addition, some contexts may offer more potentials for synergy. This is clearly demonstrated in the classic 'Robbers Cave' experiment (Sherif & Sherif, 1953), which studied the behaviours of groups of young boys in a 'summer camp' setting. Here, in the face of competitive goals (where the victory of one group meant the defeat of the other), conflict and prejudice rapidly ensued. By contrast, when the researchers set up 'superordinate' goals for the groups of boys (that they could only achieve by working together), they became much more predisposed towards cooperation and between-group hostilities ceased.

As a society, then, the more that we can generate resources, the more likely it may be that synergies can flourish. However, this is not just about generating material resources. If we go back to people's highest-order directions (Chapter 6), it is also about creating a world in which there is an abundance of respect, warmth, and safety for others, opportunities for pleasure, and in which others can feel free and able to actualise their possibilities. And it is also about creating a society in which people can see the potentials for synergies: where interdependent, cooperative goals are emphasised over individual, competitive ones (even if, to some extent, interpersonal dysergies may always exist, see Web Resource 16.1). In the face of environmental and military catastrophe, we have to work together. Whether or not people can see this essential interconnectedness and dependence on each other may be the key to our fate.

DISCUSSION: COMMON CHANGE PROCESSES AT THE INTERPERSONAL AND INTRAPERSONAL LEVELS

'The way to better [mental] health is the same as the way to a more sustainable politics', writes Mindell (2014, p. 169). In this chapter, we have focused on the development of synergies at a range of interpersonal levels. No doubt, processes across the interpersonal and intrapersonal levels are not identical (Powers, 1992). Nevertheless, there are some striking parallels, and drawing these out may help to establish common principles of change, which can then inform both intrapersonal and interpersonal work. To summarise:

- Wellbeing is associated with the actualisation of directions; distress and difficulties with their frustration or blocking.
- Any interaction can be conceptualised as zero-sum or non-zero-sum, with the latter having potential for greater or lesser degrees of synergy. Matrices, as used in game theory, can be used to map out what the potential gains and losses might be.
- Synergies are good. They mean more gains within the same set of resources. Concomitantly, dysergies are bad, because less comes out of the system than could otherwise.
- Rogue desires and goals – which operate without any due regard for other directions – are likely to create problems. Concomitantly, the capacity to stand back from any one direction, mentalise, and coordinate efforts is likely to be salutogenic.
- Empathy and acceptance are essential to the development of synergies: being able to see the other (whether internal or external) as an agentic subjectivity whose higher-order directions are valid and intelligible. This also means prizing diversity in otherness.
- To create synergies, it helps if you are motivated to create synergies; and this may require effort, leadership, and a sense of responsibility for them. This may be particularly important to get out of 'Nash equilibrium' points: where any move risks greater immediate losses.
- The formation of synergies requires trust, forgiveness, communication, dialogue, affirmation, and good will – whether to an internal or external 'other'. Chairs around a table on the interpersonal plane; chairwork on the intrapersonal plane. Explicit agreements may facilitate this process.
- Synergies require assertiveness: standing by our own directions rather than being gullible or caving in.
- Democratic and egalitarian structures are likely to be most conducive to the development of synergies (Chaplin, 1988). Totalitarian, dictatorial, and repressive voices, like 'the inner patriarch' (Stone & Winkelman, 1989), may give greater short-term clarity and focus, but ultimately are likely to invoke opposition, resistance, and conflict.

QUESTIONS FOR REFLECTION

- What factors do you think are most important to the development of synergetic relationships at interpersonal levels of organisation?
- To what extent do you think that the factors which facilitate synergies at the interpersonal and intrapersonal levels are the same?
- What might you learn from this chapter about how to help your clients create more synergetic internal worlds?

FURTHER READING

Cooper, M. (2016). The fully functioning society: A humanistic-existential vision of an actualizing, socially-just future. *Journal of Humanistic Psychology,* 56(6), 581–594. doi: 10.1177/0022167816659755. Considers the nature of an improved society from a synergistic perspective.

See also Further Reading, Chapter 9.

17

CONCLUSION

Towards better

This chapter discusses:

- The potential for therapists to act as agents of social change.
- The limitations of, and challenges to, the present framework.
- Key areas for further work.
- A summary of the framework.

THERAPISTS FOR SOCIAL CHANGE

As argued in the previous chapter, for people to flourish psychologically – in synergy with others – they need to inhabit a society that is resource-rich. Maslow (1971) writes, 'actualization of the highest human potentials is possible – on a mass basis – only under "good conditions." Or more directly, good human beings will need a good society to grow' (p. 7). Based on an analysis of highest-order human directions (Box 6.1), this means a world in which people can feel safe from threat; where basic physiological needs are met; where difference and diversity are valued; where there is freedom; where people can find meaning, purpose, and self-worth in their everyday lives; and where there is an abundance of opportunities for love, relatedness, and closeness to others. In addition, it means creating a world in which these highest-order desires can be achieved synergetically: where education, for instance, is fun, so that pupils can experience growth and pleasure simultaneously; or where work is also an opportunity for creative expression (Ford, 1992); and where people of all sexualities and identities can be radically themselves and still experience the love and acceptance of others. If our aim as therapists, then, is to enhance the wellbeing of our clients, the question of how to create a better society (discussed in Chapter 16, this volume) is essential to our work.

'My new client, I dreamed, was the world,' writes Mindell (2014, p. 12). He argues that, to bring about these social improvements, we need *worldworkers*: therapists of society who can merge psychology and politics (Mindell, 2014). And, indeed, from the earliest days of psychoanalysis, authors such as Reich, Adler, and Fromm attempted to bring a social change dimension to the work that therapists do (Rowan, 1988; Totton, 2005). One example of this is Fromm's 'socialist humanism', which attempts to synthesise personal and political change perspectives (Cooper, 2006; Fromm, 1965; see Web Resource 17.1). Such work continues today, with organisations like Psychotherapists and Counsellors for Social Responsibility (www.pcsr.org.uk), and with counsellors and psychotherapists working with some of the most displaced and marginalised people across the globe (see, for example, Proctor, Cooper, Sanders, & Malcolm, 2006).

Such worldwork is likely to need action on many fronts. Within the political domain, there is the work of campaigning on such issues as equal rights, justice, and environmental protection. Within the therapeutic domain, there is the day-to-day work of helping clients feel enabled and empowered to live the lives that they want. And then there are those areas of potential action where the therapeutic and political worlds meet. This may be in several places (see, for instance, Sanders, 2006). First, there is the development of national policies that can help to enhance intra- and interpersonal health and wellbeing. Education may be a prime focus of delivery here: with emotional and relational literacy training that can help children and young people grow into psychologically healthy, cooperative adults (see Chapter 16, this volume). Second is the use of therapeutic skills and concepts to address wider political issues, such as national and international conflict resolution. Third is looking more deeply into the ways that progressive political understandings can enhance the potential of therapy to empower clients as, for instance, with the politically-informed therapies (see Box II.1).

LIMITATIONS AND CHALLENGES

What about the limitations of, or challenges to, the framework being developed here? Perhaps the most fundamental one is that directionality tells us only part of the human 'story'. Directionality is about agency and going out to meet the world; but there is another side of human being which is about taking in the world, a 'receptivity', or what Heidegger (1966) terms *gelassenheit*. This is about how the world impacts upon us – how it shapes and structures our being – including the sociopolitical forces that flow through us (Smail, 2005). Along these lines, Maslow (1987) identifies a number of aspects of human experiencing – such as perceptions and experiences of awe – that cannot easily be constructed as agentic, future-oriented acts. When I look at the trees outside my window, for instance, I may be agentically turning my gaze to them, but the actual 'greenness' or 'treeness' that I see is not something I create. Rather, it 'strikes' me. Hence, in thinking about directionality, it is important to remember its context within the wider breadth of human experiencing. We are towards the world, but the world is also towards, and 'within', us. A full understanding of human being needs a comprehensive conceptualisation of both.

This relates closely to a more clinical critique of the present model. The book is based on the assumption that actualising our desires and goals is, in general, a good 'thing'. But does this put too much emphasis on *doing*, at the expense of *being* (e.g., Fromm, 2005)? That is, what about the value of reflection, contemplation, and living in the here-and-now (Foresight Mental Capital and Wellbeing Project, 2008; Seligman, 2002): 'the pure delight of the beckoning stillness' (Heidegger, 1971, p. 44)? This is the way of being that is considered salutogenic in many Eastern traditions, such as Buddhism and Taoism, and by mindfulness- and acceptance-based approaches to therapy, which show good evidence of efficacy (e.g., Coelho, Canter, & Ernst, 2007). Indeed, from an Eastern perspective, desires may be considered the very sources of psychological suffering (O'Hara, 2013). These are the unquenchable yearnings, 'the unceasing search into the future and concern for the future that casts its shadow over every present moment and clouds the joy of it' (Schlick, 2008, p. 71). Schopenhauer (1969), for instance, writes:

> No satisfaction is lasting; on the contrary, it is always merely the starting-point of a fresh striving. We see striving everywhere impeded in many ways, everywhere struggling and fighting, and hence always as suffering. Thus that there is no ultimate aim of striving means that there is no measure or end of suffering. (p. 309)

Hence, from this perspective, an emphasis on human directionality may be considered more pathogenic than salutogenic: something to transcend rather than to focus on. Moreover, it might be seen as reinforcing a contemporary neoliberal focus on achievement, success, and consumption: the aggrandisement of the goal-focused, highly-driven, 'Type A' personality (Snyder, 2000). In a similar vein, Little (2011) writes:

> there are times in life when the single-minded pursuit of core concerns and vital projects may require temporary suspension. During these moments of receptivity, or sharpened perceptual vision, we may find ourselves restored, and joy might even sneak up on us unanticipated and unannounced. (p. 85)

This critique, however, would be based on a somewhat caricatured view of the present framework. Ontologically, human beings are understood as being directional; but psychological distress is not only understood in terms of what we achieve, but also what our expectations for achievement are. Hence, as argued in Chapter 4, it is quite compatible with the present framework to suggest that distress comes from setting too high strivings and expectations, and that wellbeing can come through acceptance of how we are.

In addition, as Klinger (2013) points out, to 'just be' is not a goalless state. Rather, it can be considered a goal in itself. He writes, 'People go to great lengths to "just be," including taking long walks, journeying to the mountains or ocean, undertaking years of meditative training, and doing what is necessary to acquire a variety of psychoactive drugs' (p. 33).

The concept of directionality could also be critiqued from a postmodern perspective, which questions the existence of any 'true' reality. From this standpoint, directionality is not a 'thing' but a particular narrative construction of the world, no 'truer' than any other narrative. This links right back to the tensions between the present framework and the pluralistic approach (see Chapter 1), where the former can be seen as a step back towards a more totalising, universalising perspective. From a pluralistic standpoint, it might also be argued that the present framework (both in linear and phase form) is too 'neat': too linear and organised, and not consistent with the chaotic, holistic, multidirectional reality of systems in the real world. It is essential, therefore, to hold the present framework lightly, and to see it as a suggested means of understanding the world, rather than a definitive 'truth'.

FURTHER WORK

As with Grawe's (2004) comprehensive psychotherapy, the framework developed here is just the beginning of a new, integrative perspective on counselling, psychotherapy, and social change. Key areas for further work include:

- Developing, and evaluating, new practices that are specifically aligned with the framework: at each phase of the directional arc, and in terms of enhancing both synergies and effectiveness.

- Developing an understanding of the links between emotions, motivation, and neurobiological processes.
- Deepening an understanding of the interface between psychological and social change: both in terms of how sociopolitical understandings can enhance therapeutic practice, and in terms of how therapeutic understandings and methods can contribute towards social change.
- Developing and testing directionality-based methods of formulation, such as the plan formulation approach.
- Developing methods that can help to identify people's highest-order directions, particularly those that exist at an implicit level.
- Developing an understanding of how supervision might be practised from a directional standpoint.
- Developing an understanding of how training might be enhanced from a directional perspective.

CONCLUSION

'The particular language that is eventually adopted or used to describe our various commonalities matters much less to us than the development of a more ecumenical [i.e., non-sectarian, inclusive] spirit and direction,' write Miller et al. (1997, p. 216). To a great extent, the present text has been written with much the same aims. In this book, I have tried to lay out a framework for thinking about therapy – along with wider social change – that can help to align the different approaches and bring them into a more integrated conceptual framework. Of course, the aim here is not to reduce or eradicate difference, but to enhance communication and learning from across the perspectives. If all therapies, ultimately, aim to help clients find better ways of doing things, then a therapist who, for instance, mainly does that through listening may come to feel that also doing it through problem-solving, or through relational interpretations, is not so far away.

The integrative framework developed in the present book, however, is oriented around a particular approach towards human being. This is one that starts with ethics: 'How can we engage with people in a way that is deeply respectful and valuing?' Out of this, inevitably, emerges sociopolitical concerns: to treat the other respectfully means supporting them to have the freedom, rights, and opportunities that we would want for ourselves. From these two starting points comes a framework for understanding human being which can explain both wellbeing and distress, and which is consistent with much contemporary research and theory. It is also a framework which, while helping to guide therapy integration, can also be transposed to a range of levels of organisation: dyads, the family, communities, and nation states.

Across these different levels, we have seen that more synergetic configurations can, and do, endure. The same may also be true for more effective configurations. This means that there may be a tendency towards greater overall 'good' over time (see Web Resource 17.2). However, at each level of organisation, these steps forward are constantly challenged by short-termism, by a lack of knowledge of what 'better' might look like, and by fears of change. Hence, there may be a role for 'nudging' systems forward and helping to consolidate more synergetic and effective configurations. At the individual level, this may be the role of the therapist; at the social level, the political activist; and across levels, the worldworkers. Adopting such roles are not always easy, however. Systems may not only be reluctant to change; they may blame the people trying to instigate it. However, as game theory research shows, even a small cluster of people who are able to model and instigate better configurations can have a lasting effect (Axelrod, 1984). There is much cause for hope.

QUESTIONS FOR REFLECTION

- What do you consider are the main limitations of the model developed in this book?
- What aspects of the present framework would you like to see developed further?

FURTHER READING

Cooper, M. (2006). Socialist humanism: A progressive politics for the twenty-first century. In G. Proctor, M. Cooper, P. Sanders & B. Malcolm (Eds.), *Politicising the person-centred approach: An agenda for social change* (pp. 80–94). Ross-on-Wye: PCCS Books. Details a socialist humanistic political perspective.

Corning, P. (2003). *Nature's magic: Synergy in evolution and the fate of humankind*. Cambridge: Cambridge University Press. An in-depth analysis of synergy across multiple domains, and its evolution over time.

Wright, R. (2000). *Nonzero: The logic of human destiny*. New York: Vintage Books. A more accessible and readable companion to Corning's (above) text.

REFERENCES

Aarts, H., & Custers, R. (2012). Unconscious goal pursuit: Nonconscious goal regulation and motivation. In R. M. Ryan (Ed.), *The Oxford handbook of human motivation* (pp. 232–247). New York: Oxford University Press.

Ajzen, I. (1991). The theory of planned behavior. *Organizational Behavior and Human Decision Processes, 50*(2), 179–211.

Aked, J., Marks, N., Cordon, C., & Thompson, S. (2008). *Five ways to wellbeing: The evidence*. London: nef.

Allport, G. B. (1961). *Pattern and growth in personality*. NY: Holt, Rinehart, & Winston.

Alsleben, P., & Kuhl, J. (2011). Touching a person's essence: Using implicit motives as personal resources in counseling. In W. M. Cox & E. Klinger (Eds.), *Handbook of motivational counseling: Goal-based approaches to assessment and intervention with addiction and other problems* (2nd ed., pp. 109–129). Chichester: Wiley.

Altrocchi, J. (1999). Individual differences in pluralism in self-structure. In J. Rowan & M. Cooper (Eds.), *The plural self: Multiplicty in everyday life* (pp. 168–182). London: Sage.

Ames, C. (1992). Classrooms: Goals, structures, and student motivation. *Journal of Educational Psychology, 84*(3), 261–271.

Angyal, A. (1941). *Foundations for a science of personality*. New York: Commonwealth Fund.

Antony, M. M., & Roemer, L. (2003). Behavior therapy. In A. S. Gurman & S. B. Messer (Eds.), *Essential psychotherapies: Theory and practice* (2nd ed., pp. 182–223). New York: Guilford Press.

Armor, D. E., & Taylor, S. E. (1998). Situated optimism: Specific outcome expectancies and self-regulation. In M. P. Zanna (Ed.), *Advances in experimental social psychology* (Vol. *30*). San Diego, CA: Academic Press.

Aron, A., & Aron, E. N. (2013). The meaning of love. In P. T. P. Wong (Ed.), *The human quest for meaning: Theories, research, and applications* (2nd ed., pp. 185–208). New York: Routledge.

Aronson, E., Wilson, T. D., & Akert, R. M. (1999). *Social psychology*. New York: Longman.

Assagioli, R. (1965). *Psychosynthesis: A manual of principles and techniques*. London: Aquarian/Thorsons.

Astington, J. W. (2001). The paradox of intention: Assessing children's metarepresentational understanding. In B. F. Malle, L. J. Moses & D. A. Baldwin (Eds.), *Intentions and intentionality: Foundations of social cognition* (pp. 85–103). Cambridge, MA: MIT Press.

Atterton, P., Calarco, M., & Friedman, M. (2004). Introduction. In P. Atterton, M. Calarco & M. Friedman (Eds.), *Levinas and Buber: Difference and dialogue* (pp. 1–25). Pittsburgh, PA: Duquesne University Press.

Austin, J. T., & Vancouver, J. B. (1996). Goal constructs in psychology: Structure, process, and content. *Psychological Bulletin, 120*(3), 338–375.

Axelrod, R. (1984). *The evolution of cooperation.* New York: Basic Books.

Baer, R. A., & Huss, D. B. (2008). Mindfulness- and acceptance-based therapy. In J. L. Lebow (Ed.), *Twenty-first century psychotherapies: Contemporary approaches to theory and practice* (pp. 123–166). London: Wiley.

Bagozzi, R. P., & Kimmel, S. K. (1995). A comparison of leading theories for the prediction of goal-directed behaviours. *British Journal of Social Psychology, 34*(4), 437–461.

Bagozzi, R. P., & Pieters, R. (1998). Goal-directed emotions. *Cognition & Emotion, 12*(1), 1–26.

Bailly, L. (2012). Lacanian therapy. In C. Feltham & I. Horton (Eds.), *The Sage handbook of counselling and psychotherapy* (3rd ed., pp. 264–267). London: Sage.

Ballinger, L. (2017). Feminist therapy. In C. Feltham, T. Hanley & L. A. Winter (Eds.), *The Sage handbook of counselling and psychotherapy* (4th ed., pp. 521–525). London: Sage.

Bandura, A. (2001). Social cognitive theory: An agentic perspective. *Annual Review of Psychology, 52*, 1–26. doi: 10.1146/annurev.psych.52.1.1

Bandura, A., & Locke, E. A. (2003). Negative self-efficacy and goal effects revisited. *Journal of Applied Psychology, 88*(1), 87–99.

Barber, J. P., Muran, J. C., McCarthy, K. S., & Keefe, J. R. (2013). Research on dynamic therapies. In M. J. Lambert (Ed.), *Bergin and Garfield's handbook of psychotherapy and behavior change* (6th ed., pp. 443–494). Chicago, IL: John Wiley & Sons.

Bargh, J. A. (1990). Auto-motives: Preconscious determinants of thought and behavior. Multiple affects from multiple stages. In E. T. Higgins & R. M. Sorrentino (Eds.), *Handbook of motivation and cognition: Foundations of social behavior* (Vol. 2, pp. 93–130). New York: Guilford Press.

Bargh, J. A., & Ferguson, M. J. (2000). Beyond behaviorism: On the automaticity of higher mental processes. *Psychological Bulletin, 126*(6), 925–945.

Bargh, J. A., Gollwitzer, P. M., Lee-Chai, A., Barndollar, K., & Trötschel, R. (2001). The automated will: Nonconscious activation and pursuit of behavioral goals. *Journal of Personality and Social Psychology, 81*(6), 1014–1027.

Bargh, J. A., & Huang, J. Y. (2009). The selfish goal. In G. B. Moskowitz & H. Grant (Eds.), *The psychology of goals* (pp. 127–150). New York: Guilford Press.

Barker, M. (2010). Sociocultural issues. In M. Barker, A. Vossler & D. Langdridge (Eds.), *Understanding counselling and psychotherapy* (pp. 211–233). London: Sage.

Barker, M.-J. (2017). *Gender, sexual, and relationship diversity (GSRD). BACP Good practice across the counselling professions.* Lutterworth: BACP.

REFERENCES

Baumeister, R. F. (1991). *Meanings of life*. New York: Guilford Press.

Baumeister, R. F., & Leary, M. R. (1995). The need to belong – desire for interpersonal attachments as a fundamental human-motivation. *Psychological Bulletin, 117*(3), 497–529.

Beahrs, J. O. (1982). *Unity and multiplicity: Multilevel consciousness of self in hypnosis, psychiatric disorder and mental health*. New York: Brunner-Mazel.

Beck, A. T., Rush, A. J., Shaw, B. F., & Emery, G. (1979). *Cognitive therapy of depression*. New York: Guilford Press.

Bédard, J., & Chi, M. T. (1992). Expertise. *Current Directions in Psychological Science, 1*(4), 135–139.

Bednar, R. L., Melnick, J., & Kaul, T. J. (1974). Risk, responsibility, and structure: A conceptual framework for initiating group counseling and psychotherapy. *Journal of Counseling Psychology, 21*(1), 31–37.

Beitman, B. D., Soth, A. M., & Bumby, N. A. (2005). The future as an integrating force through the schools of psychotherapy. In J. C. Norcross & M. R. Goldfried (Eds.), *Handbook of psychotherapy integration* (2nd ed., pp. 65–83). New York: Oxford University Press.

Bennett-Levy, J., Butler, G., Fennell, M., Hackmann, A., Mueller, M., & Westbrook, D. (2005). *Oxford guide to behavioural experiments in cognitive therapy*. Oxford: Oxford University Press.

Berking, M., Grosse Holtforth, M., Jacobi, C., & Kröner-Herwig, B. (2005). Empirically based guidelines for goal-finding procedures in psychotherapy: Are some goals easier to attain than others? *Psychotherapy Research, 15*(3), 316–324.

Berlin, I. (1958). Two concepts of liberty. In H. Hardy (Ed.), *Liberty* (pp. 166–217). Oxford: Oxford University Press.

Berlin, I. (2003). The pursuit of the ideal. In H. Hardy (Ed.), *The crooked timber of humanity: Chapters in the history of ideas* (pp. 1–19). London: Random House.

Berne, E. (1961). *Transactional analysis in psychotherapy*. New York: Grove Press.

Berrios, R., Totterdell, P., & Kellett, S. (2015). Investigating goal conflict as a source of mixed emotions. *Cognition and Emotion, 29*(4), 755–763.

Beutler, L. E., Blatt, S. J., Alimohamed, S., Levy, K. N., & Angtuaco, L. (2006). Participant factors in treating dysphoric disorders. In L. G. Castonguay & L. E. Beutler (Eds.), *Principles of therapeutic change that work* (pp. 13–63). Oxford: Oxford University Press.

Bion, W. R. (1961). *Experiences in groups and other papers*. London: Routledge.

Blatt, S. J., Quinlan, D. M., Pilkonis, P. A., & Shea, M. T. (1995). Impact of perfectionism and need for approval on the brief treatment of depression – the National Institute of Mental Health Treatment of Depression Collaborative Research Program revisited. *Journal of Consulting and Clinical Psychology, 63*(1), 125–132.

Blatt, S. J., Zuroff, D. C., Bondi, C. M., Sanislow, C. A., & Pilkonis, P. A. (1998). When and how perfectionism impedes the brief treatment of depression: Further analyses of the National Institute of Mental Health Treatment of Depression Collaborative Research Program. *Journal of Consulting and Clinical Psychology, 66*(2), 423–428.

REFERENCES

Bleidorn, W., Kandler, C., Hülsheger, U. R., Riemann, R., Angleitner, A., & Spinath, F. M. (2010). Nature and nurture of the interplay between personality traits and major life goals. *Journal of Personality and Social Psychology, 99*(2), 366–379.

Bohart, A. C. (2001). Emphasising the future in empathy responses. In S. Haugh & T. Merry (Eds.), *Empathy* (pp. 99–111). Ross-on-Wye: PCCS Books.

Bohart, A. C., & Tallman, K. (1999). *How clients make therapy work: The process of active self-healing.* Washington, DC: American Psychological Association.

Bohart, A. C., & Wade, A. G. (2013). The client in psychotherapy. In M. J. Lambert (Ed.), *Bergin and Garfield's handbook of psychotherapy and behavior change* (6th ed., pp. 219–257). Chicago, IL: John Wiley & Sons.

Bohm, D. (1996). *On dialogue.* London: Routledge.

Boorman, J., Morris, E., & Oliver, J. (2012). Acceptance and commitment therapy. In C. Feltham & I. Horton (Eds.), *The Sage handbook of counselling and psychotherapy* (3rd ed., pp. 281–285). London: Sage.

Boss, M. (1963). *Psychoanalysis and Daseinsanalysis.* New York: Basic Books.

Boszormenyi-Nagy, I., Grunebaum, J., & Ulrich, D. (1991). Contextual therapy. In A. S. Gurman & D. Kniskern (Eds.), *Handbook of family therapy* (Vol. 2). New York: Brunner-Mazel.

Boszormenyi-Nagy, I., & Krasner, B. R. (1986). *Between give and take: A clinical guide to contextual therapy.* New York: Brunner-Routledge.

Boudreaux, M. J., & Ozer, D. J. (2013). Goal conflict, goal striving, and psychological well-being. *Motivation and Emotion, 37*(3), 433–443.

Bowlby, J. (1969). *Attachment.* New York: Basic Books.

Bowlby, J. (1979). The making and breaking of affectional bonds. In *The making and breaking of affectional bonds* (pp. 150–201). London: Routledge.

Bozarth, J. D., & Wilkins, P. (Eds.). (2001). *Unconditional positive regard.* Ross-on-Wye: PCCS Books.

Braude, S. E. (1991). *First person plural: Multiple personality and the philosophy of the mind.* London: Routledge.

Breitbart, W., Rosenfeld, B., Gibson, C., Pessin, H., Poppito, S., Nelson, C., ... & Olden, M. (2010). Meaning-centered group psychotherapy for patients with advanced cancer: A pilot randomized controlled trial. *Psycho-Oncology, 19*(1), 21–28.

Brentano, F. (2015). *Psychology from an empirical standpoint.* Abingdon, Oxon: Routledge.

Brickell, J., & Wubbolding, R. (2000). Reality therapy. In S. Palmer (Ed.), *Introduction to counselling and psychotherapy: The essential guide* (pp. 292–303). London: Sage.

British Association for Counselling and Psychotherapy. (2018). *Ethical Framework for the Counselling Professions.* Lutterworth: BACP.

Brown, L. (2008). Feminist therapy. In J. L. Lebow (Ed.), *Twenty-first century psychotherapies: Contemporary approaches to theory and practice* (pp. 277–306). London: Wiley.

Bruner, J. (2001). Foreword. In B. F. Malle, L. J. Moses & D. A. Baldwin (Eds.), *Intentions and intentionality: Foundations of social cognition* (pp. ix–xii). Cambridge, MA: MIT Press.

REFERENCES

Brunstein, J. C. (1993). Personal goals and subjective well-being: A longitudinal study. *Journal of Personality and Social Psychology, 65*(5), 1061–1070.

Buber, M. (1947). Dialogue (R. G. Smith, Trans.). *Between man and man* (pp. 17–59). London: Fontana.

Buber, M. (1958). *I and Thou* (R. G. Smith, Trans., 2nd ed.). Edinburgh: T. & T. Clark Ltd.

Buber, M. (1964). *Daniel: Dialogues on realisation* (M. Friedman, Trans.). New York: Holt, Reinhart and Winston.

Bugental, J. F. T. (1976). *The search for existential identity: Patient–therapist dialogues in humanistic psychotherapy*. San Francisco, CA: Jossey-Bass.

Bugental, J. F. T. (1978). *Psychotherapy and process: The fundamentals of an existential-humanistic approach*. Boston, MA: McGraw-Hill.

Bugental, J. F. T. (1981). *The search for authenticity: An existential-analytic approach to psychotherapy* (Exp. ed.). New York: Irvington.

Bugental, J. F. T. (1987). *The art of the psychotherapist: How to develop the skills that take psychotherapy beyond science*. New York: W. W. Norton and Co.

Bulka, R. P. (1982). Logotherapy and Judaism – some philosophical comparisons. In R. Bulka, P. & M. H. Spero (Eds.), *A psychology-Judaism reader*. Springfield, IL: Charles C. Thomas.

Burlingame, G. M., & McClendon, D. T. (2003). Group therapy. In A. S. Gurman & S. B. Messer (Eds.), *Essential psychotherapies* (2nd ed., pp. 347–388). New York: Guilford Press.

Cain, D. J. (2002). Defining characteristics, history, and evolution of humanistic psychotherapies. In D. J. Cain & J. Seeman (Eds.), *Humanistic psychotherapies: Handbook of research and practice* (pp. 3–54). Washington, DC: American Psychological Association.

Cain, D. J., Keenan, K., & Rubin, S. (2016a). Introduction. In D. J. Cain, K. Keenan & S. Rubin (Eds.), *Humanistic psychotherapies: Handbook of research and practice* (2nd ed., pp. 3–8). Washington, DC: American Psychological Association.

Cain, D. J., Keenan, K., & Rubin, S. (Eds.). (2016b). *Humanistic psychotherapies: Handbook of research and practice* (2nd ed.). Washington, DC: American Psychological Association.

Camus, A. (1955). *The myth of Sisyphus* (J. O'Brien, Trans.). London: Penguin.

Cantor, N., & Sanderson, C. A. (1999). Life task participation and well-being: The importance of taking part in daily life. In D. Kahneman, E. Diener & N. Schwarz (Eds.), *Well-being: The foundations of hedonic psychology* (pp. 230–243). New York: Russell Sage Foundation.

Carey, T. A. (2006). *The method of levels: How to do psychotherapy without getting in the way*. Hayward, CA: Living Control Systems.

Carey, T. A. (2008). *Hold that thought! Two steps to effective counseling and psychotherapy with the method of levels*. St. Louis, MO: Newview.

REFERENCES

Carrell, S. E. (2001). *The therapist's toolbox: 26 tools and an assortment of implements for the busy therapist*. Thousand Oaks, CA: Sage.

Carver, C. S., & Scheier, M. F. (1981). *Attention and self-regulation: A control-theory approach to human behavior*. New York: Springer-Verlag.

Carver, C. S., & Scheier, M. F. (1990a). Origins and functions of positive and negative affect: A control-process view. *Psychological Review, 97*(1), 19–35.

Carver, C. S., & Scheier, M. F. (1990b). Principles of self-regulation: Action and emotion. In E. T. Higgins & R. M. Sorrentino (Eds.), *Handbook of motivation and cognition: Foundations of social behaviour* (Vol. 2, pp. 3–52). New York: Guilford Press.

Carver, C. S., & Scheier, M. F. (2012). Cybernetic control processes and the self-regulation of behavior. In R. M. Ryan (Ed.), *The Oxford handbook of human motivation* (pp. 28–42). New York: Oxford University Press.

Caspar, F. (1995). *Plan analysis: Towards optimizing psychotherapy*. Bern: Hogrefe & Huber.

Cavallo, J. V., & Fitzsimons, G. M. (2012). Goal competition, conflict, coordination, and completion: How intergoal dynamics affect self-regulation. In H. Aarts & A. J. Elliot (Eds.), *Goal-directed behavior* (pp. 267–300). New York: Psychology Press.

Chaplin, J. (1988). *Feminist counselling in action*. London: Sage.

Chun, W. Y., Kruglanski, A. W., Sleeth-Keppler, D., & Friedman, R. S. (2011). Multifinality in implicit choice. *Journal of Personality and Social Psychology, 101*(5), 1124–1137.

Clark, D. M. (2011). Implementing NICE guidelines for the psychological treatment of depression and anxiety disorders: The IAPT experience. *International Review of Psychiatry, 23*(4), 318–327.

Clarkson, P. (1989). *Gestalt counselling in action*. London: Sage.

Clarkson, P. (2000). Eclectic, integrative and integrating psychotherapy or beyond schoolism. In S. Palmer & R. Woolfe (Eds.), *Integrative and eclectic counselling and psychotherapy* (pp. 305–314). London: Sage.

Coelho, H. F., Canter, P. H., & Ernst, E. (2007). Mindfulness-based cognitive therapy: Evaluating current evidence and informing future research. *Journal of Consulting and Clinical Psychology, 75*(6), 1000–1005.

Constantino, M., Glass, C., Arnkoff, D., Ametrano, R., & Smith, J. (2011). Expectations. In J. C. Norcross (Ed.), *Psychotherapy relationships that work* (2nd ed., pp. 354–376). New York: Oxford University Press.

Cooper, M. (2000). Person-centred developmental theory: Reflections and revisions. *Person-Centred Practice, 8*(2), 87–94.

Cooper, M. (2003). 'I–I' and 'I–Me': Transposing Buber's interpersonal attitudes to the intrapersonal plane. *Journal of Constructivist Psychology, 16*(2), 131–153.

Cooper, M. (2004). Encountering self-otherness: 'I–I' and 'I–Me' modes of self-relating. In H. J. M. Hermans & G. Dimaggio (Eds.), *Dialogical self in psychotherapy* (pp. 60–73). Hove: Brunner-Routledge.

REFERENCES

Cooper, M. (2006). Socialist humanism: A progressive politics for the twenty-first century. In G. Proctor, M. Cooper, P. Sanders & B. Malcolm (Eds.), *Politicising the person-centred approach: An agenda for social change* (pp. 80–94). Ross-on-Wye: PCCS Books.

Cooper, M. (2007). Humanizing psychotherapy. *Journal of Contemporary Psychotherapy, 37*(1), 11–16.

Cooper, M. (2008). *Essential research findings in counselling and psychotherapy: The facts are friendly*. London: Sage.

Cooper, M. (2009). Welcoming the Other: Actualising the humanistic ethic at the core of counselling psychology practice. *Counselling Psychology Review, 24*(3&4), 119–129.

Cooper, M. (2012). *A hierarchy of wants: Towards an integrative framework for counselling, psychotherapy and social change*. University of Strathclyde, Glasgow. Retrieved from pure.strath.ac.uk/portal

Cooper, M. (2013). The intrinsic foundations of extrinsic motivations and goals: Towards a unified humanistic theory of wellbeing. *Journal of Humanistic Psychology, 53*(2), 153–171.

Cooper, M. (2015a). *Existential psychotherapy and counselling: Contributions to a pluralistic practice*. London: Sage.

Cooper, M. (2015b). *Goals form*. University of Roehampton, London. Retrieved from www.researchgate.net/publication/286928866_Goals_Form

Cooper, M. (2015c). Social change from the counselling room. *Therapy Today, 26*(2), 10–13.

Cooper, M. (2016). The fully functioning society: A humanistic-existential vision of an actualizing, socially-just future. *Journal of Humanistic Psychology, 56*(6), 581–594.

Cooper, M. (2017a). *Existential therapies* (2nd ed.). London: Sage.

Cooper, M. (2017b). Synergy, dysergy and the alleviation of preventable suffering. In R. E. Anderson (Ed.), *Alleviating world suffering: The challenge of negative quality of life* (pp. 73–83). New York: Springer.

Cooper, M. (2018). The psychology of goals: A practice-friendly review. In M. Cooper & D. Law (Eds.), *Working with goals in counselling and psychotherapy* (pp. 35–71). Oxford: Oxford University Press.

Cooper, M., Chak, A., Cornish, F., & Gillespie, A. (2012). Dialogue: Bridging personal, community and social transformation. *Journal of Humanistic Psychology, 53*(1), 70–93.

Cooper, M., & Cruthers, H. (1999). Facilitating the expression of subpersonalities: A review and analysis of techniques. In J. Rowan & M. Cooper (Eds.), *The plural self: Multiplicity in everyday life* (pp. 198–212). London: Sage.

Cooper, M., & Dryden, W. (Eds.). (2016). *Handbook of pluralistic counselling and psychotherapy*. London: Sage.

Cooper, M., Dryden, W., Martin, K., & Papayianni, F. (2016). Metatherapeutic communication and shared decision-making. In M. Cooper & W. Dryden (Eds.), *Handbook of pluralistic counselling and psychotherapy* (pp. 42–54). London: Sage.

REFERENCES

Cooper, M., & Hermans, H. (2007). Honouring self-otherness: Alterity and the intrapersonal. In L. M. Simão & J. Valsiner (Eds.), *Otherness in question: Labyrinths of the self* (pp. 305–315). Charlotte, NC: Information Age.

Cooper, M., & Ikemi, A. (2012). Dialogue: A dialogue between focusing and relational perspectives. *Person-Centered & Experiential Psychotherapies, 11*(2), 124–136.

Cooper, M., & Knox, R. (2018). Therapists' self-reported chronic strategies of disconnection in everyday life and in counselling and psychotherapy: An exploratory study. *British Journal of Guidance & Counselling, 46*(2), 185–200.

Cooper, M., & Law, D. (2018a). Introduction. In M. Cooper & D. Law (Eds.), *Working with goals in counselling and psychotherapy* (pp. 1–13). Oxford: Oxford University Press.

Cooper, M., & Law, D. (Eds.). (2018b). *Working with goals in counselling and psychotherapy*. Oxford: Oxford University Press.

Cooper, M., & McLeod, J. (2007). A pluralistic framework for counselling and psychotherapy: Implications for research. *Counselling and Psychotherapy Research, 7*(3), 135–143.

Cooper, M., & McLeod, J. (2011). *Pluralistic counselling and psychotherapy*. London: Sage.

Cooper, M., & Norcross, J. C. (2015). *Mental health professionals and service users' preferences for therapy* [Unpublished dataset].

Cooper, M., & Spinelli, E. (2012). A dialogue on dialogue. In L. Barnett & G. Madison (Eds.), *Existential psychotherapy: Vibrancy, legacy and dialogue* (pp. 141–157). London: Routledge.

Cornell, A. W. (1996). *The power of focusing: Finding your inner voice*. Oakland, CA: New Harbinger Publications.

Corning, P. (1998). The synergism hypothesis: On the concept of synergy and it's role in the evolution of complex species. *Journal of Social and Evolutionary Systems, 21*(2), 133–172.

Corning, P. (2003). *Nature's magic: Synergy in evolution and the fate of humankind*. Cambridge: Cambridge University Press.

Corning, P. (2011). *The fair society: The science of human nature and the pursuit of social justice*. London: University of Chicago Press.

Cornish, P. (2012). The contribution of synergy to the experience of empowerment. In R. Katz & S. Murphy-Shigematsu (Eds.), *Synergy, healing and empowerment: Insights from cultural diversity* (pp. 241–256). Calgary, CA: Brush.

Correia, C. J., Murphy, J. G., & Butler, L. H. (2011). Behavioral economics: Basic concepts and clinical applications. In W. M. Cox & E. Klinger (Eds.), *Handbook of motivational counseling: Goal-based approaches to assessment and intervention with addiction and other problems* (2nd ed., pp. 49–72). Chichester: Wiley.

Correia, E., Cooper, M., & Berdondini, L. (2015). Existential psychotherapy: An international survey of the key authors and texts influencing practice. *Journal of Contemporary Psychotherapy, 45*(1), 3–10.

REFERENCES

Correia, E. A., Sartóris, V., Fernandes, T., Cooper, M., Berdondini, L., Sousa, D., Sá Pires, B., & da Fonseca, J. (2018). The practices of existential psychotherapists: Development and application of an observational grid. *British Journal of Guidance & Counselling, 46*(2), 201–216.

Cox, G. (2009). *How to be an existentialist: Or how to get real, get a grip and stop making excuses*. London: Bloomsbury.

Cox, W. M. (2000). *Personal concerns inventory* [Unpublished questionnaire]. Bangor University.

Cox, W. M., & Klinger, E. (2002). Motivational structure: Relationships with substance use and processes of change. *Addictive Behaviors, 27*(6), 925–940.

Cox, W. M., & Klinger, E. (2011a). Measuring motivation: The Motivational Structure Questionnaire and Personal Concerns Inventory and their variants. In W. M. Cox & E. Klinger (Eds.), *Handbook of motivational counseling: Goal-based approaches to assessment and intervention with addiction and other problems* (2nd ed., pp. 161–204). Chichester: Wiley.

Cox, W. M., & Klinger, E. (2011b). A motivational model of alcohol use: Determinants of use and change. In W. M. Cox & E. Klinger (Eds.), *Handbook of motivational counseling: Goal-based approaches to assessment and intervention with addiction and other problems* (2nd ed., pp. 131–158). Chichester: Wiley.

Cox, W. M., & Klinger, E. (2011c). Systematic motivational counseling: From motivational assessment to motivational change. In W. M. Cox & E. Klinger (Eds.), *Handbook of motivational counseling: Goal-based approaches to assessment and intervention with addiction and other problems* (2nd ed., pp. 275–302). Chichester: Wiley.

Cox, W. M., & Klinger, E. (Eds.). (2011d). *Handbook of motivational counseling: Goal-based approaches to assessment and intervention with addiction and other problems* (2nd ed.). Chichester: Wiley.

Crossley, N. (1996). *Intersubjectivity: The fabric of social becoming*. London: Sage.

Csikszentmihalyi, M. (2002). *Flow: The classic work on how to achieve happiness*. London: Rider.

Cullen, J. W., & Russell, D. (1989). *The self actualizing manager: An introduction to managerial psychosynthesis*. Thousand Oaks, CA: International Association for Managerial and Organizational Psychosynthesis.

Curtice, J. (2016). Is there a progressive majority? In L. Nandy, C. Lucas & C. Bowers (Eds.), *The alternative: Towards a new progressive politics* (pp. 186–201). London: Biteback.

Curtis, J., Silberschatz, G., Sampson, H., & Weiss, J. (1994). The Plan Formulation Method. *Psychotherapy Research, 4*(3–4), 197–207.

Curtis, R. C., & Hirsch, I. (2003). Relational approaches to psychoanalytic psychotherapy. In A. S. Gurman & S. B. Messer (Eds.), *Essential psychotherapies: Theory and practice* (2nd ed., pp. 69–106). New York: Guilford Press.

Custers, R. (2009). How does our unconscious know what we want? In G. B. Moskowitz & H. Grant (Eds.), *The psychology of goals* (pp. 179–202). New York: Guilford Press.

REFERENCES

Custers, R., Eitam, B., & Bargh, J. A. (2012). Conscious and unconscious goal pursuits. In H. Aarts & A. J. Elliot (Eds.), *Goal-directed behavior* (pp. 231–266). New York: Psychology Press.

Dallos, R., Wright, J., Stedman, J., & Johnstone, L. (2006). Integrative formulation. In L. Johnstone & R. Dallos (Eds.), *Formulation in psychology and psychotherapy: Making sense of people's problems* (pp. 154–181). London: Routledge.

Dawkins, R. (2009). The purpose of purpose. Lecture delivered at Michigan State University, East Lansing, MI, 2–3 March. https://www.youtube.com/watch?v=mT4EWCRfdUg

de Beauvoir, S. (1948). *The ethics of ambiguity*. New York: Citadel.

Deci, E. L., & Ryan, R. M. (2000). The 'what' and 'why' of goal pursuits: Human needs and the self-determination of behavior. *Psychological Inquiry, 11*(4), 227–268.

Deci, E. L., & Ryan, R. M. (2012). Motivation, personality, and development within embedded social contexts: An overview of self-determination theory. In R. M. Ryan (Ed.), *The Oxford handbook of human motivation* (pp. 85–107). New York: Oxford University Press.

Dennett, D. (1987). *The intentional stance*. Cambridge, MA: MIT Press.

Derrida, J. (1974). *Of grammatology* (G. C. Spivak, Trans.). Baltimore, MD: The Johns Hopkins University Press.

di Malta, G. S., Cooper, M., & Oddli, H. W. (2018). Goal-setting and -tracking in pluralistic therapy: A qualitative analysis. [Manuscript submitted for publication].

Diener, E. (1984). Subjective wellbeing. *Psychological Bulletin, 95*(3), 542–575.

Diener, E., & Lucas, R. E. (1999). Personality and subjective well-being. In D. Kahneman, E. Diener & N. Schwarz (Eds.), *Well-being: The foundations of hedonic psychology* (pp. 213–229). New York: Russell Sage Foundation.

Dies, R. R. (2003). Group psychotherapies. In A. S. Gurman & S. B. Messer (Eds.), *Essential psychotherapies* (2nd ed., pp. 515–550). New York: Guilford Press.

Dimeff, L., & Linehan, M. M. (2001). Dialectical behavior therapy in a nutshell. *The California Psychologist, 34*(3), 10–13.

Dolan, P. (2014). *Happiness by design: Finding pleasure and purpose in everyday life*. London: Penguin.

Dreyfus, H. L. (1997). *Being-in-the-world: A commentary on Heidegger's* Being and Time, *Division 1*. Cambridge, MA: MIT Press.

Dryden, W. (1999). *Rational emotive behavioural counselling in action* (2nd ed.). London: Sage.

Dryden, W. (2014). Rational emotive behaviour therapy. In W. Dryden & A. Reeves (Eds.), *The handbook of individual therapy* (6th ed., pp. 271–299). London: Sage.

Dryden, W. (2018). From problems to goals: Identifying 'good' goals in psychotherapy and counselling. In M. Cooper & D. Law (Eds.), *Working with goals in counselling and psychotherapy* (pp. 139–159). Oxford: Oxford University Press.

Duncan, B. L., Miller, S. D., & Sparks, J. A. (2004). *The heroic client: A revolutionary way to improve effectiveness through client-directed, outcome-informed therapy*. San Francisco, CA: Jossey-Bass.

REFERENCES

Dunn, M. (2014). Cognitive analytic therapy. In W. Dryden & A. Reeves (Eds.), *The handbook of individual therapy* (6th ed., pp. 361–385). London: Sage.

Dweck, C. S., & Leggett, E. L. (1988). A social-cognitive approach to motivation and personality. *Psychological Review, 95*(2), 256–273.

D'Zurilla, T. J., & Nezu, A. M. (1999). *Problem-solving therapy: A social competence approach to clinical interventions.* New York: Springer.

Eames, V., & Denborough, D. (2017). *Mapping team goals: Team of life collective narrative practice.* London: Team of Life.

Egan, G. (1994). *The skilled helper: A problem-management approach to helping* (5th ed.). Belmont, CA: Brooks/Cole.

Egan, G., & Reese, R. J. (2019). *The skilled helper: A Problem-management and opportunity-development approach to helping* (11th ed.). Boston, MA: Cengage.

Eigner, S. (2001). The relationship between 'protecting the environment' as a dominant life goal and subjective well-being. In P. Schmuck & K. M. Sheldon (Eds.), *Life goals and well-being: Towards a positive psychology of human striving* (pp. 182–201). Gottingen, Germany: Hogrefe & Huber.

Elliot, A. J., & Church, M. A. (2002). Client articulated avoidance goals in the therapy context. *Journal of Counseling Psychology, 49*(2), 243–254.

Elliot, A. J., & Friedman, R. (2007). Approach–avoidance: A central characteristic of personal goals. In B. R. Little, K. Salmela-Aro & S. D. Phillips (Eds.), *Personal project pursuit: Goals, action, and human flourishing* (pp. 97–118). Mahwah, NJ: Lawrence Erlbaum Associates.

Elliot, A. J., & Niesta, D. (2009). Goals in the context of the hierarchical model of approach–avoidance motivation. In G. B. Moskowitz & H. Grant (Eds.), *The psychology of goals* (pp. 56–76). New York: Guilford Press.

Elliot, A. J., & Sheldon, K. M. (1997). Avoidance achievement motivation: A personal goals analysis. *Journal of Personality and Social Psychology, 73*(1), 171–185.

Elliott, E. S., & Dweck, C. S. (1988). Goals: An approach to motivation and achievement. *Journal of Personality and Social Psychology, 54*(1), 5–12.

Elliott, R., Bohart, A. C., Watson, J. C., & Greenberg, L. S. (2011). Empathy. In J. C. Norcross (Ed.), *Psychotherapy relationships that work: Evidence-based responsiveness* (2nd ed., pp. 132–152). New York: Oxford University Press.

Elliott, R., & Greenberg, L. S. (1997). Multiple voices in process-experiential therapy: Dialogue between aspects of the self. *Journal of Psychotherapy Integration, 7*(3), 225–239.

Elliott, R., Greenberg, L. S., Watson, J. C., Timulak, L., & Freire, E. (2013). Research on humanistic-experiential psychotherapies. In M. J. Lambert (Ed.), *Bergin and Garfield's handbook of psychotherapy and behavior change* (6th ed., pp. 495–538). Chicago, IL: John Wiley & Sons.

Elliott, R., Watson, J. C., Goldman, R. N., & Greenberg, L. S. (2004). *Learning emotion-focused therapy: The process-experiential approach to change.* Washington, DC: American Psychological Association.

REFERENCES

Emmerson, G. (2006). *Advanced skills and interventions in therapeutic counselling*. Carmarthen: Crown House.

Emmons, R. A. (1986). Personal strivings: An approach to personality and subjective well-being. *Journal of Personality and Social Psychology, 51*(5), 1058–1068.

Emmons, R. A., & Diener, E. (1986). A goal-affect analysis of everyday situational choices. *Journal of Research in Personality, 20*(3), 309–326.

Emmons, R. A., & King, L. A. (1988). Conflict among personal strivings: Immediate and long-term implications for psychological and physical well-being. *Journal of Personality and Social Psychology, 54*(6), 1040–1048.

Emmons, R. A., & McCullough, M. E. (2003). Counting blessings versus burdens: An experimental investigation of gratitude and subjective well-being in daily life. *Journal of Personality and Social Psychology, 84*(2), 377–389.

Engel, G. L. (1977). The need for a new medical model: A challenge for biomedicine. *Science, 196*(4286), 129–136.

Enns, C. Z., & Williams, E. N. (Eds.). (2013). *The Oxford handbook of feminist multicultural counseling psychology*. New York: Oxford University Press.

Epstein, S. (1994). Integration of the cognitive and the psychodynamic unconscious. *American Psychologist, 49*(8), 709–724.

Epstein, S. (1998). Cognitive-experiential self-theory. In D. F. Barone, M. Hersen & V. B. Van Hasselt (Eds.), *Advanced personality* (pp. 211–238). Boston, MA: Springer.

Epton, T., Currie, S., & Armitage, C. J. (2017). Unique effects of setting goals on behavior change: Systematic review and meta-analysis. *Journal of Consulting and Clinical Psychology, 85*(12), 1182–1198.

Erikson, E. H. (1950). *Childhood and society*. Harmondsworth: Penguin.

Eriksson, L. (2011). *Rational choice theory: Potential and limits*. Basingstoke: Palgrave.

Evans, G. (2012). Couple counselling. In C. Feltham & I. Horton (Eds.), *The Sage handbook of counselling and psychotherapy* (3rd ed., pp. 581–585). London: Sage.

Fabry, J. (1980). *The pursuit of meaning: Viktor Frankl, logotherapy and life* (rev. ed.). San Francisco, CA: Harper & Row.

Farber, L. H. (2000). *The ways of the will* (exp. ed.). New York: Basic Books.

Feixas, G., & Compañ, V. (2016). Dilemma-focused intervention for unipolar depression: A treatment manual. *BMC Psychiatry, 16*(1), 235.

Feltham, A., Martin, K., Walker, L., & Harris, L. (2018). Using goals in therapy: The perspective of people with lived experience. In M. Cooper & D. Law (Eds.), *Working with goals in counselling and psychotherapy* (pp. 73–85). Oxford: Oxford University Press.

Ferrucci, P. (1982). *What we may be*. London: Aquarian.

Fishbach, A., & Finkelstein, S. R. (2012). How feedback influences persistence, disengagement, and change in goal pursuits. In H. Aarts & A. J. Elliot (Eds.), *Goal-directed behavior* (pp. 203–230). New York: Psychology Press.

REFERENCES

Fisher, L. (2008). *Rock, paper, scissors: Game theory in everyday life*. London: Basic Books.

Flanagan, C. M. (2010). The case for needs in psychotherapy. *Journal of Psychotherapy Integration, 20*(1), 1–36. doi: 10.1037/a0018815

Fonagy, P., Gergely, G., Jurist, E. L., & Target, M. (2004). *Affect regulation, mentalization and the development of the self*. London: Karnac Books.

Ford, D. H. (1987). *Humans as self-constructing living systems: A developmental perspective on behavior and personality*. Mahwah, NJ: Lawrence Erlbaum Associates.

Ford, M. E. (1992). *Motivating humans: Goals, emotions, and personal agency beliefs*. Newbury Park, CA: Sage.

Foresight Mental Capital and Wellbeing Project. (2008). Final Project report – executive summary. London: The Government Office for Science.

Foulkes, E. T. (1984). The origin and development of group analysis. In T. E. Lear (Ed.), *Spheres of group analysis* (pp. 5–19). London: Group Analytic Society.

Frank, J. D., & Frank, J. B. (1993). *Persuasion and healing* (3rd ed.). Baltimore, MD: The Johns Hopkins University Press.

Frankl, V. E. (1967). *Psychotherapy and existentialism: Selected papers on logotherapy*. New York: Clarion Books.

Frankl, V. E. (1984). *Man's search for meaning* (revised and updated ed.). New York: Washington Square Press.

Frankl, V. E. (1986). *The doctor and the soul: From psychotherapy to logotherapy* (R. Winston & C. Winston, Trans., 3rd ed.). New York: Vintage Books.

Frankl, V. E. (1988). *The will to meaning: Foundations and applications of logotherapy* (exp. ed.). London: Meridian.

Frankl, V. E. (1998). *The unconditional human: Metaclinical lectures* (W. J. Maas, Trans.). Unpublished translation.

Fransella, F., & Winter, D. (2012). Personal construct counselling and psychotherapy. In C. Feltham & I. Horton (Eds.), *The Sage handbook of counselling and psychotherapy* (3rd ed., pp. 388–391). London: Sage.

Freud, S. (1909). Analysis of a phobia of a five year old boy. *The Standard Edition of the Complete Psychological Works of Sigmund Freud* (Vol. *8*). London: Pelican.

Freud, S. (1923). The ego and the id (J. Strachey, Trans.) *The Standard Edition of the Complete Psychological Works of Sigmund Freud* (Vol. *19*, pp. 12–59). London: Hogarth Press.

Freud, S. (1962). *Introductory lectures on psychoanalysis* (J. Strachey, Trans.). London: Penguin.

Freud, S. (1963). The unconscious. In S. Freud (Ed.), *General psychological theory: Papers on metapsychology* (pp. 116–150). New York: Collier.

Freud, S. (1965). *New introductory lectures on psychoanalysis*. London: W. W. Norton.

Freud, S. (2002). *The 'wolfman' and other cases* (L. A. Huish, Trans.). London: Penguin.

Freund, A. M. (2007). Differentiating and integrating levels of goal representation: A life-span perspective. In B. R. Little, K. Salmela-Aro & S. D. Phillips (Eds.), *Personal *project pursuit: Goals, action, and human flourishing.* (pp. 247–270). Mahwah, NJ: Lawrence Erlbaum Associates.

Frijda, N. H., Kuipers, P., & ter Schure, E. (1989). Relations among emotion, appraisal, and emotional action readiness. *Journal of Personality and Social Psychology, 57*(2), 212–228.

Fromm, E. (1942). *The fear of freedom.* London: Routledge.

Fromm, E. (1957). *The art of loving.* London: Unwin.

Fromm, E. (1961). *Marx's concept of man.* London: Continuum.

Fromm, E. (Ed.). (1965). *Socialist humanism.* London: Penguin.

Fromm, E. (1991). *The sane society* (2nd ed.). London: Routledge.

Fromm, E. (2005). *To have or to be?* London: Continuum.

Fujita, K., & MacGregor, K. E. (2012). Basic goal distinctions. In H. Aarts & A. J. Elliot (Eds.), *Goal-directed behavior* (pp. 85–114). New York: Psychology Press.

Gendlin, E. T. (1996). *Focusing-oriented psychotherapy: A manual of the experiential method.* New York: Guilford Press.

Gendlin, E. T. (2003). *Focusing.* London: Rider.

Gibbs Jr, R. W. (2001). Intentions as emergent products of social interactions. In B. F. Malle, L. J. Moses & D. A. Baldwin (Eds.), *Intentions and intentionality: Foundations of social cognition* (pp. 105–122). Cambridge, MA: MIT Press.

Gilbert, P., & Irons, C. (2014). Compassion-focused therapy. In W. Dryden & A. Reeves (Eds.), *Handbook of individual therapy* (6th ed., pp. 301–327). London: Sage.

Gillespie, A. (2007). Time, self, and the other: The striving tourist in Ladakh, North India. In L. M. Simão & J. Valsiner (Eds.), *Otherness in question: Labyrinths of the self* (pp. 163–186). Charlotte, NC: Information Age.

Glass, C. R., Arnkoff, D. B., & Shapiro, S. J. (2001). Expectations and preferences. *Psychotherapy, 38*(4), 455–461.

Glasser, W. (1965). *Reality therapy: A new approach to psychiatry.* New York: Harper & Row.

Goldfried, M. R., Pachanakis, J. E., & Bell, A. C. (2005). A history of psychotherapy integration. In J. C. Norcross & M. R. Goldfried (Eds.), *Handbook of psychotherapy integration* (2nd ed., pp. 24–60). New York: Oxford University Press.

Goldman, R. N. (2016). Emotion-focused therapy. In D. Cain, K. Keenan & S. Rubin (Eds.), *Humanistic psychotherapies* (2nd ed., pp. 319–350). Washington, DC: American Psychological Association.

Goldstein, D. M. (1990). Clincial applications of control theory. *American Behavioral Scientist, 34*(1), 110–116.

Goldstein, K. (1940). *Human nature in the light of psychopathology.* New York: Schocken Books.

Goleman, D. (1996). *Emotional intelligence: Why it can matter more than IQ.* London: Bloomsbury.

Gollwitzer, P. M. (1990). Action phases and mind-sets. In E. T. Higgins & R. M. Sorrentino (Eds.), *Handbook of motivation and cognition: Foundations of social behavior* (Vol. 2, pp. 53–92). New York: Guilford Press.

Gollwitzer, P. M. (1999). Implementation intentions: Strong effects of simple plans. *American Psychologist, 54*(7), 493–503.

Gollwitzer, P. M. (2012). Mindset theory of action phases. In P. A. van Lange, A. W. Kruglanski & E. T. Higgins (Eds.), *The Handbook of Theories of social psychology* (Vol. 1, pp. 526–545). Los Angeles, CA: Sage.

Gollwitzer, P. M., Kappes, H. B., & Oettingen, G. (2012). Needs and incentives as sources of goals. In H. Aarts & A. J. Elliot (Eds.), *Goal-directed behavior* (pp. 115–150). New York: Psychology Press.

Gollwitzer, P. M., & Oettingen, G. (2012). Goal pursuit. In R. M. Ryan (Ed.), *The Oxford handbook of human motivation* (pp. 208–231). New York: Oxford University Press.

Gollwitzer, P. M., & Sheeran, P. (2006). Implementation intentions and goal achievement: A meta-analysis of effects and processes. *Advances in Experimental Social Psychology, 38*, 69–119.

Gordon Training International. (2016). Learning a new skill is easier said than done. Retrieved from www.gordontraining.com/free-workplace-articles/learning-a-new-skill-is-easier-said-than-done/

Grant, H., & Gelety, L. (2009). Goal content theories: Why differences in what we are striving for matter. In G. B. Moskowitz & H. Grant (Eds.), *The psychology of goals* (pp. 77–97). New York: Guilford Press.

Grawe, K. (2004). *Psychological therapy*. Gottingen, Germany: Hogrefe & Huber.

Greenberg, J. R., & Mitchell, S. A. (1983). *Object relations in psychoanalytic theory*. Cambridge, MA: Harvard University Press.

Greenberg, L. S., & Dompierre, L. M. (1981). Specific effects of Gestalt 2-chair dialog on intrapsychic conflict in counseling. *Journal of Counseling Psychology, 28*(4), 288–294.

Greenberg, L. S., Korman, L. M., & Paivio, S. C. (2002). Emotion in humanistic psychotherapy. In D. J. Cain & J. Seeman (Eds.), *Humanistic psychotherapies: Handbook of research and practice* (pp. 499–530). Washington, DC: American Psychological Association.

Greenberg, L. S., & Paivio, S. C. (1997). *Working with emotions in psychotherapy*. New York: Guilford Press.

Greenberg, L. S., Rice, L. N., & Elliott, R. (1993). *Facilitating emotional change: The moment-by-moment process*. New York: Guilford Press.

Greenberg, L. S., Watson, J. C., & Lietaer, G. (Eds.). (1998). *Handbook of experiential psychotherapy*. New York: Guilford Press.

Gregory, R. L. (Ed.). (1987). *The Oxford companion to the mind*. Oxford: Oxford University Press.

Grey, N., Byrne, S., Taylor, T., Shmueli, A., Troupp, C., Stratton, P., Sefi, A., Law, R., & Cooper, M. (2018). Goal-oriented practice across therapies. In D. Law & M. Cooper (Eds.), *Working with goals in counselling and psychotherapy* (pp. 181–203). Oxford: Oxford University Press.

Griffin, J., & Tyrrell, I. (2013). *Human givens*. Chalvington, East Sussex: Human Givens.

REFERENCES

Grosse Holtforth, M., & Grawe, K. (2002). Bern Inventory of Treatment Goals: Part 1. Development and first application of a taxonomy of treatment goal themes. *Psychotherapy Research, 12*(1), 79–99.

Grosse Holtforth, M., & Michalak, J. (2012). Motivation in psychotherapy. In R. M. Ryan (Ed.), *The Oxford handbook of human motivation* (pp. 441–462). New York: Oxford University Press.

Grouzet, F. M. E., Kasser, T., Ahuvia, A., Dols, J. M. F., Kim, Y., Lau, S., Ryan, R. M., Saunders, S., Schmuck, P., & Sheldon, K. M. (2005). The structure of goal contents across 15 cultures. *Journal of Personality and Social Psychology, 89*(5), 800–816.

Guignon, C. B. (Ed.). (1993). *The Cambridge companion to Heidegger.* Cambridge: Cambridge University Press.

Gurman, A. S. (2003). Marital therapies. In A. S. Gurman & S. B. Messer (Eds.), *Essential psychotherapies* (2nd ed., pp. 463–514). New York: Guilford Press.

Harkin, B., Webb, T. L., Chang, B. P., Prestwich, A., Conner, M., Kellar, I., Benn, Y., & Sheeran, P. (2016). Does monitoring goal progress promote goal attainment? A meta-analysis of the experimental evidence. *Psychological Bulletin, 142*(2), 198–229.

Heckhausen, H., & Gollwitzer, P. M. (1987). Thought contents and cognitive functioning in motivational versus volitional states of mind. *Motivation and Emotion, 11*(2), 101–120.

Heckhausen, J., Wrosch, C., & Schulz, R. (2010). A motivational theory of life-span development. *Psychological Review, 117*(1), 32–60.

Heidegger, M. (1962). *Being and time* (J. Macquarrie & E. Robinson, Trans.). Oxford: Blackwell.

Heidegger, M. (1966). *Discourse on thinking* (J. M. Anderson & E. H. Freund, Trans.). London: Harper Colophon Books.

Heidegger, M. (1971). *On the way to language* (P. D. Hertz, Trans.). San Francisco, CA: Harper Collins.

Hendricks, M. N. (2002). Focusing-oriented/experiential psychotherapy. In D. J. Cain & J. Seeman (Eds.), *Humanistic psychotherapies: Handbook of research and practice* (pp. 221–252). Washington, DC: American Psychological Association.

Henry, K. L., Lovegrove, P. J., Steger, M. F., Chen, P. Y., Cigularov, K. P., & Tomazic, R. G. (2014). The potential role of meaning in life in the relationship between bullying victimization and suicidal ideation. *Journal of Youth and Adolescence, 43*(2), 221–232.

Hermans, H. J. M. (2001). The dialogical self: Towards a theory of personal and cultural positioning. *Culture and Psychology, 7*(3), 243–281.

Hermans, H. J. M., & Kempen, H. J. G. (1993). *The dialogical self: Meaning as movement.* San Diego, CA: Academic Press.

Higgins, E. T. (1997). Beyond pleasure and pain. *American Psychologist, 52*(12), 1280–1300.

Hill, C. E., Kanazawa, Y., Knox, S., Schauerman, I., Loureiro, D., James, D., Carter, I., King, S., Razzak, S., Scarff, M., & Moore J. (2017). Meaning in life in psychotherapy: The perspective of experienced psychotherapists. *Psychotherapy Research, 27*(4), 381–396.

REFERENCES

Hoffman, L. (2009). Introduction to existential psychology in a cross-cultural context: An East–West dialogue. In L. Hoffman, M. Yang, F. J. Kaklauskas & A. Chan (Eds.), *Existential psychology East–West* (pp. 1–67). Colorado Springs, CO: University of the Rockies Press.

Holland, R. W., Hendriks, M., & Aarts, H. (2005). Smells like clean spirit: Nonconscious effects of scent on cognition and behavior. *Psychological Science, 16*(9), 689–693.

Hollanders, H. (2003). The eclectic and integrative approach. In R. Woolfe, W. Dryden & S. Strawbridge (Eds.), *Handbook of counselling psychology* (2nd ed., pp. 277–300). London: Sage.

Hollon, S. D., & Beck, A. T. (2013). Cognitive and cognitive-behavioral therapies. In M. J. Lambert (Ed.), *Bergin and Garfield's handbook of psychotherapy and behavior change* (6th ed., pp. 393–442). Chicago, IL: John Wiley and Sons.

Holzhey-Kunz, A. (2014). *Daseinsanalysis* (S. Leighton, Trans.). London: Free Association Books.

Houston, G. (1993). *Being and belonging: Group, intergroup and Gestalt*. Chichester: Wiley.

Howard, S. (2014). Interpersonal therapy. In W. Dryden & A. Reeves (Eds.), *The handbook of individual therapy* (6th ed., pp. 415–441). London: Sage.

Hoyt, M. F. (2003). Brief psychotherapies. In A. S. Gurman & S. B. Messer (Eds.), *Essential psychotherapies* (2nd ed., pp. 350–399). New York: Guilford Press.

Hsee, C. K., & Abelson, R. P. (1991). Velocity relation: Satisfaction as a function of the first derivative of outcome over time. *Journal of Personality and Social Psychology, 60*(3), 341–347.

Husserl, E. (1960). *Cartesian meditations: An introduction to phenomenology*. The Hague: Martinus Nijhoff.

Iacovou, S., & Weixel-Dixon, K. (2015). *Existential therapy: 100 key points and techniques*. London: Routledge.

Ilardi, S. S., & Craighead, W. E. (1994). The role of nonspecific factors in cognitive-behavior therapy for depression. *Clinical Psychology: Science and Practice, 1*(2), 138–156.

Irving, L. M., & Cannon, R. (2000). Starving for hope: Goals, agency, and pathways in the development and treatment of eating disorders. In C. R. Snyder (Ed.), *Handbook of hope: Theory, measures & applications* (pp. 261–283). San Diego, CA: Academic Press.

Ivey, A. E., & Brooks-Harris, J. E. (2005). Integrative psychotherapy with culturally diverse clients. In J. C. Norcross & M. R. Goldfried (Eds.), *Handbook of psychotherapy integration* (2nd ed., pp. 321–339). New York: Oxford University Press.

Jacob, J., Edbrooke-Childs, J., Lloyd, C., Hayes, D., Whelan, I., Wolpert, M., & Law, D. (2018). Measuring outcomes using goals. In M. Cooper & D. Law (Eds.), *Working with goals in counselling and psychotherapy* (pp. 111–137). Oxford: Oxford University Press.

Jacobsen, B. (2007). *Invitation to existential psychology*. Chichester: John Wiley.

REFERENCES

Jacobson, N. S., Dobson, K. S., Truax, P. A., Addis, M. E., Koerner, K., Gollan, J. K., Gortner, E., & Prince, S. E. (1996). A component analysis of cognitive-behavioral treatment for depression. *Journal of Consulting and Clinical Psychology, 6*(2), 295–304.

James, W. (1981). *The principles of psychology* (Vol. 1). Cambridge, MA: Harvard University Press.

James, W. (1996). *A pluralistic universe*. Lincoln, NB, and London: University of Nebraska Press.

Jaspers, K. (1932). Boundary situations (E. B. Ashton, Trans.). *Philosophy* (Vol. 2). Chicago, IL: The University of Chicago Press.

Johnstone, L., Boyle, M., with Cromby, J., Dillon, J., Harper, D., Kinderman, P., Longden, E., Pilgrim, D., & Read, J. (2018). *The Power Threat Meaning Framework: Towards the identification of patterns in emotional distress, unusual experiences and troubled or troubling behaviour, as an alternative to functional psychiatric diagnosis.* Leicester: British Psychological Society. *Download from:* https://www.bps.org.uk/news-and-policy/introducing-power-threat-meaning-framework

Johnstone, L., & Dallos, R. (2006). Introduction to formulation. In L. Johnstone & R. Dallos (Eds.), *Formulation in psychology and psychotherapy: Making sense of people's problems* (pp. 1–16). London: Routledge.

Jones, K. (2014). Psychodynamic therapy: The independent approach. In W. Dryden & A. Reeves (Eds.), *Handbook of individual therapy* (6th ed., pp. 49–74). London: Sage.

Jordan, J. V., Kaplan, A. G., Miller, J. B., Stiver, I. P., & Surrey, J. L. (Eds.). (1991). *Women's growth in connection: Writings from the Stone Center*. New York: Guilford Press.

Jordan, J. V., Walker, M., & Hartling, L. M. (Eds.). (2004). *The complexity of connection: Writing from the Stone Center's Jean Baker Miller Training Institute*. New York: Guilford Press.

Jostmann, N. B., & Koole, S. L. (2009). When persistence is futile: A functional analysis of action orientation and goal disengagement. In G. B. Moskowitz & H. Grant (Eds.), *The psychology of goals* (pp. 337–361). New York: Guilford Press.

Kahneman, D. (1999). Objective happiness. In D. Kahneman, E. Diener & N. Schwarz (Eds.), *Well-being: The foundations of hedonic psychology* (pp. 3–25). New York: Russell Sage Foundation.

Kahneman, D. (2011). *Thinking, fast and slow*. London: Penguin.

Karoly, P. (1999). A goal systems–self-regulatory perspective on personality, psychopathology, and change. *Review of General Psychology, 3*(4), 264–291.

Kaslow, N. J., Dausch, B. M., & Celano, M. (2003). Family therapies. In A. S. Gurman & S. B. Messer (Eds.), *Essential psychotherapies* (2nd ed., pp. 400–462). New York: Guilford Press.

Kasser, T., & Ryan, R. M. (1993). A dark side of the American dream: Correlates of financial success as a central life aspiration. *Journal of Personality and Social Psychology, 65*(2), 410–422.

REFERENCES

Kasser, T., & Ryan, R. M. (1996). Further examining the American dream: Differential correlates of intrinsic and extrinsic goals. *Personality and Social Psychology Bulletin*, *22*(3), 280–287.

Kasser, T., & Ryan, R. M. (2001). Be careful what you wish for: Optimal functioning and the relative attainment of instrinsic and extrinsic goals. In P. Schmuck & K. M. Sheldon (Eds.), *Life goals and well-being: Towards a positive psychology of human striving* (pp. 116–131). Gottingen, Germany: Hogrefe & Huber.

Katz, R., & Murphy-Shigematsu, S. (Eds.). (2012). *Synergy, healing and empowerment: Insights from cultural diversity*. Calgary, CA: Brush.

Kellogg, S. H., & Young, J. E. (2008). Cognitive therapy. In J. Lebow (Ed.), *Twenty-first century psychotherapies: Contemporary approaches to theory and practice* (pp. 43–79). London: Wiley.

Kelly, R. E., Mansell, W., & Wood, A. M. (2015). Goal conflict and well-being: A review and hierarchical model of goal conflict, ambivalence, self-discrepancy and self-concordance. *Personality and Individual Differences*, *85*, 212–229.

Kennedy-Moore, E., & Watson, J. C. (1999). *Expressing emotion: Myths, realities, and therapeutic strategies*. New York: Guilford Press.

Kiesler, D. J. (1996). *Contemporary interpersonal theory and research: Personality, psychopathology, and psychotherapy*. New York: Wiley.

King, L. A., & Hicks, J. A. (2013). Positive affect and meaning in life. In P. T. P. Wong (Ed.), *The human quest for meaning: Theories, research, and applications* (2nd ed., pp. 125–141). New York: Routledge.

Kiresuk, T. J. (1994). Conceptual background. In T. J. Kiresuk, A. Smith & J. E. Cardillo (Eds.), *Goal Attainment Scaling: Applications, theory, and measurement* (pp. 161–171). Hillsdale, NJ: Lawrence Erlbaum Associates.

Kiresuk, T. J., & Sherman, R. E. (1968). Goal Attainment Scaling: A general method for evaluating comprehensive community mental health programs. *Community Mental Health Journal*, *4*(6), 443–453.

Kiresuk, T. J., Smith, A., & Cardillo, J. E. (Eds.). (1994). *Goal Attainment Scaling: Applications, theory, and measurement*. Hillsdale, NJ: Lawrence Erlbaum Associates.

Kivlighan, D. M. (2002). Transference, interpretation, and insight: A research-practice model. In G. S. Tryon (Ed.), *Counselling based on process research: Applying what we know* (pp. 166–196). Boston, MA: Allyn and Bacon.

Klinger, E. (2013). The search for meaning in evolutionary goal-theory perspective and its clinical implications. In P. T. P. Wong (Ed.), *The human quest for meaning: Theories, research, and applications* (2nd ed., pp. 23–56). New York: Routledge.

Klinger, E., & Cox, W. M. (2011). Motivation and the goal theory of current concerns. In W. M. Cox & E. Klinger (Eds.), *Handbook of motivational counseling: Goal-based approaches to assessment and intervention with addiction and other problems* (2nd ed., pp. 3–48). Chichester: Wiley.

REFERENCES

Koepp, M. J., Gunn, R. N., Lawrence, A. D., & Cunningham, V. J. (1998). Evidence for striatal dopamine release during a video game. *Nature, 393*(6682), 266–268.

Koestler, A. (1967). *The ghost in the machine*. London: Pan.

Koestner, R., Lekes, N., Powers, T. A., & Chicoine, E. (2002). Attaining personal goals: Self-concordance plus implementation intentions equals success. *Journal of Personality and Social Psychology, 83*(1), 231–244.

Kruglanski, A. W., & Kopetz, C. (2009). What is so special (and nonspecial) about goals? A view from the cognitive perspective. In G. B. Moskowitz & H. Grant (Eds.), *The psychology of goals* (pp. 27–55). New York: Guilford Press.

Kruglanski, A. W., Shah, J. Y., Fishbach, A., Friedman, R., Chun, W. Y., & Sleeth-Keppler, D. (2002). A theory of goal systems. In M. P. Zanna (Ed.), *Advances in experimental social psychology* (Vol. *34*, pp. 331–378). San Diego, CA: Academic Press.

Krycka, K. C., & Ikemi, A. (2016). Focusing-oriented–experiential psychotherapy. In D. Cain, K. Keenan & S. Rubin (Eds.), *Humanistic psychotherapies* (2nd ed., pp. 251–282). Washington, DC: American Psychological Association.

Lago, C. (2005). *Race, culture and counselling: The ongoing challenge*. Maidenhead: Open University Press.

Lago, C., & Smith, B. (Eds.). (2010). *Anti-discriminatory practice in counselling & psychotherapy* (2nd ed.). London: Sage.

Laing, R. D. (1965). *The divided self: An existential study in sanity and madness*. Harmondsworth: Penguin.

Laing, R. D. (1967). *The politics of experience and the bird of paradise*. Harmondsworth: Penguin.

Laing, R. D., & Esterson, A. (1964). *Sanity, madness and the family*. London: Penguin.

Lambert, M. J., & Shimokawa, K. (2011). Collecting client feedback. In J. C. Norcross (Ed.), *Psychotherapy relationships that work: Evidence-based responsiveness* (2nd ed., pp. 203–223). New York: Oxford University Press.

Langdridge, D. (2012). *Existential counselling and psychotherapy*. London: Sage.

Lantz, J., & Gregoire, T. (2000). Existential psychotherapy with Vietnam veteran couples: A twenty-five year report. *Contemporary Family Therapy: An International Journal, 22*(1), 19–37.

Latham, G. P., & Locke, E. A. (1979). Goal setting: A motivational technique that works. *Organizational Dynamics, 8*(2), 68–80.

Law, D. (2018). Goal-oriented practice. In M. Cooper & D. Law (Eds.), *Working with goals in counselling and psychotherapy* (pp. 161–180). Oxford: Oxford University Press.

Law, D., & Jacob, J. (2015). *Goals and goal-based outcomes (GBOs): Some useful information* (3rd ed.). London: CAMHS Press at EBPU.

Layard, R. (2006). *Happiness: Lessons from a new science*. London: Penguin.

Lazarus, A. A. (1981). *The practice of multimodal therapy*. Baltimore, MD: The Johns Hopkins University Press.

REFERENCES

Lazarus, A. A. (2005). Multimodal therapy. In J. C. Norcross & M. R. Goldfried (Eds.), *Handbook of psychotherapy integration* (2nd ed., pp. 105–120). New York: Oxford University Press.

Lebow, J. L. (2008a). Couple and family therapy. In J. L. Lebow (Ed.), *Twenty-first century psychotherapies: Contemporary approaches to theory and practice* (pp. 307–346). London: Wiley.

Lebow, J. L. (Ed.). (2008b). *Twenty-first century psychotherapies: Contemporary approaches to theory and practice.* London: Wiley.

Lee, V. (2008). The existential plight of cancer: Meaning making as a concrete approach to the intangible search for meaning. *Supportive Care in Cancer, 16*(7), 779–785.

Lee, V., Cohen, S. R., Edgar, L., Laizner, A. M., & Gagnon, A. J. (2006). Meaning-making intervention during breast or colorectal cancer treatment improves self-esteem, optimism, and self-efficacy. *Social Science & Medicine, 62*(12), 3133–3145.

Leijssen, M. (1998). Focusing microprocesses. In L. S. Greenberg, J. C. Watson & G. Lietaer (Eds.), *Handbook of experiential psychotherapy* (pp. 121–154). New York: Guilford Press.

Levinas, E. (1969). *Totality and infinity: An essay on exteriority* (A. Lingis, Trans.). Pittsburgh, PA: Duquesne University Press.

Levinas, E. (1982). *Ethics and infinity: Conversations with Philippe Nemo* (R. A. Cohen, Trans.). Pittsburgh, PA: Duquesne University Press.

Levinas, E. (2003). *Humanism of the Other* (N. Poller, Trans.). Chicago, IL: University of Illinois Press.

Lewin, K. (1947). Frontiers in group dynamics: Concept, method and reality in social science; social equilibria and social change. *Human Relations, 1*(1), 5–41.

Liberman, N., & Dar, R. (2009). Normal and pathological consequences of encountering difficulties in monitoring progress toward goals. In G. B. Moskowitz & H. Grant (Eds.), *The psychology of goals* (pp. 277–303). New York: Guilford Press.

Lillienfeld, S. O., & Arkowitz, H. (2012). Are all psychotherapies created equal? *Scientific American.* Retrieved from www.scientificamerican.com/article/are-all-psychotherapies-created-equal/

Little, B. (2011). Personal projects and motivational counseling: The quality of lives reconsidered. In W. M. Cox & E. Klinger (Eds.), *Handbook of motivational counseling: Goal-based approaches to assessment and intervention with addiction and other problems* (2nd ed., pp. 73–87). Chichester: Wiley.

Little, B. R. (1983). Personal projects: A rationale and method for investigation. *Environment and Behavior, 15*(3), 273–309.

Little, B. R. (2007). Prompt and circumstance: The generative contexts of personal projects analysis. In B. R. Little, K. Salmela-Aro & S. D. Phillips (Eds.), *Personal project pursuit: Goals, action, and human flourishing* (pp. 3–49). Mahwah, NJ: Lawrence Erlbaum Associates.

REFERENCES

Little, B. R., & Gee, T. L. (2007). The methodology of personal projects analysis: Four modules and a funnel. In B. R. Little, K. Salmela-Aro & S. D. Phillips (Eds.), *Personal project pursuit: Goals, action, and human flourishing* (pp. 51–94). Mahwah, NJ: Lawrence Erlbaum Associates.

Lloyd, C., Duncan, C., & Cooper, M. (2018). A systematic review of goal progress measures for psychotherapy. [Manuscript submitted for publication].

Locke, E. A., & Latham, G. P. (2002). Building a practically useful theory of goal setting and task motivation – a 35-year odyssey. *American Psychologist, 57*(9), 705–717. doi: 10.1037//0003-066x.57.9.705

Locke, E. A., Shaw, K. N., Saari, L. M., & Latham, G. P. (1981). Goal setting and task performance: 1969–1980. *Psychological Bulletin, 90*(1), 125–152.

Lopez, S. J., Floyd, R. K., Ulven, J. C., & Snyder, C. R. (2000). Hope therapy: Helping clients build a house of hope. In C. R. Snyder (Ed.), *Handbook of hope: Theory, measures and applications* (pp. 123–150). San Diego, CA: Academic Press.

Lowen, A. (1975). *Bioenergetics*. London: Penguin.

Macdonald, A. J. (2014). Solution-focused therapy. In W. Dryden & A. Reeves (Eds.), *The handbook of individual therapy* (6th ed., pp. 387–413). London: Sage.

MacKenzie, K. R. (1992). *Classics in Group Psychotherapy*. NY: The Guilford Press.

Mackrill, T. (2010). Goal consensus and collaboration in psychotherapy: An existential rationale. *Journal of Humanistic Psychology, 50*(1), 96–107.

Mackrill, T. (2011). Differentiating life goals and therapeutic goals: Expanding our understanding of the working alliance. *British Journal of Guidance & Counselling, 39*(1), 25–39.

Macquarrie, J. (1972). *Existentialism*. Harmondsworth: Penguin.

Magnavita, J. J. (2008). Psychoanalytic psychotherapy. In J. L. Lebow (Ed.), *Twenty-first century psychotherapies: Contemporary approaches to theory and practice* (pp. 206–236). London: Wiley.

Mahalik, J. R. (2002). Understanding client resistance in therapy. In G. S. Tryon (Ed.), *Counseling based on process research: Applying what we know* (pp. 66–80). Boston, MA: Allyn and Bacon.

Malle, B. F., & Knobe, J. (2001). The distinction between desire and intention: A folk-conceptual analysis. In B. F. Malle, L. J. Moses & D. A. Baldwin (Eds.), *Intentions and intentionality: Foundations of social cognition* (pp. 45–67). Cambridge, MA: MIT Press.

Malle, B. F., Moses, L. J., & Baldwin, D. A. (2001). Introduction: The significance of intentionality. In B. F. Malle, L. J. Moses & D. A. Baldwin (Eds.), *Intentions and intentionality: Foundations of social cognition* (pp. 1–24). Cambridge, MA: MIT Press.

Mansell, W. (2005). Control theory and psychopathology: An integrative approach. *Psychology and Psychotherapy: Theory, Research and Practice, 78*(2), 141–178.

Mansell, W., Carey, T. A., & Tai, S. J. (2013). *A transdiagnostic approach to CBT using methods of levels therapy*. London: Routledge.

Marcuse, H. (1966). *Eros and civilization*. London: Sphere.

REFERENCES

Mardula, J., & Larkin, F. (2014). Mindfulness in individual therapy. In W. Dryden & A. Reeves (Eds.), *The handbook of individual therapy* (6th ed., pp. 445–468). London: Sage.

Marien, H., Custers, R., Hassin, R. R., & Aarts, H. (2012). Unconscious goal activation and the hijacking of the executive function. *Journal of Personality and Social Psychology, 103*(3), 399–415.

Marks, I. M. (1978). *Living with fear: Understanding and coping with anxiety*. New York: McGraw-Hill.

Martin, L., Campbell, W. K., & Henry, C. D. (2004). The roar of awakening: Mortality acknowledgement as a call to authentic living. In J. Greenberg, S. L. Koole & T. Pyszczynski (Eds.), *Handbook of experimental existential psychology* (pp. 431–448). New York: Guilford Press.

Marx, K. (1988). *Economic and philosophical manuscripts of 1884* (M. Milligan, Trans.). Amherst, NY: Prometheus Books.

Maslow, A. H. (1943). A theory of human motivation. *Psychological Review, 50*, 370–396.

Maslow, A. H. (1968). *Toward a psychology of being* (2nd ed.). New York: D. van Nostrand Co.

Maslow, A. H. (1971). *The farther reaches of human nature*. London: Penguin.

Maslow, A. H. (1987). *Motivation and personality* (3rd ed.). New Delhi, India: Dorling Kindersley.

May, R. (1953). *Man's search for himself*. New York: W. W. Norton and Co.

May, R. (1958). The origins and significance of the existential movement in psychology. In R. May, E. Angel & H. F. Ellenberger (Eds.), *Existence: A new dimension in psychiatry and psychology* (pp. 3–36). New York: Basic Books.

May, R. (1969a). *Love and will*. New York: W. W. Norton and Co.

May, R. (Ed.). (1969b). *Existential psychology* (2nd ed.). New York: Random House.

McAdams, D. P. (1985). The 'imago': A key narrative component of identity. *Review of Personality and Social Psychology, 6*, 115–141.

McClelland, D. C., & Burnham, D. H. (2008). *Power is the great motivator*. Cambridge, MA: Harvard Business Review Press.

McClelland, D. C., Koestner, R., & Weinberger, J. (1989). How do self-attributed and implicit motives differ? *Psychological Review, 96*(4), 690–702.

McCormick, E. W. (2012). *Change for the better* (4th ed.). London: Sage.

McCullough Jr, J. P. (2006). *Treating chronic depression with disciplined personal involvement: Cognitive Behavioural Analysis System of Psychotherapy (CBASP)*. New York: Springer.

McLennan, G. (1995). *Pluralism*. Buckingham: Open University Press.

McLeod, J. (2013). *An introduction to counselling* (5th ed.). London: Open University Press.

McLeod, J. (2018a). *Goal alignment theory*. Paper presented at the Department of Psychology Seminar Series, University of Roehampton, London.

REFERENCES

McLeod, J. (2018b). *Pluralistic therapy: Distinctive features*. Abingdon, Oxon: Routledge.

McLeod, J., & Mackrill, T. (2018). Philosophical, conceptual, and ethical perspectives on working with goals in therapy. In M. Cooper & D. Law (Eds.), *Working with goals in counselling and psychotherapy* (pp. 15–34). Oxford: Oxford University Press.

McLeod, J., & McLeod, J. (2011). *Counselling skills*. Maidenhead: Open University Press.

McLeod, J., & McLeod, J. (2016). Assessment and formulation in pluralistic counselling and psychotherapy. In M. Cooper & W. Dryden (Eds.), *Handbook of pluralistic counselling and psychotherapy* (pp. 15–27). London: Sage.

Mearns, D., & Cooper, M. (2018). *Working at relational depth in counselling and psychotherapy* (2nd ed.). London: Sage.

Meltzoff, A. N. (1995). Understanding the intentions of others: Re-enactment of intended acts by 18-month-old children. *Developmental Psychology, 31*(5), 838–850.

Meneses, C. W., & Scuka, R. F. (2016). Empirically supported humanistic approaches to working with couples and families. In D. Cain, K. Keenan & S. Rubin (Eds.), *Humanistic psychotherapies* (2nd ed., pp. 353–386). Washington, DC: American Psychological Association.

Merleau-Ponty, M. (1962). *Phenomenology of perception* (C. Smith, Trans.). London: Routledge.

Mezulis, A. H., Abramson, L. Y., Hyde, J. S., & Hankin, B. L. (2004). Is there a universal positivity bias in attributions? A meta-analytic review of individual, developmental, and cultural differences in the self-serving attributional bias. *Psychological Bulletin, 130*(5), 711–747.

Michalak, J., & Grosse Holtforth, M. (2006). Where do we go from here? The goal perspective in psychotherapy. *Clinical Psychology: Science and Practice, 13*(4), 346–365.

Michalak, J., Heidenreich, T., & Hoyer, J. (2004). Goal conflicts: Concepts, findings, and consequences for psychotherapy. In W. M. Cox & E. Klinger (Eds.), *Handbook of motivational counseling* (pp. 83–97). New York: John Wiley.

Michalak, J., Heidenreich, T., & Hoyer, J. (2011). Goal conflicts and goal integration: Theory, assessment, and clinical integration. In W. M. Cox & E. Klinger (Eds.), *Handbook of motivational counseling: Goal-based approaches to assessment and intervention with addiction and other problems* (2nd ed., pp. 89–107). Chichester: Wiley.

Michie, S., Abraham, C., Whittington, C., McAteer, J., & Gupta, S. (2009). Effective techniques in healthy eating and physical activity interventions: A meta-regression. *Health Psychology, 28*(6), 690–701.

Miller, G. A., Galanter, E., & Pribam, K. H. (1960). *Plans and the structure of behavior*. New York: Holt, Rinehart and Winston.

Miller, R. B., & Brickman, S. J. (2004). A model of future-oriented motivation and self-regulation. *Educational Psychology Review, 16*(1), 9–33.

Miller, S. D., Duncan, B. L., & Hubble, M. A. (1997). *Escape from Babel: Toward a unifying language for psychotherapy practice*. New York: W. W. Norton.

REFERENCES

Miller, W. R., & Rollnick, S. (2012). *Motivational interviewing* (3rd ed.). New York: Guilford Press.

Mindell, A. (2014). *The leader as martial artist: An introduction to deep democracy.* Florence, CA: Deep Democracy Exchange.

Mohr, D. C. (1995). Negative outcome in psychotherapy – a critical review. *Clinical Psychology: Science and Practice, 2*(1), 1–27.

Moorey, S. (2014). Cognitive therapy. In A. Reeves & W. Dryden (Eds.), *Handbook of individual therapy* (6th ed., pp. 243–269). London: Sage.

Moran, D. (2000). *Introduction to phenomenology.* London: Routledge.

Moreno, J. L. (1946). *Psychodrama* (Vol. 1). New York: Beacon House.

Moskowitz, G. B. (2012). The representation and regulation of goals. In H. Aarts & A. J. Elliot (Eds.), *Goal-directed behavior* (pp. 1–47). New York: Psychology Press.

Moskowitz, G. B., & Gesundheit, Y. (2009). Goal priming. In G. B. Moskowitz & H. Grant (Eds.), *The psychology of goals* (pp. 203–233). New York: Guilford Press.

Moskowitz, G. B., & Grant, H. (2009a). Introduction: Four themes in the study of goals. In G. B. Moskowitz & H. Grant (Eds.), *The psychology of goals* (pp. 1–24). New York: Guilford Press.

Moskowitz, G. B., & Grant, H. (Eds.). (2009b). *The psychology of goals.* New York: Guilford Press.

Munro, A., Manthei, B., & Small, J. (1989). *Counselling: The skills of problem-solving.* London: Routledge.

Murayama, K., Elliot, A. J., & Friedman, R. (2012). Achievement goals. In R. M. Ryan (Ed.), *The Oxford handbook of human motivation* (pp. 191–207). New York: Oxford University Press.

Murray, H. A. (1943). *Thematic Apperception Test manual.* Cambridge, MA: Harvard University Press.

Neenan, M. (2000). Rational emotive behaviour therapy. In S. Palmer (Ed.), *Introduction to counselling and psychotherapy: The essential guide* (pp. 278–291). London: Sage.

Neenan, M., & Palmer, S. (2000). Problem-focused counselling and psychotherapy. In S. Palmer (Ed.), *Introduction to counselling and psychotherapy: The essential guide* (pp. 208–221). London: Sage.

Nir, D. (2008). *Resolving inner conflict, building inner harmony – the Negotiational Self Workshop.* Paper presented at the Fifth International Conference on the Dialogical Self, Cambridge, UK.

Norcross, J. C. (2005). A primer on psychotherapy integration. In J. C. Norcross & M. R. Goldfried (Eds.), *Handbook of psychotherapy integration* (2nd ed., pp. 3–23). New York: Oxford University Press.

Nozick, R. (1974). *Anarchy, state, and utopia.* Malden, MA: Basic Books.

O'Carroll, P. (2014). Behavioural activation. In W. Dryden & A. Reeves (Eds.), *Handbook of individual therapy* (6th ed., pp. 329–357). London: Sage.

O'Connell, B. (2012). Solution-focused therapy. In C. Feltham & I. Horton (Eds.), *The Sage handbook of counselling and psychotherapy* (3rd ed., pp. 392–395). London: Sage.

REFERENCES

Oddli, H. W., McLeod, J., Reichelt, S., & Rønnestad, M. H. (2014). Strategies used by experienced therapists to explore client goals in early sessions of psychotherapy. *European Journal of Psychotherapy & Counselling, 16*(3), 245–266.

Oettingen, G., & Stephens, E. J. (2009). Fantasies and motivationally intelligent goal setting. In G. B. Moskowitz & H. Grant (Eds.), *The psychology of goals* (pp. 153–178). New York: Guilford Press.

O'Hara, D. (2013). *Hope in counselling and psychotherapy*. London: Sage.

Öst, L. G. (1988). Applied relaxation vs progressive relaxation in the treatment of panic disorder. *Behaviour Research and Therapy, 26*(1), 13–22.

Palmer, S., & Neenan, M. (2000). Problem-focused counselling and psychotherapy. In S. Palmer & R. Woolfe (Eds.), *Integrative and eclectic counselling and psychotherapy* (pp. 181–201). London: Sage.

Papayianni, F., & Cooper, M. (2018). Metatherapeutic communication: An exploratory analysis of therapist-reported moments of dialogue regarding the nature of the therapeutic work. *British Journal of Guidance & Counselling, 46*(2), 173–184. doi: 10.1080/03069885.2017.1305098

Park, N., Park, M., & Peterson, C. (2010). When is the search for meaning related to life satisfaction? *Applied Psychology: Health and Well-Being, 2*(1), 1–13.

Park-Stamms, E. J., & Gollwitzer, P. M. (2009). Goal implementation: The benefits and costs of if-then planning. In G. B. Moskowitz & H. Grant (Eds.), *The psychology of goals* (pp. 362–391). New York: Guilford Press.

Pascual-Leone, A., Paivio, S., & Harrington, S. (2016). Emotion in psychotherapy: An experiential-humanistic perspective. In D. Cain, K. Keenan & S. Rubin (Eds.), *Humanistic psychotherapies* (2nd ed., pp. 147–181). Washington, DC: American Psychological Association.

Paul, S. (2012). Group counselling and therapy. In C. Feltham & I. Horton (Eds.), *The Sage handbook of counselling and psychotherapy* (3rd ed., pp. 617–625). London: Sage.

Pender, F., Tinwell, C., Marsh, E., & Cowell, V. (2013). Evaluating the use of goal-based outcomes as a single patient rated outcome measure across CWP CAMHS: A pilot study. *Child and Family Clinical Psychology Review, 1*, 29–40.

Perls, F., Hefferline, R. F., & Goodman, P. (1951). *Gestalt therapy: Excitement and growth in the human personality*. New York: Julian Press.

Perugini, M., & Bagozzi, R. P. (2001). The role of desires and anticipated emotions in goal-directed behaviours: Broadening and deepening the theory of planned behaviour. *British Journal of Social Psychology, 40*(1), 79–98.

Perugini, M., & Bagozzi, R. P. (2004). The distinction between desires and intentions. *European Journal of Social Psychology, 34*(1), 69–84.

Pinsof, W. M. (2005). Integrative problem-centered therapy. In J. C. Norcross & M. R. Goldfried (Eds.), *Handbook of psychotherapy integration* (2nd ed., pp. 382–402). New York: Oxford University Press.

REFERENCES

Piper, W. E., Joyce, A. S., McCallum, M., & Azim, H. F. (1998). Interpretive and supportive forms of psychotherapy and patient personality variables. *Journal of Consulting and Clinical Psychology*, 66(3), 558–567.

Pöhlmann, K. (2001). Agency- and communion-orientation in life goals: Impacts on goal pursuit strategies and psychological well-being. In P. Schmuck & K. M. Sheldon (Eds.), *Life goals and well-being: Towards a positive psychology of human striving* (pp. 68–84). Gottingen, Germany: Hogrefe & Huber.

Polivy, J., Herman, C. P., Hackett, R., & Kuleshnyk, I. (1986). The effects of self-attention and public attention on eating in restrained and unrestrained subjects. *Journal of Personality and Social Psychology*, 50(6), 1253–1260.

Polster, E., & Polster, M. (1973). *Gestalt therapy integrated: Contours of theory & practice*. New York: Vintage.

Polt, R. (1999). *Heidegger: An introduction*. London: UCL Press.

Powers, W. T. (1973). *Behavior: The control of perception*. Chicago, IL: Aldine.

Powers, W. T. (1992). *Living control systems II*. Gravel Switch, KY: Control Systems Group.

Prochaska, J. O., & DiClemente, C. C. (1986). Toward a comprehensive model of change. In W. R. Miller & N. Heather (Eds.), *Treating addictive behaviors* (pp. 3–27). New York: Springer.

Proctor, G., Cooper, M., Sanders, P., & Malcolm, B. (Eds.). (2006). *Politicising the person-centred approach: An agenda for social change*. Ross-on-Wye: PCCS Books.

Rabin, M. (1993). Incorporating fairness into game theory and economics. *The American Economic Review*, 83(5), 1281–1302.

Rapoport, A. (1960). *Fights, games and debates*. Michigan, MI: University of Michigan Press.

Reese, H. W. (1994). Teleology and teleonomy in behavior analysis. *The Behavior Analyst*, 17(1), 75–91.

Reeve, J., & Lee, W. (2012). Neuroscience and human motivation. In R. M. Ryan (Ed.), *The Oxford handbook of human motivation* (pp. 365–380). New York: Oxford University Press.

Reinecke, M. A., & Freeman, A. (2003). Cognitive therapy. In A. S. Gurman & S. B. Messer (Eds.), *Essential psychotherapies* (2nd ed., pp. 224–271). New York: Guilford Press.

Reis, H. T., Sheldon, K. M., Gable, S. L., Roscoe, J., & Ryan, R. M. (2000). Daily well-being: The role of autonomy, competence, and relatedness. *Personality and Social Psychology Bulletin*, 26(4), 419–435.

Rescher, N. (1993). *Pluralism: Against the demand for consensus*. Oxford: Oxford University Press.

Resnicow, K., McMaster, F., & Rollnick, S. (2012). Action reflections: A client-centered technique to bridge the WHY–HOW transition in motivational interviewing. *Behavioural and Cognitive Psychotherapy*, 40(4), 474–480.

Riediger, M. (2007). Interference and facilitation among personal goals: Age differences and associations with well-being and behavior. In B. R. Little, K. Salmela-Aro & S. D. Phillips (Eds.), *Personal project pursuit: Goals, action, and human flourishing.* (pp. 119–143). Mahwah, NJ: Lawrence Erlbaum Associates.

Riediger, M., & Freund, A. M. (2004). Interference and facilitation among personal goals: Differential associations with subjective well-being and persistent goal pursuit. *Personality and Social Psychology Bulletin, 30*(12), 1511–1523.

Riemann, B. C., & McNally, R. J. (1995). Cognitive processing of personally relevant information. *Cognition & Emotion, 9*(4), 325–340.

Rilling, J. K., Gutman, D. A., Zeh, T. R., Pagnoni, G., Berns, G. S., & Kilts, C. D. (2002). A neural basis for social cooperation. *Neuron, 35*(2), 395–405.

Rogers, C. R. (1942). *Counselling and psychotherapy: Newer concepts in practice.* Boston, MA: Houghton Mifflin.

Rogers, C. R. (1951). *Client-centered therapy.* Boston, MA: Houghton Mifflin.

Rogers, C. R. (1957). The necessary and sufficient conditions of therapeutic personality change. *Journal of Consulting Psychology, 21*(2), 95–103.

Rogers, C. R. (1959). A theory of therapy, personality and interpersonal relationships as developed in the client-centered framework. In S. Koch (Ed.), *Psychology: A study of science* (Vol. 3, pp. 184–256). New York: McGraw-Hill.

Rogers, C. R. (1961). *On becoming a person: A therapist's view of therapy.* London: Constable and Co.

Rogers, C. R. (1963).The actualizing tendency in relation to 'motives' and to consciousness. In M. Jones (Ed.), *Nebraska symposium on motivation* (pp. 1–24). Lincoln, NB: University of Nebraska Press.

Rogers, C. R. (1980). *A way of being.* Boston, MA: Houghton Mifflin.

Rowan, J. (1988). *Ordinary ecstasy: Humanistic psychology in action* (2nd ed.). London: Routledge.

Rowan, J. (1990). *Subpersonalities: The people inside us.* London: Routledge.

Rowan, J. (2008). Goals. *BACP North London Magazine, 59,* 7.

Ryan, R. M. (2012). Motivation and the organization of human behavior: Three reasons for the reemergence of a field. In R. M. Ryan (Ed.), *The Oxford handbook of human motivation* (pp. 3–10). New York: Oxford University Press.

Ryan, R. M., & Deci, E. L. (2000). Self-determination theory and the facilitation of intrinsic motivation, social development, and well-being. *American Psychologist, 55*(1), 68–78.

Ryan, R. M., & Deci, E. L. (2001). On happiness and human potentials: A review of research on hedonic and eudaimonic well-being. *Annual Review of Psychology, 52*(1), 141–166.

Ryan, R. M., & Deci, E. L. (2002). Overview of self-determination theory: An organismic-dialectical perspective. *Handbook of self-determination research* (pp. 3–33): Rochester, NY: University of Rochester Press.

REFERENCES

Ryan, R. M., & Deci, E. L. (2004). Autonomy is no illusion: Self-determination theory and the empirical study of authenticity, awareness and will. In J. Greenberg, S. L. Koole & T. Pyszczynski (Eds.), *Handbook of experimental existential psychology* (pp. 449–479). New York: Guilford Press.

Rycroft, C. (1995). *A critical dictionary of psychoanalysis*. London: Penguin.

Ryff, C. D., & Singer, B. H. (2008). Know thyself and become what you are: A eudaimonic approach to psychological well-being. *Journal of Happiness Studies, 9*(1), 13–39.

Ryle, A. (1990). *Cognitive analytic therapy: Active participation in change*. Chichester: Wiley.

Samuels, A. (1986). *Jung and the post-Jungians*. London: Routledge.

Sanchez, V. C., Lewinsohn, P. M., & Larson, D. W. (1980). Assertion training: Effectiveness in the treatment of depression. *Journal of Clinical Psychology, 36*(2), 526–529.

Sanders, P. (2006). Politics and therapy: Mapping areas for consideration. In G. Proctor, M. Cooper, P. Sanders & B. Malcolm (Eds.), *Politicising the person-centred approach: An agenda for social change* (pp. 5–16). Ross-on-Wye: PCCS Books.

Sartre, J.-P. (1958). *Being and nothingness: An essay on phenomenological ontology* (H. Barnes, Trans.). London: Routledge.

Sartre, J.-P. (1996). Existentialism. In L. Cahoone (Ed.), *From modernism to postmodernism: An anthology* (pp. 259–265). Cambridge, MA: Blackwells.

Schlick, M. (2008). On the meaning of life. In E. D. Klemke & S. M. Cahn (Eds.), *The meaning of life: A reader* (3rd ed., pp. 62–71). New York: Oxford University Press.

Schmid, P. F. (2006). The challenge of the Other: Towards dialogical person-centered psychotherapy and counseling. *Person-Centered and Experiential Psychotherapies, 5*(4), 240–254.

Schmuck, P., & Sheldon, K. M. (2001). Life goals and well-being: To the frontiers of life goal research. In P. Schmuck & K. M. Sheldon (Eds.), *Life goals and well-being: Towards a positive psychology of human striving* (pp. 1–17). Gottingen, Germany: Hogrefe & Huber.

Schneider, K. J. (1999). *The paradoxical self: Toward an understanding of our contradictory nature* (2nd ed.). Amherst, NY: Humanity Books.

Schneider, K. J., & Krug, O. T. (2010). *Existential-humanistic therapy*. Washington, DC: American Psychological Association.

Schopenhauer, A. (1969). *The world as will and representation* (E. F. J. Payne, Trans.). New York: Dover.

Schulenberg, S. E., Hutzell, R. R., Nassif, C., & Rogina, J. M. (2008). Logotherapy for clinical practice. *Psychotherapy: Theory, Research, Practice, Training, 45*(4), 447–463. doi: 10.1037/a0014331

Schunk, D. H. (1990). Goal setting and self-efficacy during self-regulated learning. *Educational Psychologist, 25*(1), 71–86.

REFERENCES

Schwartz, J. (2012). Attachment-based psychoanalytic psychotherapy. In C. Feltham & I. Horton (Eds.), *The Sage handbook of counselling and psychotherapy* (3rd ed., pp. 259–263). London: Sage.

Segal, J. (2014). Psychodynamic therapy: The Kleinian approach. In W. Dryden & A. Reeves (Eds.), *The handbook of individual therapy* (6th ed., pp. 101–125). London: Sage.

Seligman, M. E. P. (2002). *Authentic happiness*. New York: Simon & Schuster.

Shapiro, D. H., & Austin, J. (1998). *Control therapy: An integrated approach to psychotherapy, health and healing*. New York: John Wiley.

Shaw, R., & Colimore, K. (1988). Humanistic psychology as ideology: An analysis of Maslow's contradictions. *Journal of Humanistic Psychology, 28*(3), 51–74.

Sheeran, P., & Webb, T. L. (2012). From goals to action. In H. Aarts & A. J. Elliot (Eds.), *Goal-directed behavior* (pp. 175–192). New York: Psychology Press.

Sheldon, K. M. (2001). The self-concordance model of healthy goal striving: When personal goals correctly represent the person. In P. Schmuck & K. M. Sheldon (Eds.), *Life goals and well-being: Towards a positive psychology of human striving* (pp. 18–36). Gottingen, Germany: Hogrefe & Huber.

Sheldon, K. M., Arndt, J., & Houser-Marko, L. (2003). In search of the organismic valuing process: The human tendency to move towards beneficial goal choices. *Journal of Personality, 71*(5), 835–869.

Sheldon, K. M., & Elliot, A. J. (1999). Goal striving, need satisfaction, and longitudinal well-being: The self-concordance model. *Journal of Personality and Social Psychology, 76*(3), 482–497.

Sheldon, K. M., & Houser-Marko, L. (2001). Self-concordance, goal attainment, and the pursuit of happiness: Can there be an upward spiral? *Journal of Personality and Social Psychology, 80*(1), 152–165.

Sheldon, K. M., & Kasser, T. (1995). Coherence and congruence: Two aspects of personality integration. *Journal of Personality and Social Psychology, 68*(3), 531–543.

Sheldon, K. M., & Kasser, T. (1998). Pursuing personal goals: Skills enable progress, but not all progress is beneficial. *Personality and Social Psychology Bulletin, 24*(12), 1319–1331.

Sheldon, K. M., Kasser, T., Smith, K., & Share, T. (2002). Personal goals and psychological growth: Testing an intervention to enhance goal attainment and personality integration. *Journal of Personality, 70*(1), 5–31.

Sheldon, K. M., Ryan, R., & Reis, H. T. (1996). What makes for a good day? Competence and autonomy in the day and in the person. *Personality and Social Psychology Bulletin, 22*(12), 1270–1279.

Sheldon, K. M., & Schmuck, P. (2001). Suggestions for healthy goal striving. In P. Schmuck & K. M. Sheldon (Eds.), *Life goals and well-being: Towards a positive psychology of human striving* (pp. 216–230). Gottingen, Germany: Hogrefe & Huber.

Sherif, M., & Sherif, C. W. (1953). *Groups in harmony and tension: An integration of studies of intergroup relations*. Oxford: Harper & Brothers.

REFERENCES

Sieroda, H. (2012). Psychosynthesis therapy. In C. Feltham & I. Horton (Eds.), *The Sage handbook of counselling and psychotherapy* (3rd ed., pp. 330–334). London: Sage.

Silberschatz, G. (2017). Improving the yield of psychotherapy research. *Psychotherapy Research, 27*(1), 1–13.

Silberschatz, G., Curtis, J. T., & Nathans, S. (1989). Using the patient's plan to assess progress in psychotherapy. *Psychotherapy, 26*(1), 40–46.

Sills, C. (2014). Transactional analysis. In W. Dryden & A. Reeves (Eds.), *Handbook of individual therapy* (6th ed., pp. 207–239). London: Sage.

Slavson, S. R. (1957). Are there 'group dynamics' in therapy groups? *International Journal of Group Psychotherapy, 7*(2), 131–154.

Sloane, R. B., Staples, F. R., Whipple, K., & Cristol, A. H. (1977). Patients' attitudes toward behavior therapy and psychotherapy. *American Journal of Psychiatry, 134*(2), 134–137.

Smail, D. (2005). *Power, interest and psychology*. Ross-on-Wye: PCCS Books.

Smith, B., & Woodruff Smith, D. (Eds.). (1995). *The Cambridge companion to Husserl*. Cambridge: Cambridge University Press.

Smith, D. L. (1976). Goal Attainment Scaling as an adjunct to counseling. *Journal of Counseling Psychology, 23*(1), 22–27.

Snyder, C. R. (2000). Hypothesis: There is hope. In C. R. Snyder (Ed.), *Handbook of hope: Theory, measures and applications* (pp. 3–21). San Diego, CA: Academic Press.

Snyder, C. R., Michael, S. T., & Cheavens, J. S. (1999). Hope as a foundation of common factors, placebos, and expectancies. In M. Hubble, B. L. Duncan & S. D. Miller (Eds.), *The heart and soul of change: What works in therapy* (pp. 179–200). Washington, DC: American Psychological Association.

Snyder, C. R., & Taylor, J. D. (2000). Hope as a common factor across psychotherapy approaches: A lesson from the dodo's verdict. In C. R. Snyder (Ed.), *Handbook of hope: Theory, measures and applications* (pp. 89–108). San Diego, CA: Academic Press.

Snygg, D., & Combs, A. W. (1949). *Individual behavior: A new frame of reference for psychology*. New York: Harper & Brothers.

Sohr, S. (2001). Eco-activism and well-being: Between flow and burnout. In P. Schmuck & K. M. Sheldon (Eds.), *Life goals and well-being: Towards a positive psychology of human striving* (pp. 202–215). Gottingen, Germany: Hogrefe & Huber.

Sornson, B. (2013). *Stand in my shoes: Kids learning about empathy*. Golden, CO: Love and Logic.

Sorokin, P. (1985). *Social and cultural dynamics*. London: Routledge.

Spangler, W. D. (1992). Validity of questionnaire and TAT measures of need for achievement: Two meta-analyses. *Psychological Bulletin, 112*(1), 140–154.

Spaniel, W. (2015). *Game theory 101: The complete textbook*. Pittsburgh, PA: William Spaniel.

Spinelli, E. (1994). *Demystifying therapy*. London: Constable.

Spinelli, E. (2001). *The mirror and the hammer: Challenges to therapeutic orthodoxy*. London: Continuum.

REFERENCES

Spinelli, E. (2005). *The interpreted world: An introduction to phenomenological psychology* (2nd ed.). London: Sage.

Spinelli, E. (2006). *Tales of un-knowing: Therapeutic encounters from an existential perspective.* Ross-on-Wye: PCCS Books.

Spinelli, E. (2015). *Practising existential psychotherapy: The relational world* (2nd ed.). London: Sage.

Steering Committee. (2002). Empirically supported therapy relationships: Conclusions and recommendations on the Division 29 task force. In J. C. Norcross (Ed.), *Psychotherapy relationships that work: Therapist contributions and responsiveness to patients* (pp. 441–443). New York: Oxford University Press.

Steger, M. F. (2013). Experiencing meaning in life. In P. T. P. Wong (Ed.), *The human quest for meaning: Theories, research, and applications* (2nd ed., pp. 165–184). New York: Routledge.

Steger, M. F., Frazier, P., Oishi, S., & Kaler, M. (2006). The Meaning in Life Questionnaire: Assessing the presence of and search for meaning in life. *Journal of Counseling Psychology, 53*(1), 80–93.

Stern, D. N. (2004). *The present moment in psychotherapy and everyday life.* New York: W. W. Norton and Co.

Stewart, I., & Joines, V. (1987). *TA today: A new introduction to transactional analysis.* Nottingham: Life Space.

Stoll, L., Michaelson, J., & Seaford, C. (2012). *Well-being evidence for policy: A review.* London: nef.

Stone, H., & Winkelman, S. (1989). *Embracing our selves: The Voice Dialogue Manual.* Mill Valley, CA: Nataraj Publishing.

Strauman, T. J., Vieth, A. Z., Merrill, K. A., Kolden, G. G., Woods, T. E., Klein, M. H., Papadakis, A. A., Schneider, K. L., & Kwapil, L. (2006). Self-System Therapy as an intervention for self-regulatory dysfunction in depression: A randomized comparison with cognitive therapy. *Journal of Consulting and Clinical Psychology, 74*(2), 367–376.

Stricker, G., & Gold, J. (2003). Integrative approaches to psychotherapy. In A. S. Gurman & S. B. Messer (Eds.), *Essential psychotherapies* (2nd ed., pp. 317–349). New York: Guilford Press.

Stuart, S., & Robertson, M. (2003). *Interpersonal psychotherapy: A clinician's guide.* London: Arnold.

Stuart, S., & Robertson, M. (2012). *Interpersonal psychotherapy: A clinician's guide* (2nd ed.). New York: CRC.

Sullivan, H. S. (1953). *The interpersonal theory of psychiatry.* New York: W. W. Norton and Co.

Swift, J., & Callahan, J. (2009). Early psychotherapy processes: An examination of client and trainee clinician perspective convergence. *Clinical Psychology & Psychotherapy, 16*(3), 228–236.

REFERENCES

Tarragona, M. (2008). Postmodern/poststructuralist therapies. In J. L. Lebow (Ed.), *Twenty-first century psychotherapies: Contemporary approaches to theory and practice* (pp. 167–205). London: Wiley.

Taylor, S., & Asmundson, G. J. G. (2004). *Treating health anxiety: A cognitive-behavioral approach*. New York: Guilford Press.

Taylor, S. E. (1981). The interface of cognitive and social psychology. In J. Harvey (Ed.), *Cognition, social behavior, and the environment* (pp. 189–211). Mahwah, NJ: Lawrence Erlbaum Associates.

Teasdale, J. D. (1985). Psychological treatments for depression – how do they work? *Behaviour Research and Therapy, 23*(2), 157–165.

Thir, M., & Batthyány, A. (2016). The state of empirical research on logotherapy and existential analysis. In A. Batthyány (Ed.), *Logotherapy and existential analysis: Proceedings of the Viktor Frankl Institute Vienna* (Vol. 1, pp. 53–74). Cham, Switzerland: Springer International.

Thompson, A., & Cooper, M. (2012). Therapists' experiences of pluralistic practice. *European Journal of Psychotherapy and Counselling, 14*(1), 63–76.

Thrash, T. M., Maruskin, L. A., & Martin, C. C. (2012). Implicit–explicit motive congruence. In R. M. Ryan (Ed.), *The Oxford handbook of human motivation* (pp. 141–156). New York: Oxford University Press.

Tillich, P. (2000). *The courage to be* (2nd ed.). New Haven, CT: Yale University Press.

Toporek, R. L., Gerstein, L., Fouad, N., Roysircar, G., & Israel, T. (2006). *Handbook for social justice in counseling psychology: Leadership, vision, and action*. Thousand Oaks, CA: Sage.

Totton, N. (2000). *Psychotherapy and politics*. London: Sage.

Totton, N. (Ed.). (2005). *The politics of psychotherapy: New perspectives*. Maidenhead: Open University Press.

Tryon, G. S. (2018). Goals and psychotherapy research. In D. Law & M. Cooper (Eds.), *Working with goals in counselling and psychotherapy* (pp. 87–109). Oxford: Oxford University Press.

Tryon, G. S., & Winograd, G. (2011). Goal consensus and collaboration. In J. C. Norcross (Ed.), *Psychotherapy relationships that work: Evidence-based responsiveness* (2nd ed., pp. 153–167). New York: Oxford University Press.

Tuckman, B. W. (1965). Developmental sequence in small groups. *Psychological Bulletin, 63*(6), 384–399.

Urmson, J. O., & Ree, J. (1989). *The concise encyclopedia of Western philosophy and philosophers*. London: Routledge.

van Deurzen-Smith, E. (1997). *Everyday mysteries*. London: Routledge.

van Deurzen, E. (1998). *Paradox and passion in psychotherapy: An existential approach to therapy and counselling*. Chichester: John Wiley and Sons.

van Deurzen, E. (2002). *Existential counselling and psychotherapy in practice* (2nd ed.). London: Sage.

REFERENCES

van Deurzen, E. (2009). *Psychotherapy and the quest for happiness*. London: Sage.

van Deurzen, E. (2012a). *Existential counselling and psychotherapy in practice* (3rd ed.). London: Sage.

van Deurzen, E. (2012b). Reasons for living: Existential therapy and spirituality. In L. Barnett & G. Madison (Eds.), *Existential psychotherapy: Vibrancy, legacy and dialogue* (pp. 171–182). London: Routledge.

van Deurzen, E., & Adams, M. (2011). *Skills in existential counselling and psychotherapy*. London: Sage.

van Deurzen, E., & Kenward, R. (2005). *Dictionary of existential psychotherapy and counselling*. London: Sage.

Vargiu, J. G. (1974). Psychosynthesis workbook: Subpersonalities. *Synthesis, 1*, 52–90.

Vermes, C. (2017). The individualism impasse in counselling psychology. *Counselling Psychology Review, 32*(1), 44–53.

Vieth, A. Z., Strauman, T. J., Kolden, G. G., Woods, T. E., Michels, J. L., & Klein, M. H. (2003). Self-System Therapy (SST): A theory-based psychotherapy for depression. *Clinical Psychology: Science and Practice, 10*(3), 245–268.

Vohs, K. D., & Baumeister, R. F. (2004). Ego depletion, self-control, and choice. In J. Greenberg, S. L. Koole & T. Pyszczynski (Eds.), *Handbook of experimental existential psychology* (pp. 398–410). New York: Guilford Press.

Vos, J. (2015). *Meaning centred group training for physically ill individuals: Basic treatment manual*. University of Roehampton. London.

Vos, J. (2016a). Working with meaning in life in chronic or life-threatening disease: A review of its relevance and effectiveness of meaning-centred therapies. In P. Russo-Netzer, S. E. Schulenberg & A. Batthyány (Eds.), *Clinical perspectives on meaning: Positive and existential psychotherapy* (pp. 171–200). New York: Springer.

Vos, J. (2016b). Working with meaning in life in mental health care: A systematic literature review and meta-analyses of the practices and effectiveness of meaning-centered therapies. In P. Russo-Netzer, S. E. Schulenberg & A. Batthyány (Eds.), *Clinical perspectives on meaning: Positive and existential psychotherapy* (pp. 59–87). New York: Springer.

Vos, J., Craig, M., & Cooper, M. (2014). Existential therapies: A meta-analysis of their effects on psychological outcomes. *Journal of Consulting and Clinical Psychology, 83*(1), 115–128.

Wadsworth, M., & Ford, D. H. (1983). Assessment of personal goal hierarchies. *Journal of Counseling Psychology, 30*(4), 514–526.

Wahl, B. (2003). Working with 'existence tensions' as a basis for therapeutic practice. *Existential Analysis, 14*(2), 265–278.

Walzer, M. (1983). *Spheres of justice*. New York: Basic Books.

Wampold, B. E., & Imel, Z. E. (2015). *The great psychotherapy debate: The evidence for what makes psychotherapy work* (2nd ed.). New York: Routledge.

REFERENCES

Watson, J. B. (1925). *Behaviorism*. New York: W. W. Norton and Co.

Wellman, H. W., & Phillips, A. T. (2001). Developing intentional understandings. In B. F. Malle, L. J. Moses & D. A. Baldwin (Eds.), *Intentions and intentionality: Foundations of social cognition* (pp. 125–148). Cambridge, MA: MIT Press.

Wiese, B. S. (2007). Successful pursuit of personal goals and subjective well-being. In B. R. Little, K. Salmela-Aro & S. D. Phillips (Eds.), *Personal project pursuit: Goals, action, and human flourishing*. (pp. 301–328). Mahwah, NJ: Lawrence Erlbaum Associates.

Wiese, B. S., & Salmela-Aro, K. (2008). Goal conflict and facilitation as predictors of work–family satisfaction and engagement. *Journal of Vocational Behavior, 73*(3), 490–497.

Wilkinson, R., & Pickett, K. (2010). *The spirit level: Why equality is better for everyone*. Harmondsworth: Penguin.

Willer, B., & Miller, G. H. (1976). Client involvement in goal setting and its relationship to therapeutic outcome. *Journal of Clinical Psychology, 32*(3), 687–690.

Williams, E. N. (2002). Therapist techniques. In G. S. Tryon (Ed.), *Counseling based on process research: Applying what we know* (pp. 232–264). Boston, MA: Allyn and Bacon.

Willutzki, U., & Koban, C. (2011). The elaboration of positive goal perspectives (EPOS): An intervention module to enhance motivation. In W. M. Cox & E. Klinger (Eds.), *Handbook of motivational counseling: Goal-based approaches to assessment and intervention with addiction and other problems* (2nd ed., pp. 437–459). Chichester: Wiley.

Wittgenstein, L. (1967). *Philosophical investigations* (G. E. M. Anscombe, Trans., 3rd ed.). Oxford: Blackwell.

Wolfe, B. E. (2008). Existential issues in anxiety disorders and their treatment. In K. J. Schneider (Ed.), *Existential-integrative psychotherapy: Guideposts to the core of practice* (pp. 204–216). New York: Routledge.

Wolitzky, D. (2003). The theory and practice of traditional psychoanalytic treatment. In A. S. Gurman & S. B. Messer (Eds.), *Essential psychotherapies: Theory and practice* (2nd ed., pp. 24–68). New York: Guilford Press.

Wollburg, E., & Braukhaus, C. (2010). Goal setting in psychotherapy: The relevance of approach and avoidance goals for treatment outcome. *Psychotherapy Research, 20*(4), 488–494.

Wong, P. T. P. (1998). Meaning-centred counseling. In P. T. Wong & P. Fry (Eds.), *The human quest for meaning: A handbook of psychological research and clinical applications* (pp. 395–435). Mahwah, NJ: Lawrence Erlbaum Associates.

Woodfield, A. (1976). *Teleology*. Cambridge: Cambridge University Press.

Wosket, V. (2012). The skilled helper model. In C. Feltham & I. Horton (Eds.), *The Sage handbook of counselling and psychotherapy* (3rd ed., 372–376). London: Sage.

Wright, R. (2000). *Nonzero: The logic of human destiny*. New York: Vintage Books.

REFERENCES

Yakeley, J. (2014). Psychodynamic therapy: Contemporary Freudian approach. In W. Dryden & A. Reeves (Eds.), *The handbook of individual therapy* (6th ed., pp. 21–47). London: Sage.

Yalom, I. D. (1980). *Existential psychotherapy*. New York: Basic Books.

Yalom, I. D. (2001). *The gift of therapy: Reflections on being a therapist*. London: Piatkus.

Yalom, I. D. (2008). *Staring at the sun*. London: Piatkus.

Zaleski, Z. (1987). Behavioral effects of self-set goals for different time ranges. *International Journal of Psychology, 22*(1), 17–38.

INDEX

Aarts, H., 74
abstract principles and values, 174
absurdity of human life, 90
acceptance-based therapy, 249
acceptance and commitment therapy (ACT), 183–4
achievement
  as a high-order direction, 86
  sense of, 51–2
action-and-feedback-focused methods of psychotherapy, 225–6
actualising of directions, 26, 32, 44, 54–8, 62–3, 73, 76, 83, 85, 94, 97–100, 103–4, 111, 116, 120, 124–7, 135, 148, 154–5, 212, 228, 232, 234, 242, 245, 249
  drive or tendency towards, 16, 154–6
Adams, Victoria, 121
Adler, Alfred, 173–4, 248
Adult Intentional and Motivational System (AIMS), 206
aesthetic people, 89
affect and affective methods, 44, 47, 50–2, 57, 62, 70, 193
agency, 19–21, 153, 172
agile method, 122
agreements, 238–9
Aked, J., 240
alcohol abuse, 221
altruism, 87, 240
Angyal, A., 16, 23
anorexia, 39, 87, 112
Antony, M.M., 184
anxiety and anxiety disorders, 49, 51, 56, 177, 184, 210; see also status anxiety
appearances, judging by, 100
appreciating achievements, 52–3
approach goals, 64–6, 73, 210
approaching our goals, 50–1
arbitrary control, 112
arbitrary inference, 102
Aristippus, 83
Aristotle, 18, 85
arms race, 131

arrow techniques, upward and downward, 186
assertiveness, 191, 245
assimilative integration, 3–4
attainability of goals, 48–50
Austin, J.T., 19, 74
authenticity, 85–6, 157, 172
autonomy
  of clients, 91, 202
  definition of, 86
avoidance goals, 64–6, 73, 87, 210, 240
avoidant attachment style, 34
awareness, 32, 183, 199
  lack of, 96–8
awareness-focused therapy, 224
Axelrod, R., 133, 233–9

backward-driven strategies, 204
Bandura, A., 182
Bargh, J.A., 38, 66–7, 113–14
Bateman, A., 150
Baumeister, R.F., 88
Beahrs, J.O., 165
Beck, A.T., 194
Beckham, David, 121
behavioural activation (BA), 183, 190
behavioural experiments, 189
behavioural therapies, 189–91
behaviourism and behavioural psychology, 2, 4, 182–3, 193
Beitman, B.D., 216, 221
Bentham, Jeremy, 83–4
Berlin, I., 12, 91
bigger picture, 233
biopsychosocial understanding of the person, 23
blocking of certain directions by clients, 159, 162
B-needs, 154
Bohart, A.C., 20, 28, 152–3, 157–60
Bomby, N.A., 216
borderline personality disorder, 193, 221
Boszormenyi-Nagy, I., 235, 239, 243

INDEX

Boudreaux, M.J., 111
Bowers, C., 31
Bowlby, J., 34
brain function, 57, 242
brainstorming, 185
Braukhaus, C., 65
Brentano, F., 23
Brickell, J., 86
British Psychological Society, 9, 20
Brown, D., 150
Brown, L., 96
Bruner, J., 146
Brunstein, J.C., 48
Buber, M., 8, 16, 22–3, 28
Buddhism, 249
Bugental, J.F.T., 36, 39, 152
Buhler, Charlotte, 198
bulimia, 39
bullying, 48
Burnham, D.H., 89

Cain, D., 169
Callahan, J., 201
Camus, A., 90
Cannon, R., 112
capitalism, 25
care, meaning of, 24
Carey, T.A., 81–2, 188, 194
Carver, C.S., 50–1
Caspar, F., 6, 57, 70, 76–7, 103, 159, 221–3, 227, 229
catastrophising, 102
causal explanations of human behaviour, 18–19
chair work, 164–7, 245
challenging goals, 211
change, common principles of, 244–5
childhood experiences, 98–9, 104
choice-making, facilitation of, 177–8
chronic strategies, 102–4
Chun, W.Y., 66
Church, M.A., 64–5, 201, 210
Circle of wants exercise, 217
clarification-oriented therapeutic approaches, 136
Clarkson, P., 30
client-directed approach to therapy, 20
client factors accounting for change, 153
client–therapist relationship, 7; see also therapeutic relationship
climate change, 233
closed transactions, 127
co-formulating, 219
cognitive analytic therapy, 3, 112, 149
Cognitive Behavioural Analysis System of Psychotherapy (CBASP), 192, 218

cognitive behavioural therapies (CBTs), 97–8, 104, 114, 158, 181–4, 187–9, 193–4, 198, 226
 particular contributions of, 193–4
cognitive errors, 99–102, 104
cognitive miserliness, 101, 103
cognitive theory, 99–101
cognitive therapies in general, 7, 69, 101, 186–8
collaboration between clients and therapists, 207–8
collaborative empiricism, 186
college grading, 126
Combs, A.W., 126–7
common elements in psychotherapy, 3, 5, 8, 12
communal goals, 239
communication, helpfulness of, 236–7
communication theory and analysis, 192
compassion-focused therapy, 187
competence, 86–7
 definition of, 86
 four stages of, 136
complementary transactions, 127
Computerized Interpersonal Conflict Assessment, 206
computers, use of, 17
conflict, 109–12
 conscious or unconscious, 110
 definition of, 109
 as a feature of human desires, 114
 between intrinsic and extrinsic directions, 124
 within and between people, 157
 see also core conflict; realistic conflict theory
conflict-free societies, 243
contingency management, 191
control theory (Power), 167, 243
 see also perceptual control theory
Cooper, Mick (author), 179, 212, 219, 246, 252
cooperative outcomes, 234–6
core conflict, 174–5, 183
Cornell, A.W., 163
Corning, P., 106, 128, 242, 252
Cornish, P., 243
cost–benefit analysis, 187
countertransference, 218, 227
couples and couples therapy, 121–3, 127, 235, 237–8
Cox, W.M., 16–17, 33, 55, 113
creative methods for expressing higher-order directions, 215
creativity, fostering of, 241
crossed transactions, 157

Csikzentmihalyi, M., 39, 90
Cullen, J.W., 217
Curtis, J.T., 223
Curtis, R.C., 148
Custers, R., 38

Dallos, R., 219
death instinct, 144
Deci, E.L., 86–7, 153
decisional balance, 191
decision-fostering intervention, 185
deep democracy, 243
defence mechanisms, 143–4
delay discounting, 33
delay documenting, 102
Dennett, D., 73
depressive position, 146
Derrida, Jacques, 25
deserted island fantasy, 215–16
diachronic relations, 106–7, 112
dialectical behaviour therapy, 193
dialectical relationships, 6–7
dialogue, 237
diary-keeping by clients, 186
dichotomous thinking, 102
diClemente, C.C., 30
Diener, E., 44, 51, 94
different-positions taken in internal dialogue, 164
dilemma-focused intervention, 164
dilemmas, 111, 114
direction, 16–17, 24–6
  sense of, 46–7, 52, 54
  social construction of, 24–5
directional arc, 30–2, 35–6, 39–41, 46–52, 55, 122, 136–7, 146, 157, 175, 183–5, 189–90, 199, 202, 204, 224, 226
directionality, 6, 10, 17–27, 32, 39, 52, 77, 79, 88
  analysis of, 26
  aspects of (the five As), 46
  critiques of, 249–50
  definition of, 26
  elements of, 30
  embodied nature of, 24
  interpersonal, 25–6, 120–3
  of nations, 124
  phase model of, 77, 189
  social construction of, 25
  structural model of, 82
  towards someone, 26
  towards something, 23–4
directions
  deliberate conflicts between, 108
  individual-level, 89, 124
  links between, 77–9, 94, 106
  lower-order, 76–80
  multiple, 76, 83
  physiological, 87
  of therapists, 227
  see also actualising of directions; higher–order directions
discrepancy between current state and desired one, 64
distal goals, 69–70
distress
  emotional, 9, 186
  psychological, 55, 78–9, 87, 101, 104, 109–10, 155, 172–3, 182, 190, 193, 249–50
diversity
  benefits of, 240–1
  celebration of, 240–1
  of therapeutic approaches, 3
D-needs, 154
Dolan, P., 51–2, 85
dopamine, 51
Dryden, Windy, 4, 69, 194
Duncan, B.L., 20, 28, 207
Durkheim, É., 47
dysergies, 107–16
  sources of, 113–16

eating disorders, 24, 79–80, 112
eclectic approaches to counselling and psychotherapy, 3–5
economic people, 89
effective goals, 209
efficiency in actualising, 94
Egan, G., 185
ego, the, 145–6
ego integrity, 52
ego states, 156
Eigner, S., 64
Eitam, B., 38
Elaboration of Positive Goal Perspectives (EPOS), 216
elephant metaphors, 5, 10
Elliot, A., 64–5, 74, 201, 210
Elliott, R., 21, 165, 169
embodiment, 22
Emmons, R.A., 44, 51
emotion-focused therapy, 162–3, 166
emotion regulation, 193
emotional literacy and emotional intelligence, 238
emotional states, 57
emotions, 44–6, 53–4, 57–8
  and the directional process, 53–4
  motivational function of, 45–6
  positive and negative, 57
  primary and secondary, 57

INDEX

empathy, 159–61, 233, 245
  future-directed, 160
empowerment, 200, 243–4, 249
empty chair work, 167
engagement with clients, 7–8, 12
Epstein, S., 66, 107
equality, benefits from, 241–3
equifinality, 19, 79–80, 227–8
Erikson, E.H., 52–3
Eriksson, L., 22
ethical duty, 91
ethics, 7–8, 136, 201–2, 251
eudaimonic perspective, 85
evaluation-focused methods, 224–5
evaluation of initial
  directions, 32–4
Evans, G., 237–8
evolutionary processes, 17, 44–5
existential theory and therapy, 7, 112, 172–9, 183
existentialism, 88–90
expectancy–value theories, 33, 234
expectation videos from clients, 216
expectations, 55–8
  about attainment of goals, 48–9
  setting of, 55
experience machine, 85–6
experiential methods for
  dramatising clients directions, 217
exposure therapy, 109, 189
expressiveness, 237
external dialogue, 166–7
extrinsic desires, 155–6, 164

family relationships, 122
family therapies, 127, 238–9
Farber, L.H., 56, 66
feasibility of reaching a goal, 33
feedback, 37–8, 189, 192
feelings, 53–4
feminist perspectives, 138, 143
Ferrucci, P., 32, 112, 215
Finkelstein, S.R., 37
Fishbach, A., 37
FIsher, L., 234–5, 238
5-year question, 216
fixed-role therapy, 190–1
flexibility
  psychological, 183
  of therapists, 227
flexible and inflexible people, 79
focusing, humanistic practice of, 163
focusing illusion, 101
focusing-oriented psychotherapy, 22
Ford, D.H., 16, 45, 54

Ford, M.E., 24, 26, 28, 34, 40, 92, 107, 209, 211
forgiveness, capacity for, 235
formulation, directional, 218–23
forward-driven strategies, 204
frame boxes, 221
framing effects, 101
Frankl, V.E., 48, 53, 172–4, 179
free association, 146–7, 157
freedom, definition of, 86
Freud, Sigmund, 21, 85, 109, 114, 142–5, 174
Freudian theory and practice, 31, 142, 144, 147
Frijda, N.H., 45
Fromm, E., 25, 68, 87, 155, 248
Fujita, K., 62
further work required in psychotherapy, 250–1
futural orientation, 19
future possibilities and limitations for
  clients, 214–15

game theory, 11, 127–32, 234–6, 245, 252
gendered differences, 89
Gendlin, E.T., 22, 163
Gestalt therapy, 7, 30
Gibbs, R.W. Jr, 120
Gillespie, A., 24
Glasser, W., 88, 167
Goal Assessment Scaling, 206
Goal Attainment and Scaling, 205
Goal-Based Outcome Measure, 205
goal-based tools, 204–7
goal conflict, 107, 110–11
goal contagion, 24
goal dimensions, 62–4, 73, 77
goal discussion, 198
goal disengagement, 39
goal hierarchies, 76
goal identification, 206–7
goal maps, 217
goal monitoring, 199–200, 203–4
goal-oriented practices, 11, 37, 57–8, 66–7, 70, 73, 107, 152, 199–202, 214
  challenges and limitations of, 202–3
  definition of, 198
  helpfulness or unhelpfulness of, 204
  tailoring of, 203–4
goal scheduling and goal balancing, 37
goal setting, 184, 198–208, 211, 218
goal stepping, 210
goal tracking, 198
goals, 62–74
  of clients and of therapists, 201

concrete or abstract, 72
difficult or easy, 71
extrinsic or intrinsic, 62–3
focus on, 6
for health, 184
helpfulness of, 208–12
important or unimportant, 70
personal and interpersonal, 64
practical considerations
  in working with, 207–8
primary or secondary, 73
realistic or unrealistic, 71
relationships between, 106
revision of, 208
self-attributed, 202
short-term or long-term, 68–9
simple or complex, 72
specific or vague, 71–2
Goals Form, 205
Goldman, R.M., 45–6
Goldstein, K., 154
Gollwitzer, P.M., 30, 32, 34
Grant, H., 74
gratitude, 52
Grawe, K., 6, 12, 33, 76–7, 79, 112–13, 136, 182, 218, 250
Greenberg, L.S., 21, 46, 57, 163, 166
Grosse Holtforth, M., 207
group properties, 120–1
group therapy, 124–7
groups, stages in the life of, 122
Grunebaum, J., 235
guided visualisations, 215
Guignon, C., 172

habits, 136
happiness, 51–2, 55–6, 64, 72, 88, 212
Heckhausen, H., 30, 34
hedonism and the hedonic treadmill, 52, 55, 83, 85
Heidegger, Martin, 24–5, 28, 172, 249
Heidenreich, T., 92, 107, 117
Hendricks, M.N., 163
Henry, K.L., 48
heterostasis, 85
heuristics, 100–2
Higgins, E.T., 64
higher needs, 64
higher-order directions, 76–80, 82–91, 99, 104, 127, 142–4, 149, 154–6, 159, 166, 173–6, 183, 185, 200, 203, 207–9
  absence of, 89–90
  diversity of, 244
  effective and ineffective means for satisfaction of, 96

helping clients with their identification of, 214–18
idiographic, 89–90
lack of awareness of, 96–7
Hill, C.E., 227
Hirsch, I., 148
Hoffman, L., 202
holarchy, concept of, 121
Hollanders, H., 3
Holtforth, M.G., 6
Holzhey-Kunz, A., 173
homeostasis and homeostatic principles, 85, 154
homophobia, 126
hopelessness, feelings of, 48–9
how? questions, 187–8
Howard, S., 150
Hoyer, J., 92, 107, 117
Hoyt, M.F., 158
Huang, J.Y., 113–14
human being, the: models of, 142–4, 152–4, 172–3, 182, 251
humanistic worldview and humanistic therapies, 114, 152–68, 183, 236
  distinctive contributions of, 168
Husserl, E., 18

id, the, 31, 145
idealistic meaning system and ideational meaning system, 88
Imel, Z.E., 49
implementation intentions, 36
implied messages, 160
Improving Access to Psychological Therapies (IAPT), 206
impulses, emergence of, 30–1
impulsive directional style, 40
individuation, 86
inequality, 241–2
in-groups and out-groups, 242
inner patriarch, 245
insight, 146
insight-based therapy, 69
instincts, definition and concept of, 142
integrative approaches to counselling and psychotherapy, 3–4, 12, 251
intelligibility, concept of, 21–2, 96
intention-focused methods, 225
intentionality, 16
interconnectedness of people, 244
internal dialogue, facilitation of, 163–6
interostatic principles, 154
interpersonal directionality, synergies and dysergies, 120

interpersonal psychotherapy (IPT), 98, 127, 191–3, 198, 226, 238
interpersonal relationships, synergetic, 125, 132
interpretation process, 147–8
  reconstructive or transferential, 147
intrapersonal synergies, 107
intrinsic goals, 164, 209
I-position, 165
Irving, L.M., 112

James, William, 83, 89, 109
Johnstone, L., 12, 26, 139
Jolie, Angelina, 121
Joostman, N.B., 39
journey metaphor, 208
Ju/hoansi community, 126
Jung, Carl Gustav, 153

Kahneman, D., 66, 100, 104
Kasser, T., 50, 63, 94
Katz, R., 126
Keenan, K., 169
Kelly, R.E., 110–11
Kennedy-Moore, E., 53
Kierkegaard, Søren, 154
Klein, Melanie, 144–5
Klinger, E., 16–17, 33, 45, 113, 155–6, 250
Koban, C., 214
Koestler, A., 76, 113, 121, 133
Koestner, R., 50
Koole, S.L., 39

laddering techniques, upward and downward, 186, 188
Laing, R.D., 21–2, 25, 172
Latham, G.P., 38, 200
Law, Duncan, 10, 212, 219
Layard, R., 20, 71, 127
Lazarus, A.A., 3, 215
learning goals, 63
Lemma, A., 150
leverage, therapeutic, 185, 220
Levinas, E., 7, 234
Lewin, K., 120
life goals, 68–9, 199
life lines, 215
limitations, acknowledgement of, 178
Little, B., 39, 44, 62, 70, 250
Little Hans, 21, 142
Locke, E.A., 38, 199–200
logotherapy, 176
longer-term goals, 209
lose-lose outcomes, 131
loss aversion, 101

lower needs, 64
Lucas, R.E., 94

McClelland, D.C., 67, 89
McCormick, E.W., 112
MacGregor, K.E., 62
Mackrill, T., 137, 201–2, 208, 216–17
McLellan, G., 240
MAcLeod, John, 4, 6–7, 10, 12, 137, 201–2, 208, 216–17, 229
Macquarrie, J., 18
macro levels of organisation, 120
magical voluntarianism, 9
mania, 221
Mansell, W., 92, 109, 111, 117, 188, 194, 214
Manthei, B., 227
Marcuse, H., 155
marginalised groups, 138
Martin, C.C., 68
Maruskin, L.A., 68
Marx, Karl, 25
Marxist theory, 120
Maslow, A.H., 51–2, 82, 87–8, 125–6, 152–5, 174, 248–9
mass production, 241
mastery-oriented therapeutic approaches, 136
May, R., 148
meaning-centred therapies, 172, 175–7
meaning of life, 53–4, 88
meaninglessness, sense of, 47
media portrayals of psychotherapy, 202
mediation, 127, 235
mental contrasting, 36
mentalisation and mentalisation-based techniques, 225, 232
Merleau-Ponty, M., 22
metacommunication, 192–3, 233
metadirections, 228
metagoals, 53, 68, 73
metatherapeutic communication about goals, 198
method of levels (MOL), 188–9
Michalak, J., 6, 92, 107, 110–11, 117, 135, 207
Miller, G.A., 81
Miller, S.D., 3, 5, 20, 28, 251
Miller, W.R., 161
Mindell, A., 233, 244, 248
mindfulness and mindfulness therapy, 193, 225, 249
mindset theory of action phases, 34
miracle question, 158
Moorey, S., 182

Moskowitz, G.B., 74
motivation, 16, 152–3
  to create synergies, 245
  explicit or implicit, 67–8
  extrinsic, 99
  of therapists, 227
motivational counselling, 6, 185; see also systematic motivational counselling
motivational interviewing, 161, 185
Motivational Structure Questionnaire (MSQ), 205
motivational structures, 76
motivational systems theory, 6
motive congruence, 68
multidirected partiality, 239
multifinality, 80, 106, 153
multimodal therapy, 3
Munro, A., 227
Murphy-Shigematsu, S., 126

Nash equilibrium, 131–2, 235, 245
Nathans, S., 223
National Health Service, 125, 206
Neenan, M., 185
negative feelings and mood, 57–8
neutrality, analytical, 148
New Years resolutions, 35
nice strategies, 239–40
Nietzsche, Friedrich, 48, 86, 88
noesis and noema, 23
nomothetic tools for the rating of progress, 205–6
non-judgmental acceptance, 239
Norcross, J.C., 12

Oddli, H.W., 203
organisation, levels of, 120–3, 132, 234, 252
organismic valuing tendency, 97
ostrich problem, 200
outcome goals, 72
over-estimation of rare events, 101
over-generalisation, 101
over-optimism, 101
Ozer, D.J., 111

pain, avoidance of, 83, 85
Paivio, S.C., 57
Palmer, S., 185
pantheoretical pathways, 5
paralysis through analysis, 40
paranoid personality, 221
paranoid–schizoid position, 145
payoff matrices, 129–30
PDSA (plan-do-study-act) cycles, 122

peak–end rule, 100
Pedder, J., 150
perceptual control theory (Powers), 81–2, 112, 188
perfectionism, 50, 55
performance goals, 63
persistence as a human feature, 19
person-centred therapy, 2, 7, 109, 152–7
Personal Concerns Inventory, 205, 208
Personal Project Analysis, 62, 205
personalisation, 102
personalised action plans, 190
phenomenology, 23–4
Pickett, K., 241–2
pipedreams, 56
Pitt, Brad, 121
placebo effect, 49
plan analysis, 221, 223
plan formulation method, 206, 223
planned behaviour, theory of, 27
planning, 35–6, 40
  definition of, 35
planning-focused therapy, 225
planograms, 185
plasticity, 19, 79
Plato, 108
pleasure, pursuit of, 83, 85
pleasure principle, 145
pluralistic approach to therapy, 4–9, 12, 89, 136–7, 250
Pohlmann, K., 26
political people, 89
politically-informed approaches to therapy, 9, 137–9, 249
Polivy, J., 38
Polster, E. and M., 48
positive regard, 116; see also unconditional positive regard
postintentional mindset, 34–5
postmodernism, 25, 250
Power Threat Meaning Framework, 9, 20–1, 26, 137
Powers, W.T., 50, 81–2, 86, 92, 109–12, 117, 126, 167, 188, 234, 243
preintentional mindset, 34–5
presenting problems, 184
priming, 67
prisoners dilemma game, 128–31, 232–9, 242
problem-focused therapy, 184–6
problem-solving training, 190
problems, psychological. see distress
process-focused goals, 72, 211–12
Prochaska, J.O., 30
progress towards goals, 50–1

projection, 143
proximal goals, 68–70
psychoanalysis and psychoanalytic
   theory, 109, 198
psychodynamic theory and therapy, 2, 4,
   69, 104, 142–8, 155, 183, 226
   distinctive contribution made by, 150
psychoeducation, 186–7, 192
Psychological Situation Analysis, 188
psychosis, 21–2, 172
psychosynthesis, 152
Psychotherapists and Counsellors for
   Social Responsibility, 248
pure form therapies, 3–4
purpose in life, 46–8, 57, 88, 90

racism, 123–4
Rapoport, A., 131, 232
rational choice theory, 22–3, 33
rational emotive behaviour therapy
   (REBT), 100–1
realistic and unrealistic goals, 210
realistic conflict theory, 116
reality therapy, 98, 167–8
receptiveness, 237
red thread metaphor, 161
Ree, J., 126
Reese, H.W., 18
reference standards, 55–6, 65,
   71, 81–2, 242
reference value, 76
referrals, 137
regression (as a defence mechanism), 143
regulatory style, 66
Reich, Wilhelm, 248
relatedness, definition of, 87
relational methods for identifying clients
   directions, 217
religious people, 89
remoralization, 49
Renaissance, the, 88
repression, 143
Rescher, N., 4, 91, 126–7
resistance in a therapeutic sense, 68
   from a humanistic standpoint, 161
   in psychodynamics, 148
resource limitations, 115–16, 243–4
response preventon, 190
Rice, L.N., 21
Riediger, M., 106
Robbers Cave experiment, 244
Robertson, M., 192
Roemer, L., 184
Rogers, Carl, 9, 16–17, 25, 152–5, 236
rogue goals, 111–12, 115, 144, 156, 245

role-plays, 192
rolling with the resistance, 161
Rollnick, S., 161
Rubicon Model, 30, 34, 136
Rubin, S., 169
Russell, D., 217
Ryan, R.M., 27, 63, 86–7, 153
Rycroft, C., 109, 144

safety as a basic human direction, 87
Salmela-Aro, K., 106–7
salutogenic goals, 39, 71–2, 80, 207–8,
   228, 245, 249–50
Samuels, A., 86
sanctions on breaking agreements, 239
Sartre, J.-P., 18, 89–90
scaling, 187
Scheier, M.F., 50–1
Schlick, M., 249
Schmuck, P., 64, 239–40
Schneider, K.J., 175
schoolism, 3–4
Schopenhauer, A., 55, 249
selective abstraction, 102
self-actualisation, 85, 154–6
   tendency towards, 155
self-attributed motives, 67
self-concordant goals, 62–3
self–criticism, 166
self-efficacy, 33, 48, 53, 138, 200, 210
self-healing process, 153
self-help groups, 126
self-interest, 232
self-organisation, 20
self-oriented meanings for therapists from
   their work, 227
self-system therapy, 65, 188
Seligman, M.E.P., 107
sensate meaning system, 88
session goals, 69
Sheeran, P., 71
Sheldon, K.M., 50, 64–5, 94, 97, 239–40
short-termism, 69, 102, 252
should statements, 102
Sieroda, H., 152
Silberschatz, G., 89, 98, 223
Sisyphus, 90
skills needed
   by clients, 190
   by therapists, 137, 226
Slavson, S.R., 125–6
Small, J., 227
small steps goals, 210–11
SMART principles, 158, 212
Snyder, C.R., 6, 44

Snygg, D., 126–7
social concerns, 242; see also sociopolitical factors
social constructionism, 24–5
social contract, 238
social people, 89
social synergies, 125–7
socialisation, 99
socialist humanism, 248
sociopolitical factors, 8, 115–16, 138, 251
Socratic dialogue, 176
Sohr, S., 64
solution-focused therapy (SFT), 158
Soth, A.M., 216
space provided for clients, 157
Spaniel, W., 127
Sparks, J.A., 20, 28
specific goals, 211
The Spice Girls, 82
Spinelli, E., 175
Stages of change model, 30
status anxiety, 242
Steger, M.F., 46
stereotypical thinking, 100
Strauman, T.J., 66
Striving Instrumentality Matrix, 206
structural diagrams, 221–3
structural models, 114, 132, 145
Stuart, S., 192
sub-directions and sub-sub-directions, 76
subjective well-being, 94, 107, 240
sublimation, 143
suicide, 47
suicide bombers, 174
sunk costs fallacy, 101
superego, the, 145
survival strategies, 21
Swift, J., 201
synchronic relationships, 106–7, 112
syncretism, 4
synergetic goals, 209
synergetic solutions, 232–8, 242–5, 251
synergy, 80, 106–10, 114–16, 125–7, 132, 135, 155
  definition of, 106
  at interpersonal level, 232
  motivation for development of, 233–4, 245
systematic motivational counselling, 161

tabling, 37
Tai, S.J., 194
Tallman, K., 20, 28, 157–8
Taoism, 249
technical eclecticism, 3

teleology, 18–20
telic perspective, 44
temperament, 44
temporal range, 68–9
tensions, 174–5
termination of directional process, 38–9
Thematic Apperception Test, 67, 206
theoretical integration, 3–4
theoretical people, 89
therapeutic relationship, 147, 175, 218, 223, 227
Thrash, T.M., 68
time-lines, 215
TIT FOR TAT strategy, 235–40
totalising frameworks, 6–7
TOTE (Test-Operate-Test-Exit) concept, 81, 173
tournaments, 232
Tragedy of the Commons, 234
transactional analysis, 127, 161
trust, 234–7, 242
two-chair work, 165, 217

Ulrich, D., 235
unconditional positive regard, 159, 239
unconscious processes, 46, 66–8, 142–3
unintended consequences, 108, 143
uniqueness of individual persons, 155
Urmson, J.O., 126
utilitarianism, 126–7

value pluralism, 91, 136
van Deurzen, E., 47–8, 56, 114, 174–6, 179
van Deurzen-Smith, E., 54
Vancouver, J.B., 19, 62, 74
Vargiu, J.G., 164–5
Vieth, A.Z., 65
voluntarism, 22
Vos, J., 179

Wade, A.G., 153
Wadsworth, M., 16
Walzer, M., 241
Wampold, B.E., 49
warfare, 124
Watson, J.C., 53
WDEP (wants-doing-evaluation-planning) principles, 168
Webb, T.L., 71
well-being, 87, 153
  eudaimonic and hedonic, 52
  psychological, 79
  sense of, 54, 58, 62–4, 68, 70, 73
  social, 126, 232, 240, 242, 248–9
  subjective, 94, 107, 240

INDEX

What You See Is All
    There Is (WYSIATI), 100
whole more than the
    sum of the parts, 106
whole less than the sum of
    the parts, 108
Wiese, B.S., 106–7
Wilkinson, R., 241–2
Willutzki, U., 214
win–win solutions, 107, 235
Wittgenstein, Ludwig, 25
Wolfe, B.E., 173
Wolitzky, D., 144
Wollburg, E., 65

Woodfield, A., 37
worldworkers, 248, 252
Wright, R., 252
Wubbolding, R., 86

X-Factor (television series), 99

Yakeley, J., 147
Yalom, I.D., 98, 172, 218
YouTube, 99

Zaleski, Z., 114
zero-sum and non-zero-sum games,
    127–32, 233, 243, 245